FAMILY, FIELDS, AND ANCESTORS

D1021743

FAMILY, FIELDS, AND ANCESTORS

Constancy and Change in China's Social and Economic History, 1550–1949

LLOYD E. EASTMAN

New York   Oxford
OXFORD UNIVERSITY PRESS
1988

Oxford University Press

Oxford   New York   Toronto
Delhi   Bombay   Calcutta   Madras   Karachi
Petaling Jaya   Singapore   Hong Kong   Tokyo
Nairobi   Dar es Salaam   Cape Town
Melbourne   Auckland

and associated companies in
Beirut   Berlin   Ibadan   Nicosia

Copyright © 1988 by Oxford University Press, Inc.

Published by Oxford University Press, Inc.,
198 Madison Avenue, New York, New York 10016-4314

Oxford is a registered trademark of Oxford University Press

All rights reserved. No part of this publication may be reproduced,
stored in a retrieval system, or transmitted, in any form or by any means,
electronic, mechanical, photocopying, recording, or otherwise,
without the prior permission of Oxford University Press.
Library of Congress Cataloging-in-Publication Data
Eastman, Lloyd E.
Family, fields, and ancestors.
Bibliography: p.   1. China—Social conditions.   2. China—Economic conditions.   I. Title.
HN733.E25   1988   306'.0951   87-12320
ISBN 0-19-505269-2
ISBN 0-19-505270-6 (pbk.)

9

Printed in the United States of America
on acid-free paper

Preface

For a century preceding the Communist victory in 1949, China was caught in the vortex of political turmoil. There was domestic rebellion, foreign aggression, warlordism, and revolution. Understandably, therefore, modern Chinese history, as taught in our classrooms, is essentially political history. Students learn of the Taiping Rebellion, the May Fourth Movement, and Mao Tse-tung's march to power. Rarely do they gain more than a glimpse of the economic and social context of these political events.

Students do, perhaps, learn that the peasants played a key role in the Communist revolution as a result of their growing impoverishment and their worsening exploitation by the landlords, that imperialism destroyed the native handicrafts and obstructed the development of a modern Chinese-owned industrial sector, and that the traditional scholar-gentry class was displaced after the abolition in 1905 of the civil-service examination system. Few students, however, get much beyond such broad generalizations about the social and economic processes that underlay China's modern political transformation.

The explanation for this failure is not that their professors view the social and economic factors as unimportant. Indeed, in their own research, they are turning in increasing numbers to study social and economic phenomena rather than, as in the past, strictly political and intellectual topics. There now exists, as a consequence, a new and extensive monographic literature that is replete with insights into these realms of China's recent historical experience. Yet this corpus of research is widely scattered and often seems to be frighteningly esoteric. There are, for example, fascinating studies of the "shed people" of Kiangsi or of rice prices in the lower Yangtze Valley. But the relevance of these to "Modern Chinese History," as presented in the classrooms, is often unclear.

The gap separating the research of the specialists from the knowledge that students acquire in the classrooms has consequently been growing wider. The purpose of this study is to narrow that gap by drawing on the insights of this new monographic literature to present a general survey of China's recent social and economic history.

When studying social and economic problems, one soon discovers that the chronological divisions that are commonly used in political history no longer "fit." It is not helpful, for instance, to think of "modern" China as commencing with the Opium War or even with the Macartney Mission of 1793. Nor do such important political events as the founding of the Qing Dynasty in 1644 or the Republican Revolution of 1911 now appear to be significant turning points. (The Communist Revolution of 1949, however, *does* appear to mark the beginning of a distinct phase of social and economic, as well as political, history. This, perhaps, is because the revolution occurred so recently that we lack the historical perspective needed to discern all the continuities that lie beneath the integuments of the Communist system.)

But if the Opium War did not mark the beginning of "modern" China, it is nonetheless true that the pace of "modernizing" change did begin to accelerate significantly after about the 1860s. Then, impelled partly—but only partly—by contacts with the West, a cluster of new social classes began displacing the traditional gentry from the top of the social structure; secret societies and bandits became feverishly active; trade and modern industry expanded. As a result of these changes, the Chinese economy and society between 1860 ahnd 1949 were progressively different, in very profound ways, from what they had been. These ninety years thus appear, at least from the vantage point of the society and economy, to constitute a distinctive historical era. Here, for convenience' sake, we label it the "early modern period."

When starting this study, I certainly had not intended that it commence in the Ming Dynasty. Yet it soon became apparent that the social and economic changes of the early modern period were not comprehensible without some discussion of the institutions and structures that were being changed. It was thus necessary to look backward, beyond 1860. But how far back? One might arguably start in the eighteenth century, for it represented the height of the Qing Dynasty, when "traditional" institutions remained strong and Western influences were still weak. Yet the feeling is overpowering, when researching the eighteenth century, that it represented the high point of a social and economic era, and it seemed desirable and even necessary to go back farther, to the beginning of that era. Inexorably, therefore, and despite the relative paucity of scholarly research on this earlier period, I was drawn back to the Ming and especially to the sixteenth century, which seems to have marked the beginning of a distinctive phase of Chinese history. It was then that a congeries of social forces—the commercialization and monetization of the economy, the development of an extensive foreign trade, the erosion of traditional divisions among social classes, the spread of literacy, and the rapid growth of the population—gained momentum and significantly altered the social landscape of the empire during the next 200 and more years.

Other scholars, working before me, have likewise discovered the importance of the sixteenth century in the periodization of China's social and economic history. Evelyn S. Rawski, for example, has written that "this era, the late imperial period (sixteenth through nineteenth centuries), was substantively different from its predecessors and was characterized by considerable continuity in key institutions and socio-economic structure.''[1] Even before Rawski, Ramon H. Myers and Frederic Wakeman, Jr., had made the same discovery.[2] We join good company, therefore, in labeling the era from about 1550 to 1860 the ''late imperial period.''

In writing a survey of China's social and economic history during a period four centuries long, there is considerable danger that the particularities of the society and the economy in different periods and in different places will be submerged in a sea of generalizations. China is approximately twice the size of Europe exclusive of Russia, and the diversities within such a wide area, over the course of four centuries, were often enormous. The society and way of life in the sparsely settled, impoverished uplands of Kweichow, for instance, obviously differed from that in the highly commercialized, relatively prosperous lower Yangtze provinces. And the family structures, personal relationships, and moral values of illiterate and financially straitened peasants were apt to diverge sharply from those of the wealthy and cultured scholar-officials. Can one, then, generalize about the society and economy of China *as a whole?*

Despite the importance of such regional, social, and historical differences, this is an introductory study, and some broad generalizations are, I believe, both desirable and unavoidable. I have generalized, therefore, but cautiously, noting exceptions whenever they seemed appropriate. This book is, consequently, more finely tuned than just a first-order approximation of Chinese social and economic realities. But generalizations remain, and readers would be well advised to bear in mind Lin Yu-tang's admonition that ''China is too big a country and her national life has too many facets, for her not to be open to the most diverse and contradictory interpretations.''[3] Or as Chinese peasants put it more simply, ''Customs change every 10 *li.*''

Acknowledgments

This book is a synthetic study, based on the research of others, and my intellectual debts are therefore even more numerous than if my sources had been largely documents in an archive. It would obviously not be practicable here to list all those whose books, articles, dissertations, and unpublished manuscripts have provided the data and interpretations from which this work is constructed. And, unfortunately, the constraints imposed by the publisher have made it impossible for me adequately to footnote my sources and thus reveal, even indirectly, my appreciation to the authors who have helped me so much in this endeavor. When you authors read the following text, however, you will doubtless recognize where you have made a contribution. When you do, you may be assured of my profound gratitude to you. In addition, I wish to thank my colleagues at the University of Illinois, especially Robert B. Crawford, Patricia Ebrey, Kiyohiko Munakata, Peter Schran, and Ronald Toby, who have been stimulating in conversation, rich with advice and information, and generous with criticisms. Others who have assisted in diverse but important ways are William S. Atwell, Richard E. Barrett, Muriel

Bell, Loren Brandt, David D. Buck, Prasenjit Duara, David Johnson, Harry J. Lamley, Liu Ts'ui-jung, Susan Mann, Ramon H. Myers, Susan Naquin, Thomas G. Rawski, James E. Sheridan, Ann Waltner, James L. Watson, Tim Wright, and Marilyn B. Young.

Urbana, Ill.   L. E. E.
May 1987

Contents

FAMILY, FIELDS, AND ANCESTORS

1

Population: Growth and Migration

For every Chinese living in 1400, there were about six in 1850. The social landscape of the country had thereby been transformed. Villages grew closer together; market towns proliferated. And all these additional people had to be fed. Millions, therefore, moved into unsettled regions of the nation, hewing down the forests and plowing the soil; yet farms became smaller as the per capita land shares dwindled to perhaps only two-thirds of the average in 1400. Thus during the Ming and Qing dynasties, the single most important factor affecting China's economy and social institutions, the very way that the Chinese lived their lives, was its large and growing population.

Exactly how large that population was is uncertain. Census taking in the sixteenth century was not the scientific enterprise it is today. Emperors were usually more interested in counting the number of taxpaying males than they were in knowing how many individuals lived within the borders of the empire. And local officials, when making their periodic reports on the populations in their areas of jurisdiction, often simply "cooked" the numbers, fabricating population data in order to meet the prejudices of and please their bureaucratic superiors.

A Demographic Transition

Despite such fallibilities in the census-taking system, the general trend of the demographic curve is clear. For about seven to eight centuries, from the Later Han Dynasty (25–220) through the Tang Dynasty (618–906), the population of the empire sometimes approached, but rarely exceeded, the 60 to 80 million mark. For a time during the Song Dynasty, in the eleventh century, it rose to about 108 million, but then fell again during the period of Mongol conquest and rule (Table 1.1).

3

Table 1.1.   Population and Cultivated Acreage Estimates for China—
National Totals

Year	Population (millions)[a]	Cultivated Acreage (million *mu*)[b]	*Mu* Per Capita (based on average population and acreage figures)
125	*56*[1]		
732	*45*[1]		
1086	*108*[1]		
1400	65–80[2]	370 ($\pm$70)[8]	5.1
1600	*160*[3]	500 ($\pm$100)[8]	3.1
1650	*125*[3]		
1779	275 ($\pm$25)[4]	950 ($\pm$100)[8]	3.5
1850	430 ($\pm$25)[5]	1,210 ($\pm$50)[9]	2.8
1934	503[6]	1,470 ($\pm$50)[10]	2.9
1953	583 ($\pm$15)[7]	1,678 ($\pm$25)[11]	2.9

Notes: a. The population figures for the years in italics are less reliable than are those for the other years.

   b. Cultivated acreage includes all land on which crops were grown, but excludes pasture land. Much of the "cultivated acreage" bore two or three crops a year, and thus the figures cited are less than the total "cropped acreage."

Sources: 1. John D. Durand, "The Population Statistics of China, A.D. 2–1953," *Population Studies* 13, no. 3 (March 1960): 249.

   2. Ping-ti Ho, *Studies on the Population of China, 1368–1953* (Cambridge, Mass.: Harvard University Press, 1959), p. 22; Dwight H. Perkins, *Agricultural Development in China, 1368–1968* (Chicago: Aldine, 1969), pp. 193–201.

   3. Perkins, *Agricultural Development*, pp. 209, 216.

   4. Ho, *Studies*, pp. 63–64; Perkins, *Agricultural Development*, p. 16.

   5. Ho, *Studies*, p. 64; John S. Aird, "Population Growth," in *Economic Trends in Communist China*, ed. Alexander Eckstein et al. (Chicago: Aldine, 1968), p. 271; Perkins, *Agricultural Development*, pp. 16, 207–8.

   6. Richard E. Barrett, "Results of Back-Projection of the 1953 PRC Census at Five-Year Intervals, 1849–1929" (Manuscript); Perkins, *Agricultural Development*, p. 16.

   7. John S. Aird, "Recent Demographic Data from China: Problems and Prospects," in *China Under the Four Modernizations, Part I:* Selected Papers Submitted to the Joint Economic Committee, Congress of the United States (Washington, D.C.: U.S. Government Printing Office, 1982). p. 178; Perkins, *Agricultural Development*, p. 216.

   8. Perkins, *Agricultural Development*, p. 16.

   9. Ibid., p. 240. This figure is actually for 1873.

   10. Ibid., p. 16. This figure is actually for 1933.

   11. Ibid. This figure is actually for 1957.

Thereafter, the empire experienced a fundamental demographic change, the population rising from some 65 to 80 million at the beginning of the Ming to roughly 430 million in 1850. This was about a fivefold increase in 450 years. During those centuries, of course, there were leaps and dips in the demographic curve. As in all traditional agrarian societies, famines and epidemics periodically took a catastrophic toll of human lives. The largest drop in population during these years appears to have been during the early and mid-seventeenth century—the years of the transition from the Ming to the Qing Dynasty—when the population-depressing effects of peasant rebellions and wars of conquest were compounded by a widespread and lethal epidemic in north China during the late 1630s and early 1640s.

Following the Manchus' consolidation of their conquest in the 1680s, the population again shot upward, this time to unprecedented levels. Most of this growth occurred during the eighteenth century, when the population more than doubled, probably rising from about 150 million in 1700 to about 300 million at the end of the century. This increase implies an average growth rate of somewhat under 1 percent annually. Such a growth rate in a traditional society, sustained over a long period of time, was extraordinary. After the 1770s, the rate of increase somewhat moderated, but the powerful effects of compound interest produced a population by the mid-nineteenth century that numbered 430 million.

Why did the population rise so sharply during the centuries after 1400, and especially in the eighteenth century? No one knows for sure, although demographers strongly believe that it was attributable less to increases in the fertility rates—which in traditional agrarian societies were unlikely to change rapidly—and more to declines in the mortality rates. Several explanations for the reduced death rates have been suggested. Perhaps fewer people were dying as a result of the prolonged periods of peace and stability that the empire enjoyed—first under the Ming Dynasty, as it recovered from the devastation of the fighting against Mongol rule, and later during the *pax Sinica* forged by the three great Qing emperors (Kangxi, Yongzheng, and Qianlong) in the late seventeenth and the eighteenth centuries. Or perhaps improved medical and health practices were a contributing factor. Immunization against smallpox, for instance, became known in the sixteenth century—about 200 years before Edward Jenner developed the smallpox vaccine in the West—and doubtless caused some decline in the deaths attributable to that dread disease. Or perhaps the introduction of food crops from the Americas (maize, potatoes, and peanuts) resulted in a plentiful food supply that enabled more Chinese to survive to adulthood and their reproductive years.

All these attempts to explain China's population increase in terms of conditions specific to China seem beside the point, however, when we note that the population of Europe between the fifteenth and the mid-nineteenth centuries rose and fell (including a period of regression in the seventeenth century) at nearly the same tempo as China's. Fernand Braudel, the eminent French historian, viewed this fact with puzzlement. "The simultaneity," he wrote, "is the problem."[1] Russia's population, incidentally, like that of China, doubled during the eighteenth century. Thus the concurrent increases of population in these several parts of the world strongly suggest that the causes of the demographic spurt may not have been unique to just one country.

Braudel proffered one possible explanation. The cause, he suggested, may have been the weather. It is well known by climatologists that the climate of the world does change over more or less long periods of time. There was, for example, the Pleistocene ice age, which ended only some 10,000 years ago. During the fourteenth century, too, the Northern Hemisphere cooled down, resulting in a long series of frigid winters and in such a proliferation of icebergs in the Atlantic Ocean that the Vikings could no longer venture to North America.

Braudel offered no evidence to support his conjecture that climatic change after about 1450 was particularly congenial to humankind. But he was assuredly correct in the assumption that even slight, long-term climatic changes can have momentous consequences. According to Geoffrey N. Parker of the University of Illinois:

> A fall of one degree centigrade in overall summer temperatures restricts the grow-
> ing season for plants by three or four weeks and reduces the maximum altitude
> at which crops will ripen by about 500 feet. Even today, each day's delay in the
> ripening of the harvest diminishes the present yield of cereal crops by 63 kilos
> per hectare, and a drop of (one degree) in average summer temperature reduces
> the growing season in northern Europe by about 30 days. In the seventeenth
> century, with more primitive agricultural methods and with more marginal land
> under cultivation, the impact of (such a fall) would have been proportionally
> greater still.[2]

In view of such consequences of climatic change, it is significant that the famines, political struggles, and population decline in China during the 1630s and 1640s—that is, the period when the Ming collapsed and the conquering Manchus established the Qing Dynasty—generally coincided with what European historians call the Little Ice Age. This was a period of reduced solar activity, known as the Maunder minimum, when the lakes in central China froze over with greater frequency than at any other time in recorded history. This cooling trend coincided, too, with the great Kan'ei famine in Japan in the late 1630s and early 1640s, which caused widespread death by starvation and disease. Braudel's speculation that the puzzling "simultaneity" of population growth in both Europe and China may have been due to a global warming trend appears, then, to be eminently plausible.

Expanding Sources of Food for the Growing Population

Whatever the causes of China's population growth, there was one momentous, inescapable fact: there were now far more Chinese than previously, and all demanded to be fed. Yet the technology of Chinese agriculture remained basically unchanged. Indeed, the methods and tools used by China's peasants during the Qing Dynasty were almost identical to those employed by their ancestors in the fifth century, and perhaps even earlier. The only significant technological improvements were in the methods of water control, as farmers over the centuries learned to drain marsh areas, protect coastal plains from flooding by ocean water, create reservoirs, and employ various devices (such as the water wheel using bamboo tubes) for raising water to higher levels. Basically, however, the Chinese increased their food supply not by using new technologies, but by improving crop yields by more extensive use of traditional methods and by opening up lands to cultivation.

Crop yields, or the amount of food harvested from a given unit of land, increased because the farmers applied the traditional technologies of cultivation ever more intensively and because the best of these technologies spread throughout the empire. Traditional methods of irrigating, for example, were more widely adopted, the total acreage of irrigated land nearly tripling, from 130 million *mu* in 1400 to 350 million *mu* in 1900. (1 *mu* = one-sixth of an acre). The application of fertilizers was another traditional method that, used more intensively, helped improve crop yields. The increased use of fertilizers was a consequence partly of the farmers' growing appreciation of the beneficial effects of fertilizers, and partly of the greater quantities of night soil (human excrement) and manure that the expanded populations of humans, pigs, and draft animals made available to them.

The diffusion of improved seeds also helped improve crop yields. Today, improvements in seeds that are drought- and disease-resistant, that grow well in various soils or climatic conditions, or that mature rapidly are developed scientifically, through laboratory-controlled testing, crossbreeding, and selecting of mutant varieties. In traditional China, nature produced the variant seeds, and peasants in the fields serendipitously discovered a new variety, gave it a try, and then—if successful—encouraged others to plant it. The new seeds were often discovered as migrants pushed into areas of the country that were agriculturally undeveloped. Once, for example, a peasant found a variety of wild rice growing on a hilltop; by the 1930s, the seed, now aptly called "seed-dropped-from-heaven," was being cultivated widely in the area. As early as the Song Dynasty, an early-ripening variety of rice had been introduced from Champa, a state in the region now encompassed by Vietnam. This variety shortened the growing season from at least 180 days to about 130 days. During the ensuing centuries, other early-ripening varieties were discovered, perhaps within China itself; they matured in 90 to 100 days. By the early nineteenth century, some strains matured in only 60 to 80 days.

The discovery of early-ripening varieties of rice, wheat, and other grains was critically important because they facilitated double cropping. In the semitropical climes of south China, fast-maturing rice permitted peasants to harvest two, and in some places three, crops each year. Farther north, the farmers could often put in two crops in one season—first a planting of rice, and then, perhaps, a planting of wheat, millet, or barley.

Crops introduced from the Americas also contributed to the nation's increased food supply. Within forty years of Columbus's discovery of the New World, peanuts brought to China, presumably by the Portuguese, were being cultivated in the lower Yangtze region and in the southeast. Other New World crops that reached China during the sixteenth century were maize (what Americans call "corn"), sweet potato, and tobacco. Irish potatoes reached China in the seventeenth century.

New World food crops became important in China because they could be planted in soils that were unsuitable for the native crops. They did not displace the traditional crops, but made possible a net increase in total farm acreage and food supply. Maize and potatoes could be planted in hilly and dry soils that had previously been untilled or that were uncongenial even to crops like millet and barley. Similarly, peanuts flourish in a sandy loam and could be planted on riverine sand bars and steep hillsides where they did not compete with rice or other grain crops. Other advantages of the American crops were their relative resistance to drought, their high yields, and their high nutritional value. Sweet potatoes, for instance, produce twice as many calories per acre as do other crops raised in non-irrigated soils.

But the Chinese added these foods from the Americas to their diet only slowly and reluctantly. Peanuts, it is true, quickly delighted the Chinese palate, but they long remained a delicacy, limited to the dishes of the wealthy. In 1787, a scholar visiting Peking observed that every formal banquet had to include at least one dish with peanuts. Not until the late nineteenth or early twentieth century, however, did the peanut become a common food among the poor.

Other New World crops were accepted with less gusto. The problem was the taste. Even today, few Chinese eat the Irish potato with any enthusiasm. Maize and sweet potatoes made a greater impact, becoming a dietary staple of peasants who, in the seventeenth and eighteenth centuries, were migrating into the uplands where the land was too barren or steep for the cultivation of the traditional crops. As a Kiangsi local gazetteer reported, "The leading crop of hills and mountains is maize . . . which provides half a year's food for the mountain dwellers. . . . In general, maize is grown on the sunny side of the hills, sweet potatoes on the shady side."[3] But in 1637, rice still constituted about 70 percent of the cereals consumed by Chinese, followed in importance by wheat. At that time, maize and potatoes were still generally regarded as a mountaineer's food, and the New World crops did not substantially alter the diet of the majority of Chinese until the twentieth century.

Migrations: An Expanding Empire

Approximately half of China's increased food supply during the four centuries after 1400 resulted from the more intensive use of traditional techniques of cultivation and from the adoption of nonindigenous crops. The other half was produced by opening up lands to cultivation.

China's cultivated acreage nearly quadrupled between 1400 and the 1930s. (Table 1.1). In areas already densely populated, this increase was often achieved by pushing the fields farther upward onto the hillsides, by draining marshes, and by creating polders (the low-lying lands reclaimed for farming along river banks and lake shores). Much the greater part of the increased farm acreage, however, was added by colonizing unsettled regions of the country. This was a continuation of China's historic experience of frontier expansion.

The "Chinese" people—called the "Han," to distinguish them from the numerous minority nationalities living in China—had emerged from the mists of prehistory in the loess plains of north China, close to present-day Sian, near the great bend of the Yellow River. As late as about 1000 B.C., these Han, these early Chinese, inhabited an area that was only about 10 percent of what is today China proper. Beyond that area lived the Yue, Shu, Li, and Zhuang (to mention but a few), who were politically, culturally, and often ethnically distinct from the Han. From these small beginnings, the Han evinced a truly amazing dynamism, moving outward during the ensuing 3,000 years with almost inexorable force, growing in numbers, and mixing with the peoples and cultures that lay in their path. This was a protracted process, continuing for millennia, and is evidenced even today as the Han people and Han culture spread into Tibet and Sinkiang.[4]

The political reach of the Han Chinese, however, often surpassed their capacity to exploit their expanding territories economically. As early as the Qin Dynasty (221–206 B.C.), for example, the Chinese had established a political administration that encompassed even present-day Kwangtung. Shortly thereafter, the area we now know as northern Vietnam was incorporated as an integral part of the Chinese empire and remained so for a thousand years (111 B.C.–A.D. 939). But those areas were long regarded as the remote and wild frontier of the empire, and the demographic and cultural heartland of the Han people remained far away in the plains of north China.

Soon, however, there began the southward migratory expansion of the Han— sometimes termed "China's march toward the tropics." During the fourth and fifth centuries A.D., large numbers of Han Chinese began fleeing the invasions of north China by the Central Asian nomads and migrated to the Yangtze Valley region. Subsequently—roughly from the eighth to the twelfth centuries—the demographic and economic center of gravity of the Chinese nation shifted decisively to the south. As a result of both natural increase and migration, the population of southeast China (mostly in the middle Yangtze region) during those centuries increased sevenfold. During the same period, the population of the former center of Han culture in north China increased by only 54 percent. By 1200, more than 75 percent of China's population lived in south China. Subsequently, the north's share of the nation's population grew again, but the majority of Chinese continue to live in the south.

This shift of population to the south was accompanied by a radical alteration in the way most Chinese fed themselves.[5] In north China, they grew mainly millet, wheat, and barley in their rain-fed fields. In the south, wet-rice cultivation was possible. The yield of rice is roughly twice that of millet, and thus rice quickly became the principal food crop of the Han Chinese. Important changes in Han culture ensued: new methods of agricultural cultivation, new forms of social organization, new cuisine. In short, the economy and society, the very culture of the Chinese people, were significantly modified by this shift of the Han population to the south.

After 1400, the demographic expansion continued to transform the nation's social geography. Early in the Ming Dynasty, the overwhelming majority of Chinese still resided in the quarter-moon crescent that stretches from Peking in the north to Canton in the south (See Figure 1.1). Farther to the west and south, in the "developing" regions, Chinese habitation and culture had spread into the lowlands, the river valleys, and the plains. But vast sections of even those regions— such as the Hwai River area and the lowlands of Hupei—were still sparsely populated, with cultivable land begging to be put to productive use. Elsewhere, beyond the outposts of Chinese culture, in the hill country and mountains, the land remained virtually in a pristine state—untamed, the soil unbroken by the peasant's hoe. Much of China's hinterland in the late sixteenth century resembled the hill country of Kiangsi, which was still covered by virgin forests and where deer

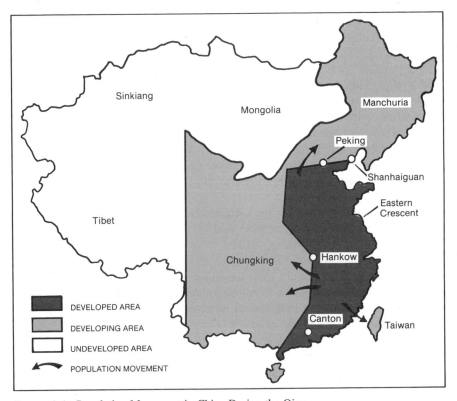

FIGURE 1.1. Population Movement in China During the Qing
Source: Yeh-chien Wang, *Land Taxation in Imperial China, 1750–1911* (Cambridge, Mass.: Harvard
    University Press, 1973), p. 85. Reprinted by permission.

grazed and tigers preyed. Aside from a few aboriginal tribespeople, not many
humans were to be found there—only some adventurous hunters and diggers of
medicinal roots, perhaps a bandit gang here and there, and an occasional Taoist
recluse. Even a century later, a Dutch visitor still found Taiwan "intersected by
many beautiful rivers, containing [an] abundance of fish, and . . . full of deer,
wild swine, wild goats, hares and rabbits, with woodcocks, partridges, doves and
other kinds of fowl. . . . The land is exceedingly rich and fertile, though very
little cultivated."[6]

As China's population multiplied after 1400, migrants moved, wave after wave,
into these frontier regions. During the Ming Dynasty, the imperial government
actively sponsored the colonization of strategically important areas along the Burma
border, in the southwest, to the Great Wall, in the north. Sometimes, the government forcibly moved settlers to those areas; other times, they encouraged the people to migrate voluntarily by promising them exemptions from taxes, by providing
them with seeds, tools, and draft animals, and even by building dikes and irrigation networks for their use. In these various ways, the Ming moved more than 1
million persons into Yunnan. In similar fashion, the Qing Dynasty in the seven-

teenth century hastened the redevelopment of Szechwan, which had been badly depopulated, in large part as a result of the atrocities of the rebel Zhang Xian-zhong in the late Ming period.

The greatest waves of interregional migrations, however, were private and voluntary, and they reached full tide during the Qing Dynasty as the pressure of population mounted. The settlers initially moved in three general directions. The largest wave flowed toward the west—toward Kiangsi, Hupei, Hunan, and Szechwan, with a spillover into the southwestern provinces of Yunnan, Kweichow, and Kwangsi. The second wave moved toward the northwest, along the Han River Valley, from northern Hupei, through southern Shensi, and into Kansu. The third and smaller wave of migration was eastward, from Kwangtung and, especially, Fukien to the island of Taiwan.

How many people joined these vast interregional migrations during the six-teenth to the mid-nineteenth centuries is uncertain. Suggestive, however, is the fact that the population of Szechwan, which was the largest recipient of new settlers, more than quadrupled (partly because of natural increase, but largely be-cause of immigration) in just three generations, growing in the years 1786 to 1850 by over 35 million. Thus China experienced a fundamental realignment of demo-graphic patterns as a result of these internal migrations.

During the latter half of the nineteenth century, the migratory flows shifted. The developing areas in the west and northwest had, since about 1800, begun to suffer the pressures of overpopulation, and thus they ceased to attract migrants from the eastern crescent. Instead, peasants and others seeking improved eco-nomic circumstances now moved into Manchuria, overseas, or—improbable though it might seem—back into the eastern crescent. The lower Yangtze region—notably Anhwei, southern Kiangsu, and northern Chekiang and Kiangsi—had suffered ter-rible destruction during the Taiping (1851–64) and Nien (1853–68) rebellions, with the result that some districts there were virtually depopulated, and the once-fertile fields were untended and overgrown with wild grasses. To land-hungry peasants elsewhere, these regions provided an inviting prospect, and millions mi-grated from the previously developing areas of Honan, Hunan, and northern Kiangsu back into this sector of the eastern crescent.

The northern and southern sectors of the eastern crescent had not suffered as severely from the mid-century rebellions as had the lower Yangtze region, and thus the population pressures there continued to build. Because the "developing" areas to the west had now filled up, the surplus population in the eastern crescent was forced to look elsewhere for a livelihood. For northern Chinese, especially those in Chihli (present-day Hopei) and Shantung, the seeming land of opportunity was Manchuria. For southern Chinese, especially those in Fukien and Kwangtung, emigration to Southeast Asia and the lands beyond became the primary alternative to the crowded conditions at home.

Manchuria was the homeland of the reigning dynasty, and the Manchus throughout most of the Qing period had banned migration there by Han Chinese. Although some Chinese hunters and adventurers had moved into the region in violation of the ban, and the dynasty had several times charitably opened the area to refugees from famines in north China, the population of Manchuria in 1800 was still only about 1 million. As population pressures mounted in China proper during the nineteenth and twentieth centuries, therefore, this area appeared as a huge, empty receptacle awaiting China's poor and hungry. Between 1860 and 1907, the reigning dynasty little by little removed the legal barriers to migration there. The dynasty's motive for doing so was, in large part, to counter the Russians' growing ambitions in the area by placing a sizable Chinese population there and thus to strengthen China's prior territorial claim. The chief boost to migration into Manchuria came after 1902, when the first railway began operating across the vast distances of the Manchurian plain. Thereafter, the railways facilitated immigration and linked the region to Chinese and international markets. The total population of Manchuria leaped from 3 million in 1860, to 17 million in 1907, to 47 million in 1953.

During the Ming and Qing dynasties, until 1893, migration outside the borders of the empire was prohibited. Yet as early as the fifteenth and sixteenth centuries, Chinese had moved abroad to such commercial centers of Southeast Asia as Manila and Malacca, and the imperial proscription on migration was largely ignored. Not until the mid-nineteenth century, however, did economic conditions force emigration to foreign soil on a large scale. Some emigrees went as contract laborers to the United States and Latin America—often suffering unspeakable conditions of transportation and employment; others went to the islands of the Indian Ocean and to South Africa; but the majority of southern Chinese settled in Southeast Asia, where they soon became a large and prominent minority of the population, numbering about 13 million by the mid-twentieth century.

The Pioneer Experience

Chinese who had migrated within China found that the tenor of life in the frontier areas was markedly different from that in the eastern crescent. On the frontier, life was characterized by "rootlessness, violence, and heavy involvement in a commercial agricultural economy."[7] There, a knowledge of the *Book of Rites* or the *Analects* of Confucius counted for little, and the dominant figure was the local strongman, often a powerful landlord who was backed by a gang of armed henchmen. The Chinese frontier, like the American West in the nineteenth century, was not a place for the refined or the weak.

Land developers, known variously as "settler-chiefs" or "mountain-lords," often led the way in opening up and controlling the new frontier areas. These men were usually wealthy or well-connected entrepreneurs who laid claim to large areas in the mountains, gaining title to the lands either by force or by purchase from the non-Han natives in the area. Then they recruited other settlers to clear and work the land, provided them with seeds and livestock, and perhaps financed the construction of irrigation works. These settler-chiefs were thus instrumental in facilitating the migration process by providing land, money, and manpower.

Clearing and cultivating the new lands was often accomplished by the slash-and-burn method. The virgin soil, in this way, produced bumper harvests for a few years. But slash-and-burn agriculture usually resulted in a terrible ravishing of the natural environment because the settlers rarely took precautions against erosion; they planted the maize and sweet potatoes in straight rows along the hillsides, and the rains soon washed away the fertile topsoil. Then the settlers had to move on to new slopes. This process was graphically described by the official Yan Ruyi in the early-nineteenth century:

> The mountain people fell trees and cultivate in the shade of the dead trees. The fertility of the soil will double the grain for one or two years. After the fourth or fifth year, the soil is already gouged and slack, the mountain is steep and the fierce waters of the sudden rains in summer and autumn leave only stone "bones" everywhere. They must again seek land to cultivate. The original land, left vacant, gradually grows grasses[;] shrubs rot and become mud, or are felled and burned to ash; only then can it be tilled again. One cannot rely on old forests for a steady living but must move to seek one's livelihood; thus the mountain people cannot but wander.[8]

In this way, much of China's most valuable resource, the fertility of the land, was tragically and permanently lost.

Most settlers could barely scratch out a subsistence by tilling these marginal lands in the hills. They supplemented their meager incomes, therefore, by supplying raw products to the market. Timber, for example, was available in profusion in the mountains and was in strong demand in the eastern crescent for construction purposes, firewood, and paper making. Early settlers in the frontier areas frequently engaged in forestry, clearing the hills of their forest cover and floating the logs downstream, first on the small streams and later on such major rivers as the Yangtze, where perhaps as many as 100 men were needed to guide just one huge raft of logs downstream. Sadly, this intensive logging during the early stages of migration rapidly squandered the nation's timber resources, denuding the mountains and accelerating soil erosion in the uplands.

Other raw products sent to the developed areas were tea, hemp, ramie, indigo, lacquer, seeds of the tung tree (for tung oil, used as a drying agent in varnishes), and even bears' paws (a culinary delight). Yunnan sent copper, which the government minted into coins. From the northwestern provinces came wool, leather, and gypsum, while Manchuria became a large supplier of grain, timber, and furs. Rather like the less-developed countries in the world today, which supply the industrialized nations with raw materials, the developing areas became prime suppliers of raw products to the eastern crescent.

Settlers in these frontier areas tended to be a "hardy and self-reliant lot." But "theirs was the self-reliance of the group, not of the individual. Only by working with his fellow settlers could the pioneer succeed." Such cooperation was often necessary for defense against the non-Han tribespeople, who resented the new arrivals. The settlers thus banded together in villages fortified with bamboo palisades. They worked the fields together, too, armed with "knives, daggers, and matchlocks."[9] Cooperation was also often needed to clear the forests or to construct and maintain irrigation networks. The political and economic realities of the pioneer experience did not, therefore, contribute to the development of individualism as a personality trait, but fostered the strong Chinese proclivity for "reliance upon others," which is discussed in Chapter 2.

Violence in the life of the frontier did not disappear, however, with the defeat of the non-Han tribes. As an area filled up and the choicest lands were occupied, quarrels erupted over the distribution of such increasingly scarce resources as land and water. The potential for conflict and misunderstanding was heightened because the several groups of settlers within an area were frequently of diverse origins, perhaps coming from different provinces or prefectures, often speaking distinctive and mutually unintelligible dialects, and preferring to maintain their own native customs.

Gradually, of course, the authority of the imperial bureaucracy extended into the developing areas, and at least a veneer of China's higher culture appeared after schools had been established and some of the youth had studied for and succeeded in the civil-service examinations. The frontier traditions of the strongman, of communal fighting and private feuding, nonetheless persisted with a remarkable tenacity—a high incidence of collective violence still found in the uplands of Kiangsi and in Taiwan in the early twentieth century.

Selected Readings

(See also the works cited in the notes)

Aird, John S. "Population Growth." In *Economic Trends in Communist China,* ed. Alexander Eckstein et al., pp. 183–327. Chicago: Aldine, 1968.

Averill, Stephen C. "The Shed People and the Opening of the Yangzi Highlands." *Modern China* 9, no. 1 (January 1983): 84–126.

Barclay, George W. et al. "A Reassessment of the Demography of Traditional Rural China." *Population Index* 42, no. 4 (October 1976): 606–35.

Barrett, Richard E. "Population Process in China Since the Nineteenth Century." Draft manuscript, July 1984.

Dunstan, Helen. "The Late Ming Epidemics: A Preliminary Survey." *Ch'ing-shih wen-t'i* 3, no. 3 (November 1975): 1–59.

Gottschang, Thomas Richard. "Migration from North China to Manchuria: An Economic History, 1891–1942." Ph.D. diss., University of Michigan, 1982.

Ho Ping-ti. *Studies on the Population of China, 1368–1953.* Cambridge, Mass.: Harvard University Press, 1959.

Lee, James. "Migration and Expansion in Chinese History." In *Human Migration: Patterns and Policies,* ed. William H. McNeill and Ruth S. Adams, pp. 20–47. Bloomington: Indiana University Press, 1978.

Mei, June. "Socioeconomic Origins of Emigration: Guangdong to California, 1850–1882." *Modern China* 5, no. 4 (October 1979): 463–501.

Meskill, Johanna Menzel. *A Chinese Pioneer Family: The Lins of Wu-feng, Taiwan, 1729–1895.* Princeton, N.J.: Princeton University Press, 1979.

Perkins, Dwight H. *Agricultural Development in China, 1368–1968.* Chicago: Aldine, 1969.

Schran, Peter. "China's Demographic Evolution 1850–1953 Reconsidered." *China Quarterly* 75 (September 1978): 639–46.

Wiens, Herold J. *China's March Toward the Tropics.* Hamden, Conn.: Shoe String Press, 1954.

2

The Family and the Individual in Chinese Society

If a Chinese died before his father, the father beat the coffin—symbolically punishing the son for unfilially having abandoned his duties of caring for his parents in this world and the next. This ritual act, although a small and seemingly insignificant part of the funeral ceremonies, highlights the differences in the relationship between fathers and sons, and hence in the very concept of the family, in China and the contemporary West. In China, children were not cherished as individuals whose destiny was to fulfill their own unique potentials, but were valued because they—and especially the sons—would help with work in the fields, produce sons who would carry on the family name, and provide for their parents in their old age *and* after death.

So important was the institution of the family that the term "familism" has been coined to characterize Chinese social values and organization. Familism was "the basis of a kind of society distinctive from any other kind in the world"—a system in which all ideas and behavior were judged by whether or not they contributed to the well-being of the family. If they did, they were good; everything else was bad.[1] Perhaps this is an exaggeration because there were realms of Chinese social life outside the family. The paramount importance of the institution of the family in Chinese life cannot, however, be doubted. It was "the strategic core of the social order."[2]

The Family

The traditional Chinese family—the Chinese term is *jia* or *jiating*—is conventionally defined as an economic unit composed of persons who are related by blood, marriage, or adoption and who partake of common property and a common purse. The family was, however, a protean institution, assuming diverse shapes, sizes, and generational depth—ranging from two persons of the same generation to fifty or more persons from four or five generations.

Social anthropologists customarily distinguish three forms of the Chinese family. There was, first, the *small,* or *conjugal,* family, which was made up of *at most two generations.* The conjugal family typically consisted of a father and mother and their *unmarried* children and usually numbered about three to six persons. Approximately 60 percent of all Chinese families were of this type. Second was the *large,* or *joint,* family, in which a husband and wife lived in the same household and shared a family budget with their unmarried children, with *two or more married sons* and their sons' wives and children, and possibly with their grandsons' wives and children. And, finally, the third form of the family represented an intermediate stage between the joint and the conjugal families. This was the *stem* family, in which the parents, unmarried children, *one married son,* and the son's wife and children lived in one household. A stem family may be regarded as an incomplete, or broken, joint family.

This threefold typology of Chinese family organization is useful for descriptive purposes. It conceals, however, the dynamic character of Chinese family life, for a Mom-and-Dad family group might, during its lifetime, evolve through all three forms. "The Chinese family . . . was like a balloon, ever ready to expand whenever there was wealth to inflate it."[3] Thus a man and wife who at marriage set up a household formed a conjugal family—and their family continued to be conjugal in form as long as their children living with them remained unmarried. Later, when their elder son took a wife and brought her into his parents' home, the family became stem in form. And if a second son took a wife and continued to live with his parents, a joint family was established. But the deaths of the parents or the decision to divide the household resulted in further changes in the form of the family.

The Chinese family was, at one and the same time, an *economic unit* in which the members produced and consumed in common, a *religious unit* that was responsible for performing the rites required for the well-being of both living and deceased members of the family (this latter aspect of the family will be discussed in the chapter on popular religion); and it was *a social-security organization* that provided for the care of its needy and aging members. The values and outlook instilled in the Chinese family were consequently fundamentally different from those found in the contemporary West. In the West, parents nurture their child so that he or she can become an independent and self-fulfilling adult; in China, parents nurtured their son—a daughter was a separate problem—so that he could subsequently support them and perpetuate the family in an unending line of descent.

As a result of the dictates of familism, a Chinese husband and wife felt impelled to have at least one son and preferably more. And all the sons, together with their wives and progeny, should if at all possible continue to live together within a single household. "Five generations under one roof" represented the family ideal. Probably no more than about 6 to 7 percent of Chinese families, however, attained that ideal.

Elementary demographics suggest one reason why five- or even three-generation families formed only a minority of all families. With a national life expectancy at birth of only about thirty years, many parents did not live much past the marriages of their sons. Many families, moreover, were fortunate to have just one son survive to adulthood—in which case, by definition, they were incapable of forming joint families.

The absence of a system of economic primogeniture was another important reason why the joint family remained but a distant ideal for most Chinese families. Without economic primogeniture, a practice that the Chinese had abandoned in about the second century B.C., all sons were entitled to an approximately equal share of the inheritance when their father died. Landholdings tended, therefore, to become smaller with each passing generation. (Because Chinese did practice ritual primogeniture, however, the eldest son often received an additional share of inheritance so that he could care for an aged parent, if one survived, and perform the ancestral sacrifices.)

There were, of course, limits to this process of division. In the poorest families, some sons were cut off without any inheritance and were thus forced to seek their livelihood as, perhaps, tenant farmers or peddlars. There was also a counter tendency because a Chinese, whenever possible—perhaps as a result of wealth derived from success as an official, as a merchant, or simply as a skillful farm manager—bought land to add to his patrimony. The system of partible inheritance meant, however, that most farms were too small to support the parents and all their married sons. It was customary, therefore, for just the eldest son to continue to reside in the family home and look after the aging parents; younger sons had to move out soon after they took a wife. Almost always, however, at least one of the sons lived with his parents after his marriage. In the system of familism, this was a moral given.

Paradoxically, the estates of the wealthy, which were large enough to support a joint family, were particularly vulnerable to the process of division. The wealthy tended to marry at a younger age than the poor, and thus to produce more children. It was also the wealthy, and not the poor, who took concubines, whose sons were entitled to shares of their fathers' bequests—although the shares were sometimes, but not always, less than those allotted to sons born of the first wives. Children in wealthy households, moreover, received better nutrition and health care and so had a reasonably good chance of surviving to adulthood, whereas poor families considered that fate was kind if even two children out of six or seven births grew to maturity.[4] Higher birth rates and lower death rates, then, meant that more sons in wealthy families grew to maturity and thus had claims on shares in their families' estates.

Occasionally, the patriarch of a wealthy family, wielding a firm hand, succeeded during his lifetime in holding his sons, and his sons' wives and children, together under one roof. Thus was created a joint family. Sometimes his sons, after his death, continued to live together—thereby forming a fraternal joint family. But few fraternal joint families remained together for very long. The eldest brother often expected deference from his younger siblings, but without a system of economic primogeniture, no one brother had greater legal authority or economic rights than any other brother. Quarrels thus easily developed over such matters as administration of the jointly held property or the disposition of the profits therefrom. Understandably, then, Chinese brothers often got along badly. There was, it seems, "a built-in tendency [for brothers] to be rivalrous when they are adult."[5]

Exacerbating these fraternal tensions were the jealousies and enmities among the brothers' wives. Sisters-in-law were generally even more resentful than the brothers when they felt that the conjugal family of one brother was receiving more than its fair share of the family income or was not performing its share of the family work. The wives would complain incessantly to their husbands of the injustice of it all, instilling suspicion in the minds of the already rivalrous brothers, until the enmities became unbearable. Then the brothers, even if they continued to reside in partitioned quarters within the same house, would "divide the family stove"—each of the brothers' families establishing its own kitchen, instead of cooking and eating communally. At the same time, they would divide the family assets and thereafter live as separate economic units.

The relatively short duration of most joint families resulted also from the inexorable laws of upward and downward mobility. In every society, some sons rise during their careers to positions more exalted than those of their fathers, but there is inevitably a downward flow as well. This might be explained by chance; some sons are just less capable than their fathers. But Chinese, who had an irrepressible penchant for viewing all social and political phenomena through moral lenses, usually ascribed the fall of families to the profligacy and immorality of the junior generation. Reared in the lap of plenty, the sons of the successful were thought to lack the dedication and drive of their fathers and grandfathers, so that when they became financially independent following the death of their fathers, they were likely to squander their families' wealth on conspicuous consumption, gambling, concubines, or (in the nineteenth century) opium smoking. Popular belief held that this process—from rags to riches, and back to rags again—required only three generations. Exceptions to this adage can, of course, be found. Yet the forces of downward mobility, together with the absence of economic primogeniture, the disputatious nature of family members, and high mortality rates, suffice to explain why most families failed to attain the ideal of the joint family.

The disintegrative tendencies within individual families were sometimes resisted, however, by the formation of lineages (zu). Lineages, also known as common-descent groups, were an extension of the principles of familism beyond the immediate family to include all relatives living in the same community who could trace their descent patrilineally to one ancestor. Lineages sometimes could count 2,000 to 3,000 living male members.[6] Organizations of lineages were strongest in south China, where the residents of entire villages often belonged to just one lineage. Lineages also existed in the north, but there they were rarely as powerful or wealthy as in the south.

Powerful lineages commonly compiled genealogies of their members as a means of maintaining their distinct identities, boosting their prestige, and performing their corporate functions (such as conducting ancestral rites, disciplining errant members, and distributing charity to needy members.) Without a genealogy, a descent group easily became scattered and lost its sense of corporate identity; with a genealogy, it possessed a collective memory, could determine the order of status relationships within the lineage (which was essential to the proper conduct of the ancestral rites), and, by no means least important, had a basis for determining who was eligible for benefits from the lineage estate.

Most important to the continued existence of a powerful lineage was the possession of some form of corporate property, revenue from which was used to construct ancestral temples, pay for the education of the lineage youth, and, in some cases, finance lineage defense. The possession of substantial lineage properties, held in common and in perpetuity, helped combat the tendency of individual families within the common-descent group to disintegrate and decline after a few generations. In Anhwei province, for example, a few families dominated the society and politics of Tongcheng *Xian* for 400 to 500 years, some of them from the early years of the Ming Dynasty to the twentieth century. This defiance of the forces of downward mobility was achieved largely by means of lineage organizations, which were valuable supports for the values of familism.

The Changing Status of Women

In China throughout the imperial period, man and woman were not created equal. It mattered little that long before, in the pre-dawn of history, Chinese society had probably been matriarchal; by historical times, women were one of the most disparaged and exploited segments of society. The Confucian ideal of womanhood, repeated constantly over the centuries, had been expressed by an exception to the rule, a famous woman scholar—Ban Zhao (d. A.D. 116). The younger sister of the great historian Ban Gu, she prescribed the conduct appropriate to a virtuous woman:

> To be humble, yielding, respectful and reverential; to put herself after others . . . these qualities are those exemplifying woman's low and humble estate. To retire late and rise early; not to shirk exertion from dawn to dark . . . this is called being diligent. To behave properly and decorously in serving her husband; to be serene and self-possessed, shunning jests and laughter . . . this is called being worthy of continuing the husband's lineage. If a woman possesses the above-mentioned three qualities, then her reputation shall be excellent.[7]

During the early centuries of the empire, the position of women was markedly better than it would be in late imperial times. Women during the centuries from the Han to the Tang dynasties, for example, could often mingle socially quite freely with men; they were not disgraced if they were divorced; and the attitude toward female chastity both before and after marriage was relatively relaxed. Even as late as the Song Dynasty, a woman of the upper classes could, if she had no brothers, be the heir to her father's property. After about the thirteenth century, however, the subjugation of women increased sharply. The consolidation of neo-Confucianism by the end of the Song reinforced the rigid, patriarchy-fortifying standards of feminine behavior expressed by Ban Zhao. And following the overthrow of Mongol rule in 1368, a powerful resurgence of veneration for native Chinese ways fostered the spread of the puritanical Confucian ideals of womanhood even among the commoners. Female virginity and chastity now became virtual cults, and a woman who had been raped could best prove her virtue by committing suicide. Remarriage of widows was denounced—although Confucian scholars sometimes debated among themselves whether a widow could best demonstrate her moral righteousness by killing herself, thus ensuring her fidelity to her husband to the very end, or by remaining alive to serve her in-laws and children.

Such, at any rate, were the orthodox ideals during late imperial times. Not always, however, did the social realities conform to these ideals. Widows in the Ming and Qing periods, for example, did frequently remarry—sometimes out of economic necessity, sometimes because their in-laws forced them into remarriage so that the in-laws could claim their dowry and the dead husbands' patrimony. And among the lower classes in the villages, female chastity appears to have been something less than a cardinal virtue.

Some women, moreover, may even have improved their position in late imperial times. Beginning in the late-sixteenth century, educational facilities spread and book publishing became popular. To some extent, women shared in the increased educational opportunities of the time, although estimates indicate that female literacy rates in the early nineteenth century ranged, indeterminately, between only 1 and 10 percent. Upper-class women were doubtless the principal beneficiaries of the improved access to education, and in the late eighteenth and early nineteenth centuries, some women became noted as poets, calligraphers, and painters. Women such as these, it is claimed, associated easily even with scholars, and at least a few men—such as the poet Yuan Mei (1716–98) and the reformist official Gong Zizhen (1792–1841)—came to sense the idiocy of the old saw that "only the untalented woman is virtuous." These men, as a consequence, criticized the patriarchal ideology that emphasized female inferiority, urging that women be given greater educational opportunities and that the oppressive codes of womanly chastity be abandoned.

Research on the history of women in late imperial China is only now beginning, and generalizations here should be regarded as tentative. It appears, however, that until the late nineteenth century, such liberating tendencies were of limited effect and that the position of women during the early Qing period may well have fallen lower than at any other time in China's long history.

Girls and Childhood

Even at birth, a girl generally brought little joy to the hearts of her parents, for the dictates of familism demanded sons to perpetuate the family line. Sons would also help with the farm work, support their parents in their declining years, and after their deaths perform the required ancestral sacrifices. A girl, by contrast, was a burden and an expense; she would have to be fed and clothed until she was seventeen years old or so, and then, just when she became old enough to help in the house and in the fields, she would at considerable expense be married out to be given in marriage to a stranger's family. Conventional wisdom was summed up in the adage "The birth of a girl child is like a thief in the night."

There were exceptions. If the girl were the mother's first-born, her arrival might be greeted with some satisfaction because her birth proved the mother's fecundity and offered hope for the birth of a son in the future. Older, more experienced friends of the young mother sometimes even saw a bright side when the first child was a girl, assuring the mother that the girl would later be a big help in caring for her future brothers. Indeed, most families probably hoped that one—but no more than one—of their children would be a girl.

Yet too many daughters were regarded as a curse, especially for poor families, which could ill-afford to feed the hungry mouths of unproductive members. Occasionally, therefore, the mother of a female newborn placed her head down in a bucket of water, suffocated her, or (perhaps more commonly) simply abandoned her to die. There has, however, been much exaggeration about the frequency of female infanticide. Certainly, in times of adversity, hard-pressed parents were more likely to dispose of a newborn child, but then even male infants were sometimes killed. The incidence of infanticide has been calculated for the years 1851 to 1948 at about 5 percent of female births and about 2.5 percent of male births.

If the newborn girl was not put to death by her parents or was spared the numerous other perils of early mortality from natural causes, she would be constantly reminded as she grew up that she was merely a "worthless girl." The treatment she received, however, generally depended more on her position in the sibling order than on her sex. Even a girl, if the first-born, would be constantly in the arms or on the back of an adult. This adult might be the mother (who invariably offered the infant a breast at the least sign of restiveness or unhappiness) or the father (who felt satisfaction at the birth of the first child) or perhaps the grandmother or grandfather (who delighted in the first or second of their grandchildren, regardless of sex). A girl born farther down the sibling order, however, received less attention and careful nurturing. Girls tended to be weaned a few months earlier than boys; if girls became ill, the parents usually delayed seeking the advice of a doctor, or beseeching the protection of the gods, longer than if boys became sick. It was also common that a poor woman who had recently given birth to a girl would serve as a wet nurse in a well-to-do family, leaving her infant daughter to subsist as best she could on rice gruel rather than on her mother's milk.

Still, Chinese children of both sexes enjoyed considerable indulgence during their early years. Toilet training, for instance, was notably relaxed, without the anxious reminders and reprimands usually visited on American children. Nature was pretty much allowed to take its course until children were two to three years old; then, mothers might mildly tease children who soiled themselves. Within the limits of their individual patience, parents also reacted tolerantly to their children's disobedience or fits of temper. As long as children did not endanger themselves or younger siblings, there was no uniform effort to train them in the ways of adult comportment. Boys, especially, were indulged in this way.

This age of indulgence ended—and ended abruptly—about the age of six, give or take a year or so. Suddenly, about the time when boys began working in the fields or attending school, children were no longer permitted to act childishly; suddenly, they were treated as though they possessed all the reasoning powers of adults, and they began the serious business of preparing for adult life. For boys, this change was more traumatic because—in contrast to girls, who had already learned to accept the responsibility and constraints of caring for siblings—theirs had been a relatively pampered and unrestrained existence. The father, who had often been warm, informal, and sometimes playful with his son, now became a strict disciplinarian. He demanded punctilious obedience; deviations from his wishes would be harshly punished. Chinese fathers never conceived of the notion, so widespread in the United States today, that they should be pals with their sons. Rather, they tended to be stern, harsh, and remote, convinced that this demeanor was necessary if they were to be effective teachers and role models. For the child, the father thus loomed as an awesome and dour figure, best avoided if at all possible. Thereafter, true warmth between a father and his sons was the exception rather than the rule.

Corporal punishment, for both boys and girls, was another part of growing up. The prevailing pedagogy was that punishment of improper conduct was the only way to encourage proper behavior. And punishment usually implied physical punishment. As one Chinese mother remarked: "Do you think that they will listen to you when you scold them? What good does that do? All you can do is grab one and really hit him hard. Then the others will be good too." Not all punishment, however, was inflicted in accordance with the principles of an implicit pedagogy. Many mothers, harassed by onerous household duties and often bearing a deep resentment at their own unkind fate, frequently gave vent to their anger by unreasoningly and spitefully striking out at their children. As one mother laughingly remarked when chided about hitting her child in a vulnerable spot: "I never [look where I'm hitting the child]. When I'm mad how can I look? I just hit them wherever I can with whatever I have in my hand." To this, a second mother responded:

> I'm that way too. You have to hit them when you are mad, or they will run off and you'll forget about it. Like yesterday. . . . I was so hot and so mad that I just grabbed the oldest one and beat her up. I think I really hurt her, but they made me so mad I just grabbed the closest one and hit her, and then they were all quiet.[8]

Such beatings, inflicted in the heat of anger, were often severe, leaving bruises and sometimes drawing blood.

For girls, the most painful stage of the transition to adulthood began on the day that their mothers bound their feet. Footbinding probably originated among dancing girls in the palace during the late Tang or the Five Dynasties period (ninth to tenth century A.D.) The dancers achieved artistic effect by lightly binding their feet. Admiration for small-footed women then spread among ladies of the court, who emulated the dancers by moderately compressing their feet. It was probably during the period of Mongol rule—the Yuan Dynasty (1271–1368)—that the prac-

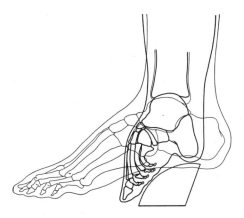

FIGURE 2.1. Footbinding. A foot misshaped by binding is juxtaposed in the sketch with a woman's normal foot. From *East Asia: Tradition and Transformation,* by John K. Fairbank, Edwin O. Reischauer, and Albert M. Craig, p. 142; copyright © 1973 by Houghton Mifflin Company; used by permission.

tice spread to the common classes. By the early Ming, large- and natural-footed women had become objects of derision, and by the nineteenth century, some 50 to 80 percent of Chinese women probably bound their feet. Those who retained their natural feet were usually from the lowest social classes or were members of certain ethnic and cultural minorities, such as the Manchus, Miao, and Hakka. There were also regional differences; footbinding was relatively uncommon in villages of, for example, Szechwan, Fukien, and Hunan, whereas even female beggars and water carriers in Honan and Shensi had tiny feet.

Footbinding was crippling. Using a bandage some 2 inches wide and 10 feet long, the four small toes were first forced down and under, so that they folded against the sole of the foot (the large toe was not bound); then the bandage was brought back around the heel so tightly that the front and back of the foot were drawn in toward each other, forcing the instep of the foot to arch upward. Progressively, the binding was tightened; the pain was unremitting, and blood and pus soaked the bandages. Flesh atrophied and was peeled off; occasionally, even a toe or two was sloughed off. When properly done, the "golden lotus"—as bound feet were euphemistically called—would measure only 3 inches from heel to end of the large toe. By then, the girl no longer suffered the agonies of pain, but she had been crippled for life and was unable to move unaided far beyond the household walls.

Sexual allure was a major reason why women bound their feet. Men waxed rhapsodic over the beauty of the embroidered small shoes worn by women with bound feet; they were sexually aroused by the foot-bound woman's swaying walk and uplifted buttocks; and they dreamed of caressing those golden lotuses, which fired their imaginations no less than did the woman's sexual organs. For a Chinese male in traditional times, a pretty face was fine, but a diminutive foot was exquisite. Small feet were not only objects of beauty, but also symbols of style, social class, and proper upbringing. Women with unbound feet, therefore, did not easily find quality husbands.

There is, however, a darker, sociological explanation for men's having encouraged women to bind their feet. By thus severely restricting women's movements, footbinding physically reinforced the rigid ideals of female virtue and isolation that neo-Confucians had formulated in the twelfth century. A woman confined to the household had no need for learning; she acquired no experience of the outside world; and she was thus kept ignorant and palpably inferior to men. Thus footbinding was a means of subjugating women and ensuring male dominance.

Women and Marriage

In contrast to the "European pattern" of marriage prevalent in western Europe from at least the eighteenth century—whereby most women customarily did not marry until their early or even mid-twenties, and many did not marry at all—Chinese women married early and nearly universally. Because of the support structures provided by the system of familism, Chinese could marry while still financially dependent on their parents. In the European pattern, by contrast, the young commonly had to be financially independent before marrying, which usually meant waiting until the death or retirement of their parents. Most societies to the east of a line drawn from Leningrad to Trieste approximated the Chinese pattern of early and universal marriage, although Japan, significantly, more closely fit the European pattern.

By the time a girl reached the age of seventeen or so, she was ready for the major turning point in her life: marriage.[9] Despite the importance of this event to her personally, she might never be consulted about it. Nor would her future husband have a part in the decision. Marriage in China was regarded as a family matter—*by* the family and *for* the family. For the groom's family, the primary goal was to acquire a woman who, with the groom, could produce male offspring in order to perpetuate the family line. It was desirable, too, that she be temperamentally suited to the work and situation of her new family. A girl who was lazy or who had a foul temper could be a curse on the family forever; if she was sickly, she could be a burden; and if she was too attractive, she might have extramarital love affairs that would sully the family reputation.

The social and economic status of the bride's family also entered into the groom's parents' decision. The status of the girl's family should be high, but not too high. "Marriage," as Mencius said, "is a bond between two surnames," and each family recognized that an advantageous marriage could enhance its reputation and provide innumerable economic and political benefits. If the bride's family status was too lofty, entertaining her parents (as was occasionally necessary) could be embarrassing and excessively costly; if its status was too low, the in-laws' requests for loans and favors could be a nuisance. For parents arranging their son's marriage, whether or not he would be happy with a particular girl was not an important consideration.

For the girl's family, the social and economic advantages to be gained from a marriage also weighed heavily in their consideration of a prospective husband. Because the girl was marrying away, however, her family would be less affected by the marriage than would the groom's family, and thus her parents had more latitude to think of her future welfare. Would her life working with the boy's mother, for instance, be tolerable? Was the boy hard working and thrifty, or did he (or his father) inveterately gamble or whore? (Occasional visits to prostitutes, though, were not considered a serious liability.) There were also questions about the size and amounts of the bride-price and dowry—sensitive issues that, like all the other items in the marriage negotiations, required the meditation of a match-maker.[10]

Ideally, the prospective bride and groom did not know each other, and had not even seen each other, before the day of the wedding. Most objectionable was the formation of a romantic attachment to each other before the marriage. Should youth have the right to choose their own mates, they were apt to be guided by considerations of love, beauty, or sexual attraction, thus elevating transient and unimportant individual desires above the needs and well-being of the family. When a marriage was properly arranged, therefore, the bride, after arriving at her new home, was first formally presented to her in-laws, and to other elder members of the family. Only after this was she taken to the bedroom, where, for the first time, she met the man who was to be her husband.

For the groom, life was little changed by marriage. He still resided in his natal home; everything there was familiar to him, and he was relatively secure in knowing what the future held for him. For the bride, this was the most traumatic period of her life. She was now uprooted from her natal home and set down in an unfamiliar house, amid total strangers, uncertain of what to expect in coming days and years. If, in the best of circumstances, she found her husband considerate and not too repulsive, if, indeed, she and her husband developed a liking for each other, then she would have a small haven of companionship. Usually, however, affection between husband and wife developed, if ever, only in the late stages of their married life. But as newlyweds, the two remained cool and distant. Outside the bedroom, husband and wife had little to do with each other; they rarely spoke to each other in public, except when he commanded her to do something, and any display of affection between the two (in the unlikely event that they did feel affection for each other) was sternly frowned on.

Marriage was simply not regarded as a means of enhancing the personal pleasure or happiness of the newly married couple. Instead, it was a means of promoting the goals of familism. Its purposes were to perpetuate the family by producing male heirs and to acquire a young woman who would ease the burden of work in the kitchen and assist in caring for her parents-in-law during their declining years. Affection between the son and his wife could cause them to place their own wishes and happiness above those of the larger family; it could weaken the mother's control over her son; or it could even cause the young couple to establish a separate household. Affection between the son and his wife, therefore, especially during the early period of their marriage, was thought to be inimical to, rather than conductive to, family unity and strength.

Far more important in the bride's new life than her husband was her mother-in-law. These two women were thrown into intimate and constant contact. They cooked together, cleaned the house together, engaged in farm and handicraft work together. In this relationship, the mother-in-law was the dominant partner, and rare indeed was the bride who could meet the exacting standards of the older woman. Often, it is true, the mother-in-law would commence the relationship by being tolerant of and even friendly to her son's bride. But the young girl was relatively inexperienced about household work, and, in any case, the work she had learned in her parents' home was done differently in her new home. Further-more, the bride at least potentially represented a threat to the mother-in-law's domination of her son—the significance of which will soon become clear when we discuss the uterine family—so there were strong psychological, as well as practical, reasons why a rift soon opened up between the two women.

Sooner or later, therefore, tension and conflict between the two women almost inevitably appeared. And in bringing about the submission of the younger woman, the mother-in-law was nearly always harsh, tyrannical, and even cruel. Conse-quently, the first year or so of marriage was probably the most stressful period in a woman's life. If she was maltreated and beaten by the mother-in-law, she had virtually no appeal. Her husband and father-in-law were reluctant to intervene. She might complain to her own father and mother, but conflicts between mother-in-law and daughter-in-law were anticipated—the absence of such conflicts was actually regarded as abnormal and somewhat suspicious—so an occasional beating of the daughter-in-law was not considered out of the ordinary. Thus her parents would be exceedingly reluctant to intervene on her behalf. The most effective check on the mother-in-law's mistreatment of the daughter-in-law was probably the gossip of neighborhood women, for when tales of gross cruelty spread to her acquaintances in the village street, the mother-in-law could suffer severe loss of face.

A large number of young brides found their new life intolerable. Escape, how-ever, was not easy. It was unthinkable that a bride could return to her parents' home, at least for long, because she no longer belonged there; her presence would be a burden and an embarrassment. She could theoretically obtain a divorce. Di-vorce was sternly disapproved of, however, and the woman would probably have no source of support unless she remarried; yet the only available bachelors who would accept "used goods" were usually those so impoverished that they had remained unmarried because they could not afford the bride-price. If she was still young and pretty, she could become a prostitute.

Or she could commit suicide. It is a tragic fact that of the women who com-mitted suicide in China, the greatest number by far were those in their late teens and early twenties—that is, young women in the age group that included those who were recently betrothed or married (Figure 2.2). To a distraught and ill-treated young bride, suicide was probably more attractive than we might suppose. By committing suicide, she knew that she would be inflicting a fearful revenge on her marital family. She knew that she would return as a ghost to torment her tormentor—say, her mother-in-law who would suffer the anguish of hell knowing that an angry ghost would be lying in wait to inflict harm at her every turn. The

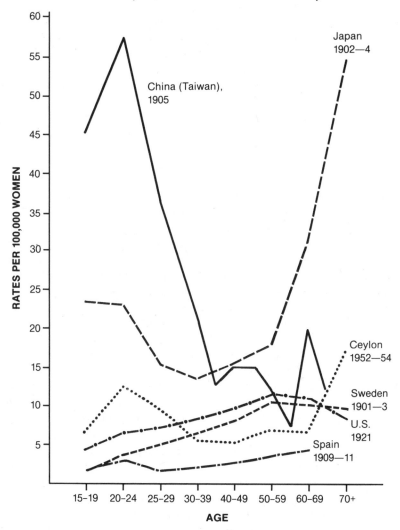

FIGURE 2.2. Women's International Suicide Profiles
Source: Margery Wolf, "Women and Suicide in China," in Margery Wolf and Roxanne Witke, eds., *Women in Chinese Society,* (Stanford, Calif.: Stanford University Press, 1975), p. 118. Reprinted by permission.

bride would also have the satisfaction of contemplating the lawsuit that her natal family could be expected to bring against her husband's family, the possibly ruinous financial settlement, the terrible loss of face that the mother-in-law would incur, and the wonderful irony of the mother-in-law having to be one of the weeping mourners at her funeral.

Relief from the tense and often unpleasant circumstances of a bride's early married life often came with the birth of her first child. She hoped that the child would be a boy, but even the birth of a daughter demonstrated that she was not barren, and thus offered promise of producing male descendants for the marital family. Moreover, before giving birth, she had never really been accepted as a part of her new family. Now she secured a place in the family, and her position for life was relatively assured.

Still, she did not identify with this family as fully as did her husband. From her husband's point of view, the family was an uninterrupted line of descent, extending from the earliest known progenitor into the infinite future. He felt himself securely and irrevocably part of that line, the heir and the beneficiary of those preceding him in the family line whose chief responsibility, therefore, was to perpetuate that line and to serve as trustee for the family's honor and accumulated properties.

From the young woman's point of view, the concept of family probably had a very different meaning. Since early childhood, she had understood that she was not truly part of her natal family, that she "belonged to others." Indeed, if she died before marriage, her parents were confronted with the embarrassing problem of how to dispose of her soul. Ritually speaking, she did not belong to any family. Her tablet could not be placed on her father's family altar—as could that of a son who died before marriage—because, as one villager declared, "The ancestors would surely be angry if you put an ugly thing like that on the altar." [11] Frequently, therefore, a small sachet of incense ashes, representing the girl's soul, was placed in a dark corner of the house, although people in some regions of China feared that placing the girl's soul anywhere on family property would bring bad luck.

For a considerable period after marriage, the young woman still felt herself an outsider, her husband's family regarding her with some suspicion and, possibly, even hostility. Moreover, she did not yet feel any bonds of emotional attachment to her husband's ancestors. She was, therefore, at least initially, isolated.

Only after the young woman had borne children of her own did she acquire a true sense of belonging to a family. But her concept of family—what has been termed the "uterine family"—was initially very different from that of her husband. Rather than encompassing the line of descent of her husband's family—the "surname family"—her family consisted essentially of herself and her progeny. A woman's uterine family would expand when her sons married, brought home daughters-in-law, and produced grandchildren. A daughter-in-law's place in this uterine family was ambivalent, however, because she at least potentially challenged the mother-in-law's control over her (the mother-in-law's) son and thus threatened the mother-in-law's sense of security. This was why a Chinese mother so adamantly opposed a love match between her son and his bride: a marriage based on romantic attachment threatened to dismember, rather than enlarge, her uterine family.

Even the woman's husband was only ambivalently associated with her uterine family. "Father is important to the group," it has been remarked, "but he is not quite a member of it, and for some uterine families he may even be 'the enemy.' " [12] If, for example, he continued to be dominated by his mother, he would offer little support to his wife's uterine family. And because he valued the family as a line of descent, he might squander financial resources on surname-family ostentation or in assisting brothers and other relatives who were suffering financial distress. Such expenditures, which accorded with the values of the family as a line of descent, were simply squandered from the vantage point of the woman whose sole property and possessions were those of the uterine family.

As old age approached, however, the woman's concept of the uterine family gradually came to coincide with her husband's concept of the patrilineal family. As frequently happened, she and her husband had now formed true bonds of common interest and even mutual affection. Now, with her mother-in-law in the grave, she had become the dominant female in the household; her place in the family was unalterably secure; and by this time, she felt pleasantly familiar with the ways of the household, neighborhood, and village. She was no longer the frightened outsider, but the family matriarch, now perhaps with daughters-in-law of her own whom she could tyrannize.[13]

Variant Forms of Marriage

The form of marriage we have just discussed, in which a woman of sixteen to eighteen years of age was married and moved out of her parents' home, is known as the "major form of marriage." There were also two other forms of marriage: the "minor form," in which a girl was "adopted" into the home of her betrothed while still very young; and "uxorilocal marriage," in which an adult man married into the woman's natal home.[14] These forms of marriage were perhaps even more revealing of the social values associated with familism than was the more orthodox, socially respected, major form of marriage.

In the minor form of marriage, the intended bride usually moved into the household of her future husband's family while still merely an infant, often six months old or less and usually less than one year old. There she was raised almost as a daughter, probably nursing at the breasts of her prospective mother-in-law. Customarily, however, she was treated sternly and even callously by her adoptive "parents." She was often weaned earlier than if she had been a natural daughter, thus making her more susceptible to disease; she was also apt to receive less careful medical attention. Maltreatment and arduous labor were the normal part of her growing up. Indeed, the childhood mortality rate of "adopted daughters" was far higher than that of girls raised by their own mothers.

For fifteen years or so, her relations with her prospective husband were essentially those of a sister and brother. Soon after she began menstruating, a brief and spare wedding ceremony was held, or perhaps not even that. Then she and her "brother" were told that it was time to sleep together.

Legally speaking, there was no difference between the major and minor forms of marriage. But psychologically speaking, the differences were enormous. The relationship between husband and wife in the minor form of marriage was even less emotionally intimate or satisfying than that in the major form of marriage. Husband and wife, having been raised as brother and sister, frequently felt extreme aversion to consummating their marriage. Being "brother" and "sister"— at least psychologically—they commonly were disgusted by the thought of having sexual relations with each other, and the father and family sometimes had to compel the two to sleep together on their wedding night.

But if a minor marriage was unsatisfactory for the husband and wife, it had considerable advantages from the mother-in-law's point of view. It was less of a financial burden than if her son married in the major, or orthodox, manner. Feeding and clothing an "adopted daughter" during the years prior to the actual marriage was, of course, an expense, but was far less costly than were the extravagances a major marriage, which required expenditures for the bride-price, gifts for the bride and her family, and feasting that often consumed as much as an entire year's income.

But frugality was not the sole, or even the most important, reason why parents often favored the minor form of marriage. This is evidenced by the fact that wealthy and high-status families "adopted" their sons' future brides—and gave away their own infant daughters to the families of prospective husbands—with approximately the same frequency as poor families. Indeed, the compelling reason that a family adopted a future daughter-in-law was that the adoptive "mothers" wished to avoid the disagreeable conflicts with a daughter-in-law that almost inevitably accompanied a major marriage. An "adopted daughter," being brought up in the marital rather than the natal home, became socialized at an early age to the ways of her future husband's family and complaisant to the wishes of her prospective mother-in-law. There was, moreover, little likelihood that a romantic bond would develop between the son and his "sister"-wife. A daughter-in-law who was acquired through the minor form of marriage thus posed no threat to the mother-in-law's uterine family.

Uxorilocal marriage, the second form of unorthodox marriage, was less common than minor marriage, but was by no means rare. This form of marriage was usually contracted by a married couple that had produced no natural male heir. They thus faced the prospect of ending the family line, of having no children to care for them in their declining years, and of being without anyone to sacrifice to them after their deaths. For a Chinese, the prospect of such a future was the most worrisome possible.

There were, however, a couple of solutions to this problem. One was to adopt a son. The couple could adopt a boy from, for example, a brother or the wife's sister, or could purchase a boy from a distant village. This solution was often less than fully satisfactory, however, because boys adopted from relatives or nearby acquaintances would sometimes neglect their adoptive parents in favor of their natural parents. And boys purchased from strangers were expensive—and their loyalty was uncertain.

A uxorilocal marriage provided another, and some thought preferable, solution to this problem. This solution was most easily arranged when the couple, although they had no son, had produced a daughter. They would search for a man willing to marry their daughter uxorilocally. (A couple with no children at all sometimes adopted a girl, which was easier than adopting a boy, and then arranged a uxorilocal marriage for her.)

Uxorilocal marriages took a variety of forms. In some instances, the groom was like a male daughter-in-law, breaking his ties with his natal home, taking his wife's surname, and agreeing that all offspring of the marriage would belong to the descent line of the wife's father. In other cases, the uxorilocally married man might retain his own surname, assign only some of his children to his wife's father's line, and agree to live in the in-laws' household for only a limited number of years. Such a groom usually acquired no property rights, and the property of his in-laws was bequeathed not to him, but to his wife and to those of his children who had been assigned to his father-in-law's descent line.

Whatever the precise contractual arrangements, the husband in such a marriage was generally a sorry creature, because the values of families dictated that a son ought to perpetuate his own line of descent and serve his own parents and ancestors. A man who had deserted his parents was ipso facto unprincipled and immoral. He was usually scorned by fellow villagers; even his in-laws, who should have felt beholden to him, treated him much like a mere servant. Nonetheless, there was rarely a dearth of candidates for uxorilocal marriages. In almost every village, a sizable reserve of single men were too poor to afford a bride-price and had no prospect of inheriting property from their fathers. Marrying uxorilocally was one way—albeit a demeaning way—for such a man to acquire a wife and an economic stake in life.

Uxorilocal and minor marriages were not found uniformly throughout the whole of China. Both were rare in north China, for instance, but were relatively common in the southeastern provinces of the country, stretching from Kiangsu and Anhwei along the Yangtze River to Kwangtung in the south—where minor marriages frequently accounted for between 20 and 40 percent of all first marriages. In some areas, such as southern Kiangsi, the figure reportedly rose to as high as 70 and even 80 percent. The most meticulous and well-documented study of marriage practices is of an area known as Haishan in northern Taiwan, just south of Taipei. There, 40 percent of first marriages in the early twentieth century were in the minor form, and 10 percent were uxorilocal. Just 150 miles south of Haishan, however, minor marriages were rare, running from almost nil to about 15 percent—although 10 percent of the first marriages were in the uxorilocal form. Thus diversity was the norm, and to generalize about marriage, as about so many questions in "China as a whole," is perilous.

Concubinage and Marital Infidelity

Another possible solution for a barren marriage was for the husband to take a concubine. Indeed, the man who took a concubine, whether to gain male heirs or for his own pleasure, acquired an added increment of prestige, because concubines were luxury items usually affordable by only the upper classes. China's was a monogamous society, in the sense that a man married but one wife at a time,[15] but there was no legal obstacle to or moral stigma against taking one or more concubines.

Concubines were invariably recruited from the lower classes. Often, they were peasant girls, purchased from their parents to provide sexual services for their masters. Sometimes, too, they had been maidservants in the household who had captured the fancy of the master, or they had been female entertainers or even prostitutes. Taken into the master's household without benefit of wedding or other ceremony, the concubine was legally and socially much inferior to the master's first wife. She was often required to perform menial and unpleasant jobs in the household and to serve as the first wife's personal maid. She could be expelled, or even sold, from the household at the whim of the master. The status of a concubine was, however, not merely that of a domestic servant whose duties included sexual services. Like a first wife, she could be selected only through surname exogamy; her children were legal heirs of the master, even though they did not always enjoy full equality with the first wife's children; and after her death, her tablet was placed on the family altar—although perhaps in a place of lesser honor and perhaps for no more than one generation.

The status of a concubine was actually determined less by legal or ritualistic regulations than by her personal relationship with her master and the first wife. Because the master himself customarily selected the concubine—whereas his wife had been chosen for him by his parents without regard for his own feelings or preferences—true romantic love sometimes blossomed between concubine and master. And if she bore him a son, especially if the first wife was barren, she might enjoy a position of considerable favor in the household. Indeed, if she bore a son, but only then, she qualified to have her name entered in the lineage genealogy. Generally, however, society disapproved of excessive emotional attachment between the master and his concubine, and commonly they were together only when the master sought sexual gratification.

Decisive for the concubine's status in the household, in many cases, was the attitude of the first wife. Some wives encouraged their husbands to take concubines, perhaps to be relieved of what for them may have been the irksome task of engaging in sexual intercourse with their husbands, or perhaps to add prestige to the family name. The *grand dame* in *The Dream of the Red Chamber,* for example, urged her husband to take a concubine, insisting that "other distinguished people can have several concubines, why not we?" In such cases, the concubine's life may have been tolerable and even pleasant. More commonly, however, the first wife probably was jealous of her. Then, like that of a maltreated daughter-in-law, her life would be hell. If purchased from her parents, she could seek no solace or relief from her natal family. And even her master might be reluctant to intervene between the rivalrous women, regarding affairs in the women's quarters as being outside his jurisdiction. Thus concubinage could be a disruptive influence in Chinese family life.

As the institution of concubinage suggests, Chinese placed little value on a husband's sexual fidelity to his wife, and a male's search for sexual variety was generally condoned as long as he did not approach the women of relatives and neighbors. This was true of all social classes. While poor villagers sought diversion in the tawdry whorehouses of a nearby market town, the elite patronized the expensive houses of entertainment in the larger towns and cities. Many men, probably, found their only exposure to romantic love in the brothels, for such love was seldom found at home. Whoring was, it is true, regarded as a vice. But it was a minor vice, and brothels were frequently used by both merchants and government officials as places to conduct business. Scholars were reputed to have written some of their best poetry in the company of prostitutes. The high level of tolerance that Chinese felt toward prostitution is suggested by the case of a well-known author whose friends praised him as a filial son because he gratified his father's desires by entertaining him in a brothel.

Because of this tolerant attitude, girls and women who became prostitutes were not the objects of strong moral censure, as they have been in the West. Many had entered their profession as a result of their families' economic destitution, and they were often able to contribute significantly to their families' incomes. In such cases, everyone made moral allowances. Villagers usually knew of the economic plight of their neighbors, and they therefore rarely condemned a girl who "obeys her parents and sacrifices her own opportunity for a normal life by becoming a prostitute. If she behaves herself in the village, they tend to regard her as a particularly filial young woman who has paid her debt to her parents more completely than other young women." [16]

Prostitutes were not the only women who failed to conform to the Confucian ideal of female chastity. Widows who refused to remarry, for example, were often honored by the commemorative arches erected by the government, but such exemplars of chastity, like the joint family, were probably found more often in wealthy, elite families than among the poor. Young, economically straitened widows frequently remarried.[17] Furthermore, at the turn of the twentieth century, 40 percent of the women in the northern Taiwan area of Haishan who had been widowed before the age of thirty-four bore illegitimate children. Extramarital affairs there were "common and tolerated if not approved." [18]

The incidence of marital infidelity varied with the form of marriage. Of 315 women married in the major form in Haishan, for example, 16.5 percent had presumably committed adultery. By contrast, of 236 women married in the minor fashion, 37.7 percent had presumably had sexual relations with men other than their husbands. Why was adultery more common among women married in the minor than in the major fashion? The explanation may be that "adopted daughters," failing to find satisfactory sexual relations with their "brothers"-husbands, sought gratification elsewhere. The true reason may not have been sheer lust, however, because these unfaithful wives, it has been suggested, were actually motivated by the desire to produce male heirs for their husbands' families. Because their "brother"-husbands avoided them sexually, they may have sought sex with other men—perhaps even at the mother-in-laws' bidding—in order to become pregnant.[19] Familism *would* be served!

Sexual life in China's villages was, therefore, something less than prim and proper. Indeed, several studies of rural life convey images of a raw sexuality—full of rapes, liaisons, and seductions.[20] Mao Tse-tung, in a famous report on the peasant movement in 1927, noted that women "enjoy considerable sexual freedom. Among the poor peasantry, triangular and multilateral relationships are *almost universal*." [21]

Such active extramarital sex was probably more common among the poor peasants than it was among the elites, who were supposedly more restrained by decorous Confucian ideals of womanhood. Whether or not this is true, it is safe to say that the traditional image of Chinese women being isolated from social and, especially, sexual contact is as inappropriate as the descriptions of the typical Chinese family of five generations living contentedly under one roof.

The Content of Social Interactions

When analyzing social behavior, in China or in any other society, it is useful to distinguish between the structure and the content of a social relationship. The structure of a relationship may be the same in two cultures, but the content—the premises and instincts that vivify the relationship—may be different and thus produce a qualitatively distinct social relationship. The father–son or husband–wife relationship in late imperial China may have been structurally the same as that between a father and son or a husband and wife in the United States today, but the psychological attributes of those relationships resulted in significantly different interactions.

Because the content of social relationships among Chinese differs markedly from that of relationships among Westerners, Westerners have often been perplexed and sometimes annoyed in their interactions with Chinese. A Russian diplomat gave vent to his exasperation with the Chinese in 1972, declaring:

> Do not think that you will ever understand the Chinese! Do not believe that you will ever get to know them! The Chinese are unknowable, the Chinese cannot be understood! You know what? I'll tell you: the fact of the matter is that they are basically immoral! They live for form, for appearance, for "face," and not on the level of conscience! The moral, individual, personal conscience, sir! (Deeply moved, he struck his breast, presumed seat of the spiritual faculty to which he was alluding.) Moral individual conscience is the treasure and unique legacy of our Western Christian civilization! I can tell you, sir, there is a thousand times more in common between an illiterate Siberian woodcutter and an American professor, between a French peasant and a Moscow academician, than there is between any one of them and his Chinese counterpart![22]

This Russian was undoubtedly venting some exceptional frustration. Yet even those who have formed deep and lasting friendships with Chinese, and have delighted in their warm generosity and fullness of life, recognize that the patterns of interaction and the motivations impelling social action in China are often distinctive from those in Western society.

Generalizing about the wellsprings of human behavior, especially in a society as large and complex as that of China, is a perilous task. It is also important to realize that different individuals as well as members of different socioeconomic classes (such as untutored peasants and sophisticated literati) undoubtedly displayed somewhat different characteristics in their social relationships. Throwing caution to the winds, however, one might identify several characteristics of Chinese social behavior.

China was, in the first instance, a status-oriented society. Chinese were acutely aware that society was a hierarchical structure within which each person occupied a clearly defined niche. The relationship of one Chinese to another was thus determined by the relative location of their niches. Although occasionally two persons might occupy niches at the same level of the social hierarchy, their relationship thus being that between equals (for example, two very close friends), most status relationships were vertically structured; the niche of one implied a role of superiority and authority vis-à-vis the inferior and dependent role of the other.

The most characteristic of Chinese status relationships were found within the family, and Chinese responses to social interactions throughout the course of their lives were profoundly influenced by the socialization process within the family. A Chinese father was, as we have seen, typically remote, stern, and unchallengeable in his relations with his son, while the son (at least overtly) was respectful, servile, and loyal to his father. In varying degrees, interactions between other family members—husband and wife, mother and daughter, mother-in-law and daughter-in-law, brother and sister, and brother and brother—displayed the vertical, unequal relationship between an authority figure and a dependent. The content of relationships outside the family—between, for example, teacher and student, employer and employee, government minister and bureaucratic subordinate—were fundamentally the same as those within the family.

Relative status within the social hierarchy was determined by the criteria of age, sex, wealth, proximity to power, and education. Among family members, age and sex were the determining factors. Thus elder brothers were dominant over their younger brothers, and brothers were superior to their sisters. Outside the family, wealth and proximity to power tended to be the decisive factors. Because such a high value was placed on education, it became a factor that could modify any of the relationships noted above. These five factors affecting status relationships were variables, however, and a different mix might produce subtly different shades of relationships. Thus a well-educated young man of moderate means might enjoy superior status in his relationship with a wealthy but relatively uneducated landlord or merchant, but the same young scholar would presumably assume an attitude of deference toward the wife of a high official. Although the mix of variables might produce innumerable combinations, the resulting relationships were almost always vertical, not horizontal.

Chinese did, of course, enjoy intimate friendships in which there was an assumption of equality and no anticipation on the part of either friend that he could exploit the friendship for his own benefit. Still, to a remarkable degree, it is true that "Chinese society has been based on the . . . assumption: no two persons are ever equal; always one is higher than the other."[23]

This pattern of superior–subordinate, or authority–dependency, relationships profoundly influenced the way that Chinese interacted with one another. The superior in the relationship—a father with his son, or a mother-in-law with her daughter-in-law—tended to be stern, demanding, and, sometimes, willfully inconsiderate. Teachers, for instance, tended to act as though they were omniscient, brooked no challenge from their students, and severely punished disobedience and displays of independence; corporal punishment in the classrooms was common. The attitude of factory foremen in the 1940s was representative of that of Chinese authority figures:

> Whenever they pass by [they] have a habit of shouting at workers to 'hurry up,' without even looking at the work at all. These same supervisors when they give

orders are blustering and rude as if ordering slaves. Other officers, even assistant engineers, often go beyond their duty to give workers superfluous directions, seemingly merely to show that they have the power to give orders.[24]

Subordinates in these relationships, by contrast, tended to be excessively submissive. They displayed an "indirection in dealing with superiors, great reluctance to criticize, and an overwillingness to please those in power."[25] Of Chinese social behavior, it has been said that "the first outstanding quality is an explicitly submissive attitude toward authority."[26]

Chinese were, therefore, acutely sensitive to questions of status. When meeting a person for the first time, they quickly tried to learn about the person's background: What office or position did he hold? What was his family background (was the father an official or a scholar, rich or poor, or a nobody)? Was he wealthy? What schools had he attended, and what degrees had he earned? Having established the other person's status in the social hierarchy by dint of his relative age, wealth, proximity to power, and education, it was possible to adopt the socially correct attitude toward him.

A second major characteristic of Chinese social behavior was the tendency of individual Chinese to form around them networks of useful personal relationships, or *guanxi*. For reasons that were probably related to the socialization of children within the family, Chinese rarely sensed that they could cope with the world as independent individuals. They tended to shun personal autonomy, therefore, and to seek sources of support, guidance, and protection from others. "The Chinese ideal of mutual dependence," wrote a Chinese, "is the exact opposite of the American spirit of self-reliance."[27] Establishing *guanxi* with persons of wealth, power, or influence was particularly desirable; even relationships with one's neighbors, fellow workers, and classmates were cultivated with the expectation that those *guanxi* might at some time be exploited to their own advantage.

Guanxi by itself was merely a connecting link; what imparted force and substance to the relationship was *ganqing*. *Ganqing*, sometimes translated as "feelings" or "sentiment," was the emotional, or affective, quality of the relationship. Thus two people might have a *guanxi* relationship, but the *ganqing* between them might be good, bad, or absent; the utility of their relationship would thus vary with the quality of the *ganqing*.

Given the values of the society, however, some *guanxi* connections predisposed Chinese to assume a good *ganqing* relationship. Family and kin relationships were the most obvious of these, because there was virtually a moral imperative that relatives help and trust one another. This was one reason that Chinese did not require the elaborate system of social services and charities found in the United States today, for family members customarily assisted relatives who were unemployed, ill, or aged.[28] It was also the reason that nepotism—the often debilitating practice whereby, for instance, a government official or factory foreman arranged for the employment of an uncle or a wife's brother, regardless of that person's qualifications—was so common in China. Other forms of *guanxi* that at least carried a likelihood of good *ganqing* were those between teacher and student, among school classmates, and, when living away from the native village or province, among fellow villagers and fellow provincials.

Regardless of the nature of a *guanxi* relationship, it would lose force and usefulness if the partners in the relationship did not work to maintain social contact and endeavor to improve the relationship. Usually, the higher the status of one partner in such a relationship, the harder the other worked to cultivate good *ganqing*. This could be done in numerous ways. Adopting an appropriately respectful and subservient manner would, of course, help ingratiate the subordinate with the superior. Doing favors and giving gifts were other preferred ways of cultivating *ganqing;* hosting banquets for persons who might be useful was a particularly common way of maintaining good *guanxi*. Chinese frequently lavished such large sums of money on entertaining and gifts that their homes and families suffered deprivation. They did so, however, with the clear sense of future benefits to be derived from well-lubricated *guanxi*. As a Chinese scholar explained, "When a Chinese acts, he normally anticipates a response or return. Favors done for others are often considered what may be termed 'social investments,' for which handsome returns are expected."[29]

A third major characteristic of Chinese social behavior was concern for "face." Face was a form of self-esteem that depended on the judgment of others. One enjoyed "face" when one had prestige and a good reputation in the eyes of others. The Chinese employed two terms—*lian* and *mianzi*—both of which we translate as "face," although the connotations of the two are different. *Lian* meant the self-esteem that one derived as a result of having a reputation for being of good moral character. Because the Chinese placed an extremely high value on proper moral conduct, they were deeply concerned that they not "lose face" *(diulian)*. One who made a pretense to high moral character but was caught out in telling a lie or cheating, for example, would lose *lian*. The Chinese, however, imbued a broad range of actions with a moral content, so that *lian* encompassed also what we might call social propriety, or social behavior appropriate to one's social status. Thus the rich man who was regarded as being excessively stingy might lose *lian* in the eyes of his neighbors. One of the strongest controls over a mother-in-law's mistreatment of her daughter-in-law was her fear of losing *lian*—of incurring the negative judgment of other women in the village.

If, of course, one were of low social status and had few moral pretenses, one would be correspondingly less concerned about losing *lian*. Lowly peasants or workers, for instance, might become involved in land disputes or brawls without losing *lian,* because social standards were lower for them. People of high status, by contrast, were expected to have such dignity and self-control that they would not become involved in such a fracas. If such a person purposely acted in defiance of the moral and social standards appropriate to his status—for example, a wealthy landlord who unfeelingly ousted a poor widowed mother from her land—he was open to the damning charge that "he has no concern for face" *(ta bu yao lian)*.

Having *mianzi,* like having *lian,* meant the condition of enjoying the esteem of others. *Mianzi* was derived, however, not from the positive moral assessments of others, but from the possession of such attributes of status as wealth, power, education, or rich and powerful friends. Because China was a status-oriented society, most Chinese ardently desired good *mianzi*. The rich villager who performed such charitable acts as establishing a village school, building a bridge to facilitate public transportation, or hiring an opera troupe to entertain fellow villagers, was not only doing a good deed, but also demonstrating to the villagers that he could afford such largesse; thus he would gain *mianzi* in their eyes. Even relatively poor peasants prepared large feasts at the time of a son's wedding or a father's funeral—entailing expenditures that often caused real financial hardship—in order to preserve their and their families' *mianzi*. If they scrimped unduly on such festive occasions, they would lose both *mianzi* and *lian* (because niggardliness conveyed moral as well as status implications).

The desire for *mianzi,* however, was not always regarded as a positive trait (whereas the desire for *lian* was always applauded) and might even lead to ridicule. Even the phrase "to want *mianzi*" *(yao mianzi)* was often derogatory, because it suggested that a person was seeking to attain a status above that which was properly his. Exemplifying such a desire for *mianzi* is the story of the Manchu who, after the Revolution of 1911, did not easily adjust to his reduced status and increased poverty. Visiting a teahouse, he had only enough cash to buy one piece of pastry. Having eaten the cake, the poor fellow was still hungry, so he thought to eat the sesame seeds that had fallen from the cake onto the table. But how could he, a one-time aristocrat, get those seeds into his mouth without simply scraping them up like a common peasant? His solution was to wet his finger with saliva, and then pretend to write Chinese characters on the table top—in the process, eating the seeds that adhered to his finger. Some seeds, however, had fallen into a crack in the table top. These he extracted by feigning anger and pounding the table with his fist, whereupon the seeds flew from the crack. He then continued to write his characters, thus assuaging his hunger. This story is amusing to Chinese because the Manchu, seeking *mianzi*, was trying to cling to a status that he had clearly lost. He appears ridiculous as a result.[30]

It should be obvious, but we often forget, that social institutions and behavioral traits of a people change over the course of time. European society in the sixteenth and seventeenth centuries, for instance, was vastly different from what it is today. Indeed, it was similar in many respects to Chinese society in late imperial times. Marriages in England were commonly arranged by the parents on the basis of "a pragmatic calculation of family interest." "In the early sixteenth century," it has been said of the British propertied classes, "children were bought and sold like cattle for breeding, and no-one thought that the parties concerned had any right to complain."[31] Among the lower classes, too, spouses felt little romantic attachment for each other. In France, peasants deemed their horses to be more valuable than their wives; throughout France, "if the horse and the wife fall sick at the same time, the . . . peasant rushes to the blacksmith to care for the animal, and leaves the task of healing his wife to nature." A wife could be easily replaced, but losing a horse could mean economic ruin.[32]

Even toward their infant children, European fathers and mothers of the sixteenth and seventeenth centuries felt little attachment. Perhaps because children died so frequently in their early years, it would have been psychological folly for parents to invest much emotion in their offspring. Even for children who survived infancy, the parents displayed little affection, the dominant theory of parenting being that the elders must "crush the will" of the youth. "Extreme deference" from the children was demanded, and punishment was meted out with brutal whippings that often drew blood or with beatings that raised blisters. Among the British elite, the eldest son did enjoy greater favor than his siblings because his parents valued him as the one to carry on the family name and inherit the property. But even with such favored children, parental love was rare. "The key to all understanding of interpersonal relationships among the propertied classes at this time is a recognition of the fact that what mattered was not the individual but the family."[33]

Europeans did not practice footbinding, but young girls were squeezed into iron- or whalebone-reinforced corsets that misshaped their bodies and sometimes severely crippled them. When a two-year-old girl died in 1665, medical examination revealed that "her iron bodice was her pain, and had hindered the lungs to grow. . . . her breastbone pressed very deeply inwardly, and . . . two of her ribs were broken, and the straightness of the bodice upon the vitals occasioned this difficulty of breathing and her death."[34]

These comments about European society before the eighteenth century serve as a healthy reminder that the features of Chinese social life in the late imperial period that we may find objectionable were not unique to Chinese or Asian cultures. They remind us, too, that social practices and values are not static and unalterable. Although we still lack a clear sense of the changes in family life, marriage, and the position of women that occurred between the sixteenth and nineteenth centuries in China, we do know that social change began to accelerate in the late nineteenth and early-twentieth centuries. Those social changes will be more comprehensible after we have examined changes in the economy. First, however, we must examine a powerful support for familism, the popular religion.

Selected Readings

(See also the works cited in the notes)

Baker, Hugh D. R. *Chinese Family and Kinship*. New York: Columbia University Press, 1979.

Ebrey, Patricia. "Concubines in Sung China." *Journal of Family History* 11, no. 1 (January 1986): 1–24.

Freedman, Maurice. *Chinese Lineage and Society: Fukien and Kwangtung*. London: Athlone Press, 1966.

———. *Chinese Organization in Southeastern China*. London: Athlone Press, 1958.

Fried, Morton H. *Fabric of Chinese Society: A Study of the Social Life of a Chinese County Seat*. New York: Praeger, 1953.

Gallin, Bernard. *Hsin Hsing, Taiwan: A Chinese Village in Change*. Berkeley: University of California Press, 1966.

Gronewold, Sue. *Beautiful Merchandise: Prostitution in China, 1860–1936*. New York: Institute for Research in History and the Haworth Press, 1982.

Harrell, Stevan. "The Rich Get Children: Segmentation, Stratification, and Population in Three Chekiang Lineages, 1550–1850." In *Family and Population in East Asian History,* ed. Susan B. Hanley and Arthur P. Wolf, pp. 81–109. Stanford, Calif.: Stanford University Press, 1985.

Ho, Ping-ti. *The Ladder of Success in Imperial China: Aspects of Social Mobility, 1368–1911.* New York: Columbia University Press, 1962.

Hsieh, Andrew C. K., and Jonathan D. Spence. "Suicide and the Family in Pre-Modern Chinese Society." In *Normal and Abnormal Behavior in Chinese Culture,* ed. Arthur Kleinman and Tsung-yi Lin, pp. 29–47. Dordrecht, Netherlands: Reidel, 1981.

Jacobs, Bruce J. "A Preliminary Model of Particularistic Ties in Chinese Political Alliances: *Kan-ch'ing* and *Kuan-hsi* in a Rural Taiwanese Township." *China Quarterly* 78 (June 1979): 237–73.

Lang, Olga. *Chinese Family and Society.* New Haven, Conn.: Yale University Press, 1946.

Lee, Bernice J. "Female Infanticide in China." In *Women in China: Current Directions in Historical Scholarship,* ed. Richard W. Guisso and Stanley Johannesen, pp. 163–77. Youngstown, N.Y.: Philo Press, 1981.

Leung, Angela Kiche. "L'Accueil des Enfants Abandonnés dans la Chine du Bas-Yangzi auz XVIIe et XVIIIe Siècles." *Études Chinoises* 4, no. 1 (Spring 1985): 15–54.

Levy, Howard S. *Chinese Footbinding: The History of a Curious Erotic Custom.* New York: Bell, 1967.

Levy, Marion J., Jr. *The Family Revolution in Modern China.* Cambridge, Mass.: Harvard University Press, 1949.

Liu, Ts'ui-jung. "The Demography of Two Chinese Clans in Hsiao-shan, Chekiang, 1650–1850." In *Family and Population in East Asian History,* ed. Susan B. Hanley and Arthur P. Wolf, pp. 13–61. Stanford, Calif.: Stanford University Press, 1985.

Mann, Susan. "Widows in the Kinship, Class, and Community Structures of Qing Dynasty China," *Journal of Asian Studies* 46, no. 1 (February 1987): 37–56.

Pasternak, Burton. *Guests in the Dragon: Social Demography of a Chinese District, 1895–1946.* New York: Columbia University Press, 1983.

Ropp, Paul S. *Dissent in Early Modern China: Ju-lin Wai-shih and Ch'ing Social Criticism.* Ann Arbor: University of Michigan Press, 1981.

Waltner, Ann. "The Adoption of Children in Ming and Early Ch'ing China." Ph.D. diss., University of California, Berkeley, 1981.

———. "The Loyalty of Adopted Sons in Ming and Early Qing China." *Modern China* 10, no. 4 (October 1984): 441–59.

———. "Widows and Remarriage in Ming and Early Qing China." In *Women in China: Current Directions in Historical Scholarship,* ed. Richard W. Guisso and Stanley Johannesen, pp. 129–46. Youngstown, N.Y.: Philo Press, 1981.

Wolf, Arthur P. "Introduction," In *Religion and Ritual in Chinese Society,* ed. Arthur P. Wolf, pp. 1–18. Stanford, Calif.: Stanford University Press, 1974.

Wolf, Margery. "Child Training and the Chinese Family." In *Family and Kinship in Chinese Society,* ed. Maurice Freedman, pp. 37–62. Stanford, Calif.: Stanford University Press, 1970.

———. "Women and Suicide in China." In *Women in Chinese Society,* ed. Margery Wolf and Roxane Witke, pp. 111–41. Stanford, Calif.: Stanford University Press, 1975.

3

Gods, Ghosts, and Ancestors: The Popular Religion

The Chinese are a highly rationalistic people, spared the religious prejudices and superstitions that have tarnished the history of the Western world. Such, at any rate, is how numerous observers have depicted them. Hu Shi, for example, who was the country's preeminent scholar in the 1920s and 1930s, insisted that "the Chinese people [are] less other-worldly than the other historical races of the earth. . . . They had no time to indulge in speculating about the ways of the gods."[1]

In fact, however, Chinese of all economic classes and social rank were, over the centuries, deeply concerned about mystical forces and the supernatural. Spirits and gods were thought to be everywhere—usually unseen, but nonetheless real. The largest and most ornate buildings in every town and village were customarily temples; along the roadways and even beside paths in the fields, untold numbers of small shrines housed effigies of various deities; virtually every home contained at least one altar and place of sacrifice. Spirit gates stood just inside the entrance to family compounds to prevent the entry of evil spirits. And in any town or village, regardless of the day of the year, a visitor could see incense and spirit-money burned, food sacrificed, and firecrackers exploded—evidence of an active belief in denizens of a supernatural world. The sense that supernatural beings were omnipresent was expressed by the small boy who, before relieving himself along-side a dark street, warned the spirits lurking in the spot: "I am going to urinate. Please stand aside."[2]

The origins of this Chinese view of the supernatural universe are veiled in the mists of prehistory. Already in the Zhou Dynasty (ca. 1027–256 B.C.), however, when the historical record becomes fairly firm, the basic ingredients of the popular religion that persisted down to the twentieth century were in place. These ingredients included ancestor worship, a vast array of gods and spirits that could affect the fate of mortals, and a belief in the efficacy of divination and sacrifices as means of influencing these gods and spirits.

41

This indigenous religion of the Chinese was nothing if not eclectic. By the Han Dynasty, for instance, it had added such cosmological refinements as the *Yin–yang* and Five Elements concepts. The religion also absorbed the deities and practices of innumerable local cults that the Han people encountered as they spread out from the north China plain. In subsequent centuries, it was further enriched by the theologies and deities of Taoism and Buddhism.

For nearly 800 years, from about the second to the tenth century, the indigenous cult, together with Confucianism, was largely eclipsed by those two religions, both of which periodically enjoyed imperial favor and attracted large followings among the common people. The influence of Buddhism, in particular, became pervasive, and China throughout most of the Tang Dynasty was virtually a Buddhist nation, the church enjoying tremendous power, both economically and politically, and exerting profound influence on the religious sentiments of all Chinese.

Between the ninth and twelfth centuries, however, both Taoism and Buddhism entered a period of decline. Occasionally thereafter, as during the period of Mongol rule, emperors looked to Taoist priests for advice and comfort, but religious Taoism had been largely abandoned by the common people. Buddhism, too, lost much of its vitality. Its monasteries ceased to be centers dedicated to the salvation of the creatures of the world, and instead became retreats for individuals seeking to escape the travails of the world. The intellectual and moral quality of the priests fell, and doctrinal creativity, or even concern, nearly vanished. Of the several Buddhist schools, only two that emphasized religious practice rather than philosophical contemplation—Chan (Zen) and Pure Land—retained any vigor, but even they were doctrinally corrupt and institutionally weak by late imperial times.[3]

As Taoism and Buddhism declined, both Confucianism and the indigenous religion experienced a powerful resurgence. They did so, however, only after incorporating many of the concepts and characteristics of those religions. The popular religion, for instance, appropriated such Buddhist concepts as the transmigration of souls and the law of causal retribution (karma). It also added the Buddhist bodhisattvas to its pantheon of gods. From Taoism, the popular religion acquired various notions of occult magic and the practice of deifying prominent personalities, both legendary and historical. Despite these syncretic tendencies, the basic ingredients of the popular religion throughout the late imperial and early modern periods were still those known in the days of Confucius, some 2,000 years earlier.

The Demographics of the Supernatural Realm

The popular religion was spectacularly polytheistic. By the late imperial period, animistic spirits of mountains and trees, Buddhist bodhisattvas, and Taoist mythic heroes resided amiably together in one capacious pantheon. Mortals who believed in these deities ignored the theological inconsistencies of this supernatural congregation, for they were interested primarily in the magical efficacy of this or that god in responding to their appeals for help, healing, or male offspring.

In the popular imagination, these numerous deities reigned in an underworld whose denizens were *usually* invisible to the human eye. Yet to most Chinese, this was a very real world that could directly influence human affairs. Humans, in turn, could influence affairs in the spiritual world.

The spiritual world, as conceived by believers in the popular religion, reflected the social landscape of human existence. It was inhabited by bureaucrats and ordinary citizens, police and soldiers, beggars and ruffians. Some were good; some, bad. Although all these supernatural beings possessed powers transcending those of mere mortals, they were also endowed with human characteristics. They felt emotions—such as pride, jealousy, anger, and pleasure. And they had needs—for food, money, and housing. Because of their ability to intervene in the lives of the living, it was important for the human condition to win the favor and to forestall the malevolence of the supernatural beings.

Gods, ghosts, and ancestors—these were the three basic kinds of supernatural beings. In the popular imagination, gods *(shen)*, the most powerful and awesome of the three, were often like bureaucrats. Indeed, a sizable part of the pantheon was virtually a mirror image of the Chinese imperial bureaucracy, rising in a pyramidal hierarchy from god-bureaucrats with local territorial jurisdiction to a supreme god, analogous to the emperor in Peking.

Near the bottom of the spiritual bureaucratic hierarchy was the stove, or kitchen, god, which acted as a police officer in each household. In traditional China, each family had a stove on which the cooking was done and which symbolized the corporate unity of that family, whether it was a conjugal family of the peasantry or a vast joint family of the upper gentry. Whenever brothers split the family property and established separate households, hot coals from the old stove were transferred to the new stoves of the younger brothers, who then placed above the stoves placards bearing the picture or name of the stove god. Every New Year, this god returned to the spiritual realm, where it reported on the conduct of the family under its jurisdiction. Because all gods, like members of the imperial bureaucracy, were thought to be susceptible to fawning praise and timely bribes, Chinese families at the beginning of the New Year's celebrations often smeared the mouth of the stove god's effigy with glutinous rice cakes or other sweets, or offered sacrificial food and wine by its placard, hoping that the god would thereby be induced to submit a favorable report.

The next ranking official in the supernatural bureaucracy, in the view of most Chinese, was the earth god (Tudigong)—prominent in the popular religion since at least the first century A.D. Much like a *xian* magistrate, an earth god had jurisdiction over a specific locality, which often encompassed one or several villages or perhaps a ward of a city. Its responsibility was, first, to protect its area of jurisdiction from wandering ghosts that might do mischief in the lives of the mortals residing there. At the same time, it had to keep a sharp eye on the residents themselves, recording their activities and reporting to higher level spiritual bureaucrats. Knowing this, villagers informed it of such important events as births, deaths, and marriages. When they planned to erect or tear down a building, they also sought the earth god's permission. The relationship between an earth god and its worshipers was therefore close, yet its responsibilities were strictly local and territorial. When a peasant moved to a different village, he would have no further relation with the earth god of his former home, and would thereafter be under the jurisdiction of the earth god of his new locality.

Shrines to earth gods were ubiquitous. A shrine the size of a small room was often erected in a central place in a village. But peasants individually or as a group might also erect lesser earth-god shrines—perhaps no larger than a doghouse—alongside a path or in a field, so that they could carry out the prescribed rituals more conveniently than by walking to town. Some families kept an effigy of the earth god on their family altars.

Above the stove and earth gods rose myriad more powerful and exalted—but also more distant—gods. Shang-ti-kung were sometimes regarded as the earth gods' immediate bureaucratic superiors; city gods (Chenghuang) governed in the administrative towns; other gods were general inspectors, such as circuit censors in the government bureaucracy, roving from place to place and reporting to the central authorities. At the top of this proliferating spiritual hierarchy was the Jade Emperor, whose position in the supernatural realm was like that of the mortal Chinese emperor.

Many gods, however, were not conceived of as bureaucrats. They were more like sages, wise and magically efficacious. For example, Guanyin, the goddess of mercy of Buddhist origin, was particularly successful in bringing sons; Mazu, who was also known by her officially bestowed title of Tianhou (the Empress of Heaven) and who was originally the patron goddess of seafarers, had the powers to heal, produce rain, and generally provide good fortune; and Guandi, the god of war, symbolized loyalty and was efficacious in bringing wealth to his worshipers.

There were other gods of virtually every conceivable type and purpose. As a longtime foreign resident of China wrote in 1910, there were

> deities or spiritual patrons for all the forces of nature, diseases (from devil-possession to toothache), wealth and rank and happiness, war, old age, death, childbirth, towns and villages, trades, mountains and rivers and seas, lakes and canals, heaven and hell, sun, moon and stars, roads and places where there are no roads, clouds and thunder, every separate part and organ of the human body, and indeed for almost everything that is cognisable by the senses and a great deal that is not.[4]

The gods, be it noted, were something less than omnipotent. Gods they were, but they differed from humans in degree rather than in kind. Many gods, in fact, were thought to be simply the spiritual emanations of former prominent mortals. The god in charge of Shanghai, for example, was thought to be Qin Yubo, a member of the Hanlin Academy during the Ming Dynasty, and a city god in Kiangsi had been magistrate of the city in which he now reigned invisibly.

Less exalted than the gods were the souls of ordinary men and women. Depending on their fates, they existed either as ancestors or as ghosts. Actually, the number of souls residing in a living mortal was a matter of some debate. Some Chinese believed that thirty-six souls inhabited each human body. But Zhu Xi, the great Confucian scholar of the Song Dynasty, stated flatly that there were ten souls: seven of which were *yin* in nature and three of which were *yang*. (Note that even this most eminent of Confucian philosophers shared the popular belief in supernatural beings!)

For simple peasants, however, it was usually sufficient to observe the existence of but two souls. One of these, the *yin* soul, was essential to life, but was relatively unimportant after death. It lingered around the coffins and graves of the deceased, but eventually it dissipated and faded from existence. The *yang* soul, by contrast, was immortal and more complex. After the death of a human, it was dispatched to Hell *(diyu),* where it confronted a tribunal of spiritual mandarins, who recounted the soul's earthly wrongdoings and declared judgment on it. Then the soul was subjected to horrible but condign punishments, such as being boiled in oil, sawed in half from the crotch through the head, or mashed in a rice grinder. After enduring the prescribed agonies, the soul was given a potion that erased the memory of these sufferings, and then—the idea obviously originating in the Buddhist concept of transmigration of souls—was reincarnated on earth.

Many Chinese believed that by performing prescribed rituals during the coffining, at the funeral, and at specified times during the forty-nine days following death—the time needed by the soul to pass through Hell—those terrible punishments could be avoided. Offerings (bribes?) to the officials of Hell, in the form of spirit-money burned at the funeral, could ease the soul's passage through those torments, as could dressing the corpses in clothes embroidered with sutras and other efficacious symbols. The ever-pragmatic Chinese thus found ways to pass through the spiritual world, just as they did through their worldly existence, and Hell thus probably held fewer terrors for them than it did for devout Christians in the West. Note, however, that male descendants were essential if a person's soul was to avoid the fearsome tortures.

Despite the implicit contradiction to their belief in the reincarnation of the *yang* soul of the dead, the Chinese believed that the *yang* soul also continued to reside in a part of the supernatural realm, where it required food, housing, clothes, and money. These could be provided only by humans of the mortal realm, delivered by means of ceremonial offerings. Souls that were served by filial descendants and were well supplied with these needs were *ancestors;* souls that were not provided with the necessities of celestial existence became *ghosts,* which were by nature hungry, mean, and malicious.

Rituals that were intended to provide for the needs of souls in the afterlife constituted what is known as ancestor worship, which has been aptly termed the "essential religion" of the Chinese.[5] To Chinese, it was supremely important that they present offerings to their recent forebears, especially parents and grandparents, so that these forebears could enjoy the comforts of ancestorhood in the afterlife, rather than roaming the underworld as ghosts. With characteristic pragmatism, however, Chinese did not feel it necessary to worship *all ancestors* for *all time*—if for no other reason than that a family's altar could not accommodate the tablets of all the forebears. Consequently, the family worshiped only especially important or powerful ancestors (such as the lineage founder or one who had served as a court official) and those ancestors known and remembered by the living (grandpa and grandma received sacrifices, surely, and perhaps even great-great-grandpa—but rarely ordinary ancestors more distant than that). Tablets of

FIGURE 3.1. Scroll of the type frequently displayed during funerals. This one depicts gods of the spiritual underworld—conceived here in the image of imperial bureaucrats—sitting in judgment upon the recently deceased, who are being punished for the misdeeds they committed while in the world of the living. Scroll belongs to the author.

46

lesser and more remote forebears could be ritually disposed of by burning or burying. Presumably, the souls of these ancestors would then dissipate into non-existence and were not in peril of becoming hungry ghosts.

For the living, of course, it was of utmost importance to make preparations so that after their own deaths, they would be provided the required offerings. And for this, they needed at least one son. Daughters were virtually useless for the purpose, since they were destined to leave the family when they married. For a son, the obligation to care for the souls of his parents was nearly absolute. He had received the gift of life from his parents, and if he were so unfilial as not to provide for them in the afterlife, their spirits might inflict illness, death, and other misfortunes on him and his family. Ordinarily, however, the ancestors were thought to be benevolent, looking out for the well-being of their descendants. But reciprocity was demanded![6] Because the consequences for a soul of not receiving offerings from the mortal world meant the difference between being an ancestor and being a ghost, the failure to produce male offspring—or at least the failure to obtain a male heir through adoption or a uxorilocal marriage—was considered a terrible tragedy.

Souls in the underworld that received no offerings or whose human forms had died unusual or violent deaths were generally fated to be ghosts. Souls of dead infants, for instance, were customarily thought to be ghosts. Should an infant die, the parents often assumed that the child had been a ghost *in the guise of a child* that had come to do them harm. The body of such an infant consequently did not warrant proper burial. In Shantung, dead infants were simply buried in shallow holes for dogs to exhume and eat. As the people of Shantung contended, ''An evil spirit inhabited the child's body, otherwise it would not have died so young. If the dogs eat it, the bad spirit enters the dog and cannot again enter another child who may be born to the same parents.''[7]

The souls of unmarried women, of older youth who had died before producing a son, and of those who had died by suicide, drowning, or sudden accident were also in peril of becoming ghosts. Yet not all these unfortunate persons, not even all deceased infants, became ghosts if their parents or other people whose welfare might be adversely affected by the malevolent spirit, employed a little ingenuity. It was not uncommon, for example, for the tablet of a deceased son who had survived beyond infancy to be placed on the ancestral altar, where he could be worshiped by his younger siblings. Even if the deceased was the youngest of the siblings, families adopted the fiction that the first to die had actually been the eldest.

The soul of a deceased daughter, unfortunately, could not be provided for so easily because, not regarded as a member of her natal family, she warranted no offerings from her siblings or siblings' children. One solution for parents who were concerned for the soul of their dead daughter was to place a tablet or a sachet of incense ashes (representing the deceased) in the care of a Buddhist monastery, a shaman, or a ''maidens' temple,'' where, in return for a financial consideration, monks would perform the requisite rituals. Another solution was to arrange a ''ghost marriage'' for the dead girl. Through various means, the girl's parents could arrange for a living man to ''marry'' her soul; she would then become a member of his family line, and his descendants could properly send sacrifices to her. A common scheme employed to bring about such a marriage was for the family to trap a husband by placing a purse containing the girl's name and horoscope by the roadside; should a man pick up the purse, it was clear that he was fated to marry her. It was particularly fortunate if the fellow was already married and had a son, for it was assumed that the deceased girl would automatically become the man's "first" wife, and the man's son would then assume the responsibility of worshiping her.

Ghosts were malevolent souls: they were hungry and mean because no one in the mortal realm provided them with the necessities of a comfortable existence in the spiritual world; or they were angry and mean because they had died a violent or an unjust death. They might also be malevolent, however, simply because they were strangers, and—as in human society—strangers were inherently suspect and thought to be capable of inflicting harm. Here we encounter a supernatural paradox: one person's ancestor might be another person's ghost. One young peasant, for example, reported having seen a white apparition moving across the fields toward his village; the fellow was convinced that the apparition was the soul of the mother of the Lim family traveling to receive offerings at the death-day rites to be given her by the Lims the next day. This ancestor of the Lim family was to him, however, a ghost and therefore a cause of trepidation.

Chinese generally conceived of ghosts as beggars, ruffians, or bandits. They scorned them, therefore, but they also realized that ghosts were not to be trifled with. In the material world, beggars were often regarded as small-scale blackmailers who, if not given alms, might inflict some kind of harm. Ghosts, similarly, might bring illness or misfortune on ungenerous humans who failed to propitiate them with offerings. Thus Chinese regularly—for example, on the second and sixteenth day of each lunar month—presented offerings to ghosts lurking in the neighborhood. They also referred to ghosts by the euphemism "Good Brothers" *(hao xiongdi)* because calling them ghosts *(gui)* might needlessly antagonize them and thereby invite trouble.

Religious Worship and Festivals

In presenting offerings, Chinese distinguished clearly among the three kinds of supernatural beings. Ancestors were presented offerings as venerated members of the family; they were invited into the home, where they dined on foods such as those they had consumed when alive. Food already cooked and ready to be eaten was set on the table before the ancestral altar; the meats were sliced and seasoned, and the soup was hot. Dishes that the ancestors had especially favored during their earthly existence—perhaps peppery foods for grandpa and rice cakes for grandma—were served. Because ancestral offerings were like meals to be consumed in the home, cooked rice and chopsticks were also laid out for the ancestors' use.

Such intimacy, appropriate among family members and persons of approximately equal social standing, was wholly improper in offerings to the gods and ghosts. The exalted status of the gods precluded the familiarity of a family meal, just as it was inappropriate in human society for a *xian* (county or district) magistrate to dine with a peasant family. Offerings to the gods, therefore, were presented as gifts, which the gods would consume later in the privacy of their own abodes. The offerings usually consisted of three or five kinds of cooked meats presented whole—perhaps a duck, a fish, or a slab of pork—together with vegetables that were neither sliced nor spiced. The precise form and size of the offerings differed, depending on the rank of the god. Offerings to the lowly earth god, for example, were the simplest and closest in form to food ready to be ingested by humans, whereas offerings to the Jade Emperor were significantly larger and relatively unprepared (such as a raw chicken plucked clean except for some of the tail feathers, a whole pig with the entrails draped around the neck, and stalks of sugar cane with roots and leaves still attached). Three cups of wine and perhaps a bowl of fruit were also presented, but neither rice nor chopsticks were needed because the gods would not be eating in the presence of the worshipers.

Ghosts, being disreputable beings and undiscriminating eaters, could usually be offered food in virtually any form—cooked and sliced, or raw and whole. These offerings had to be accompanied by a wash basin and towel, for ghosts had no residences of their own in the supernatural world where they could wash before consuming the offerings. In the twentieth century, families also set out cigarettes and beer for the ghosts, because—like the gangs of ruffians to whom they were sometimes compared—they were thought to enjoy smoking and drinking. Ghosts, moreover, received their offerings outside the house or temple. Being strangers, they were regarded with suspicion and ought not, therefore, be invited into the family dwelling. Like real-life beggars, they were fed outside the back door. Ghosts were kept at a distance, too, because they were thought to be ritually polluted, and thus whatever they touched would be contaminated. Bowls used for the ghost offerings, for instance, had to be turned upside down and left exposed to the weather for three days before they could be used again by family members.

Most rituals of the popular religion were performed privately within the home. Yet public religious observances, which contributed greatly to the color and vitality of community life, were a prominent feature of Chinese social life. By contrast with those in the West, the public rituals were rarely performed by believers gathered under the direction of a member of the clergy. Temples were not assembly halls for believers, but were the gods' official residences where believers might individually visit to worship and beseech help. Ornately decorated, painted in brilliant hues (which, however, often faded from lack of proper maintenance), and frequently topped by majestically rising roofs with outward-reaching, swooping eaves, the temples consisted usually of a large hall, which one entered through a high multidoored gateway. At the rear of the hall, facing the gateway, stood an effigy of the temple's primary god. At his side and along the lateral walls were statues of lesser gods and of the gods' wives, concubines, and spiritual assistants. A large temple might have several such halls, one behind the other and interconnected, with the primary god ensconced in the farthermost hall. Temples, both large and small, frequently housed dozens of gods, often in total disregard of ''denominational'' affiliations. So-called Taoist temples—which were the primary temples of the popular religion—were the most eclectic. They often housed images of Buddhist bodhisattvas, Confucian sages, the local earth god, and a wide assortment of gods from the Taoist tradition. Buddhist temples tended to be more discriminating, but even they frequently contained effigies of non-Buddhist deities, such as Guandi or the Three Rulers of Heaven, Earth, and Water (the Sanguan).

Worshipers, who might come to a temple at any time of day or night, did not require the ministrations of a priest. Instead, they proceeded individually to the effigy of the god that they thought to be especially efficacious in dealing with their particular problem or concern. Should a god acquire a reputation for being especially potent, then its temple would prosper. The number of worshipers would be large, perhaps even coming from other villages, and the financial contributions would be correspondingly large. Some gods, such as Guandi and Tianhou, became so popular that branch temples proliferated over wide sections of the country; other gods had only a local reputation and existence. Should a god acquire a reputation for failing to respond to appeals of worshipers, villagers would soon neglect it, and its temple would fall into disuse. In this way, gods that were at one time popular could fade into oblivion.

In Ming and Qing China, there was no sabbath or regular day of rest. But there were festivals, most of which had religious overtones, that gave the masses of peasants and workers respite from the daily tedium. The chief festival of the year was the New Year. Beginning with a day of housecleaning during the twelfth lunar month, when families turned their households upside down to scour away the accumulated dirt and dust of the preceding year—and, symbolically, to exorcise all evil forces—the New Year's celebration lasted for more than half a month. The New Year was a time of family togetherness, relaxation, and feasting—on meat and other dishes that most families, during the rest of the year, could not ordinarily afford. It was a time when many businesses closed their doors for a week or so, all debts were to be repaid, the spirits of the ancestors were worshiped, friends were visited, and red envelopes containing money were given to the children. Throughout the night of New Year's Eve, most families remained up and about, cracking melon seeds, drinking hot wine, playing finger games, or gambling. Early the following morning, the entire family performed the kowtow and other obeisances before the ancestral altar. Then the young people paid their respects to their parents and other living elders in the family.

Several of the annual festivals, like the New Year were celebrated primarily in the home and among the family, rather than in a temple. Such "domestic" festivals included, for instance, Qingming, in the early spring, when families swept and cleaned the graves of the ancestors; the Dragon-Boat Festival, in the heat of summer, when southern Chinese staged boat races and everyone ate *zongze,* a triangular dumpling of glutinous rice, wrapped in bamboo leaves; and the Mid-Autumn Festival, when families and friends ate moon-cakes and viewed the autumnal full moon.

Temple festivals, in contrast to the major domestic festivals, were seldom celebrated at the same time throughout the nation. Instead, the birthday of each important god in each temple was usually the occasion for an annual village festival. Guanyin, the most popular of the Buddhist deities, was actually feted three times during the year; the popular Taiwanese god Zushigong was a trinity composed of three brothers, each of whose birthdays was marked by a festival. Even the lowly earth god enjoyed a special festival in its honor, on the second day of the second lunar month, although it was also worshipped, albeit less elaborately, on the second and sixteenth of each month (except during the New Year festivities).

These festivals of the gods tended to be the most lively, colorful, and exciting events in the life of a Chinese community. Only rarely was the popular religion solemn, and temple festivals often generated a carnival-like atmosphere. A major temple festival was often the occasion for numerous guests—including married daughters and their families, men working in the cities, and relatives and friends— to return to the village and renew acquaintanceships. Not infrequently, temple celebrations were the occasion also of an annual fair, at which peasants sold or bought draft animals, farm products, and manufactured goods. Always the festival was a time for feasting, so that the food market was more crowded, noisy, and alive than usual. Peddlars from afar set up stalls, selling candies, lottery chances, and perhaps the mildly narcotic beetle nut.

The religious aspects of a temple festival were hardly less lively. On the morning of one typical village festival, for example, a corps of young men carried the village gods, each seated in a resplendent sedan chair, to the four corners of the village to inspect the camps of spirit-soldiers, who throughout the year protected the village from evil spirits. As this procession proceeded on its tour of inspection, the men and boys beat loudly on drums and gongs and set off firecrackers to frighten away intruding ghosts, while villagers waited outside their homes and held incense to greet the passing gods. At the camps, the head of the procession performed a dramatic ritual: burning spirit-money, snapping a whip, and spitting mouthfuls of wine in all directions to clear ghosts from the area.

Meanwhile, each family in the village brought sacrifices to the temple, which they set out in massive quantities on tables and benches in the temple courtyard. Most visitors to the temple performed obeisances to the gods, and the smoke of incense weighed heavily in the air. By this time, too, a performance of native opera had begun, performed by a traveling troupe on a stage especially erected near the temple and accompanied by the loud clanging of cymbals and the whining of stringed instruments. These dramatic performances had no special religious content, but were ostensibly staged for the entertainment of the gods—although the plays obviously delighted the villagers, most of whom knew the stories by heart.

After the evening meal—consisting of food earlier sacrificed to the gods and subsequently retrieved from the temple—there was more opera. But the focus of attention now was the fire-walking ceremony, a performance that was thought to enhance the magical potency of the gods. After the lighting of a huge bonfire, the red-hot coals were spread in a large circle, perhaps 50 feet in diameter. Then a group of young men—selected by the gods through divination and prepared by means of special purification rites—three times carried the godly effigies in sedan chairs around the coals. A ritual master tossed salt over the coals and snapped his whip, and then, at a steady trot, the young men carried the gods directly across the fiery coals.

Another major temple festival, the Festival of the Hungry Ghosts—reminiscent of Halloween in the West—was distinguished by its dedication not to the gods or ancestors, but primarily to the ghosts. According to custom, the king of the underworld opened the Gates of Hell on the first day of the seventh lunar month. Then, all those souls that had died violent deaths or that received no offerings from living descendants were temporarily released from their unhappy confinement in the underworld and were free to roam among the living. To pacify these hungry ghosts and to prevent them from inflicting harm, Chinese placed elaborate food offerings outside the temples; and priests—usually Buddhist, but sometimes Taoist—performed propitiatory rituals within. Large and colorful paper models of houses, palaces, horses, carriages, and the like were erected; they, together with spirit-money, were burned during the celebration to provide for the needs of the ghosts. Opera was also staged for the entertainment of the visitors from the underworld.

The knowledge that hungry ghosts were roaming about during the seventh month caused villagers considerable concern. Swimming and boating were thought to be especially dangerous, because ghosts who had died by drowning might try to obtain their own release from Hell by drowning someone, thereby procuring a substitute. In China, as in the West, ghosts become particularly active in the dark. After nightfall, therefore, venturing outdoors was thought to be risky; throwing water on the ground might disturb and anger the malicious spirits; and it was especially forbidden to hang clothes out on bamboo poles, for they might obstruct the nocturnal wanderings of the ghosts. Chinese popular religion was never overly solemn, however, and the Festival of the Hungry Ghosts, which was in most parts of China second in importance only to the New Year, was always accompanied by light-hearted celebration and feasting.

Finally, on the last day of the seventh month, the Hungry Ghosts were called back to the underworld, and the Gates of Hell were closed for another year. Some of the "Good Brothers" remained behind, of course, so that mortals were never entirely free from worry about these troubled and vengeful souls.

The Clergy

Since it was diffused through families, communities, and other social organizations, the popular religion had no regular clergy in the usual sense of that term. Most religious observances required no clergy. Individual worshipers prayed or attempted to divine the will of a god without priestly intervention; and group worship, such as in a family, lineage, guild, or similar social unit, was directed by the secular leader of that group. Indeed, many temples in China either were untended or were staffed by a layman who served as a caretaker.

On special occasions, however, such as a funeral, a time of serious illness, or a temple festival, the people may have felt that they needed the assistance of those who possessed a specialized knowledge of religious ritual and affairs of the underworld. Then they called in one or more religious specialists: Buddhist or Taoist priests, shamans, or geomancers.

The Buddhist clergy during late imperial times had only limited contact with society at large. Most priests and nuns had severed their ties to the secular world and dedicated themselves to attaining redemption for themselves within the confines of a temple or monastery. They were not preachers who sought to win converts to the Buddhist faith, and, except when they officiated at funerals in the homes of the relatively wealthy, they seldom ventured into the world beyond the temple gates. Even when the common people worshiped in Buddhist temples and monasteries, ministrations by the priests were unnecessary. Most Chinese regarded Buddhist objects of veneration—most notably, the bodhisattva Guanyin and, to a lesser extent, the Amida Buddha and Sakyamuni Buddha—as deities who possessed magical powers, but they were no different in essence from countless other gods in the vast pantheon of the popular religion. The Buddhist church, in turn, was hardly less syncretic during the late imperial period than was the popular religion. It admitted into its temples, for instance, effigies of non-Buddhist deities, such as earth gods, and provided divination blocks and fortunetelling slips, all of which were alien to the pure Buddhist tradition.

Taoist priests were of two types. There were the monastic priests, who practiced the religion full time, resided in monasteries, and were celibate. Far more common, however, were the priests who lived more integrally within secular society than either Taoist or Buddhist monks. Most such popular Taoist priests married and raised families and, except when performing religious ceremonies, dressed as ordinary laymen. Because they often could not earn a livelihood in their religious vocation, most worked at regular jobs—usually as merchants or artisans, rather than as peasants, because the demands of farming might prevent them from responding to calls to serve in their priestly role.

Yet Taoist priests, like the Buddhist clergy, stood on the periphery of the popular religion. Although most public temples of the popular religion were regarded as Taoist, Taoist priests did not usually reside in the temples. Instead, they lived in private homes and hired out their services. They were liturgical specialists. In the homes of clients, they conducted marriages and funerals, healed the ill, and exorcised evil spirits; when called to the temples, they performed rites celebrating the gods' birthdays, rites of spiritual cleansing, and so on. They were, in other words, rather like lawyers or physicians in Western society, independent entrepreneurs whom the public occasionally employed because of their command of a body of arcane knowledge. Their services would be needed, however, only as long as they kept their magic a secret. Rather then preaching to the masses, therefore, they jealousy guarded those secrets, usually passing on their esoteric skills to no one but their sons.

To become a Taoist priest required at least minimal literacy and an extended novitiate. An acolyte spent years learning the dances, chants, *mudra* (hand symbols), and other rituals; he had to memorize hundreds of ceremonial texts; and he was required to master the magic that would enable him to exorcise malevolent spirits and heal the sick. The most skilled of the priests obtained ordination in the

Taoist church. These Taoist masters had learned the techniques of internal al-
chemy *(neidan),* which involved meditation and breath control, and were able to
summon forth a large number of spirits from the cosmos. These spirits—one of
which, the god of the star *tan,* was described as being "ten feet tall, has a red
face, a red beard, red shoes, and protruding eyes, and bears a long sword"—
could cure diseases, exorcise demons, and (on one's enemies) inflict black magic.[8]
Taoist adepts also had to acquire magical powers that would, for example, enable
them to climb, unharmed, a ladder of sword blades, cutting edge upward. Depending on their level of proficiency in such occult matters, they held ranks and
titles in a graded hierarchy.

Communicating with the underworld by means of spirit possession was the
special skill of the shamans. These spirit mediums were usually from the lowest
strata of society and rarely required special training. Three Cantonese shamans,
for example, had become spirit mediums after having gone through severe crises
in their lives, such as the deaths of children or husbands, after which they felt
themselves suddenly possessed by the spirits of the deceased relatives. At the
insistence of those spirits, which the women claimed to have resisted in vain, they
finally became shamans.

The role of shamans in the popular religion derived from the widespread belief
among Chinese that angry spirits—malevolent ghosts and displeased ancestors—
were common causes of illness and bad fortune among mortals. Should, for instance, an ancestor feel that its descendants were neglecting the necessary offerings, a ghost be angry at having suffered a cruel and early death, or a deceased
first wife be jealous of her husband's second spouse, then their souls could inflict
all manner of suffering on the living. Not always, of course, did the living know
the source of their suffering. That is where a shaman could help. By communicating with the spirits in the underworld, they could discover the identity of the
aggrieved ancestor or ghost and learn what was needed to placate the angered
soul.

The techniques employed by the various shamans differed. In a group séance
conducted in a Cantonese lineage, for example, a female shaman sent her own
soul down to the spiritual world. After the shaman had entered a deep trance, her
soul set off on the long and arduous journey, during which it encountered souls
of the dead who, when living, had resided in the village. The soul of an old man,
for instance, reported (through the voice of the shaman) that he was well, and he
merely admonished his living relatives: "Daughter-in-law, obey your mother-in-
law; son, obey your mother. Be careful in doing things; do not quarrel." Other
souls were more troubled. The ghost of a girl who had died at age two complained
that she had died because her parents had been negligent and had called in a
doctor too late to cure her illness. Villagers at the séance scolded the girl's ghost,
saying that she was too young to understand such things. Nonetheless, the girl's
parents thereafter burned silver spirit-money on the first and fifteenth of each month,
hoping that the girl's soul would be content and not bring harm to living members
of the family. Yet another ghost was the soul of Bean-Curd Jong's wife, who had
been a shrew in her earthly existence and since her death had repeatedly caused
trouble and harm to the villagers. The shaman's soul discovered that Bean-Curd

Jong's wife had now kidnapped the souls of three living children in the village, causing them to become ill. Speaking through the entranced shaman, the ghost complained that she was hungry and would release the children's souls only after she received a ransom. Gold spirit-money was accordingly burned as an offering to the troublesome ghost. The children's mothers were irate, however, and they shouted a warning to the ghost: "Don't do this again. If you do, spirit soldiers will be sent to catch and beat you. All those children have their own parents, why do you bother them? You must stop doing these evil things." As this scolding reveals, souls of the dead were not always treated with respect and were thought to be amenable to much the same kinds of persuasion as were living mortals.[9]

Some shamans induced trances not in themselves but in their clients, causing their souls to make the trip to the underworld. Yet other shamans—known as *tongji*—became spirit mediums when, after entering a trance, their bodies were possessed by a god. Then, as a god, the *tongji* became an oracle, giving instructions on how to cure an illness, exorcise a malevolent spirit causing fires in a village, or solve other problems caused by spirits of the underworld. A *tongji* dramatically demonstrated his special powers—ostensibly to hasten the descent of the god into his body—by self-mortification. While in a trance, he might pierce his tongue with a thick needle, thrust daggers through his cheeks or into his upper arms, or flagellate his back and forehead with a sword or prick-ball (a ball on a cord, with sharp spikes protruding). Villagers regarded the blood of a *tongji* as coming from the god itself. When absorbed by a piece of spirit-money, the blood served as a charm against evil forces; when mixed with water and drunk, it served as a powerful curative.

Geomancers were another kind of religious specialist whose services were thought to influence the fortunes of the living. Chinese geomancy, or *fengshui* (literally, "wind and water"), was a quasi-science based on the belief that life-breaths, or cosmic humors *(shengqi)*, concentrated in certain places in the landscape and that humans could derive good fortune by aligning their affairs to take advantage of the life-breaths. *Fengshui* was often employed, for instance, in the siting and aligning of buildings and even of cities. Most frequently, however, geomancers were employed to determine the location of burial sites.

Precisely how the geomantic forces worked in a tomb is a matter of controversy. The interpretations of the geomancers themselves and of the common people seemingly differed. In the geomancers' view, various configurations of the landscape—the shapes, sizes, and directions of hills and waters—represented the forces of *yin* and *yang*. A geomancer, using a specially designed compass, sought an auspicious arrangement of the Dragon and Tiger, the Five Elements, the Eight Trigrams, the Twenty-eight Lunar Mansions, and other symbols. In places where these symbols conjoined favorably, the life-breaths flowed. By burying the bones of an ancestor in precisely the center of this flow of life-breath, the living descendants could expect to derive wealth, professional success, good health, and numerous sons.

Geomancers insisted that these benefits resulted simply from the placement of the bones in that spot; the spirits of the ancestors had no influence on those results. In their view, the dead were passive agents, pawns in a kind of ritual game played by their descendants with the help of geomancers. The accumulation of [Life-] Breaths followed automatically from the correct siting of the grave. The dead themselves could choose neither to confer nor to withhold the blessings that flowed through their bones.[10]

Ordinary villagers, however, generally believed that the siting of a grave was important because the spirit of the deceased would be comfortable and content if the forces of *fengshui* were favorable. But it would be uncomfortable and displeased—and would therefore bring ill-fortune to the descendants—if the *fengshui* was bad. It was important, therefore, that the bones of the deceased be kept dry and protected from ants, that the view from the tomb be pleasant (which to Chinese meant a pleasing combination of hills and streams), that the air be clean, and that the tomb be exposed to the warmth of the sun. In short, ordinary Chinese who were not professional geomancers believed that correct *fengshui* meant simply that the tomb was a comfortable and pleasant place to reside, whether one were alive or dead. As one villager remarked, "If the ancestor in the grave is happy, he will help us. If he is uncomfortable, he will punish us with sickness or trouble." [11]

Whatever differences of interpretation may have divided geomancers from the common people, the consequences of their differing geomantic calculations were identical. Geomancers—however much they might use their compasses to calculate the balance of the forces of *yin* and *yang*—invariably selected sites that were aesthetically pleasing. Thus villagers, who would have been thoroughly mystified by the calculations and terminology of the *fengshui* experts, were satisfied that father's or mother's spirit in the grave rested comfortably and contentedly.

That there was a difference between the beliefs of the geomancers and those of their clients was by no means unique within the popular religion. A broad gap also separated the ideas of Buddhist and Taoist priests from those of typical adherents of the popular religion. This was because the knowledge of the religious specialists was esoteric; it was transmitted sparingly and selectively. Taoist ritual was "not meant to be directly understood and witnessed by all the faithful. The esoteric meaning . . . is concealed from all but the initiated." [12] Indeed, the various Taoist sects hid their secrets of the occult even from one another; each claimed that its own rituals and magic were more efficacious than those of the others; and the rivalry among Taoist sects sometimes escalated into large-scale fights.

Buddhist priests were generally less secretive about their beliefs, but neither were they evangelistic in spreading the Buddha's teachings. As noted earlier, most adherents of institutional Buddhism isolated themselves in monasteries. "Priests," it has been aptly remarked, "were not preachers." [13] Both Taoism and Buddhism, therefore, stood at the edges and not at the heart of the popular religion, and the religious ideas of the priests differed significantly from those of believers in the popular religion.

Although followers of the popular religion occasionally required the services of priests or spirit mediums, the social status of those religious specialists was generally low, they had only a modicum of literary education, and their morals were often suspect. Being unmarried, Buddhist priests were often suspected of homosexuality—yet their supposed lust for women was legendary. Because some Taoist sects allegedly engaged in sexual orgies, Taoist priests were also rumored to be guilty of sexual misconduct. Excessive social contact with priests could, therefore, taint a person's reputation. A lineage genealogy in the nineteenth century warned members: "Recently people have associated with Buddhist and Taoist priests, nominally in order to obtain male heirs and a long life (through religious worship). Little do they know that such social association might lead to the collapse of the family reputation. Neither should nuns be allowed to enter the homes, for as [the twelfth century Confucian philosopher] Zhu Xi has said, 'female priests are the medium for licentiousness and thievery.' "[14] With such a low reputation, the large majority of priests came from families too poor to support them at home.

The Social Utility of Popular Religion

That the popular religion persisted so long, and penetrated society so pervasively, fully testifies to its capacity to satisfy basic human religious longings. There is no gainsaying, therefore, the importance of the popular cult in the emotional life of the Chinese people. But like religions everywhere, the popular religion of China also performed important social, secular functions.

The social role of the indigenous religion differed, however, from that of the world's major organized religions—such as Buddhism, Christianity, Islam, and Judaism—which are *institutionalized* religions. Christianity, for example, is characterized by an independent theology, priesthood, and forms of ritual worship, and Christian churches are distinct and separate social institutions. In China, the popular religion tended to be *diffused;* its theology and ritual had no existence separate from the major social institutions, such as the family, lineage, merchant guild, and village. Even the "priests" of this popular religion were normally none other than the leaders of those institutions. The popular religion lacked, therefore, the independent organizational strength of, say, Christianity or Islam, but it may have had an even more pervasive social influence, contributing directly to the well-known conservatism of Chinese society.

The popular religion served, for instance, as a major support of familism. As a result of the cult of ancestor worship, the Chinese family was not merely a social and economic unit, but also a religious institution. In this way, the family was imbued with a sacred character, and the values of familism—filial piety, respect for the aged, and the paramount importance of the family as an institution over the will and desires of individual family members—were strongly reinforced.

The Chinese imperial state similarly acquired a sacred and inviolate character as a result of the diffused nature of the popular religion. The chief legitimizing principle of the imperial government was the concept of the Mandate of Heaven. Heaven, in the popular view, was the supreme transcendental force that determined the affairs of both nature and man. Heaven thus chose the emperor, who was accordingly known as the "Son of Heaven" and who alone was permitted to perform the sacrifices to Heaven and intercede with it on behalf of humankind.

This association of the head of government with the highest of the supernatural forces provided a powerful sanction for imperial rule.

Beneath Heaven, a vast number of subordinate gods and spirits shared with lesser officials of government the tasks of ruling the empire. "While it is the magistrates who rule in the world of light," read a stele of the late imperial period dedicated to a city god, "it is the gods who govern in the world of shadows. There is close cooperation between the two authorities."[15] Besides the city gods, whose temples were prominent in every city in the empire, the government associated itself with innumerable other deities of the popular religion, including the gods of earth and grain, the river god, the insect god, Guandi, Mazu, and the spirits of wind, clouds, thunder, and rain.

There existed, in fact, a state cult that was a part of and virtually indistinguishable from the religion of the commoners. Thus whenever the Board of Rites recognized that a deity of the popular religion was particularly efficacious, had performed especially valuable services for the state, or represented moral values that the state wished to foster, that deity would be awarded an honorific title and admitted to the pantheon of state-recognized gods. Temples to the deity would also be erected. On one occasion, for example, a river god was proclaimed an official deity as a reward for having assisted in the transport of grain to Peking by way of the Grand Canal. At a more exalted level, Guandi, the so-called god of war, was repeatedly honored and his temples were periodically renovated by the government in recognition of his powers of protecting the people and the state, and because he symbolized the virtues of loyalty to the dynasty and sincerity in dealings among men.

Nor did the government take the matter of the state cult lightly. Prefectural and *xian* magistrates who did not punctually conduct the required sacrifices to the state-recognized deities in the areas under their jurisdiction were to be punished with 100 blows of the bamboo. And during the Taiping Rebellion, the Xianfeng Emperor repeatedly issued decrees beseeching the aid of the gods in suppressing the rebels. In 1864, when the Taiping capital of Nanking was finally captured, the Tongzhi Emperor, in elaborate imperial ceremonies, presented sacrifices to Heaven and to earth, declaring that the victory was "due solely to [the]favored protection from Heaven and affection from the spirits of the sage ancestors."[16]

Although some especially rationalistic Confucians attempted over the centuries to debunk such beliefs in the powers of the supernatural, most emperors and officials seem to have genuinely shared the popular belief in a transcendental realm whose inhabitants could affect the affairs of mortals. These emperors and officials were also keenly aware, however, that this religion served the very practical function of helping to maintain peace, order, and obedience among the common people. The Confucian view, repeated frequently, was that "in the world of light there are rites and music (moral regulations), and in the world of shadows there are spirits and gods. Where rites and music failed to rule (the people), the spirits and gods succeeded without exception."[17] But the state encouraged popular worship of only those deities who promoted law-abiding conduct among the people. Worship of deities with a potential for promoting political unrest—such as the

"Eternal Mother," who was the patron goddess of most heterodox folk sects during late imperial times (Chapter 10)—was sternly forbidden.

The social utility of the popular religion also had a lighter side, for its ceremonies and festivities provided about the only occasions throughout the year when the common people could relax, socialize, and enjoy a colorful spectacle. Life for the masses, who ordinarily engaged in a relentless struggle for subsistence, must have been stultifyingly dull and grim. Their work was heavy, the food uninteresting, and entertainment rare. During religious festivals, however, relatives came for food, conversation, and games. The village itself became a veritable stage for drama and excitement. Meat and sweets, seldom a part of the ordinary villagers' diet, were eaten by all but the most impoverished. And temple opera, fire-walking ceremonies, and the magical feats of the Taoist priests and *tongji* provided topics of conversation for weeks to come.

One thing the popular religion did *not* supply, as do institutional religions in the West, was a distinct and independent set of moral values. From an early time, Confucianism had been the dominant source of China's ethical precepts, and the moral priesthood—those who were primarily responsible for interpreting the rules of morality and passing judgment on right and wrong actions—consisted of the Confucian scholars and officials. The Taoist and Buddhist clergy who served the popular religion were generally so poorly educated and of such suspect morality that they lacked the social and moral stature necessary to perform that role.

Popular religion did, however, help enforce the secular moral code. Confucians placed heavy stress, for instance, on the values associated with familism, but they realized that the rationalistic philosophy of Confucianism could not enforce those values among the unlettered commoners. Ancestor worship, with its belief that angry ancestors could inflict retribution if they and the family were not well served, helped maintain the dominance of familistic values. Similarly, popular religion reinforced such moral values as honesty, respect for life and property, and preservation of social harmony by threatening wrongdoers with dire punishment in the Hells of the underworld. Even the most rationalistic of Confucians, consequently, appreciated the social utility of the popular religion for providing supernatural sanction for their moral code.

Changes During the Twentieth Century

During the late nineteenth and early twentieth centuries, powerful forces of change entered China, and the popular religion came under assault from all sides. The physical and financial expressions of religion suffered terrible blows when, during the last thirteen years or so of the dynasty, the Qing government attempted to modernize administration and education at the local levels. Succeeding governments continued the process. To provide buildings for public offices and the new police departments, and classrooms for the new schools, the governments ordered that temples be taken over. To finance their new administrative activities, they confiscated temple lands. This storm of administrative and educational modernization took an especially heavy toll of the temples in north China, but the ravages were felt to some degree nationwide.

Nor did the antireligious tempest let up. Beginning about 1917, the New Culture Movement attacked all traditional beliefs and values, including the superstitions associated with the worship of ancestors and deities. During the 1920s, a nationwide anti-Christian movement spilled over into an assault on all religions. And the Nationalist government, which came to power in 1927, attempted to suppress much of the popular religion. In Chekiang, for instance, the provincial government proclaimed that "superstition is a hindrance to progress. The appeal to the authority of the gods is a policy to keep people ignorant."[18] Although the Nationalists remained tolerant of the Taoist "pope," Buddhism, and Christianity, they declared that the temples and idols of the stove god, the god of wealth, and other "useless gods" should be "razed to the ground so that nothing remains."[19] They also inveighed against wasteful expenditures on such religious paraphernalia as incense and spirit-money. The ability of the Nationalist government to enforce such ordinances was usually slight, although it is significant that the burning of incense was effectively banned in 1939, even in the semiautonomous province of Yunnan.

Still, the political disapproval of the Nationalist government doubtless had less impact on the popular religion than did the corrosive effects of modern scientific thought, increasing urbanization, and social change. Intellectuals in the cities were the first to be influenced by these secularizing trends, but their scorn of the deities spread to workers, merchants, and other urbanites. By the 1930s, craft guilds in the cities and large towns were increasingly ignoring their patron deities, and the large religious processions, which they had once promoted, were disappearing from the urban social scene.

The ideas associated with science and modern materialism penetrated less forcefully into the villages in the interior; in some regions before 1927, temples were actually being erected and existing ones, repaired. But "increasing contacts with the outside world, modern education, and many other influences had apparently weakened the hold of the gods on the people."[20] Those "other influences" probably included rampant militarism because soldiers were frequently billeted in village temples, which they vandalized terribly, at times even breaking up the structural timbers in scrounging for firewood. As a result also of harsh economic conditions during much of the century, villagers may have been spending less money on the deities.

Popular religion nonetheless remained remarkably tenacious. Studies undertaken in villages during the 1930s and 1940s reveal that if popular attachment to the gods had indeed declined, the decline was only relative, and that religious beliefs continued to hold a sway over the lives of the common people.

Selected Readings

(See also the works cited in the notes)

Ahern, Emily M. *The Cult of the Dead in a Chinese Village*. Stanford, Calif.: Stanford University Press, 1973.

Baity, Philip Chelsey. *Religion in a Chinese Town*. Taipei: Orient Cultural Service, 1975.

de Groot, J. J. M. *The Religious System of China*. 6 vols. Leiden: Brill, 1892–1910.

Eberhard, Wolfram. *Chinese Festivals*. New York: Schuman, 1952.

Goodrich, Anne Swann. *Chinese Hells: The Peking Temple of Eighteen Hells and Chinese Conceptions of Hell*. St. Augustin: Monumenta Serica, 1981.

Jordan, Donald K. *Gods, Ghosts, and Ancestors: The Folk Religion of a Taiwanese Village*. Berkeley: University of California Press, 1972.

March, Andrew L. "An Appreciation of Chinese Geomancy." *Journal of Asian Studies* 27, no. 2 (February 1968): 253–67.

Potter, Jack M. "Cantonese Shamanism." In *Religion and Ritual in Chinese Society*, ed. Arthur P. Wolf, pp. 207–31. Stanford, Calif.: Stanford University Press, 1974.

Saso, Michael. "Orthodoxy and Heterodoxy in Taoist Ritual." In *Religion and Ritual in Chinese Society*, ed. Arthur P. Wolf, pp. 325–36. Stanford, Calif.: Stanford University Press, 1974.

Thompson, Laurence G. *Chinese Religion: An Introduction*. 3d ed. Belmont, Calif.: Wadsworth, 1979.

Weller, Robert P. *Unities and Diversities in Chinese Religion*. Seattle: University of Washington Press, 1987.

Wolf, Arthur P. "Gods, Ghosts, and Ancestors." In *Religion and Ritual in Chinese Society*, ed. Arthur P. Wolf, pp. 131–82. Stanford, Calif.: Stanford University Press, 1974.

Yang, C. K. *Religion in Chinese Society: A Study of Contemporary Social Functions of Religion and Some of Their Historical Factors*. Berkeley: University of California Press, 1961.

4

Agriculture: An Overview

China was traditionally an agrarian society. On the farms and in the villages was the essence of Chinese life. And so it remained throughout the period prior to the Communist revolution. While much of the Western world since the seventeenth century experienced a series of economic revolutions—agrarian, commercial, and industrial—agriculture continued to dominate Chinese life, much as it had in previous millennia. To say this, however, is not to agree with Karl Marx that China had been ''vegetating in the teeth of time'' before the arrival of the Westerners.[1] True, the technology employed in the farm economy remained virtually unchanged, but the level of commercial activity in the empire rose dramatically during the late imperial period, and this profoundly altered the lives and production of peasants in the villages.

The Methods of Peasant Agriculture

In China proper, agriculture meant a cultivating, not a pastoral, economy. Animals were used for pulling and hauling; they were also valued for the fertilizer they produced; and most farms had a pig, a few chickens, and perhaps a pair of ducks. Rather than deriving their food energy primarily from meat, which requires the mediation of animals that consume plant products, the Chinese obtained it more efficiently by ingesting the plant products directly. Fully 90 percent of their food energy came from grains and vegetables, and only 2 to 3 percent from meat. This diet profoundly influenced the character of the farm economy as well as the culture of the entire nation.

As a nation larger than the United States, China had not just one, but several agricultural regions. The fundamental division in China's agriculture, however, was that between north and south, between the so-called rice-growing region, to

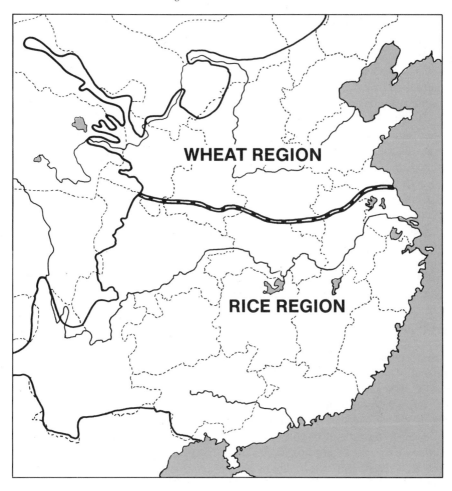

FIGURE 4.1. The Two Main Agricultural Regions of China
Source: John Lossing Buck, *Land Utilization in China* (Chicago, Ill.: The University of Chicago Press, 1937), p. 25.

the south of the Hwai River, and the wheat-growing region, to the north (Figure 4.1). Naturally, the boundary between the two areas was not as sharp as these terms suggest: geographically and economically, they shaded into each other, and many crops other than rice and wheat were cultivated in these regions. For our purposes, however, the terms are useful and generally valid.

Between these two agricultural regions, there were important economic and cultural differences. Farms in the north were nearly twice as large as those in the south, and tenancy was markedly lower. Only about 18 percent of the cultivated land in the north during the 1930s was irrigated, whereas 62 percent was irrigated in the south. Transportation of farm commodities in the south was facilitated by a vast system of interlacing rivers and canals. In the north, transportation was by

cart and on the backs of humans or animals; it was, consequently, far more arduous, slow, and expensive than in the south. Culturally and linguistically, the
south was fragmented: because of the crosscutting mountains and greater ethnic
diversity, villagers living only a few miles apart often spoke discernibly different
dialects and were marked by distinct social customs. In the northern plains, the
culture was considerably more homogeneous.

Despite the considerable differences between the two regions, there were also
many similarities. Whether in north or south, the typical farm was small, seldom
larger than the acreage that could be worked by a peasant and members of his
immediate family. During the 1930s, the average-size farm in north China was
5.1 acres; in the south, it was only 2.8 acres. With such exiguous plots, the work
of China's peasants tended more to resemble gardening than what Westerners
regard as farming.

Occasionally, a family succeeded in accumulating a relatively large area of
farmland. A farm of 400 or 500 acres was considered huge, although a very few
families, lineages, or temples owned 1,000 or more acres. Even in such rare
instances of large landholding, however, the lands were not tilled as consolidated
estates. Instead, the owner usually retained only a small portion—often about 1
acre or so—primarily to feed himself and his dependents. The rest he rented in
small parcels to scores of tenant farmers. Some rich farmers who held 15 to 30
acres farmed their lands directly, using hired labor to do most of the actual work.
These "managerial estates" were, however, in a minority; they were seldom found
in south China and even in the northern provinces of Hopei and Shantung in the
1930s, they accounted for only about 10 percent of the cultivated area.

A comparison with the United States is enlightening. In the United States in
the 1930s, the average farm family of 4.2 people lived on 157 acres; in China,
the average farm family of 6.2 people drew its sustenance from about 4.2 acres.
Little wonder, therefore, that the levels of food consumption, standard of living,
farm technology, and style of life of farmers in the two societies differed so vastly.
The minuscule size of the farms also helps explain the intensive nature of Chinese
agriculture; fully 90 percent of the farm area was devoted to crops, and only 2
percent of the farm area was set aside for pasturage or woodland. Because of the
small amount of pasturage available, young children or aged adults often led an
ox or other animal on a rope while it grazed alongside a field divider, a road, or,
possibly, an ancestral grave—evidence of the cheapness of human labor and the
farmers' use of all available resources.

Despite the small acreage of the farms, they tended to be fragmented into even
smaller plots. Farms in the early 1930s in both north and south China were broken
into an average of 5.6 parcels of land (Figure 4.2). These parcels were often
widely separated from one another; the average distance from a farm plot to the
farmer's home was four-tenths of a mile. A plot on one side of the village, however, was sometimes as much as 1 mile away from another of the farmer's fields
on the other side of the village. Dispersion of plots tended to be somewhat greater
in the wheat- than in the rice-producing region.

It has often been assumed that farmers purposely dispersed their fields, believ-
ing that they benefited from the resulting diversity of soil and water conditions.

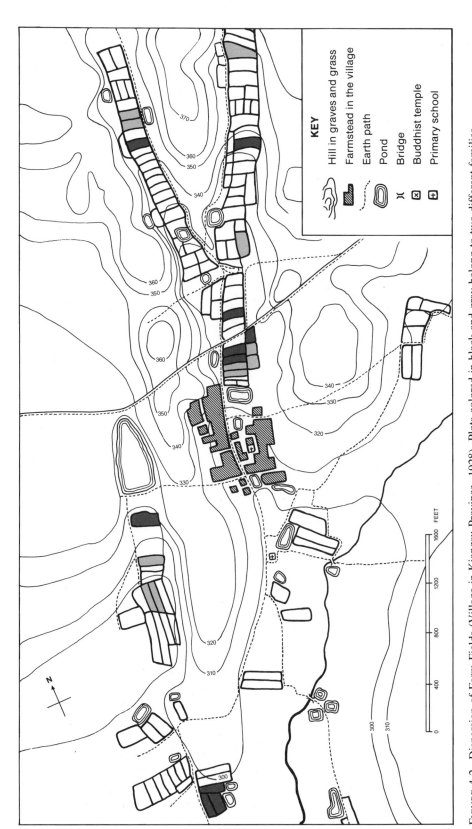

KEY

	Hill in graves and grass
	Farmstead in the village
	Earth path
	Pond
)(	Bridge
⊠	Buddhist temple
⊕	Primary school

N

370
360
350
340
360
350
360
350
340
330
320
340
350
340
330
320
330
310
320
310
300
310
300

0   400   800   1200   1600   FEET

FIGURE 4.2. Dispersion of Farm Fields (Village in Kiangsu Province, 1928). Plots colored in black and gray belong to two different families.
Source: John Lossing Buck, *Chinese Farm Economy* (Nanking: University of Nanking, 1930), facing p. 26.

Each peasant, it has been argued, needed some wet land and some dry land for his different crops, and dispersion served as insurance against recurrent natural disasters, such as floods and droughts. In fact, however, farmers purchased land whenever they had accumulated sufficient savings; and because the turnover rate of land was low, they had to buy whatever land was then available. Fragmentation of the farms was purely adventitious, therefore, and not the result of rational choice.

Chinese farming was, above all else, labor intensive. Machinery powered by wind or water was rare. Animals—notably oxen, water buffalo, and donkeys, but also horses, mules, and (in the north and northwest) camels—were used as beasts of burden. But they were expensive to buy and keep, and fully one-third of farms could not afford a draft animal. Human labor, by contrast, was plentiful and cheap. On the many farms without an ox or a buffalo, men and women—but especially men, for women with bound feet were of little use in the fields—were widely used to pull the plows and serve as beasts of burden. Pumps, used to raise water to irrigate the fields, were turned by family members walking the circular treadles. The terracing of fields, the preparation of fertilizer, and multiple cropping also characterized China's labor-intensive farming.

Terracing enabled farmers to cultivate hillsides and mountain slopes that would otherwise be untillable. Except on naturally level fields, terracing was essential for the creation of rice paddies, which had to be flooded during most of the growing season. Even in the wheat-producing areas, terracing increased the total farm acreage, minimized erosion, and helped retain precious rain water until it had

FIGURE 4.3. Tilling a Field. Lacking draught animals, many peasants, together with members of their families, had to pull the farm implements themselves. Photo courtesy The Peabody Museum, Salem, Mass.

FIGURE 4.4. Raising Water by Treadle Pumps. The woodblock print from a seventeenth century work on Chinese technology *(Tiangong kaiwu),* above, and a late-nineteenth century photograph, on page 68, illustrate the persistence through the centuries of the traditional agricultural technology. Photo courtesy of the Peabody Museum, Salem, Mass.

soaked down to the crops' roots. But terracing required stupendous effort. The farmers not only had to move large quantities of earth, but also, especially in creating rice paddies, had to buttress the terraces with stone retaining walls. It is impossible for us to conceive how much human labor was expended over the generations in converting entire hillsides and valleys into terraced fields, connected by stone-paved paths and interlaced with intricate networks of irrigation canals. Yet much of the Chinese landscape in north as well as in south China— approximately one-quarter of the cultivated acreage—was transformed and made usable by terracing. Terraced fields were often no larger than a small room; some were no bigger than a table top. But when the addition of just a few square feet of cultivable land could mean the difference between empty or full ricebowls, a farmer and his family did not begrudge the labor to build yet another terrace.

Soil maintenance likewise required prodigious and continual labor. Although much of the land had been tilled for at least 1,000 years, it continued to be productive because the farmers worked unremittingly to restore nutrients to the treasured soil—far more so than in, say, the United States or Russia, where lands showed signs of exhaustion after just two or three generations. Wherever feasible, mud from canals and streams was dredged up and spread over the fields. Compost was arduously accumulated each year and then—often at the rate of 50 to 60 tons

FIGURE 4.5. Rice fields in southern Hunan, 1934. Terracing transformed the face of much of rural China and, like fertilizing and multicropping, required prodigious human effort. Some terraced rice paddies were no larger than a table top. Photographed by Count Wulf Diether zu Castell. Courtesy of Black Star.

per acre of field—was worked into the soil. The peasants' one notable failure to use organic waste for compost was in their setting aside of straw and plant stems, which were used for fuel. A large source of humus was thereby lost, although the ashes were subsequently added to the fields.

By far, the most treasured fertilizers were animal manure and night soil. The peasants' attitude was reflected in such popular sayings as "Collecting manure is collecting gold," and "The manure pit is a treasure pot." Animal droppings, consequently, were collected diligently. In the cities and towns, professional night-soil collectors paid money for the privilege of carrying away human feces, which were, in turn, sold to farmers. Nothing was wasted.

F. H. King, in his classic 1911 description of Chinese agriculture, strongly applauded the Chinese use of night soil. He said that Americans, by contrast, each year dumped into their lakes and rivers some 3,000 to 6,000 tons of nitrogen, 1,000 to 2,000 tons of potassium, and 400 to 1,500 tons of phosphorus for each million of adult population. "And this waste," he remarked sarcastically, "we esteem one of the great achievements of our civilization." [2]

There is no doubt that the use of night soil tremendously enhanced the fertility of the Chinese soil. But it also exacted an enormous toll, for night soil was the carrier of numerous and often deadly fecal-borne parasites, such as blood fluke, hookworm, and liver fluke. Hookworm eggs, for example, are discharged from the host animal (or human) in the feces. If conditions are right, the eggs hatch, and the worm seeks contact with the skin of an unsuspecting farmer. Penetrating the skin, the worm eventually takes up residence on the farmer's intestinal wall, where it feeds itself by sucking blood. Several hundred of these half-inch parasites will consume about a half pint of blood each day. Initially, the farmer becomes anemic and weak, and, if not treated, soon dies.

The life cycle of each of these parasites varies somewhat from that of the others; but together, they were the leading cause of death in China. About one-quarter of all deaths were attributable to these parasitic worms, which were spread through the use of night soil. This awful fact led a leading agricultural economist, John Lossing Buck, to differ vehemently with King regarding the Chinese use of night soil. "From an economic viewpoint," Buck wrote, "it would probably be cheaper to throw away night soil than to incur the losses concurrent with ill-health which result from its use." [3] Actually, with proper fermentation of night soil and with care in cooking the foods nurtured with it, night soil is perfectly safe to use. And Chinese farmers today, even after the increased availability and use of chemical fertilizers, still believe that organic fertilizers, night soil included, are more efficacious in the long run for maintaining soil fertility than are the chemical varieties. They are doubtless correct.

Multiple cropping was another labor-intensive activity that substantially increased the total productivity of the available land. In south China, two and, in some regions, even three rice crops in succession could be harvested each year from one field. To fit the multiple rice crops into the limited growing season, peasants started the rice plants in seedbeds and, after twenty-five to fifty days, through back-breaking labor, transplanted the seedlings to the fields. In the north, too, multiple cropping was common. There, the farmers often planted wheat in the fall. After harvesting the wheat in the spring, they planted maize, cotton, soybeans, or some such crop that could be reaped in the late summer. The combination of crops thus planted varied enormously, depending chiefly on the climate and the length of the growing season in the various areas.

Another method of multiple cropping was intercropping, by means of which additional crops could be squeezed into the limited space and limited growing year. Beans, for instance, might be planted alongside rows of wheat that had been planted the previous fall. After the wheat was harvested, cotton might be planted in those rows, but the beans would mature and could be picked before the cotton overshadowed them. Many such mixes of crops could be planted. All, however, required painstaking, individualized attention, and defied large-scale, mechanized production. About one-quarter of the fields in the north and about two-thirds in the south were planted with more than one crop each year.

In more favorable circumstances, the labor-intensive methods employed by

Chinese peasants would have been regarded as uneconomical. But when the peasants were struggling close to the ragged edge of subsistence, they were often forced to work unimaginably long and hard merely to increase their output by even the smallest of increments. This condition has been described as "self-exploitation."[4]

The Chinese peasants' tendency toward "self-exploitation" was manifested in ways other than by laboring hard at building terraces, fertilizing the fields, multiple cropping, and so on. They also often paid uneconomical rents on land—in the sense that working the land would not repay them with a reasonable hourly wage— but they paid the rents because farming that additional land added something, if only a little, to the family granary. Similarly, most peasant families devoted long and wearisome hours to various forms of handicraft production. A weaver, for example, often earned enough to pay for only one-fifth of the food she consumed; yet from the vantage point of the family, that one-fifth was better than nothing at all. Necessity, that is, could be far more exploitative of the peasant than could the most mean-hearted landlord.

The Changing Patterns of Landholding and Farm Labor

The Chinese farm economy with which Westerners in the nineteenth and early twentieth centuries were most familiar consisted of small, privately held farms that were freely bought and sold. Those who worked the soil were free peasants— landowners and tenants who enjoyed legal and social, if not economic, equality with each other.

It had not always been so. Before the Tang Dynasty (618–907), for example, large aristocratic families dominated the countryside, administered huge rural estates, and held their farm laborers in virtual slavery. During the Tang and Song dynasties, however, the power of the aristocratic families gradually collapsed. At first, many of their estates were confiscated by the government, and heavy taxes on the land weakened their economic power. The political power of the aristocratic families further diminished during the Song Dynasty as the newly emergent gentry class became the chief source of the emperors' bureaucrats. With the collapse of the aristocrats' political power and the disappearance of their estates, the peasants working the fields gradually sloughed off their status as slaves, and by about the fourteenth century, most of them had gained the freedom to own and rent land and to move about at will.

Even during the sixteenth and seventeenth centuries, however, some in the rural population were still held in a feudal type of bondage and were known as *nupu,* usually translated as "serf" or "bondservant." The way these bondservants lived and the conditions of their indenture are still not fully understood. It is possible, however, to gain some insights into these matters, and into the general question of landholding, by examining the evolution of the rural economy in one relatively small area of China—the Lake Tai Region of east-central China, about 50 miles inland from Shanghai.[5]

At the outset of the Ming Dynasty, the Emperor Taizu adopted a policy of breaking up the estates of many large and powerful landlords, confiscating their properties, scattering their families, and distributing their lands to the poor. As a consequence, the dominant form of landholding in the Lake Tai Region in the late fourteenth century was the small, privately owned family farm. It is unlikely that many bondservants could be found in the area at that time.

Beginning with the reign of the third Ming emperor, Yongle (1403–1424), this system of small freeholders began to break down. Yongle inaugurated a number of expensive governmental undertakings, including the seven famous and costly maritime expeditions (1405–1432) to Southeast Asia, India, and the east coast of Africa; in 1421, he moved the imperial capital from present-day Nanking to Peking, where he started a huge construction program, building palaces, government offices, and the great city wall. To pay for these grandiose projects, the Peking government boosted the land taxes, visiting extreme hardship on small peasant landowners. Unable to bear the new tax burden, many of these peasants took refuge with powerful landlords who were able to resist the government's financial exactions. In taking refuge, however, the peasants were forced to commend themselves, their families, and their lands to the large landlords, who now became their masters.

As a result of this process, there arose on the landscape large rural estates, often encompassing between 1,000 and 3,000 *mu* (approximately 150 to 450 acres). The lords of these manors rarely engaged in agricultural work, but lived lives of leisure in grand villas while subordinates managed and worked the estates. Some of the workers on the estates—but probably not all—were bondservants. A large gentry landlord near Wusih, for instance, had 3,000 bondservants on his huge estate of 300,000 *mu*; another had 500 bondservants, while several others owned 100. It was common for an estate's bondservants to be employed only in fields near the villa or as domestic help, while fields more remote from the villa were farmed by hired laborers or tenant farmers. Not all land in the region had been absorbed into these large estates, however, and thus small freeholders, tilling their own farms, could still be found outside the large manors.

The bondservants' conditions of servitude varied greatly. Some bondservants, especially those who were held in hereditary bondage and who worked under the direct supervision of the master, were little more than slaves. "What I have seen of the way masters treat their serfs," wrote one observer in the Lake Tai Region,

> is not the way one treats a human being. Not only do they show no sympathy for their hunger, cold, and overwork, they even prohibit the children of serfs to wear mourning dress and weep when their parents die. They also take sexual liberties with the daughters and wives of their serfs.[6]

The vast majority of bondservants, though—and this was especially true of those who were field servants working outside the purview of the masters—were barely distinguishable from free commoners. The status of these field servants was often nonhereditary, and most had become bondservants by commending themselves and their property to the care, protection, and ownership of the landlord for only their lifetime, or perhaps for only a specified number of years. Some men even accepted bondservant status in order to acquire a wife, agreeing to serve a master for, say, twenty years in exchange for an arranged marriage.

Some bondservants, moreover, were both powerful and rich. Merchants, for example, sometimes became bondservants in exchange for commercial loans—retaining ownership of their businesses even after accepting some degree of servitude. And many bondservants served as the managers of their masters' estates. Such bondservants often acquired substantial wealth, property, and, perhaps, bondservants of their own. Some even took the civil-service examinations, thus becoming members of the gentry and sometimes serving as officials in the imperial bureaucracy. Bondservant status thus defies easy description. For most of bondservants, the demands of servitude were probably not much harsher than were the lives of small peasant freeholders.

During the sixteenth century, the entire economy—and with it, the pattern of social relationships—of the Lake Tai Region began to change. Until then, the economy of the region had been basically agricultural, rural, and self-sufficient. The great manorial lords lived in their rural villas rather than in the towns, and the commoners relied almost solely on agriculture for their livelihood. But a domestic trade in cotton and cotton textiles and a foreign trade in silk developed, greatly stimulating commercial and manufacturing activity and pumping silver into the economy. As a result of these changes, the economic and political center of gravity in the region shifted decisively from the countryside to the towns. Manorial lords began to invest in commercial and manufacturing ventures in the urban centers. There they lost touch with their rural estates, which provided a lesser return on their capital than did commercial activities. A class of merchant magnates, usually of humble and rural origin, now emerged in the towns and became a part of the urban elite. During the Qing Dynasty, this became the dominant pattern, with the overwhelming majority of the region's elite living in the towns.[7] This shift meant not only a rise in absentee landlordism, but also an increasing focus of elite interests on commerce rather than on agriculture.

The lives of Lake Tai's peasants were also transformed by the process of commercialization. Beginning in the sixteenth century, farm households in the region took up cotton spinning, silk reeling, and weaving as sources of supplementary income, and most families soon were devoting as much attention to handicraft production as to farming. As a result, men could work more intensively throughout the year, and women were able to contribute to their families' incomes. Peasants' standards of living consequently improved. And because the peasants derived approximately half their annual income from handicrafts and could readily shift from one to the other, they were relatively protected from downturns in either the agricultural or the commercial sector.

All this worked to change the peasants' relations to the land and to the landlords. Now the peasants acquired a sense of independence from the landlords. And because they were now devoting so much time to handicrafts (and also because of a population decline in the seventeenth century), there developed a labor shortage, which forced the landlords to be more solicitous of their farm help. "Nowadays," wrote a landlord to a friend,

> because there is plenty of land for rent . . . even if we try with special care to
> win support from our tenants, I am not sure we can make it. . . . Even if we
> can find replacements, the new tenants may not be better than the previous ones.
> . . . Therefore, to dismiss a tenant household should be the last solution in deal-
> ing with the problem.[8]

The peasants thus improved their bargaining stance vis-à-vis the landlords.

The mid-seventeenth century was also a time of peasant uprisings in the region. Particularly during the period of the Qing conquest, both tenants and bondservants turned on their former lords and masters. Following the fall of Nanking
to the Manchus in 1645, for example,

> hundreds and thousands of people who lived along the lakeside flocked together.
> They carried plough tails [and] sticks, and shouted loudly for revenge. . . . They
> were looking for the people they hated to destroy their walls and gates, to burn
> down their houses and to kill them. . . . The incident lasted almost a month,
> while the previously influential families either fled or hid out.[9]

Frightened by these uprisings, landlords elsewhere in the region emancipated their
bondservants, who became free tenant farmers.

As a result of the growing commercialization during the sixteenth and early
seventeenth centuries, and culminating in the peasant uprisings of the 1640s, the
system of small, free peasant households became the dominant form of agricultural production in the Lake Tai Region. Although a few bondservants could still
be found, they served primarily as domestic servants rather than as field laborers.

Social and economic changes in the Lake Tai Region were not necessarily
representative of conditions elsewhere. Lake Tai was but a small and atypical
region in the empire. The Kiangnan area, of which Lake Tai was a part, was
considerably more prosperous, more commercialized, and more influenced by foreign trade than was any other part of China in the sixteenth through eighteenth
centuries. Nonetheless, the social and economic dynamic at work in the Lake Tai
Region also seemingly had an effect, in greater or lesser degree, elsewhere in the
empire, because the system of bondservants—which had, in any case, never provided more than 20 percent of the total field workers—had largely disappeared
during the early years of Qing rule. Thereafter, the prevailing pattern of landholding and farm labor was of small peasant freeholders and tenants, a system that
persisted essentially unchanged until the Communist takeover in 1949.

Despite the dominance of the system of a free peasantry by the fourteenth
century and the virtual disappearance of bondservants on manors in the seventeenth century, varying degrees of "feudal" subservience persisted into the twentieth century. In some areas, for instance, tenants were expected to present "gifts"—
such as a chicken, a duck, or eggs—to their landlords at festival time; they might
also be required to help out with various chores during a wedding or funeral in
the landlords' household. And instances of actual slavery, particularly of domestic
workers, could occasionally be found right down to 1949.[10]

Tenancy in the System of Small-Peasant Agriculture

Within the system of small freeholders that gradually evolved after the Tang Dynasty, every farmer aspired to own his own land. This was among his dearest ambitions, for by owning his land, he could hope to bring prestige and economic well-being to his family and to guarantee that succeeding generations would remember him in their performance of the ancestral rites. Yet each year, some peasants lost all or part of the land that they or their ancestors had painstakingly acquired. As a consequence, fully 32 percent of all peasant households by the 1930s owned no land. About 42 percent of all the farmland in the nation was rented. And because rents often ranged from .50 to 70 percent of the main harvest, and sometimes higher, the high incidence of tenancy has often been regarded as the most invidious element in China's agricultural economy.

Peasants usually lost their land as a result of indebtedness. For those who lived near the subsistence level, only a little hard luck—illness, a year or two of poor harvests, or a sharp drop in market prices—easily sufficed to plunge even the most diligent and frugal landowning peasant into debt. A wedding or funeral, necessitating costly forms of conspicuous consumption, also impelled numerous farmers to visit the local moneylender. At interest rates of 30 to 40 percent a year, and sometimes higher, peasants frequently could not pay back loans, resulting in foreclosure and the loss of the land offered as collateral. Seldom, be it noted, did Chinese borrow to make capital investments—to increase productivity by purchasing a draft animal, tools, and other means of production. Dire necessity, rather, was the chief reason for indebtedness and, consequently, of the peasants' loss of land.

A paradox, however, exists. Natural disasters—such as droughts, floods, and locusts—and hence the cause of much of the peasants' worst suffering, were more common in north than in south China. One would expect, then, that the incidence of tenancy would be higher in the north than in the south—but just the opposite was true. Obviously, factors other than indebtedness contributed to the incidence of peasant tenancy.

High tenancy rates were found primarily in areas where the land produced substantial surpluses, where transportation to markets was economical, and where large amounts of investment capital could be accumulated. These factors generally point to south rather than north China. Indeed, tenancy rates in the neighborhoods of Canton and Shanghai in the 1930s were 85 percent and 95 percent, respectively. In north China, fields on the relatively infertile and dry plains produced barely enough to sustain the cultivator and his family. A unit of rice paddy in south China, by contrast, yielded approximately three to five times more food energy per unit of land than did staple crops in the north. The south, as a consequence, more often produced surpluses. Transportation in north China, primarily by cart and pack animal, was arduous and expensive over long distances, whereas the waterways of the south provided relatively cheap conveyance. Finally, high tenancy rates were often found in areas where commerce was more highly developed. Although officeholders, moneylenders, and even bandits invested their wealth in land, most absentee landlords had derived their capital from commercial activities.

Despite the tendency of China's wealthy to invest in agriculture, the returns on investments in farmland were low. The annual return on landholding was customarily only about 5 to 6 percent of the value of the land, whereas the return on commercial investment was often 10 to 20 percent, and moneylending usually brought a return of at least 30 to 40 percent. The wealthy nonetheless often invested in land because it was regarded as a relatively safe way to store one's wealth. Landholding, moreover, was a genteel and socially respected form of investment, whereas commercial investment, however profitable, hinted of money grubbing, which Confucian society contemned. Not profit, therefore, but considerations of security and prestige were the principal reasons the urban wealthy continued to invest in land.

The Varieties of Rental Arrangements

Although landlords realized that their returns on investments in rented land was relatively small, tenants generally felt that the rents they paid were extremely burdensome. Yet tenancy was a diverse phenomenon, and the welfare of tenants was often affected more by the form of tenancy than by tenancy as such.

Rents were customarily paid either in *fixed amounts* of money or grain, or as a *percentage* of the final harvest. Each system had advantages and disadvantages for both landlords and tenants. From the point of view of the landlord, the advantage of charging a fixed rent, whether in cash or in kind, was that he was assured a steady income, regardless of the vicissitudes of nature and the size of the harvest. This system had an advantage for the tenant, too; if he worked hard to improve the productivity of the land, all incremental increases in the harvests would accrue to him alone, with no need of sharing them with the landlord—which was, of course, from the landlord's point of view, a disadvantage. Conversely, the system could weigh especially heavily on the tenant in a year of poor crops, for he still had to pay the fixed rent and might, therefore, have woefully little left to feed himself and his family. In south China, approximately 85 percent of the rents were paid in fixed amounts.

In the north, however, the system of sharecropping was more common than it was in the south, although it accounted for only one-third of the rental arrangements. Under this system, the landlord customarily supplied the tenant with some of the necessities for farming the land, such as seeds, tools, or, possibly, the use of a draft animal. Depending on what the landlord provided, rents might take 50, 60, or even 70 percent of the harvest. Sharecropping generally repaid the landlord with a larger return than did any of the other types of rental arrangements, but the system required that the landlord or his representative exercise close supervision at harvest time because of the ease with which tenants could cheat the landlord out of the proper share of the rent. Probably for this reason, sharecropping was less popular in the south, where landlords frequently did not reside in the villages, but in the cities.

The length of a rental contract was also critical to a tenant's security and well-being. Tenants favored long-term contracts because they thereby acquired a degree of security and benefited from their efforts to improve the farm, such as increasing the applications of fertilizer and maintaining and developing irrigation networks. Landlords, in this matter, were in something of a dilemma. Long-term contracts prevented them from adjusting the rents upward if prices or productivity increased or from changing the tenant if the current one was lazy or became ill. Short-term contracts, on the contrary, might discourage tenants from making capital improvements or adequately maintaining the farm property.

In north China, for reasons that are still unclear, rental contracts were usually for only a short term, often for only one year. In the high-tenancy areas of the south, by contrast, contracts tended to run for relatively long periods of time. Even within a village, however, there were often great disparities in the terms of the tenants' contracts: some contracts perhaps specifying no time limit; others possibly stipulating periods of five or ten years.

Some tenants enjoyed permanent rights of tenure. The usual form of permanent tenure, known as the "one-field, two-lords" *(yitian liangzhu)* system, was found most extensively in the rice-growing region of the south. In this system, the landlord held what were known as the "subsoil rights," while the tenant held the right to cultivate the surface of the soil in perpetuity. Because the tenant usually could not be dispossessed and his rights were heritable, he was virtually the owner of the land. He could, moreover, rent the land to a third party; if the terms of that contract provided for permanent tenure, as sometimes happened, the system known as the "one-field, three-lords" system had evolved. In any event, whether with three lords or two, the position of the first lord, the so-called landlord, was usually unenviable. He not only found it difficult to evict the topsoil owner, even if payment of the rent was in arrears, but also as de jure owner, had to pay the taxes. In most areas, therefore, ownership of the topsoil rights was highly attractive, often selling for considerably more than the subsoil rights.

The system of permanent tenure originated at least as early as the Yuan Dynasty, and some scholars would trace the origins back to the Song. Although the precise chronology of the system is hazy, it seems certain that permanent tenancy was often established under the frontier conditions created when Chinese migrants pushed into unsettled regions of the country. In some cases, land developers sought laborers in the sparsely settled, newly opened areas to clear the land, construct rice paddies, and build irrigation networks. To lure workers to their projects, the developers held out the promise of farmland with rights of permanent tenure. In other cases, the first migrants to an area appropriated larger amounts of land than they themselves could till, and held out the lure of permanent tenure as a means of attracting others to cultivate the land.

Actually, the system of permanent tenancy was so advantageous to tenants that it spread to even the long-settled areas of the country. We know, for example, that some tenants purchased the right from their landlords and that others, whose families had rented the same land for several generations, simply claimed the right of permanent tenure. Whatever the precise origins of the one-field, two-lords system, it had spread extensively throughout the rice-growing region by the twentieth century. By some accounts, fully 20 percent of the tenants in Fukien, 30 percent in Chekiang, 40 percent in southern Kiangsu, and 44 percent in Anhwei held rights of permanent tenancy in the 1930s. These figures may be exaggerated. But if they are at all close to accurate, they have important implications for our understanding of the problem of tenancy in China. Because tenants who held the right of permanent tenure were virtually owners of the land in all but name, a high incidence of permanent tenure would mean that the true proportion of farmers who were renters was considerably lower than 70 percent, as usually claimed.

In any event, how onerous was the system of tenancy for those peasants who did not hold rights of permanent tenure? Was it, as countless reformers and revolutionaries over the years have suggested, the chief source of rural inequities and penury? Or can one make a case in its defense?

Certainly, the rents were generally burdensome, but tenants were not totally impotent in their relations with landlords. They might, for example, simply default on their rents, and the landlords were surprisingly powerless to respond. The records of a landlord family in the lower Yangtze region, for example, show that between 1895 and 1921, over 90 percent of the family's tenants failed to pay their rents in full. Even more striking is the fact that twenty-nine of the eighty tenants who rented from that family had fallen in arrears for ten or more years. The records of a bursary—a landlords' tax-collecting agency—in Kiangsu also reveal that 20 to 30 percent of the tenants' accounts were in arrears at any one time. To induce tenants to pay on time, landlords sometimes discounted the rent by 30 to 40 percent, if it was paid promptly. Landlords sometimes had tenants arrested for failing to pay their rents. In theory, too, they could evict them. In fact, however, at least in some regions of the country, custom protected tenants from such harsh measures, and the landlords had to swallow the losses.

Nor did farmers become tenants solely out of desperation. Farm efficiency tended to be greater on relatively large farms than on smaller farms—the optimum size was about 13 acres—because a smaller percentage of the land was set aside for farmsteads, field boundaries, and burial mounds. Thus farm size was usually a more accurate indicator of a farmer's livelihood than was the method of landholding. Many well-to-do peasants, consequently, were part tenants, renting fields in addition to those they owned in order to increase the size of their farms. Sometimes, too, farmers were simultaneously landlords and tenants. If their plots were small and scattered, for example, they might rent some of their fields to other villagers, while paying rent for plots adjacent to their own in order to consolidate their fields.

For all these reasons, it is manifest that landlordism was not synonymous with exploitation, nor tenancy with penury. This is not to suggest that tenants lived a life of ease, because the majority of peasants, tenants or owners, seldom lived far above the minimal level of subsistence.

Selected Readings

(See also the works cited in the notes)

Bray, Francesca. *Agriculture,* in Joseph Needham, *Science and Civilization in China.* Vol. 6, *Biology and Biological Technology.* Cambridge: Cambridge University Press, 1984.

Buck, John Lossing. *Land Utilization in China*. Nanking: University of Nanking, 1937.

Esherick, Joseph. "Number Games: A Note on Land Distribution in Prerevolutionary China." *Modern China* 7, no. 4 (October 1981): 387–411.

Huang, Philip C. C. *The Peasant Economy and Social Change in North China*. Stanford, Calif.: Stanford University Press, 1985.

Jing Su, and Luo Lun. *Landlord and Labor in Late Imperial China: Case Studies from Shandong*, trans. and with an introduction by Endymion Wilkinson. Cambridge, Mass.: Harvard University, Council on East Asian Studies, 1978.

King, F. H. *Farmers of Forty Centuries: or Permanent Agriculture in China, Korea, and Japan*. Madison, Wis.: Mrs. F. H. King, 1911.

McDermott, Joseph P. "Bondservants in the T'ai-hu Basin During the Late Ming: A Case of Mistaken Identity." *Journal of Asian Studies* 40, no. 4 (August 1981): 675–701.

Perdue, Peter C. *Exhausting the Earth: State and Peasant in Hunan, 1500–1850*. Cambridge, Mass.: Harvard University, Council on East Asian Studies, 1987.

Perkins, Dwight H. *Agricultural Development in China, 1368–1968*. Chicago: Aldine, 1969.

Rawski, Evelyn Sakakida. *Agricultural Change and the Peasant Economy of South China*. Cambridge, Mass.: Harvard University Press, 1972.

Wiens, Mi Chu. "The Origins of Modern Chinese Landlordism," in *Shen Kang-po Hsien-sheng Pa-chih Jung-ch'ing Lun-wen-chi* (Festschrift in honor of the eightieth birthday of Professor Shen Kang-po), pp. 285–344. Taipei: Lien-ching, 1976.

5

The Agricultural Sector in the Early Twentieth Century: The Problem of "Peasant Immiseration"

"There are districts," wrote the economic historian R. H. Tawney in 1933, "in which the position of the rural population [in China] is that of a man standing permanently up to the neck in water, so that even a ripple is sufficient to drown him."[1] Nearly all observers during the late 1920s and the 1930s shared Tawney's forlorn view of conditions in China's villages. Rural surveys were taken, and citified intellectuals wrote articles describing the conditions they had witnessed while visiting their native villages. Overwhelmingly, these surveys and reports painted a picture of rural suffering, demoralizing impoverishment, and cultural benightedness. Most of the reports, too, concluded that life for the great majority of peasant households had become harsher over the years. "One thing is clear," wrote China's leading sociologist, Fei Xiaotong, of the Yangtze Valley region in 1936, "the conditions of the peasants are getting worse and worse." "The essential problem in Chinese villages . . . is that the income of the villagers has been reduced to such an extent that *it is not sufficient even to meet the expenditure in securing the minimum requirements of livelihood. It is the hunger of the people that is the real issue in China.*"[2] According to Fei, with the exception of a few landlords and large-scale farmers who were growing rich, the peasants generally were being plunged into a life of misery. This process, in which the average income of the majority of peasants was falling close to or below the minimum subsistence level, is known as immiseration.

Those who have contended that Chinese peasants were experiencing a process of immiseration generally belonged to one of two distinct schools of interpretation. The first of these might be termed the Exploitation School, which stressed that peasant immiseration resulted primarily from exploitation by the landlord class and foreign imperialists. By charging extortionate rents and interest rates, manipulating the tax-collecting system in its favor, and dominating the marketing of farm produce, the landlord class was becoming richer while the vast majority of peasants was becoming poorer. As the wealth of the landlords grew, they bought more land, thereby reducing even more farmers to the status of tenants or hired hands. Imperialism, meanwhile, had forced its economic presence on China, causing instability in the villages by making the rural economy dependent on the vagaries of capitalists' whims and of world market forces. The argument of the Exploitation School was in essence, therefore, that if imperialism were eliminated and if landholdings were equitably distributed, want and hunger would disappear from China.

The second school of interpretation might be termed the Overpopulation, Primitive-Technology School. Rejecting the view that exploitation lay at the root of the problem, representatives of this school stressed that there were just too many people relative to the available resources. Farms were too small, and the methods of cultivating the soil and marketing the product were backward and unscientific. Eliminating landlordism and giving fields to every peasant would only exacerbate the problems, because the farms were already too small and inefficient. Improvement could be realized, they argued, only by introducing new knowledge and technologies, which would lead to an improvement of the seeds and a restoration of the tired soil, and would enable the farmer to work more productively.

A look at the several factors involved in this debate will, perhaps, enable us to choose between these schools of interpretation.

Overpopulation

Much of the discussion about peasant immiseration in the twentieth century has been based on the Malthusian premise that the growth of human populations naturally tends to outrun the increase of the food supply. The Overpopulation, Primitive-Technology School, especially, was convinced that as a result of population pressures and limited food supplies, the population was being reduced to starvation levels. "The fundamental fact," wrote Tawney in 1932, "is of terrible simplicity. It is that the population of China is too large to be supported by existing resources."[3] Or as Albert Feuerwerker wrote more recently, "Every other factor [causing China's agrarian crisis] pales before the stark fact of a critically adverse population–land ratio."[4] These are succinct expressions of the position of the Overpopulation, Primitive-Technology School.

Statistical evidence lends plausibility to this grim conclusion. During the Ming Dynasty, for example, a farm of 100 *mu* in Hopei and Shantung had been considered small, and many measured 200 or 300 *mu*. As a result of the rising population, however, average farm size by the mid-1930s had fallen to 17.5 *mu* in Hopei and only 14.3 *mu* in Shantung. In China as a whole, average farm size probably declined by about 32 percent between 1890 and the early 1930s.

But the view that China was suffering from overpopulation, in the sense that per capita food consumption of the average Chinese was falling below the subsistence level, was probably excessively pessimistic. Why? In a society at or near the Malthusian crisis level, the population will not increase significantly—particularly over many years—because all population increments over and beyond the levels sustainable by the available food supplies will sooner or later be removed by what Malthus called "positive checks"—famine, disease, and war. Yet few deny that China's population was, for a premodern society, increasing rapidly from 1873 to 1953. Indeed, the only real dispute is about the *rate* of population increase during that period—some specialists insisting, for example, that it was increasing at an annual average of 0.7 percent, while others suggesting that it could not have averaged more than 0.5 percent a year.

There is also the anomaly that between the 1930s and the 1970s, the life expectancy at birth of the average Chinese improved from about thirty-two years to approximately sixty-two years—even though, during those four decades, there was no significant improvement in either average food consumption or efficiency of food distribution.[5] This suggests that the high mortality rates in the pre-Communist period were not attributable to food shortages, as the Malthusian-inspired historians have contended. Instead, they were caused largely by appalling hygienic conditions and primitive medical treatment, which resulted in the spread of fatal diseases that are now relatively easily prevented and controlled. Approximately one of every three children died within the first year after birth. An estimated 10 percent of the newborn died, for example, from neonatal tetanus—a disease that is totally preventable with antiseptic care of the umbilical cord and vaccination of mothers during pregnancy. Nearly 50 percent of all children died before they reached the age of five, often from diarrhea, malaria, and childhood pneumonia. Among adults, vaccine-preventable diseases (smallpox, polio, measles, diptheria, and, especially, tuberculosis), waterborne diseases (dysentery, hepatitis, cholera, and typhoid), and parasitic diseases (caused by hookworm, liver fluke, and intestinal fluke) were the major killers. Following the "epidemiological transition" instituted by the People's Republic after 1949, parasitic and infectious diseases were largely eliminated, and by 1987 the population had shot up over the 1 billion mark.[6] It appears certain, therefore, that epidemiological factors, and not a paucity of food, were the principal causes of the high death rates in pre-1949 China.

Even if China was able to feed itself during the early twentieth century, it appears probable that demographic pressures were contributing to the reduction in the standard of living of a sizable part of the nation's rural population. This is suggested by the fact that the so-called coarse grains—maize, potatoes, barley, millet, and sorghum—were becoming the food staples of the poor. Whereas rice in the seventeenth century had provided about 70 percent of the nation's food, it accounted for only about 36 percent in the 1930s. Maize, potatoes, and other New World crops, on the contrary, accounted for about 20 percent of the food. A Chinese recalled that in his childhood village in Shantung, for instance, sweet potatoes were consumed by the poor "at every meal every day throughout the year."[7] Less impoverished families added millet to their sweet-potato diet, while the relatively prosperous added wheat. Only the richest families ate mostly wheat. In some other areas of north China, the chief item in the diet was noodles, gruel, or steamed buns made from millet and corn meal. Even in the relatively well-off province of Kwangtung in southern China, the sweet potato served as the main food for three to four months of every year. That large and growing segments of the population were being forced to subsist on a diet consisting predominantly of sweet potatoes, maize, and millet—however distasteful and boring it may have been—reveals the enormous strains that the growing population imposed on the food-producing capacity of the nation.

The Increasing Incidence of Tenancy

A major tenet of the Exploitation School was that the ownership of farmland was being progressively concentrated in the hands of relatively few landlords. And as the bulk of peasants lost their lands, the gap between the rich and the very poor became wider and wider.

The Exploitation School's view is reflected in a recent study of the peasant economy of north China that stresses the invidious effects of increased commercialization. The cultivation of cash crops, this study asserts, required significantly larger capital investments than did subsistence farming, and thus the farmer was far more vulnerable in an economic crisis resulting from poor harvests or a downturn of the market. "A ruined cotton crop," the study concludes, "was much more devastating to the smallholder than a ruined sorghum crop, often *starting him on a downward spiral in which he was forced to offer his land as security for a loan, only to lose it and become first a tenant, then a part-laborer, and finally a landless wage worker.*" [8]

Plausible though this scenario might seem, the evidence offered in support of the view that land was being increasingly concentrated in the hands of the few is notoriously unreliable.[9] And there are strong reasons to think that landlordism was not a spreading phenomenon. Land had never paid large returns on investment— seldom more than 5 percent and often as little as 2 percent—and in the 1920s and 1930s, the lure of investing in land diminished even further. Tenants were becoming increasingly recalcitrant, and thus rents were more difficult to collect; Communist agitation threatened landlords with expropriation of their properties; and the real burden of the land tax (which had fallen by approximately two-thirds during the nineteenth century) rose substantially during the early 1930s. After 1925, therefore, land values fell. Investments in urban industry and bank securities, and deposits in bank accounts, were both safer and assured a larger return.

True, the incidence of tenancy in the 1930s was relatively high, although not so high as in such European countries as France, Denmark, and Ireland. But tenancy was not a new or growing problem. In the Yangtze and Pearl River deltas, for example, tenancy was already extensive in the nineteenth century. And a recent study of those regions during the 1920s and 1930s reveals that "there is no evidence that the proportion of rented land increased by any significant extent after 1870."[10] Evidence that the incidence of farm tenancy was increasing significantly during the Republican period is, therefore, unconvincing. If China's peasants were undergoing a process of immiseration, we must continue to look elsewhere for the causes.

The Commercialization of Agriculture

Even in the period before Western contact, few Chinese peasants had been wholly self-sufficient. They customarily raised most of their own food, but they sold the surplus, however small, and they often set aside one or two plots of land specifically for a marketable crop, such as peanuts, water chestnuts, or melons. With the cash therefrom, they paid taxes and bought salt, tools, and utensils that they could not produce. Moreover, already in the sixteenth century, peasants in some areas were specializing in one cash crop, such as tea, silk, or cotton. And those who were, of course, had to buy much of their food from other areas, which thus produced rice, wheat, and other grains as cash crops. There was, therefore, in the late Ming and early Qing periods a surprisingly flourishing interregional trade.[11] Still, as a percentage of total farm output, the amounts of produce that were marketed remained small.

By the latter decades of the nineteenth century, the extent of rural marketing had already increased substantially, and by the 1920s and 1930s had probably increased at least five times over the levels of the early nineteenth century. Spurred by the growth of cities, cheaper transportation (notably railroads), and increased foreign demand, more Chinese farmers began to specialize in producing cash crops. In north China, where cotton had long been produced commercially, output increased some three- to fivefold in just the first 36 years of this century—more than in the entire preceding 300 years. Similarly, soybeans, peanuts, tobacco, rapeseed (a rich source of vegetable oil), and tung oil (favored abroad for its quick-drying qualities in varnish and paints) became major cash crops.

The extent of specialization for the market varied from place to place, depending on, for example, the availability of transport facilities, soil conditions, and the distance to cities and major markets. During the 1920s and 1930s, some regions along the Yangtze River marketed over 50 percent of the farm produce, though the national average was closer to 30 to 40 percent.

The effects on the farmers' livelihood of this increased orientation to the market is much debated. In normal circumstances, peasants would probably have benefited substantially from crop specialization and agricultural commercialization. Increased specialization usually resulted in increased productivity. And by concentrating on crops for which the soils and climate were especially suitable, farmers could significantly increase their yields. Goods produced for the market, moreover, usually brought substantially higher returns than did staple foods. The net return on a unit of rice land in a village near Hong Kong, for example, was HK$107; a field of the same size, when devoted to vegetables to be marketed, produced a net profit of HK$2,251. Raising mulberry leaves to feed silkworms brought a return perhaps ten times that of rice; and the net income from cotton in north China was at least twice that from sorghum.

But there were dangers in specializing for the market. Farmers who abandoned subsistence farming to concentrate on a commercial crop became vulnerable to market forces over which they had little or no control. The prices of crops they sold were determined by the inexorable and unfeeling law of supply and demand—the price of cotton, say, falling because of bumper harvests in the southern United States or because industrialists in London and New York had decided to cut back on the production of shirting. Similarly, the cost of farmers' food, which they had produced themselves but now had to buy on the market, could suddenly rise, depending, for example, on the harvests that year or on the threat of war in a nearby province.

Small-scale farmers, in particular, could be placed in thrall to the uncertainties of the market. Unable to subsist on their farms by producing just staple grains, they felt compelled to plant a relatively large proportion of their fields in cash crops, which promised potentially higher returns. Large-scale and richer farmers, by contrast, generally set aside enough of their crop area that they could produce sufficient food for their families' own consumption.

Producing cash crops also required larger capital investments than did growing most food staples. Cash crops usually needed generous applications of fertilizer to preserve soil fertility; interest on money borrowed to purchase the fertilizer was costly; and rents on land turned to commercial crops were customarily increased. As a consequence, to cite but one example, the costs of raising tobacco were three to five times higher than those of producing most food crops. Therefore, in the event of crop failure, decline in prices, or disruption of the market, the potential for damage to the welfare of farm families was notably greater than if they had continued to engage in subsistence farming.

> Even in comparatively good years, wide fluctuations in price made dependence on the market for food a risky business. A farmer who planted all of his land to cash crops might physically survive a 50 per cent increase in the price of rice, but his losses might well be sufficient to deprive him of his savings, his land, or both.[12]

The vicissitudes of the market, and their impact on China's farmers, are dramatically illustrated by the experience of the silk industry. The growing of silkworms and mulberry leaves had, of course, a long history in China, but silk production increased rapidly after 1870. As a result of the growing foreign market, the volume of exported raw silk tripled by 1928 and that of silk fabrics increased eightfold. Attracted by the potential for substantial profits, a large number of peasants shifted from growing grains and other food crops to producing silk. In the traditional silk-producing areas of Chekiang, for instance, cocoon output between 1870 and 1928 rose by a third. In Haining *Xian,* also in Chekiang, fully 45 percent of the cultivable land was devoted to mulberries. Peasants in Kiangsu and Kwangtung doubled their production of cocoons, while production in peripheral silk-producing regions rose even faster—in Shantung increasing four and a half times and in Anhwei, eight times.

Beginning in 1887 and continuing until the late 1920s, silk was China's leading export commodity, and China's farmers benefited enormously from this growing demand for the cash crop.

> The large-scale expansion of silk output, essentially new to many areas, such as Kiangsu, Kwangtung, and Shantung, brought a new source of income to peasant

households in these regions. In the old districts in northern Chekiang, it brought revived prosperity as more households undertook silk production and the value of their output rose.[13]

The perils of producing for the market became starkly evident during the late 1920s and the 1930s. After some sixty years of prosperity, the bottom of the market dropped out. China's competitive position in the world silk market was eroded, in the first place, by its failure to maintain the quality of its product. Foreign manufacturers thus turned to Japan, since they were confident that the Japanese silk thread they purchased would be of uniform thickness and strength. Consequently, even though Japan had entered the world's silk trade much later than China, it was by 1930 exporting silk valued at £42.5 million, while China's was valued at only £13.5 million. The failure to maintain quality control was not limited to the silk industry, but was a major crippling factor in all sectors of China's exporting industry.[14]

Other blows to China's silk industry came in rapid succession. In the late 1920s, rayon began competing with silk (nylon entered the competition in 1939). And after 1931, China was struck first by foreign invasion and then by economic depression (see pp. 96–98). Under these successive blows, China's silk industry staggered. In 1934, for instance, when the market price of cocoons fell by about 60 percent, the total value of cocoon production in the silk-producing center of Wuxing *Xian* in Chekiang was only 9 percent of that in 1930. Many farmers in the silk-growing regions, therefore, tore out their once-treasured mulberry bushes and planted food crops. Farm incomes in the silk-producing areas dropped precipitously—a *xian* survey in Chekiang revealing that family incomes there fell to 57 percent of the 1930 level. Few farm families could incur deprivation of that magnitude without experiencing extreme want and suffering.

The experience of the silk producers—which was repeated, with minor variations, by producers of such other cash crops as tobacco and tea—illustrates the variable impact of commercialization on the peasants' livelihood. Generally, commercialization was a major reason why the agricultural sector was able to support a growing population during the late nineteenth and early twentieth centuries. But during periods of market downturns and economic dislocations, those peasants who had become dependent on cash crops could, like the silk producers in the 1930s, suffer terribly.

Handicrafts

Disguised unemployment and underemployment were common phenomena in China's villages. Because of the minuscule size of the farms and the seasonal fluctuation of the demand for work on the farms, men customarily worked on their fields for only about 110 days of each year. Women and children, too, except in the busy seasons, had considerable free time on their hands. Most rural families, as a consequence, attempted to increase their exiguous incomes by engaging in some form of subsidiary work, such as peddling, raising pigs, hiring out as farm laborers, and working as transport coolies. Of all the subsidiary occupations for farm families, however, the most prevalent was handicrafts.

Virtually all writers on China from the 1920s to the 1940s contended that foreign imports and competition from China's modern domestic industries had seriously damaged the nation's handicraft industry, thereby contributing in a major way to the ruination of the peasants' livelihood. Even today, Chinese Communist historians perpetuate the interpretation that

> the opening of the free ports and the tariff agreement [after the Opium War] gave the foreigners unlimited opportunity to push the sales of their goods and grab new raw materials. British textiles flooded the Chinese market, penetrated the country-side, bringing ruin to the peasants' cottage industries. . . . Under the battering blows of foreign capitalism, China's self-sufficient feudal economy started giving way, and a semi-colonial and semi-feudal economy began to take shape.[15]

But that longstanding interpretation has recently come under attack. It has become clear, for instance, that some traditional handicrafts remained strong even into the 1930s. Indeed, handicrafts in 1933 still accounted for over 65 percent of the gross value-added of the cotton cloth produced, over 66 percent of the silk piece goods, 89 percent of the edible vegetable oil, and 95 percent of the wheat flour. Other traditional handicrafts, such as oil pressing and rice milling, were actually stimulated by the expanding market economy. Yet other traditional han-dicrafts grew as a result of the opening of the export trade with the foreigners. Among these were gathering pig bristles (for brushes) and chicken and duck eggs (whose whites were used for confectionery and photographic purposes), plaiting straw (for hats and mats), tung oil, animal hides and skins, soybean oil (for food), and bean cakes (for fertilizer). In a few instances, new handicrafts were created to manufacture imitations of such Western products as matches, soap, and ciga-rettes.

An analysis of cotton textiles, which was the largest and most important of the traditional handicrafts, reveals the difficulties of assessing trends in China's handicraft industry and of evaluating their effects on the peasants' standard of living. Initially, during the eighteenth century, cotton-textile handicrafts were stimulated by strong demand from abroad. The so-called nankeen, the native cloth produced near Nanking, was much admired in Europe, for it was of a higher quality than the cotton cloth manufactured in the new British mills in Lancashire. From 1734, when the statistical record began, until 1800, exports of nankeen cloth rose steadily, and thereafter remained strong until about 1830. Then, however, Chinese exports of cotton cloth virtually halted, the handicraft production unable to compete with the rising efficiency of the modern factories in Europe and the United States. But starting about 1890, surprisingly, the export of handcrafted cotton cloth revived, rising from 750,000 pounds each year from 1886 to 1890 to an average of 8.4 million pounds annually during the peak period of 1921 to 1925.

Domestically, too, handcrafted cotton textiles proved to be remarkably resis-tant to the competition of machine-made cloth. Chinese consumers, at least ini-tially, favored native cloth, which was woven from coarse hand-spun yarn ranging from six to ten counts. This native cloth was about three times heavier, and thus warmer and more durable, than the British cloth, which was woven of 20- to 30-count yarn. It was also cheaper. Thus while imports of foreign cloth did increase during the nineteenth and twentieth centuries, most of it was purchased in the cities, where it was regarded as a substitute for silk and linen. In the rural areas, the vast majority of Chinese continued to use the hand-woven product.

The cotton-textile industry comprises two major components: the spinning of raw cotton into yarn, and the weaving of that yarn into bolts of cloth. The former, handicraft spinning, was largely eliminated by competition from machine-spun yarns. As late as 1875, for instance, almost 100 percent of the yarn used in China was hand-spun; by 1905, only 50 percent was hand-spun; and by the late 1930s, only 14 percent was hand-spun. Millions of Chinese, as a consequence, were deprived of their customary occupation. This would seem to bear out the assertions of the Exploitation School.

There is, however, more to the story. Hand spinning disappeared largely because it was excruciatingly slow; to hand spin sufficient yarn for just one hour of weaving required at least three hours. To spin that much yarn by machine, by contrast, required only about five minutes and thus offered a means of breaking what had traditionally been a major bottleneck in the production of cotton cloth. The machine-spun yarn, moreover, was markedly stronger than the handcrafted product, so that weavers, using it as the warp in their looms, could make much longer bolts of cloth than had been possible with hand-spun yarn. Weavers were able to prepare the warps in their looms less frequently and thereby saved much energy and time. Meanwhile, Chinese consumers gradually became accustomed to this lighter cloth, so machine-spun yarn virtually wiped out the traditional method of spinning yarn.

At the same time, the ready availability and cheapness of machine-spun yarn brought about an unprecedented expansion of handicraft weaving. The traditional weaving centers began producing cloth in far greater quantities than had ever been possible when only hand-spun yarn was available. In Nantong *Xian*, near Shanghai, for instance, the weavers in 1933—which was actually a poor year because production had dropped off sharply from the pre-Depression years—consumed 21,094,500 catties of yarn. To produce that much yarn by hand would have required the work of 2,344,000 spinners, yet the total population of Nantong was only about half that number. "This suggests that [cloth] output prior to the use of machine-spun yarn must have been only a small fraction of the 1933 level and an even smaller fraction of the peak output."[16]

Machine-spun yarn also made possible the spread of weaving into new areas. According to a Japanese consul in 1898,

> The inhabitants[near Foochow] were formerly ignorant of the art of weaving cotton cloth. . . . Cotton yarn has recently begun to be imported from India, and many more women have mastered the art of weaving. There are said to be more than ten thousand looms at present in the various parts of Foochow Prefecture."[17]

As a result of this weaving boom, the total output of hand-woven cloth in the 1920s and early 1930s was several times greater than it had been before the introduction of machine-spun yarn. Approximately two-thirds of all cotton cloth used in China in the 1930s was still woven on hand looms.

What was the effect on the livelihood of the spinners when machine-spun yarn displaced their handcrafted product? Obviously, many of them were put out of work—at least 2 million man-years of labor each year were thereby lost. Yet about one of every ten of the displaced spinners could now turn to weaving, and they benefited from the switch because the wages to be earned from weaving were substantially higher than from spinning. Other spinners took up alternative handicrafts, such as straw braiding or animal husbandry. Still others took advantage of the ample supply of inexpensive machine-spun yarn to engage in two new handicrafts: knitting and lace making. Significantly, too, the development of machine spinning in China generated a greatly expanded demand for raw cotton, whose production increased by approximately 50 percent between 1900 and the early 1920s. Thus some of the displaced spinners found alternative sources of income, and it may even be argued that the economy as a whole benefited from the ruin of hand spinning. But there can be no doubt that this development created real, *if* only temporary, hardship for many tens of thousands of villagers.

The intrusion of foreign manufactures and modern methods of manufacturing, moreover, was not usually as destructive to other handicrafts as it was to cotton spinning. True, hand-reeled silk gradually lost out to filature silk after 1895; Chinese tea failed to compete on the export markets with that of Japan and Ceylon; and kerosene replaced vegetable oils for lighting. Yet even as late as 1933, about 75 percent of all China's industrial output, in terms of value-added, was still produced by handicraft industries (machine-powered factories, mining, and utilities made up the remaining 25 percent). Exports of handicrafts likewise remained remarkably strong, increasing in value (as measured in constant prices) an estimated four times between 1875 and 1928. And in 1930 to 1931, both the quantity and the value of exported handicraft products reached an all-time high.[18] It is clear, therefore, that China's handicraft industry, taken as a whole, not only was not destroyed during the period of contact with the Western powers, but actually produced more goods of greater value than in the late imperial period.

The Increasing Harshness of Social Relationships

Although life as a peasant in China was probably always hard, the rigors of rural life in the traditional period were often mitigated by local elites—the gentry, village leaders, and landlords—who felt a sense of noblesse oblige toward the less fortunate peasants. The attitude of these traditional elites, according to modern China's preeminent sociologist, Fei Xiaotong, "was not one of the exploitation of resources but rather of companionship with and adaptation to nature." They would therefore "share in the life of the countryside," providing leadership and organization in their communities. It was these men of learning, deeply imbued with Confucian morality, who bore most of the responsibilities of "informal government," establishing schools, maintaining roads and dikes, settling disputes, and so on.[19]

During the nineteenth and twentieth centuries, however, these traditional local elites ceased to reside in the rural areas. They were, in a sense, *eroded* from the social landscape. Some fled the villages during the upheavals of the mid-nineteenth century for the security of the cities; others invested in urban commerce and industry and left the villages behind them. This process of "social erosion" accelerated during the twentieth century. A major milestone in this process was the abolition of the civil-service examinations in 1905. The men who had studied for those examinations adhered to a common ideology—the moral and social values of Confucianism—and they served as leaders in society by dint of their concern for community welfare, their prestige as learned men, and their ability to meet and communicate with government officials. With the abolition of the examinations, this group lost much of its sheen of superior status. No longer was the social hierarchy clearly defined, and no longer was Confucian learning the paramount social value.

Yet another reason for social erosion was that young, educated men no longer took up residence in the rural areas. Having gone to the towns and cities to attend middle school and the university, they acquired an education that had little relevance back home; moreover, they became accustomed to the amenities and culture of city life. "The college graduate of today," wrote Fei Xiaotong, "feels that in the country there is no one to talk with, no one who understands him, and he often even feels alienated from his own kin."[20] Another Chinese scholar observed that "recent decades of change had so widened the socio-economic gap between the urban centers and the countryside that the modern educated man almost always remained in the city and refused to return to the home village to supply it with community leadership."[21]

As the educated and responsible leadership was eroded from the local landscape, several new strata of local elites surfaced. These new leaders—merchants, usurers, unschooled landlords, militia leaders, bandit chieftains, and the like—had long resided in the villages, but they assumed the leadership of their communities only as the old gentry disappeared. They were, by contrast with their predecessors, a heterogeneous lot. Their influence derived not from education, but from wealth, physical force, and audacity.

In the Cantonese village of Nanching during the 1920s and 1930s, for example, the leading personage had once been a successful bandit and opium trafficker. Although he was virtually illiterate, he enjoyed power and influence in the village because he was wealthy and had ready access to government circles through his former bandit boss, now an official in the provincial government. The natural crassness and selfishness of such leaders as these was seldom tempered by education or moral training. They had, it was said, "not one drop of ink in them" and "no political ideology to teach the villagers . . . except the silent message that these were times when the strong man won regardless of class background or moral conduct."[22]

Not all local leaders were former bandits or militarists, for the new local elites were extremely diverse in character and background. Yet, according to proponents of the theory of social erosion, they were alike in being largely devoid of the beneficent paternalism that in an earlier day had eased the passage of their fellow villagers through life's many adversities.

The validity of the theory of harshening social relationships, however, has never been established conclusively, and it may be criticized for romanticizing the traditional period. The old gentry were not always as moralistic and charitable, as personally disinterested and concerned for community welfare, as the theory of social erosion implies. In times of famine, for instance, they often hoarded their grains, pressing the market price upward, so that they could make a killing on the market. In such cases, commercial instincts overwhelmed whatever Confucian concepts of noblesse oblige they may have held.[23]

It is also questionable that social relationships were quite as harsh in the Republican period as Fei Xiaotong insisted. Certainly, the literature that came out during the Communists' land-reform movement often portrayed landlords as having been not just lacking compassion, but as having frequently been bestially and depravedly cruel. William Hinton, in his classic book *Fanshen: A Documentary of Revolution in a Chinese Village,* told of a peasant who had "struck back at a landlord who raped his wife. He was hung by the hair of his head and beaten until his scalp separated from his skull. He fell to the ground and bled to death." Hinton also claimed that tenants who did not pay their rent on time were beaten, and, if that did not suffice to produce payment, the landlord "drove the peasant off the land or out of the house."[24]

Yet Morton Fried, an anthropologist who, like Hinton, studied conditions in the villages during the late 1940s, portrayed a very different relationship between landlords and tenants. Without idealizing the relationship, Fried apparently saw none of the vicious landlord behavior that Hinton reported in such lurid detail. He even told of one landlord who lacked the heart to evict an older tenant who was notoriously lazy, incompetent, and an opium smoker. In fact, landlords in the area disagreed among themselves whether they even possessed the right to evict a tenant.[25]

Obviously, then, there was a broad range of human responses to the changing conditions of rural China during the early years of the twentieth century. Yet, on balance, we are left with the deep impression that human relationships had probably become more exploitative, that those with power and wealth did feel less empathy toward those less fortunate than themselves. As a Chinese historian has remarked, "The view that the Chinese elite became increasingly amoral and detached from society from 1902 to 1949 is, to my mind, an indisputable statement of fact."[26] Social erosion, therefore, probably did make the lives of most peasants more strained and difficult. But the greatest source of economic stagnation and personal suffering in twentieth-century China—greater, indeed, than any of the factors thus far discussed—was the orgy of warfare, violence, and political instability that beset the nation shortly after the Revolution of 1911.

Political Breakdown and Chronic Violence

Not long after the overthrow of the Qing Dynasty and the establishment of the Republic, China plunged into the period of warlordism. This was an age of almost complete political breakdown, and power devolved into the hands of men wielding the gun. For such men, social reform and economic construction had no place on their political agendas, and the administrative decay that had become evident in the nineteenth century now became extreme. Water-conservancy projects fell into disrepair. Earthen dikes were weakened by erosion and easily broke when the waters rose. The dredging of silt from river beds was also neglected, thereby reducing the water-carrying capacity of the rivers—a phenomenon that caused floods in times of heavy rains and drought in times of little rain (because there was less water in the rivers to be used for irrigation). Pests, such as locusts, snout moths, and rats, as well as smut, rust, and other crop diseases, also struck more often, leading to the loss in the early 1930s of an estimated 10 to 20 percent of China's potential farm production.

Floods, droughts, and other natural calamities had been increasing in frequency since the thirteenth century. During the Song Dynasty, for instance, areas along the Huai River had suffered a major flood only once every 30 years, but during the Qing Dynasty, those areas suffered a major flood every 5.3 years. Deforestation and more extensive cultivation had been major reasons for this increase in the earlier centuries. Political breakdown, however, was probably the principal reason that natural disasters struck more often, and became almost the norm, during the latter half of the nineteenth century and, particularly, in the Republican period. Pest control, for instance, is at least as much an administrative as a technological problem. Similarly, floods and droughts were partially caused by, and their effects were certainly exacerbated by, administrative ineptitude.

Famine, therefore, assailed the peasantry with increasing frequency during the period of political breakdown in the early twentieth century. And the famine-relief measures that had traditionally been performed by the state—such as the maintenance of charitable granaries in every *xian* and the transfer of resources from grain-plenty to grain-hungry regions—were by now defunct. Thus when calamity did strike, suffering and devastation usually were more severe than they had been in the periods when imperial rule had been strong and effective.

Warlords worried little about the problems of the peasantry and were concerned instead to establish control over a territory and to exact revenues from it. Warfare, therefore, became endemic. By one count, a state of war existed in an average of seven provinces every year from 1912 to 1923, increasing during the next six years to an annual average of war in fourteen provinces.

With the political breakdown, bandit gangs proliferated, wreaking even greater human suffering and economic uncertainty, if not physical devastation, than did the regular armies of the warlords (Chapter 10). The tide of banditry, in turn, necessitated formation of local defense forces and wide-scale building of fortresses and village walls, all of which were funded by increased tax levies on the villagers.

Inevitably, the fighting, the pillage, and the expenditures for guns and defense works had an economic impact. Did they, however, cause the immiseration of the peasantry? Most historians of Chinese warlordism think that they did. Warlords, for example, taxed the peasants unmercifully. In most provinces, they simply added surtaxes to the regular land tax, and these new levies often totaled several times the regular tax. In Szechwan Province, the warlords relied not on surtaxes, but on the quaint practice of collecting the land tax that would come due in future years. Thus in 1918, the warlord might collect the land tax for the years 1925 to 1928; then, the next year, he would collect for the years 1929 to 1934; and on and on. By 1934, several of the Szechwan warlord regimes had collected the land tax for fifty, sixty, and sixty-six years in advance, and one had even collected for the year 2008–seventy-four years in advance!

The number of troops formally enrolled in the various armies—not including the armed men in bandit gangs, secret societies, and defense militia—more than tripled, from 570,000 men at the time of the Revolution of 1911 to 1,830,000 men in 1928. These troops were obviously a growing burden on the nation's economic resources, but when on the march or in battle, they became a veritable scourge on the countryside. Such troops usually commandeered their food and supplies from local inhabitants. They confiscated carts and draft animals to pull their equipment, tore up wooden floors for fuel, and forced peasant men into service as laborers and porters. Nor were women spared, there being no defense against rape except hiding while the troops were in the area. In such anarchic conditions, the soldiers were virtually indistinguishable from bandits, enriching themselves with whatever movable wealth they could find.

Troops customarily moved along the main lines of communication, especially along river valleys and railways, which became "conduits of violence" as the warlord armies marched and countermarched across the land. The West River, linking Kwangtung and Kwangsi, was just such a conduit of violence, where "Cantonese, Kwangsi and Yunnanese soldiers [moved] up and down the river and its tributaries with a grim frequency, sometimes fighting each other, sometimes not, always inflicting terror and more or less damage [on] the inhabitants of the riverine towns and villages."[27] Along the upper Han River, too, north and west of Hankow, warlords and bandits impeded navigation on the river so that trade during the 1920s and 1930s virtually stopped, and peasants who had relied on cash crops were being reduced to penury.

While it is easy to deplore the wanton killing and destruction, the pillage and rape wreaked by the warlord soldiers, the bandits, and the predatory secret societies, one ought not exaggerate their economic effects. Chinese armies enrolled fewer than 2 percent of the men aged fifteen to forty-four, and expenditures on the military probably amounted to no more than 3.5 to 4 percent of the country's gross domestic product—which appears very slight in comparison with military expenditures in the world today. Moreover, the violence of the warlord era was episodic: some warlords were more extortionate and destructive than others; wars were more extensive in some areas than in others; and some years were worse than others. Kwangsi, for example, suffered its worst ravages of warlordism in the early 1920s and again in 1929 and 1930, while the peasants of Shantung and Szechwan suffered most severely in the early 1930s.

Yet the economic effects of administrative breakdown and frequent warfare during this period were very real. For instance, a congeries of taxes, in addition to the customary land tax, proliferated and weighed heavily on the peasants' livelihood. Irregular levies, known as *tanpai,* for example, were imposed on villagers—twenty, thirty, or even more times a year—by the various administrative levels of the government to meet unusual or unexpected expenses, or simply to remedy a budgetary deficit. There existed no systematic control over the assessing or collecting of these irregular levies, and so they multiplied wildly. Since they could be levied at any time of the year, in almost any amounts, they caused the peasants enormous grief and distress.[28]

The decline of railway tonnage during the 1920s is further evidence of the destructive effects of the civil wars on the economy. From the levels of 1921, for instance, the total of freight hauled in north China declined by over 21 percent in 1922, 38 percent in 1926, and 36 percent in 1928. These declines were caused by a series of regional warlord conflicts that disrupted rail traffic, damaged tracks, and resulted in the commandeering of large amounts of rolling stock for military use. Other consequences of these warlord struggles in north China were the sharp drop in the production of raw cotton and the inflation of the price of cotton that did reach the mills in Tientsin. In addition, because most of the mills in Tientsin had been established with investments from one warlord group or another, the reversals of military and political fortunes in these wars led to the loss of financial backing by several factories in the city. So badly did the economy of Hopei and Shantung deteriorate as a result of these wars that the stream of peasants seeking refuge and a better life in Manchuria reached flood tide.

Perhaps the least palpable effect of political instability on the peasants' standard of living, but one that nonetheless had profoundly negative consequences, was the pall of insecurity that hung over the economy. Even during the intervals of peace, the fear of future violence that had been engendered by past experience and the recognition of continuing weak political institutions dissuaded the wealthy from making capital investments in the interior. Railroad construction was postponed; a major cotton-textile firm abandoned an ambitious program to build mills, processing plants, and cotton-collection warehouses in the provinces of north China; and an untold number of wealthy landlords sent their money to the treaty ports rather than investing in their home areas, where the sense of insecurity was chronic. This drain of the nation's wealth from the countryside to the treaty ports had incalculable consequences, depressing the rural areas and skewing the nation's financial and industrial development in favor of the foreign-dominated cities along the eastern seaboard.

An Interim Assessment: Conditions as of 1930

The preceding review of the several major factors affecting the peasants' livelihood—population growth, incidence of tenancy, commercialization of agriculture, the fate of handicrafts, social erosion, and political breakdown—suggests that there are no easy, simple answers to the question of whether the majority of peasants were suffering immiseration in the early twentieth century. Nonetheless, we found no conclusive evidence to support the view that rural living standards in China as a whole had fallen significantly. Of the two schools of interpretation discussed at the opening of this chapter, the less persuasive was the Exploitation School. Neither landlordism nor imperialist destruction of handicrafts had as negative an impact as that school contended. And the increase in commercialization—contrary to the view of that school—actually had strong, albeit not uniformly, positive effects. The Overpopulation, Primitive-Technology School was closer to the mark, although the problem of overpopulation was not as serious as proponents of that school usually implied.

Indeed, because the arguments of these two schools of interpretation are so weak, some contemporary economists are arguing not only that the peasants were not suffering a process of immiseration, but also that their standard of living was actually rising in the early modern period. The strongest evidence for this surprising assertion is that per capita cloth consumption nearly doubled between the 1870s and the late 1920s. Specifically, it rose from about 4.7 square yards per person in the years 1871 to 1880, to 5.3 square yards in 1901 to 1910, and reached a peak of 8.2 square yards in 1923 to 1927. (Thereafter, cloth consumption declined slightly, falling to 7.6 square yards per person in 1931 to 1933, and 7.9 square yards in 1934 to 1936.) Because—as shown in numerous studies on other countries—cloth consumption is a good indicator of rising or falling standards of living, these data suggest that China's income levels were rising between 1870 and 1927.

This conclusion seems to be corroborated by the results of a survey done by John Lossing Buck in 1928, which reported that over 80 percent of the informants in 216 localities across the country asserted that their standard of living "in recent years" had been either stationary or rising. The survey noted that *"the general improvement in the clothing worn was the most commonly remarked evidence of a better plane of living* given by 56 per cent of the informants who reported a rise. An improving quality of food was reported by 27 per cent of the cases."[29]

It would be premature, however, on the basis of this limited, and possibly misleading,[30] evidence to conclude that the peasants' living standards were rising during the early twentieth century. Nevertheless, that evidence does at least add plausibility to our earlier conclusion that rural living standards were not appreciably falling in those years.

If, however, the peasants' living conditions did not change radically between 1900 and the late 1920s—despite rising population levels, heavier tax burdens, worsening "natural disasters," increasing political instability, and reduced social services by the government and local elites—it is nevertheless clear that their livelihood was under heavy stress. This is indicated by their sharply increased consumption of sweet potatoes, maize, and other "coarse grains," which enabled them to maintain acceptable nutritional levels, but resulted in a *psychological* lowering of the standard of living.

Further evidence of the stress on the peasants' livelihood is revealed in the fact that more peasants were being forced to find subsidiary work to supplement their farm incomes. As a result of the growing population, a substantial proportion of the peasant households in the early twentieth century did not farm enough land (with the technology then in use) to feed themselves. In Hopei and Shantung, for instance, nearly half the peasant families farmed less than 10 *mu* of land—yet 15 *mu* were generally needed to sustain most such families. For these families, salvation lay in the growth of the market economy and in taking up subsidiary occupations. Many small-peasant families switched to commercial crops, which, sold on the market, brought in sufficient profit that they could buy the grain they ate. Other small peasants, who continued to grow rice or wheat, often sold those relatively expensive grains and purchased maize, potatoes, barley, or millet for their own consumption.

Many small-peasant families sent a member or two off the family farm to work for wages. Some 7 to 15 percent of the farm population in the early 1930s—estimates vary—took employment with larger, more successful farmers, who cultivated more land than just they and their families could handle. Another safety valve for the straitened farm households was employment in the cities. As commerce and manufacturing increased, peasant families with surplus hands sent the husband, a son, or a daughter to work in the mills, on the docks, or in the various service industries in the cities. From 1900 to 1938, the populations of Shanghai and the cities in the north grew by about 10 million (the cities in the south grew less rapidly), much of which increase was attributable to the influx of peasants seeking employment. Handicrafts, too, provided another means by which the farmers adjusted to their shrinking per capita farm holdings. Indeed, the smaller the farm, the more intensively the family members worked at handicrafts—both because they had more time to devote to sideline occupations and because of economic necessity. The importance of these various forms of subsidiary occupations is shown in the fact that in one area (along the Peking–Hankow Railroad), fully 34 percent of the net income of farm families in the early 1930s was derived from such subsidiary occupations as handicrafts, animal husbandry, coolie labor, and shipping and marketing.

Thus although China was not caught in a Malthusian trap in the early twentieth century and the living standard of the average peasant was not changing radically, it is clear that even in the best of times, the living standard was exceedingly low—a fact reflected in the low life expectancy. When, in addition, we note that every peasant within his or her lifetime could expect to experience famine an average of four times and that armed violence was a real or potential destructive force in the lives of all, we realize how difficult and tenuous was life for a Chinese peasant.

The Depression of the 1930s

During the 1930s, China was struck by a series of blows that further destabilized the delicate ecology of the peasant economy. In the summer of 1931, the Yangtze River flooded—it has been called "one of the greatest natural calamities on record"—the water covering an area the size of New York State, creating 14 million refugees, and inflicting an average loss of over Ch$500 per family. Japan's invasion of Manchuria in September 1931 and attack on Shanghai in early 1932 likewise set off far-reaching economic reverberations, severing China proper from a large and profitable market for its consumer goods, cutting off the rich source of remittances from immigrants in Manchuria to their families back home, and deeply disturbing investors' confidence. During 1934 and 1935, too, large areas of the country suffered ruinous harvests as a result of unusually bad weather. In 1934, for instance, drought turned rice paddies in Kiangsu and Anhwei into cracked cakes of dried mud, and the rice harvest in those provinces fell to 50 percent of normal. Elsewhere in the country, wind, hail, and other natural disasters hurt farm production, which in the nation as a whole fell that year by over 24 percent from the average of the previous five years. In 1935, both the Yangtze and the Yellow rivers flooded, while thirteen provinces were afflicted by drought.

Exacerbating all these difficulties was the monetary crisis that beset China in the 1930s. For the three years beginning in 1929, the economy had been spared the ill effects of the world Depression because the Chinese currency was based on silver. Following the stock-market crash, the world price of silver, relative to gold, had plummeted; this had the fortuitous effect of devaluing the Chinese currency. As a consequence, Chinese exports thrived vis-à-vis their foreign competition, and foreigners holding silver saw China as an attractive target of investment. Silver, therefore, poured into the country. The resulting inflationary trend boosted prices for farm goods, pushed down interest rates, and encouraged farmers to borrow money and to buy land, property, and other goods.

This brief period of relative prosperity ended abruptly in the winter of 1931/32. Japanese military actions contributed to this downturn, but probably no less hurtful was the decision by Great Britain and Japan in late 1931 to abandon the gold standard in order to regain their competitive advantage in the world market. Thus no longer did the silver currency ensure China's producers a favorable position relative to their British and Japanese rivals; the flow of silver into the country slowed, interest rates rose, and prices fell.

United States policy soon worsened these deflationary trends, because in 1933 it, too, devaluated its currency. And in 1934, Congress passed the Silver Purchase Act, which pushed the world price of silver to artificial heights. The flow of silver out of China, which since late 1931 had been only a trickle, now turned into a torrent—the country's silver reserves dropping from Ch$602 million in April 1934 to only Ch$288 million in November 1935. This hastened the deflationary process within China, reducing the prices of farm goods to new lows. Meanwhile, the prices of goods that farmers purchased fell more slowly, with the result that the purchasing power of the farmers—the ratio of prices received to prices paid—fell drastically. (See Table 5.1).

In addition to all these factors, the Depression hit the manufacturing sector, so that sales of rural handicrafts dropped sharply and family members working in urban factories were laid off. In Shanghai alone, 1.2 million workers were unemployed in 1934. The result was, of course, that numerous farm households lost critically important increments to their incomes. Banditry, moreover, continued to be pervasive, and troop exactions persisted. The state-building activities of the new Nationalist government were also increasing the peasants' tax burden. As even Chiang Kai-shek remarked in 1935, "Government expenditures grow steadily higher. Whenever a program is begun, new taxes arise. Surtax charges are often attached to the regular taxes . . . and miscellaneous taxes are also created. . . . As a result tax items are numerous. The people have suffered immensely under this heavy tax burden."[31]

The forces playing on the peasants' standard of living in the 1930s were complex, and most evidence suggests that the net effect was very nearly catastrophic.

Table 5.1.   Index Numbers of Prices Received and Prices Paid by Farmers,
1926–1935

Year	Prices Received	Prices Paid	Ratio of Prices Received to Prices Paid
1926	100	100	100
1927	93	104	89.4
1928	93	113	82.3
1929	122	135	90.3
1930	126	142	88.7
1931	118	152	77.6
1932	117	154	75.9
1933	57	108	52.7
1934	49	106	47.2
1935	79	121	65.3

Source: Yang Sueh-Chang, "China's Depression and Subsequent Recovery, 1931–36: An Inquiry into the Applicability of the Modern Income Determination Theory" (Ph.D. diss., Harvard University, 1950), p. 162. Indices of prices for the period are seldom in agreement. For a different set of index numbers (for the period through 1933) that reveals the same general—but not such a drastic—decline, see Chi-ming Hou, *Foreign Investment and Economic Development in China, 1840–1937* (Cambridge, Mass.: Harvard University Press, 1965), p. 266. Reprinted by permission.

The Depression was not, however, necessarily continual—as revealed in 1936 to 1937, when the rural situation briefly, but distinctly, improved. Favorable weather brought bumper crops. And the Nationalist government's decision in 1935 to abandon its silver-based currency in favor of a managed currency set off an inflationary trend that was to become ruinous in the 1940s, but was initially mild and economically invigorating. The revival of the peasants' purchasing power, in turn, created strong markets for industrial products. Sadly, the war with Japan soon broke out. It lasted for eight years and was followed by nearly four years of civil war between the Nationalists and the Communists. For almost twenty years after 1931, therefore, the nation's peasants suffered conditions substantially worse than any they had known during the first three decades of the twentieth century.

The Myth of Immiseration Before 1931

Why, if rural conditions were not worsening during the decades before 1931, have representatives of the Exploitation and the Overpopulation, Primitive-Technology schools argued so vehemently that the peasants were truly suffering a process of immiseration throughout that period? One explanation, I think, is that most of the major surveys of conditions in China's villages were undertaken only in the 1930s, and they, with a few exceptions, accurately reported that the peasants were living in miserable poverty and that conditions had recently worsened.

But viewing peasant life from the vantage point of the 1930s distorted the true picture of the peasants' living standards in the early years of the century. Those who reported a decline in village conditions inferred that because rural conditions were manifestly dreadful in the 1930s, and had worsened over the past few years, those conditions were the culmination of a long and steady process of deterioration. But extrapolating backward in this way led to erroneous conclusions. Although rural life before the 1930s had by no means been cushy, the existing evidence argues against a continual decline in living conditions between the late nineteenth century and 1930.

Another probable explanation for the myth of immiseration is that the doom sayers—being so convinced that conditions had worsened in the early part of the twentieth century—neglected the obvious fact that rural conditions in the nineteenth century were already wretched. As noted in Chapter 1, the era of economic prosperity and growth during the Qing Dynasty had ended in about the 1770s. The desolation of peasant life thereafter is suggested by the rising incidence of secret-society uprisings and peasant revolts, which climaxed in the terrible mid-nineteenth-century rebellions—the Taiping, Nien, and Moslems—that wreaked enormous devastation and loss of life. Nor did rural conditions seem to have improved during the latter decades of the nineteenth century. Arthur H. Smith, that acute missionary observer of Chinese social life, wrote in 1899 that

> the most prominent fact in China is the poverty of its people. There are too many villages to the square mile, too many families to the village, too many "mouths" to the family. Wherever one goes, it is the same weary tale with interminable reiteration. Poverty, poverty, poverty, always and evermore poverty.[32]

He told of poverty that drove even the smallest children to slave at some form of work, however dismal and insignificant it may have appeared to his readers. Every blob of manure was harvested, anything that could be burned as fuel was saved. "Not a stalk," said Smith, "not a twig, not a leaf is wasted."[33]

During the first three decades of the twentieth century, these conditions persisted—and worsened during the years after 1931. Although further research on the years 1931 to 1949 is required, it appears likely that immiseration now became a reality, no longer a figment in the imagination of academic sociologists.

Selected Readings

(See also the works cited in the notes)

Ash, Robert. *Land Tenure in Pre-Revolutionary China: Kiangsu Province in the 1920s and 1930s,* Research Notes and Studies, No. 1. London: University of London, School of Oriental and African Studies, Contemporary China Institute, 1976.

Bell, Lynda S. "Explaining China's Rural Crisis: Observations from Wuxi County in the Early Twentieth Century." *Republican China* 11, no. 1 (November 1985): 15–31.

Bianco, Lucien. "Peasant Movements." In *Cambridge History of China,* Vol. 13 ed. John K. Fairbank and Albert Feuerwerker, pp. 270–328. Cambridge: Cambridge University Press, 1986.

Brandt, Loren L., Jr. "Population Growth, Agricultural Change and Economic Integration in Central and Eastern China, 1890s–1930s." Ph.D. diss., University of Illinois, 1979.

Esherick, Joseph. "Number Games: A Note on Land Distribution in Prerevolutionary China." *Modern China* 7, no. 4 (October 1981): 387–411.

Faure, David. "The Plight of the Farmers: A Study of the Rural Economy of Jiangnan and the Pearl River Delta, 1870–1937." *Modern China* 11, no. 1 (January 1985): 3–37.

Fei, Hsiao-t'ung. *Peasant Life in China: A Field Study of Country Life in the Yangtze Valley.* New York: Dutton, 1939.

Feuerwerker, Albert. "Economic Trends, 1912–49." In *Cambridge History of China,* vol. 12, pp. 28–127. Cambridge: Cambridge University Press, 1983.

———. "Economic Trends in the Late Ch'ing Empire, 1870–1911." In *Cambridge History of China,* Vol. 11, pp. 1–69. Cambridge: Cambridge University Press, 1980.

Myers, Ramon H. *The Chinese Peasant Economy: Agricultural Development in Hopei and Shantung, 1890–1949.* Cambridge, Mass.: Harvard University Press, 1970.

Perkins, Dwight H. *Agricultural Development in China, 1368–1968.* Chicago: Aldine, 1969.

6

Commerce in the Late Imperial Period: The Instruments and Geography of Trade

Customary wisdom holds that Chinese in traditional times deeply disparaged commerce and merchants. Merchants were, after all, ranked lowest in the orthodox Confucian ordering of social classes: scholar, farmer, artisan, and merchant. It became a cliché, following the great Han Dynasty historian Ban Gu (first century A.D.), that trade was a "licentiously corrupt occupation *(yinye)*." For Chinese, agriculture was the root, or source *(ben)*, of society; what peasants harvested was obviously of value to society. Merchants, by contrast, grew rich from the productive efforts of others; they were, therefore, parasites on the body social. The customary Confucian disparagement of commercial activity was summed up in Mencius's condemnation of profit during his famous audience with King Hui of the state of Liang:

> Venerable sir, [said the king to Mencius,] since you have not counted it far to come here, a distance of a thousand *li,* may I presume that you are provided with counsels to profit my kingdom?"

> Mencius replied, "Why must your Majesty use that word 'profit'? What I am provided with are counsels to benevolence and righteousness, and these are my only topics."[1]

From this story, young Chinese for centuries learned that a true gentleman, a *junzi,* ought to concern himself with morality, not profit. Conversely, those who concerned themselves with profit—that is, merchants—could not be *junzi.* Even as late as the nineteenth century, the official and historian Xu Zi could assert approvingly that "when the profits of commerce are small, those who plow and weave will be numerous."[2]

Confucians, sensibly, did not push their deprecation of profit to extremes. Mencius himself advised rulers to avoid taxing the merchants, which policy would

101

have the happy result that "then all the traders of the kingdom will be pleased, and wish to store their goods in [the ruler's] market-place."[3] During the imperial period, therefore, officials generally recognized that, in practice, the flow of goods was vital to the well-being of society and that merchants—except when they exacted "unreasonable" or unfair profits—performed a useful social function. Emperors often adjured their officials to "pacify the people and facilitate commerce *(anmin tongshang)."* Thus in general, the orthodox Confucian attitude toward commerce was marked by a profound ambivalence. Confucians recognized the economic utility of mercantile activity, yet they were convinced that the fundamental way to attain a properly ordered, harmonious society lay in pursuing the Confucian virtues, which deprecated money grubbing.

Whatever moral scruples Confucian literati might hold regarding mercantile activity, the Chinese people themselves had, as the British missionary Arthur H. Smith remarked in 1899, a "singular penchant for trade."[4] They were, observed another old China hand, "a race of traders than whom there has not been in the world a shrewder and a keener."[5] Thus a powerful materialistic streak ran through the Chinese psyche, evidenced in numerous greetings, such as that extended at the New Year: "Congratulations, and may you become rich *(gongxi facai)."* Never was there a want of people who hoped to escape the rigors of farming by turning to peddling or setting up a shop or stall. Even as early as the Tang Dynasty, therefore, commerce flourished throughout the nation:

> Boats [wrote one Cui Rong] gather on every stream in the Empire. To one side they reach into Szechwan and the Han River valley; they point the way to Fukien and Kwangtung. . . . Great ships in thousands carry goods back and forth. If they once lay unused, it would spell ruin for ten thousand merchants.[6]

Later, during the eighteenth century, a Jesuit priest wrote in awe:

> The riches peculiar to each province, and the facility of conveying merchandise, by means of rivers and canals, have rendered the domestic trade of the empire always very flourishing. . . . The inland trade of China is so great that the commerce of all Europe is not to be compared therewith; the provinces being like so many kingdoms, which communicate to each other their respective productions. This tends to unite the several inhabitants among themselves, and makes plenty reign in all cities.[7]

Such a volume of trade should dispel any persisting notions that late imperial China was a simple society consisting of isolated villages in which peasants subsisted solely on the fruits of their own labors. In fact, peasants frequently purchased such goods as salt, vegetable oil, needles, iron tools, and cooking utensils, and patronized such specialists as blacksmiths, coffin makers, "tooth-artists" (dentists), and fortunetellers. In return, they marketed their farm produce and handicraft manufactures. Before the twentieth century, some 20 to 30 percent of farm output was marketed.

Most goods were sold close to their place of origin, usually no more than 100 miles distant. But there was also a substantially smaller long-distance trade, most of which catered to the needs and wishes of the social and economic elite. Fine porcelains, for instance, were shipped from the kilns in Kiangsi; choice teas (common peasants usually contented themselves with hot water) came from northern Chekiang and southern Kiangsu; and the finest textiles were woven in such cities of the lower Yangtze region as Soochow and Hangchow. Books, stationery, jades, and sugar were among the other luxury items often shipped long distance. The urban population—probably numbering some 6 percent of the whole during the late imperial period—was also dependent on the trade networks for food and other supplies.

Commerce on such a scale required transportation, a system of weights and measures, currency, and banking facilities. These are the instruments of trade discussed in the following pages. A caveat, however, is in order: China's commercial economy experienced ups and downs over the centuries, yet most of the available information about it pertains to the nineteenth century, which was a period of relative economic privation, political turmoil, and governmental ineffectiveness. Much of the sixteenth through the eighteenth century (exclusive of the downturn in the mid-seventeenth century), however, was a time of economic florescence. The reader should bear in mind, then, that if our data were drawn from, say, the eighteenth century, the descriptions might impart a more positive impression.

Transportation

China's transportation system—as Westerners found it in the late nineteenth century—was inconvenient, inefficient, and costly. To ship a picul of rice for 200 miles by pack animal, for instance, cost as much as to produce that rice; to transport a ton of coal the same distance cost twenty times the price of the coal at the mine. Thus shipment of cheap but heavy goods over long distances was uneconomical, and only a small part of the total produce of the nation was consumed more than a few miles from the place of origin. Goods transported by land were generally carried on the backs of men or animals (mules, horses, oxen, camels). A man with a tote pole, with the burden balanced evenly on either end, could carry a load of about 80 to 105 pounds; using a back pack, a porter sometimes bore loads of as much as 200 pounds. Wheeled vehicles were much more efficient, of course, although the poor condition of the roadways often prevented their use, especially in south and west China. The two-man wheelbarrow, which could be fitted with a sail, often carried 500 or more pounds; the smaller one-man barrows carried about half that load. Even the fastest land transport, using pack horses, customarily averaged only about 30 miles a day.

The term "roads," when applied to the paths and tracks that constituted the land-transport network, was usually a misnomer. Like Topsy, they had not been made, but just "growed"; they were paths worn down over the generations by countless feet, hooves, and wheels. They had not been mapped out by governmental planners, but followed the lines of least resistance through fields, hills, and streams. Constantly at odds with the travelers were the peasants, who received no compensation if a road crossed their land, and who were, moreover, required to pay taxes on their land even if it was used as a public road. The peasants thus placed obstacles or dug pitfalls in the way of travelers who might be tempted to cross their fields; at the very least, they endeavored to push the paths to the outer edges of their land, thereby avoiding the cutting up of their fields and forcing the neighboring farmers to contribute part of the roadway. Such a response was understandable, but it resulted in mayhem for travelers because the flow of traffic was forced to conform to the contours of each and every field rather than to the geometric principle about the shortest distance between two points. "In traveling on village roads," wrote Arthur Smith in the late nineteenth century, "it is often necessary to go a great distance to reach a place not far off."[8] Major interprovincial roads were formed by linking the various village roads. These were wider perhaps, but seldom in better condition than the lesser roads.

Nor were most roads either paved or graded. Huge potholes lurked to ambush the unwary traveler, and long sections of roadway had over the centuries become so deeply eroded that after heavy rains, they became the beds of rushing streams. "Along such a way," reported an observer in the 1890s, "the cart sways like a ship in distress at sea, the mules floundering about from one track to another and the cart going almost on its beam ends in the course of every few yards."[9] Indeed, in the loess highlands of north China, repeated use over the centuries had so worn down the roadbeds that they formed vertical-walled ravines that were often 60 or even 80 feet below the surface of the surrounding countryside. In many places, these ravines were so narrow that only one cart could pass at a time. Carters, before entering such a defile, would have to shout loudly, warning approaching carters to wait at the occasional wide spot so that they could squeeze past each other.

In the south and west, more than in the north, the natural topography dictated the course of the roadways. Most roads followed valleys and stream beds, and water-filled rice paddies did not permit travelers the carefree meandering over the fields allowed by the flat and arid northern plain. Not infrequently, the paths were paved with stone slabs, but most were too narrow and steep for carts and too uneven for wheelbarrows. Most goods, therefore, were moved by porter or pack animal.

In an earlier day, the imperial governments had assumed responsibility for at least some of the roadways. In the third century B.C., for example, the First Emperor, ruler of the Qin Dynasty, had reportedly constructed a large highway network, the roads being 50 paces wide and shaded along their entire length by pine trees. So extensive was this highway system, according to the official history of the Han Dynasty, that "later generations were even unable to find a crooked path upon which to place their feet."[10] It would be a mistake, no doubt, to infer from this that early imperial China enjoyed a network of transcontinental freeways. Still, it was by no means uncommon for cities in the Song Dynasty to be linked by bricked roadways, and the road system during the Song Dynasty seems to have ramified through much of the nation. A thirteenth-century geography of the empire noted, for example, that from the commercial center of Xinzhou, in the lower

Yangtze region, "the roads to Fukien, Hunan and Hupei, and Kiangsi all lead off from here. In times past, it was an out-of-the-way place. Today, it is a centre of communications."[11] Many of these roadways between cities were paved with bricks, although sometimes they were imperfectly maintained.

The Yuan (1271–1368) was seemingly the last of the dynasties to devote any persistent attention to the roads, however, and by the late Qing, all but an occasional remnant of these imperial roadways had disappeared. Indeed, the imperial highway connecting Tongzhou and Peking had been so heavily used since the fourteenth century that the close-fitting granite blocks surfacing the road had been worn into ruts 1 foot and more in depth, making that imperial roadway even less usable than the nearby farmers' fields. Arthur Smith remarked sarcastically that an imperial highway "is not one which is kept in order by the emperor, but rather one which may have to be put in order for the emperor."[12]

Only rarely did the government in late Qing times undertake to repair the roads. In Szechwan, it was reported that "roads where Customs' dues are collected are kept in decent condition, it being to the officials' benefit to keep them so."[13] Such pragmatism was by no means universal, however, and in most of the empire, maintenance work, when performed at all, was done by individuals or local associations seeking merit in the Buddhist chain of causation by performing good works. The only lasting results of most such efforts were stone tablets by the roadsides, which the benefactors invariably erected to commemorate their own names and acts of charity.

Bridges were occasional exceptions to the government's general disregard for the roadways. Although a terrible paucity of bridges was everywhere evident, those that did exist had usually been constructed under government supervision and at least partly with government money. Some of these were architectural marvels. The Loyang Bridge near Foochow, for instance, had been built during the Song Dynasty, was over 3,600 feet long, and had 47 blue-granite buttresses and stone railings carved with representations of lions and pagodas. Few were as imposing as this, and what most impressed Westerners traveling in China during the nineteenth century was the sorry condition of most bridges. When the stone lintel between bridge piers broke, for example, it was customary for local residents to make good the breach by throwing tree trunks or (in north China) millet stalks over the gap. Such sections might in the best of times be perilous to cross, and at high water, they were often washed away. Because of the dilapidated condition or the total absence of bridges, travelers frequently had to ford the streams or, when waters were swollen, abandon their journeys.

Transport was far more economical and convenient by water than by land. Even the small sampans that scooted along the narrow streams of south China could carry loads of about 1,600 pounds, and the junks on the major rivers bore loads up to 70 tons. As a consequence, water shipping cost only about one-third, or even one-fifth, of what a comparable distance over land would cost. Still, transporting rice 1,000 miles down the Yangtze from Hunan to Kiangsu and Chekiang at least doubled the original cost.

One disadvantage of river transport, of course, was that going upstream was more arduous than going downstream. The difficulties of going against the current in the Yangtze Gorges, for example, were legendary. Scores of haulers were needed to pull the boats only inches at a time. A Westerner in the late nineteenth century recounted that on one occasion, the towline of his boat broke; in just fifteen minutes, it was back where it had started two and a half hours earlier. Generally speaking, shipments by water required three times as long to go upstream as downstream. Still, the fact that south China was more commercialized than the north and west was attributable largely to the relative advantages of water over land transport.

Most water routes, however, suffered from the same kind of neglect as the roads. Although local magistrates were theoretically responsible for maintaining the waterways, they received no funds from the central government for that work. Few river and lake routes benefited, therefore, from regular dredging, removal of dangerous rocks, cleared towpaths, or channel markings. That the imperial government after about the Yuan Dynasty no longer took an active interest in such a crucial national utility as transportation might appear puzzling. In fact, however, it was an inevitable consequence of the late imperial government's laissez-faire approach to local affairs, discussed later in this chapter.

In the late nineteenth century, this whole system of transport, on water and land alike, exerted a great deal of drag on commerce. In earlier times, the system probably had worked more smoothly. This possibility is suggested not only by the vestiges of numerous ancient roads and bridges that in late Qing times had fallen into utter disrepair, but also by recent research into the history of price behavior in China.[14] Astonishingly, according to that study, the seasonal variations in rice prices in the Yangtze delta region in the years 1713 to 1719 were smaller and less precipitous than they were between 1913 and 1919. Already in the early eighteenth century, this area was an administrative, shipping, and manufacturing center, and a high proportion of the land in the two *xian* of Shanghai and Jiading was planted in cotton rather than in food crops. Thus it was heavily dependent for its supply of rice on shipments from other regions.

One would expect that market mechanisms and transportation would have been less efficient in the eighteenth than in the twentieth century. Shanghai in the early twentieth century was, after all, favored by modern banking and warehouse facilities, steam and rail transport, and the availability of grain imports not only from other regions of China, but also from Southeast Asia, Australia, and North America. Regional fluctuations in rice prices between 1913 and 1919 should certainly, therefore, have been markedly less than they had been 200 years earlier.

How, then, can one explain the greater price stability in the early eighteenth century? "The single most important factor which might help explain the amazing price stability of the Soochow rice market in the early 1700s," this study of price behavior concludes, "was the existence of a very large-scale, long-distance rice trade serving Soochow and, through it, the great commercial and urban areas of Southern Kiangsu, Chekiang, and Fukien."[15] Annual imports of rice to the area, for example, amounted to between 170,000 and 280,000 tons, and this rice regularly came not only from nearby Anhwei and Kiangsi, but even from Taiwan, Shantung, Manchuria, and Szechwan (which in early modern times seldom shipped rice to the lower Yangtze). The precise mechanisms of this vast trade are still unknown, but it is patent that in the early eighteenth century, (1) a large number of rice cultivators were producing for the market, (2) the marketing system succeeded in collecting large amounts of grain and in responding to the pressure of supply and demand over a vast territory, and (3) the transportation system was efficient enough that transporting a relatively low unit-value commodity like rice was still profitable. These findings lead to the conclusion that the transport technology and market mechanisms in the early eighteenth century were "very sophisticated and effective." In light of this, the study asserts, we must break free from "the mocking, belittling, condescending . . . European view [that the Chinese economic system in the late nineteenth and early twentieth centuries] was in fact traditional China for all time." [16]

Weights and Measures

Qin Shihuang, the First Emperor, is said to have unified the system of weights and measures in the third century B.C. By late imperial times, that reputed unity had been replaced by mind-boggling confusion.

In linear measurements, there was a systematic ordering of the several units: 1 Chinese yard *(zhang)* equaled 10 Chinese feet *(chi);* 1 foot equaled 10 Chinese inches *(cun);* and 1 inch equaled 10 *fen.* There, however, the logic of the system ended. In Shanghai, 1 tailor's foot equaled 13.85 inches (United States inches); 1 carpenter's foot equaled 11.1 inches; and the foot used officially to measure land was 12.1 inches, whereas the foot used privately to measure the transfers of land equaled 13.2 inches. The city of Canton was divided into two *xian,* and the foot used in the *xian* on the east side of the city equaled 14.7 inches, while that on the west side equaled 14.8 inches.

Theoretically, too, 1 picul *(dan)* of weight was supposed to equal 100 catties *(jin).* But in Amoy, a leading port in Fukien, 1 picul of indigo was divided into 110 catties; 1 picul of white sugar, into 95 catties; and 1 picul of brown sugar, into only 94 catties. One picul of rice consisted of 100 catties in Shanghai, but in Amoy, it consisted of 140 catties, and in Foochow, of 180 catties. Even the imperial government did not maintain uniformity, for the prescribed measure of tribute rice ordinarily had 120 catties, but in Nanking, the tribute-rice picul had 140 catties.

In measuring distances, the Chinese could easily have identified with the Dutch, who measured the length of a canal-boat run by the number of pipes they smoked during a trip. The standard unit of measuring distance was the *li,* which was understood to be equivalent to one-hundredth of the distance that a porter, fully laden, could walk on flat terrain in a ten-hour day. In theory, 1 *li* was considered to equal 1,800 Chinese feet, or about one-third of an English mile. Uneven terrain, however, confuted all theory. Thus the distance *going* to a village in the hills might be 50 *li;* but the distance *returning,* going downhill, might be only 25 *li.*

Similar aberrations characterized the measures of volume and area. The pint *(dou),* used to measure volumes of grain or liquids, ranged from 176 to 1,800 cubic inches. Merchants, moreover, customarily used a long pint when buying and a short pint when selling. The *mu* was the standard unit of area; it varied from 3,840 square feet to 9,964 square feet. In some places, an areal measure called "buffalo-land" *(niutian)* was used. Morton Fried, the anthropologist, was told in 1948 that this unit was equivalent to the amount of land that a water buffalo could plow in a day's time. Inquiring further, Fried was told that 1 unit of buffalo-land was equal to anywhere from 40 to 50 *mu*. Puzzled by this imprecision, Fried pressed his informant, who explained with irrefutable logic that the actual size of a unit of buffalo-land "depends on the size of the buffalo." [17]

To Chinese in the shop or on the farm, the confusion implied by such imprecision and inconsistency of weights and measures was probably more apparent than real. Thus the foot used to measure Soochow silk was different from the foot used to measure cotton cloth or wood or whatever, but Soochow silk was *always* measured by the Soochow foot. Guild rules strictly enforced this practice. Similar standardization was enforced in other towns and professions. Moreover, to put the Chinese practice into perspective, it may be helpful to recall that Americans live with similar inconsistencies without being overcome by a sense of confusion. We speak, for example, of living ten minutes from school—often without specifying whether we cover that distance by foot, bicycle, or car. And the two-by-four that we purchase at the lumberyard actually measures 1¾ inches by 3¾ inches. There was, moreover, a great deal of common sense underlying the Chinese system of weights and measures. Peasants, with the wisdom of the ages, knew what Oscar Handlin, a Harvard professor of history, discovered only in his own lifetime:

> A straight line is the shortest distance between two points in the plains—not in the mountains. Whoever has viewed the way in which paths switch back and forth up the slopes, or snake around natural obstacles, will understand why linear measurements have little meaning here. Indeed, away from the plains I lose altogether the habit of calculating distance in blocks, meters, or miles; the gauge of hours and minutes is far more significant. [18]

Money

China since the fourth century B.C. has regularly used coins and bullion as mediums of exchange. The round copper coins, such as those still used in the twentieth century, had been used as money without interruption since Han times (206 B.C.–A.D. 220), and Chinese began using true paper money as early as the eleventh century. With such a venerable experience in money matters, China might be expected to have evolved, by late imperial times, a rational, smoothly working monetary system. No less than the weights and measures, however, China's money was chaotic and constituted a major obstacle to commercial development.

Since the early Ming Dynasty, China used both silver and copper as the primary mediums of exchange. But these metals were two distinct currencies; copper was not used as a subsidiary coinage for the more valuable silver. Instead, silver was used for large transactions, wholesale purchases, and payments of large salaries; copper was used for smaller transactions and retail purchases. Although either silver or copper could, in intermediate and indefinable sectors of the market, serve as the medium of exchange, the system has been aptly called "parallel bimetallism."

There was but one copper coin, called a "cash" *(qian)*. Minted by one of the several central or provincial government mints, each copper cash was about 1 inch in diameter, had the distinctive square hole in the center, and was marked with the name of the reigning emperor. Cash were minuscule in value, being equivalent in the nineteenth century to a farthing, or one-quarter of a British penny. The low value of the cash created major problems: even a heavy pocketful of cash would not suffice to make a sizable purchase, and much time could be wasted counting the cash in each monetary exchange. A complicating factor was that the values of individual copper coins were not precisely uniform, because the government occasionally altered the size of and the amount of copper in each cash. Centuries of use, moreover, had sometimes worn down the cash so that they were thinner and lighter than a "standard" cash. Counterfeiters also frequently debased coins. Thus value of each cash being paid could become the subject of extended bargaining in any commercial exchange.

The potential inconveniences of such a currency were partly circumvented by grading the cash and stringing them together, first in substrings uniformly worth 100 cash, and then in strings *(chuan)* of ten substrings, with a total value of 1,000 cash. This painstaking task—which required not only grading the cash by size, weight, thickness, copper content, origin, and wear and tear, but also arranging the cash on the strings so that they tapered in neatly descending gradations of size—was customarily performed by money-changing shops *(qianpu)*, which specialized in this service. These shops obtained remuneration for this work by deducting, say, 1 cash from each substring. Thus a string of cash might actually contain only 990 cash, yet it would suffice in the market to buy a commodity priced at 1,000 cash; 990 unstrung cash, however, would not suffice.

But local practices differed. In some areas, money-changing shops might deduct 2 or more cash from each substring (so that a full string might contain 980, 970, or even—as in Taiyuan—as few as 820 cash). Or the cash on each string in one area might be of poorer quality than in another locality. Indeed, even within one area, several kinds of strings might be concurrently in use—each string identified by notches indicating the number and quality of cash strung on it. In such areas, some markets (say, the fuel market) might accept 980-cash strings, whereas other markets (say, the meat market) might accept only 990-cash strings. Lacking the proper string, the buyer might have to pay several unstrung cash to make up the difference, or go to a money-changing shop to purchase the acceptable type of string of cash. There were innumerable other complications. In Chihli and several northern provinces, for instance, a "small-cash" system of account was used, so that 1 standard cash had the value of 2 unit-of-account cash. That is, a commodity listed by a shop as being for sale for 100 cash could be purchased with just 50 of the copper coins. Other examples could be given, but perhaps we have already said enough to suggest the basic complexity of the cash system. Unfortunately, the silver system was hardly less confusing.

The basic unit of silver as a medium of exchange was the ounce *(liang)*, translated by foreigners as "tael" (pronounced "tail"). Just as in the United States, where prices are fixed in dollars and payment is made in dollars, so in China—at least in theory—prices were stated in *liang* of silver and payments were made in *liang* of silver. Because the government in late imperial times assumed no responsibility for the silver sector, as it did for the copper sector, however, it did not mint silver coins. Silver therefore, circulated in ingots of varying sizes, shapes, and weights. And because silver was not available in pure form, the ingots also varied in degrees of fineness, or purity. Further complicating the situation was the fact that the *liang,* as a unit of weight, varied from place to place, just as did other Chinese weights; and the method of assaying the "touch" of silver was somewhat primitive, thus precluding precise measurement of the silver's purity.

Silver circulated in specially formed ingots, the most important of which was the "shoe of sycee," weighing about 50 *liang* and so-named because of its supposed resemblance to a horse's hoof (the word "sycee," from the Chinese *xisi,* or "fine silk," was simply a term for a silver ingot). Each ingot of lesser weight had its own distinctive shape. Curiously, bar ingots obtained in trade with foreigners were not used as currency and had to be melted down and formed into proper, self-respecting Chinese ingots before being accepted as currency.

Because the government did not involve itself in the operations of the silver system, the task of molding the shoes of sycee and other ingots fell on privately owned money-changing shops that specialized in assaying and selling silver. When molding the ingots, the money-changing shops—much as they did when stringing cash—subtracted a specified amount of silver (depending on local practice) from each ingot as payment for their services, so that a shoe of sycee with a nominal value of 50 *liang* might actually weigh only 49.5 *liang*. Having molded the shoe, the money-changing shop inscribed on it the nominal weight and degree of fineness. It could now be used as money.

This new shoe of sycee, with a nominal value of 50 taels, when thrust into the marketplace, encountered a world of stunning complexity. In Peking, for example, six other taels circulated—one weighing 552.4 grains and being 980 fine, another weighing 541.7 grains and being 1,000 fine, and so on. In Tientsin, nine taels were generally recognized; Canton also had about nine taels; and in Chungking, the most infamous of all the major cities, at least sixty taels circulated. If the price of the commodity was quoted in, say, the *Zaoping* tael (weighing 565.65 grains, with a touch of 944 fine) and the purchaser possessed silver molded into *Zaoping* shoes, then the transaction could proceed smoothly. As often happened, however, the purchaser held silver in one or several other kinds of taels of different weights and fineness. Then abstruse negotiations and calculations ensued, until the parties agreed on the amount and purity of silver that would be equivalent to that expressed by the *Zaoping* standard.

A further difficulty of the silver currency was the absence of subsidiary coinage. When silver was needed in amounts less than that of the molded ingot, parties to the transaction might slice off shavings from an ingot. The original ingot was thereby debased, but the fragments thus obtained served as the small-value currency.

China's bimetallic monetary system remained largely intact until about 1800;

thereafter, several other forms of money challenged the supremacy of silver bullion and copper. Of the several new competitors, silver dollars were the strongest.[19]

Since the sixteenth century, Spanish silver dollars—first the piaster ("pieces of eight"), and later the Carolus dollar—had been pumped into the economy, and by the late eighteenth century, they circulated widely in south China, especially in the cities but also in the interior along the silk routes. Initially, Chinese had treated dollars as bullion, assaying and weighing the dollars as they would any other silver fragment, or melting them down and molding the silver into ingot. The Spanish dollar, being of uniform shape, weight, and fineness, was more convenient to use than was the traditional tael, and thus by the early nineteenth century had become the standard coin in Canton, circulated as far north as Peking, and was even accepted in some regions as payment on taxes.

After about 1850, however, the "Mex," or Mexican dollar, became the most commonly accepted silver dollar, and gradually thereafter, especially in the south, it began to displace sycee. Merchants began stating their prices in Mex, and provincial governments in the south also began paying some employees in dollars. In 1910, the imperial government, now minting a silver dollar of its own, adopted it instead of the tael as the official unit of account. Not until 1933, however, was the tael finally and fully abolished and replaced by the silver dollar as national legal tender.

Paper notes were another major rival to the system of bimetallism, which was not only complex, but also physically cumbersome. A string of 1,000 cash, equivalent to about 1 tael of silver, for instance, weighed approximately 9 pounds—not the sort of thing one conveniently carried to the market. Large wholesale purchases were often made with boxes of silver shoes, containing sixty of the 50-*liang* ingots; these boxes weighed over 240 pounds and could be lifted only by two men. Obviously, a more convenient system was needed, and during the eighteenth and nineteenth centuries, paper notes were increasingly used as a substitute for the metal currencies.

Although Chinese had begun using paper money during the Song Dynasty, the Ming had halted the practice in the mid-fifteenth century. Thereafter, except for two brief returns to paper currency by the Qing, in the Xunzhi (1644–61) and Xianfeng (1851–61) reigns, no Chinese government again issued paper currency until the early twentieth century. The private sector moved to fill the void, and during the 100 or so years preceding the Opium War, several different paper instruments of credit, such as bank drafts, were used to facilitate currency exchanges. True paper money began circulating after various banks and money-changing shops issued paper receipts for deposits of silver and copper; these receipts, backed by a 100 percent reserve, soon began circulating as money. The banks quickly discovered that the receipts, once issued, often circulated for a long time without being returned for conversion to specie. They saw no need, therefore, to maintain a 100 percent metal reserve. The opportunities presented by this practice were obvious, and the banks—and even rice, salt, and grocery merchants—were tempted to issue large amounts of paper.

Because these paper notes were light in weight and did not have to be assayed or weighed and because specie was frequently in short supply, the paper notes were widely accepted. As a result, paper added substantially to the total money supply. Probably one-third, or perhaps even more, of the money circulating in the early nineteenth century was in paper notes. But the counterfeiting of these notes was easy, and hence rampant. Furthermore, some of the bankers and merchants who issued the notes were either unskilled or unscrupulous, and government regulation was loose and ineffective. Popular confidence in paper notes, consequently, sometimes faltered, and currency panics could then lead to runs on the note-issuing institutions, forcing them into bankruptcy. Thus the use of paper currency was a source of some business instability, and the silver-tael system was never threatened, despite its considerable inconveniences.

Not all the several mediums of exchange were used uniformly throughout the nation. Indeed, early in the nineteenth century in the land-locked provinces of west China, neither silver dollars nor paper notes were much in evidence, and the traditional bimetallism of copper cash and silver bullion persisted largely unchanged. A second monetary area was in south and central China—from Canton, in the south, to the Yangtze River farther north, and west to Hunan Province—where the impact of foreign trade was most felt. There, silver dollars were widely available and shared the market about equally with silver bullion and copper. A third monetary area was in north China—stretching in a belt from southern Manchuria, in the east, to Shensi and Kansu, in the west—where copper cash were used for small transactions and paper notes representing copper cash were widely used for transactions in excess of 1,000 cash. This division of the country into three monetary regions should not be construed too rigidly, however, because each kind of money could be found in all the regions.

Banking

The complexity of the monetary system and the growing commercialization of the economy spawned a variety of shops and businesses that specialized in handling money. The most ubiquitous of these, being located in even small market towns, were the money-changing shops *(qianpu)*, which assayed and molded silver bullion, exchanged out-of-town money for strings and ingots that conformed to local standards, and, of course, strung copper cash. Some of these shops were one-man operations, perhaps handling only copper, whose places of business were small stalls set up along streets near marketplaces. Others were large and more permanent, often acquiring such additional banking functions as lending money and issuing paper notes.

Probably beginning in the eighteenth century, and expanding greatly in the nineteenth century, were two banking systems that performed many of the functions of commercial banks in the West. These were the local native banks *(qianzhuang)* and the Shansi, or remittance, banks *(piaohao* or *piaozhuang)*.

The *qianzhuang* probably represented an evolutionary step beyond the simple money-changing shops. Usually begun by a wealthy businessman using his own capital, although sometimes formed by two or three partners, these native banks performed a greater variety of functions than did the cash shops and held larger cash reserves. Like the money-changing shops, they tended to be parochial in orientation, although the scale of their operations varied enormously. Of the 120 *qianzhuang* in Shanghai in 1858, for instance, 50 had a nominal capital of only 500 to 1,000 taels each; but 10 had a capital of 30,000 to 50,000 taels. Most of them, probably, had no more than one office, although some had branches in distant cities. Essentially, however, they were *local* banks, serving a restricted area and clientele, and it was a rare occurrence if a *qianzhuang*'s paper notes circulated outside the local trading area.

In function, the *qianzhuang* were basically merchants' banks, although they also served gentry and other elite groups. They advanced loans, held deposits, issued paper notes, and occasionally remitted funds to banks in distant cities. They also performed an important role in creating credit for merchants by issuing a commercial paper called *zhuangpiao*. Merchants, lacking the needed capital to purchase goods on the wholesale market, could obtain a bank's *zhuangpiao*, which served in effect as a promissory note. After a specified period, usually five to fifteen days, the wholesaler could cash the *zhuangpiao* at the bank; the merchant, for his part, repaid the bank after selling off the goods acquired by means of the *zhuangpiao*. Although the *qianzhuang* never devised the use of bank checks, they did create a system of cash transfers between local banks using account books. The necessity of having to present the account book to the bank whenever paying or receiving funds appears cumbersome to us, but it represented a marked improvement over the older system of dealing directly in silver bullion, which had to be transported, assayed, and weighed.

Although the *qianzhuang* had stepped out of tradition in the functions they performed, they tended to be highly traditional in their organization and operations. The managers, for instance, were typically relatives of the owners or, at a minimum, natives of the same hometown. Lesser employees were also relatives, or relatives of friends, of the owners or managers. An important employee of each *qianzhuang* was the *paojie* (literally, "street runner"), whose job was to become personally familiar with potential customers and their business affairs. As in other social contexts, Chinese bankers felt most comfortable with a personal or friendly, as opposed to a legalistic, relationship in their operations. Thus relying on the *paojie* to establish and maintain that form of relationship with their clients, the banks usually advanced loans without demanding collateral. (If a borrower defaulted, of course, the *qianzhuang* did not hesitate to claim his property, and many *qianzhuang* grew into veritable trading companies with the properties thus acquired.)

Even in their relations with one another, the *qianzhuang* emphasized personal ties. Because the owners and managers of *qianzhuang* in any one city tended to come from the same native place—Ningpo natives, for example, dominated the Shanghai *qianzhuang*—the *qianzhuang* tended to cooperate, rather than compete, with one another. If one *qianzhuang* was hard-pressed for liquid assets, for instance, other *qianzhuang* might advance funds so that it could weather the crisis. The *qianzhuang* also put up a common front to the government and, in the nineteenth century, to foreign merchants.

Shansi banks differed from the *qianzhuang* in both size and function. They often had a nominal capital of 100,000 to 500,000 taels, with as many as thirty or so branches scattered from one end of the country to the other. In their operations, they did not issue paper notes, and they generally placed little emphasis on loans and deposits. A contemporary noted that they made loans "more for friendship than for business." Seemingly to discourage depositors, they paid only 5 to 8 percent interest on deposits—considerably less than the 12 percent or so paid by the *qianzhuang* and the 36 percent and more charged by pawnshops. Sometimes, indeed, they paid no interest at all; yet because of their solid reputation, they still attracted deposits. The main business of the Shansi banks, however, was interregional remittances.

Until the creation of the Shansi remittance banks, merchants who engaged in long-distance trade usually had to ship silver bullion in bulk over the primitive and bandit-infested transport lines. This was slow and inconvenient. It was also expensive, for the agencies that specialized in transmitting bullion *(piaoju)* had to hire many armed guards to accompany the shipments (and, it was reported, to pay protection money to the bandit gangs).

The origins of remittance banking are perceived but dimly. In the view of many historians, the first Shansi bank was established only in the early nineteenth century when Lei Lütai, a Shansi dye merchant in Tientsin experiencing difficulties shipping silver bullion to Szechwan to pay for his dyes, reportedly established a money-order service for himself and other merchants. In fact, however, remittance banking existed long before Lei Lütai's time. In the Ming Dynasty, a form of remittance draft called the *chiji* had been widely used in long-distance trade. We also know that Shansi bankers were already prominently engaged in interregional banking in Ningpo during the early eighteenth century. Whatever the precise origins of the Shansi banks, their service of sending remittances for a fee of 2 to 6 percent had become highly popular as interregional trading expanded during the nineteenth century. By one estimate, they handled more than half of the empire's banking until the 1890s, when the creation of the modern postal system deprived the remittance banks of their raison d'être.

The banking functions of the Shansi banks and the *qianzhuang* were generally different and complementary. Shansi bankers, for instance, usually lent funds to the *qianzhuang* rather than to individual merchants, and much of their remittance business was provided them by the *qianzhuang*. The Shansi banks, therefore, functioned much like bankers' banks, and their relationship with the *qianzhuang* was for the most part cooperative rather than competitive.

In time, however, the Shansi banks' largest customer became the imperial government, which lacked remittance facilities of its own. By remitting revenue from the land tax, providing salaries to officials around the country, and even holding government funds on deposit and dispensing them on official instructions, the Shansi banks became closely identified with the Manchu government. It was perhaps fitting, therefore, that both the dynasty and the Shansi banks faded out of existence at about the same time.

The Periodic-Marketing System

The structure within which much of China's domestic trade during the late imperial period was carried on was the periodic-marketing system. Since the 1930s, scholars have recognized this system as a significant feature of traditional agrarian societies, but it was Stanford University anthropologist G. William Skinner, one of the most stimulating and influential China scholars of recent years, who first methodically analyzed the periodic markets in the Chinese context.[20] According to Skinner, since most peasant families in traditional times were largely self-sufficient, there was not enough consumer demand to warrant keeping rural markets open throughout each working day. Instead, most market needs could usually be satisfied if a market—"standard market" in Skinner's terminology—opened only periodically, typically for only a few hours in the morning once every three to five days. Nor could every village, which usually had populations of only 200 to 400 inhabitants, support a market. Instead, a rural market customarily served not only the village in which it was located, but also from six to forty other villages. Because Chinese villages were clustered, even the most distant peasant household typically lived no more than 3 miles from a periodic market—a distance that could be walked comfortably every market day. Even in the most sparsely settled areas of the country, a peasant family would rarely be more than 8 or 9 miles from the closest periodic market.

On market days, traveling merchants, often shouldering their merchandise on tote poles or pushing it along in carts, came to the market and laid out the merchandise in stalls along the main street or in a temple courtyard. Purveyors of services—such as tool sharpeners, dentists, medical doctors, barbers, scribes, and fortunetellers—likewise set up shop. Teashops, eating establishments, and wine houses also opened to serve the gathering crowds. Meanwhile, peasants from the surrounding villages trudged the paths on their way to the market town. Usually, at least one member of every household in the marketing area—that is, the villages served by a standard market—went to the market every market day to sell a chicken or duck, surplus eggs, such grain or vegetables as could be spared, or perhaps handicraft products. At the same time, he bought food, tools, or other goods that the family needed but did not produce.

The standard market was only the lowest rung in a hierarchically ascending marketing system through which goods traveled upward from producers at the local level, and downward from wholesalers to retailers to individual consumers. Above the standard-market towns, in ascending order, were the intermediate-market towns, the central-market town, the local city, and the regional city—each higher level servicing larger marketing areas, performing larger wholesale functions, and handling more specialized and exotic goods than the markets lower in the hierarchy. Intermediate markets, for example, customarily served as the wholesale depots for the itinerant peddlers who worked the standard-market towns. Central-market towns, in turn, served as wholesalers to the intermediate markets. Each higher level market, of course, also served as a standard market for the inhabitants of that standard-marketing area.

A standard market's schedule of market days was never established by happenstance, but was fixed so that there would be minimal conflict with market days in the nearby intermediate markets. This quickly becomes apparent when we trace the route of a peddler whose place of resupply was in the intermediate-market town of Zhonghezhen in Szechwan, just south of Chengtu. Figure 6.2 is a schematic representation of the economic landscape shown in Figure 6.1. On the first day of the ten-day marketing period, our peddler would set up shop in Zhonghezhen. On the second day, he might travel to Huanglongchang; on the third day, go to Shiyangchang; and on the fourth day, return to his base of supply in Zhonghezhen. During the next circuit, he might go to Liulichang (fifth day), Gaodianzi (sixth day), and back to Zhonghezhen (seventh day). Next, he might travel to Daoshiqiao (eighth day), Xindianzi (ninth day), and back to Zhonghezhen (tenth day) for a day of rest before resuming the entire ten-day schedule on the eleventh day.

Two points have to be noted. First, neighboring standard-market towns could share a marketing schedule because residents of one standard-marketing area normally went to only their own standard market (or occasionally the intermediate market). But standard markets virtually never had the same marketing schedule as

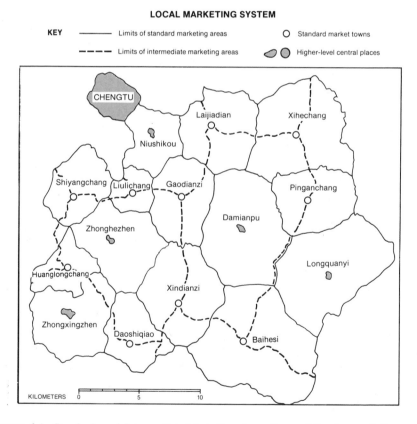

FIGURE 6.1. Standard- and Intermediate-Marketing Areas Located Southeast of Chengtu, Szechwan

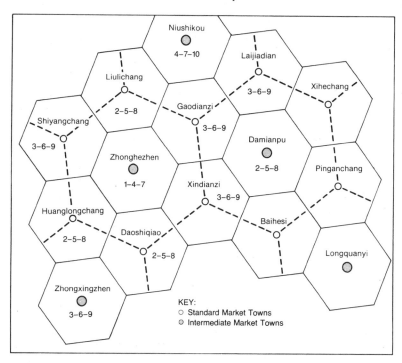

FIGURE 6.2. The Marketing Areas in Figure 6.1 Reduced to Diagrammatic Form
Source: G. William Skinner, "Marketing and Social Structure in Rural China," *Journal of Asian Studies,* 24, no. 1 (November 1964): 25, 28. Reprinted by permission.

the intermediate markets to which they were oriented, because that would have prevented itinerant merchants from maximizing their trading opportunities. Standard markets were customarily oriented around two or three intermediate-market towns; thus as is evident in Figure 6.2, the standard-market town of Gaodianzi was oriented to the three intermediate markets of Zhonghezhen, Damianpu, and Niushikou. (Note that Gaodianzi's schedule of markets on the third, sixth, and ninth days of the ten-day schedule conflicted with the marketing schedule in none of the three intermediate markets.) Second, the siting of six standard markets around each intermediate-market town was a regular feature of the periodic-marketing system, except where this was not feasible because of such topographical features as impassable rivers or valleys that ended in cul-de-sac. This feature was not peculiar to China, but was characteristic of periodic-marketing systems throughout the world, because the arrangement was maximally efficient for both consumers and merchants in largely self-sufficient agrarian societies.

With the passage of time, the relationship and size of standard markets and intermediate markets inevitably changed. As the population grew and the economy became more commercialized, the demands on the marketing structure increased. On the average, about eighteen villages were included in each standard-marketing area, but as the population of that area increased, more and more villages might form around a standard-market town—sometimes reaching as many as forty villages within one standard-marketing area. Particularly during the late imperial period, as the commercial activities of the peasants grew, this placed great strains on the marketing system. For a time, the system responded simply by increasing the number of marketing days within each ten- or twelve-day marketing cycle. Eventually, however, new standard markets tended to emerge—often with the former standard market being transformed into an intermediate market. Although initially a new standard-marketing area might comprise only six or eight villages, an equilibrium would eventually be reached so that the number of villages in that standard-marketing area again approached the average of eighteen.

This proliferation of marketing towns was a nearly constant feature of late imperial times. Occasionally, however, standard-market towns did revert to the status of ordinary villages. In the neighborhood of Ningpo in Chekiang Province, for example, there were 26 rural markets in 1227; by the late nineteenth century, that number had increased to about 170—6 of the original 26 having died, but some 150 having been added. In Szechwan, Jintang *Xian* supported only four markets in 1662; in 1762, it had thirteen; and in 1920, it had thirty-two. Figure 6.3 illustrates this process of market proliferation from the fifteenth to the twentieth century in the vicinity of Shanghai.

Besides its manifest importance to the commercial sector, the periodic-marketing system played a powerful role in molding the contours of society at the local level. Because the average peasant frequently patronized the standard market in his own area, but had minimal exposure to life outside that area, his social horizons and the social influences on him were largely delimited by the borders of his standard-

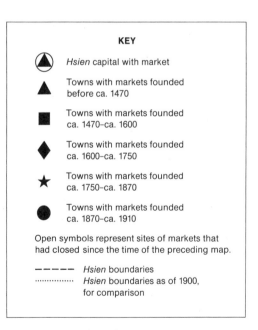
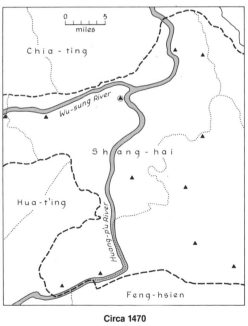

KEY

🔺 (circled) *Hsien* capital with market

🔺 Towns with markets founded before ca. 1470

◼ Towns with markets founded ca. 1470–ca. 1600

◆ Towns with markets founded ca. 1600–ca. 1750

★ Towns with markets founded ca. 1750–ca. 1870

● Towns with markets founded ca. 1870–ca. 1910

Open symbols represent sites of markets that had closed since the time of the preceding map.

– – – – – *Hsien* boundaries
.... *Hsien* boundaries as of 1900, for comparison

Circa 1470
A

FIGURE 6.3. Proliferation of Local Markets in the Vicinity of Shanghai

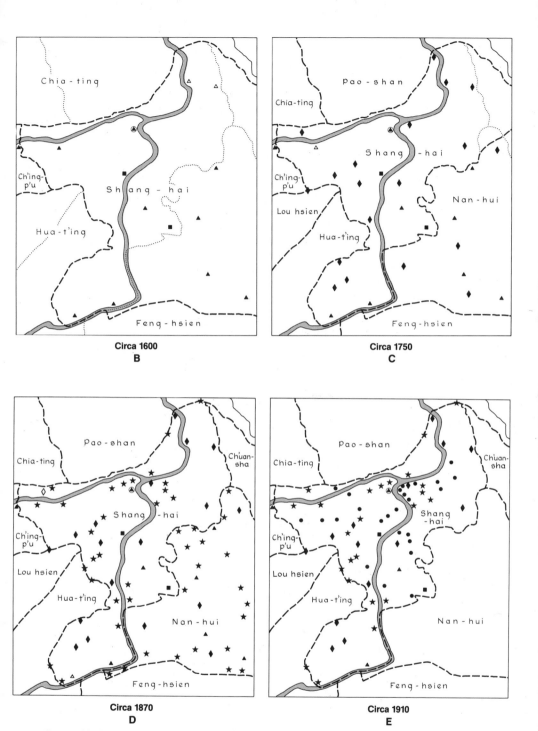

Circa 1600
B

Circa 1750
C

Circa 1870
D

Circa 1910
E

Source: Mark Elvin, ''Market Towns and Waterways: The County of Shang-hai from 1480 to 1910,'' ed. G. William Skinner, in *The City in Late Imperial China* (Stanford, Calif.: Stanford University Press, 1977), pp. 470–71. Reprinted by permission.

Note: Romanization of place names are in Wade-Giles.

marketing area. The people he knew, the customs he observed, the religion he practiced—all tended to be bound to and, in greater or lesser degree, be distinctive of his standard-marketing community. This was his social universe.

All peasants within such an area tended, for instance, to speak a particular dialect, which often differed to some extent from the dialects spoken in neighboring standard-marketing areas. Similarly, the type of straw-hat worn by the peasants and the style of embroidery done by girls preparing hangings for their bridal beds were made uniform within the area as a result of years and even centuries of cultural "inbreeding." Conversely, linkages with other standard-marketing communities tended to be weak. Seldom did peasants marry girls from outside their own area; relations among lineages celebrating a common ancestor—but located in different marketing areas—soon became attenuated; secret-society lodges and religious temples also were organized on the basis of and were largely limited to the standard-marketing area. For the peasants, therefore, each standard-marketing area tended to be a distinctive *culture-bearing* unit.[21]

The Eight Macroregions

A second of Skinner's analytic insights is that of China's eight "macroregions." China, according to Skinner, did not constitute an integrated marketing system because the country was too large, the topography too fragmented, and the system of transportation too inefficient. It was instead divided into eight distinct regions, each of which had but slight commercial intercourse with the others.[22]

The topography of China breaks the nation into eight drainage basins, the boundaries of which are formed by the vast mountain ranges that serve as watersheds (except where rivers cleave through the mountains). In the vastness of China, when transport and commerce were still premodern, these boundaries obstructed regular economic intercourse. Although a modicum of trade among these eight physiographic regions prevented them from being completely isolated from one another, each region formed a natural and virtually self-sufficient economic area. Figure 6.4 shows these eight macroregions and the river systems within them. A comparison with a political map (Figure 6.5) shows that except for the Upper Yangtze region, which more or less corresponded to Szechwan, the regions generally had little relation to political boundaries.

No less important than the distinction among the eight macroregions was the distinction, within each region, between the core and the periphery. The river valleys of each macroregion had, over the course of time, become the foci of all major resources within the macroregion, such as the best arable land, the largest population, transportation nodes, and capital investments. As one traveled outward from these riverine cores to the watershed highlands at the peripheries, the density of these resources thinned out, so that there was less production, wealth, and population; these peripheral areas were also less stable politically.

The greater fertility (and hence the greater productivity, wealth, and population) of the riverine lowlands was partly a consequence of the natural topography of the region, but the distinction between core and periphery was in substantial

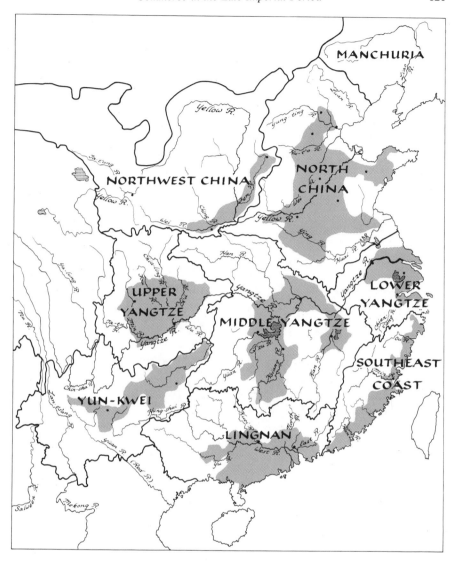

FIGURE 6.4. Physiographic Macroregions of Agrarian China in Relation to Major Rivers, with Regional Cores Indicated by Shading
Source for Figures 6.4 and 6.5: The City in Late Imperial China, ed. G. William Skinner (Stanford: Stanford University Press, 1977), pp. 214–15. Reprinted by permission.

degree wrought by human activities. Wood was the basic building material in China—even more than in other civilizations that used a large amount of stone and brick in their structures. Wood was used not only in residences and shops, but also in large public structures, such as temples, towers, government *yamen* (offices), and covered markets. Through the long course of China's history—as a result of accidental fires, wars, and rebellions—building timbers were reduced to

FIGURE 6.5. Physiographic Macroregion in Relation to Provinces, and Showing Metropolitan Cities, 1843

ash, and trees had to be cut down to provide material for new structures. Initially,
the forests in the lowlands had provided the timber, but woodcutters progressively
had worked their way into the highlands in the peripheral areas. Wood was also
transferred from the highlands to the valleys to be used as charcoal (for example,
in making roofing tiles) and in the manufacture of paper products. In this way,
much of the fertility of the highlands was transferred to the core lowlands. Deforestation resulted also in erosion of the highlands, the topsoil in the peripheries
being washed down to the core zones. The accumulation of both ash and silt

enhanced the productivity of agriculture in the core areas, which in turn influenced the development of cities, commerce, and transportation. The process influenced, that is, the entire pattern of China's historical development.

Because the eight macroregions were isolated from one another, however, they went through cycles of economic development or decline at different times and to different degrees. Thus in the mid-nineteenth century, the Lower Yangtze region, followed closely by Lingnan and the Southeast Coast, was overwhelmingly more commercialized than were the regions in north and west China. These differences point out the difficulties, indeed the dangers, of generalizing about the economy—and, consequently, about the society—of China as a whole. Add to this the discrepancies between the core and the periphery of each macroregion—in the extent of commercialization, prosperity, urbanization rates, and so on—and it soon becomes evident that generalizations drawn from, say, the core of the Lower Yangtze region, might have little relevance for most of the rest of China.[23]

Foreign Trade and the Economics of Silver

Chinese junks, those cumbrous-looking but amazingly efficient sailing vessels, had since before the Tang Dynasty sailed to Japan, Sumatra, Java, and even southern India in the search for gems, pepper, cloves, sandalwood, and exotica for the imperial court. During the Song Dynasty, this trade proliferated, reaching new ports and increasingly including imports of such staples as rice, sugar, and iron ores, and exports of books, porcelains, and fine manufactured goods.

The rulers of the Ming Dynasty, however, were profoundly anticommercial in outlook, and they attempted to restrict this rich and variegated trade by forcing it within the framework of the tributary system. Although the Ming emperors conceived of the tributary system primarily as a means of maintaining diplomatic intercourse, trade was a crucial element in it. Commodities were exchanged, first of all, in the form of gifts between the Chinese emperor and the head of the tributary state. This was the tributary exchange per se, and consisted largely of "local products" and items of curiosity. Second, official members of each tribute mission to China were permitted to engage in a limited amount of buying and selling for personal profit, which trade was usually conducted for three to five days in a fair held at the hostels where members of the tribute mission resided while in Peking. Because the Ming government regarded the trade as a favor to the visitors, no tariffs were levied on either imports or exports; the government also purchased as much as 60 percent of the envoys' merchandise, often paying prices several times the actual value of the goods.

Third, there was a large private trade conducted by merchants traveling with the formal tribute mission. In the case of Japanese tribute missions during the Ming, for example, each tribute ship carried between 150 and 200 merchants—more than half of the entire mission's retinue. These private traders were permitted to transact business in Peking along with the official envoys, but they could also carry on commerce at their port of call—which, in the case of the Japanese, was Ningpo—and along the route to Peking. Foreign traders made immense profits from this trade, but the Ming government strictly limited the number of missions that each tributary state could dispatch to China, perhaps to only once every three, four, or even ten years.

The only foreign trade that was legal during the first 142 years of the Ming Dynasty was that conducted by the tribute missions. But the pressures to trade were enormous. The attraction of the magnificent Chinese empire to foreign traders was irresistible, and the profit-making instincts of the Chinese themselves were too strong to be denied. A substantial foreign trade developed, therefore, outside the tributary framework. This was amusingly revealed in 1493, when the governor-general in Canton complained to Peking about the frequency of tribute missions and the work and expense involved in caring for them. When officials in Peking checked their records, they found that only two tribute missions, from Siam and Champa, had arrived in the previous six years. That is, all the other so-called tribute missions in Canton had actually been private traders in disguise.

The character of China's foreign trade changed radically during the latter half of the Ming period. First, finally recognizing the sizable private trade that was being conducted despite the ban, the emperor in 1509 opened Canton to merchants from the tributary states, even when not accompanying an official mission. Second, the dynasty in 1567 finally opened a port in Fukien to private Chinese merchants who were trading with Southeast Asia. The government did attempt to restrict this trade to about ninety junks a year, however, and it also levied a tariff on the imported goods. This was the period, incidentally, when Chinese began emigrating on a significant scale to the various ports throughout Southeast Asia.

The third major change in China's foreign trade in the sixteenth century was the participation by Europeans. The Portuguese, reaching China in 1514, were the first. Despite their arrogant, violent, and uncouth ways, their trade flourished. At first, they traded at a number of places, including Canton and various Fukienese ports, but gradually after 1535 they concentrated in Macao. Not until 1557, however, did they obtain permission from *local* Chinese authorities to reside there. By the early 1560s, the Portuguese population in that town had reportedly reached about 900 (there were also several thousand Malaccans, Indians, and Africans, although few, if any, Chinese). Eventually, other Europeans challenged the Portuguese preeminence in the China trade, the Spaniards arriving in 1575, the Dutch in 1604, and the British in 1635.

Because of China's large land mass and basic economic self-sufficiency, foreign trade was always peripheral to the economy as a whole. Exports, however large in absolute quantities, never accounted for more than a minuscule portion of total Chinese production, and the vast majority of the Chinese people were not directly affected by this trade. The balance of trade, however, was overwhelmingly in China's favor. From Kyoto to Lisbon to Acapulco, foreigners looked favorably on Chinese goods—especially silk fabrics and raw silk—because of their high quality and moderate prices. Describing Chinese silks shipped to New Spain in the sixteenth century, the historian W. L. Schurz wrote:

> There were delicate gauzes and Cantonese crepes, the flowered silk of Canton, called *primavera* or "springtime" by the Spaniards, velvets and taffetas and the

nobleza or fine damask, rougher grosgrains, and heavy brocades worked in fantastic designs with gold and silver thread. Of silken wearing apparel, there were many thousand pairs of stockings in each cargo—more than 50,000 in one galleon—skirts and velvet bodices, cloaks and robes and kimonos. And packed in the chests of the galleons were silken bed coverings and tapestries, handkerchiefs, tablecloths and napkins, and rich vestments for the service of churches and convents from Sonora to Chile.[24]

In return for such treasures, the foreigners exported to China such merchandise as woolen cloth and gold thread from Europe; copper, sulfur, and swords from Japan; and pepper, coral, and sappanwood (used as a red dyestuff and for medicinal purposes) from Southeast Asia But the market in China for most such goods was small—copper being a significant exception, for it was needed by the state to mint coins. Foreign traders at this time paid for their Chinese purchases largely in silver.

For the Chinese, the inflow of silver that began in the 1530s was more than welcome because their own silver mines were being exhausted as early as the mid-fifteenth century. Exports of the precious metal into China had begun after large silver deposits were discovered in Japan. Much of China's trade with Japan during the sixteenth century was illegal in the eyes of the Ming court, yet so strong was Japan's desire for China's silks, and China's desire for Japan's silver, that no imperial ban could wholly obstruct the traffic. Japanese smugglers penetrated the southern coast of China; Chinese from at least the 1540s sailed to southern Japan; and the Sino-Japanese trade was carried on indirectly by both Chinese and Japanese merchants in the ports of Southeast Asia. Beginning about 1542, too, the Portuguese became an important intermediary in the commerce between the two countries. Describing this trade in the 1580s, an English traveler wrote:

> When the Portugales goe from Macao in China to Japan, they carrie much white Silke, Gold, Muske, and Porcelanes; and they bring from thence nothing but Silver. They have a great Carake which goeth thither every yeere, and shee bringeth from thence every yeere above six hundred thousand crusadoes [or ducats, about 19,500 kilograms]; and all this silver of Japan, and two hundred thousand crusadoes more in silver which they bring yeerly out of India, they imploy to their great advantage in China; and they bring from thence Gold, Muske, Silke, Copper, Porcelanes, and many other things very costly, and gilded.[25]

Because most of the trade between China and Japan was conducted clandestinely, no precise measure of the volume of Japanese silver exported to China in the sixteenth century is available. By one credible estimate, however, the trade during the last forty years of the century averaged between 34,000 and 49,000 kilograms a years. That, however, was a mere beginning. As a result of improved mining technology in Japan and political consolidation by the house of Tokugawa, the Sino-Japanese trade in the early seventeenth century reached unprecedented heights. By conservative estimate, Japan's annual exports of silver from 1615 to 1625, the peak years, averaged between 130,000 and 160,000 kilograms. This amounted to 30 to 40 percent of all the silver then being mined in the world, outside of Japan. Most of it ultimately reached China.

Beginning in 1571, another rich source of silver opened to the Chinese. The Spanish that year established their administrative capital of the Philippines in Manila, and soon thereafter Chinese traders from Kwangtung and Fukien arrived with cargoes of silk, spices, and porcelains. The most valuable of these goods were transshipped to Latin America, where they frequently displaced imports from Europe. As the viceroy of Peru complained to the Spanish king in 1594:

> Chinese merchandise is so cheap and Spanish goods so dear that I believe it impossible to choke off the trade to such an extent that no Chinese wares will be consumed in this realm, since a man can clothe his wife in Chinese silks for two hundred reales (25 pesos), whereas he could not provide her with clothing of Spanish silks with two hundred pesos.[26]

To Chinese merchants in the Philippines, the Spaniards generally paid silver, which came from such fabulously rich South American mines as that of Potosí in Peru—some 58,000 to 86,000 kilograms passing into Chinese hands in a good year in the early seventeenth century. Lesser, but by no means negligible, quantities of Spanish American silver also arrived in China by means of the Portuguese and Dutch traders. These Europeans obtained the silver in Europe, and spent it for Chinese goods in Malacca, Macao, India, and Java. Much of this silver then ended up in China.

During the late sixteenth and early seventeenth centuries, therefore, China was the recipient of large infusions of silver; the combined imports from Japanese, Spanish, and other sources probably averaging on the order of 230,000 kilograms each year. This may be compared with the approximately 345,000 kilograms that were being imported annually from Spanish America to Europe. As in Europe, these silver imports had far-reaching consequences for Chinese life, contributing to a strong inflationary tendency, the increased monetization of the economy, and, through these, an expansion of commercial and manufacturing activity (Chapter 7). By the late sixteenth and early seventeenth centuries, therefore, China (or sizable regions thereof) had become a silver "junkie," addicted to large and steady fixes of the precious metal to maintain an economic high.

Beginning in the 1630s and continuing for fifty years, a series of complex political and economic events caused the supply of silver to dwindle. Marauding Dutch and English privateers preyed on Spanish and Portuguese shipping along the China coast, thereby sharply curtailing China's commerce with silver-rich Iberian states. During the late 1620s and the 1630s, too, the Tokugawa authorities in Japan placed strict restrictions on the foreign trade, banned its subjects from leaving the country, and expelled the Portuguese. In the 1630s, the Spanish king, concerned about the drain of silver to the Far East, also imposed limits on the trade. Most serious of all, however, was the trade embargo imposed by the Chinese themselves, because for over twenty years, from 1661 to 1684, the rulers of the

newly established Qing Dynasty closed all ports from Shantung, in the north, to
Canton, in the south, in order to combat the Ming loyalists based on Taiwan.

The results of these several events were disastrous, contributing to the collapse
of the Ming Dynasty in 1644 and to the economic distress that ravaged the country
during the difficult decades that marked the transition from the late Ming to the
early Qing periods. Symptomatic of China's economic crisis in the mid-seventeenth century was the precipitous fall of prices (Figure 6.6). Although the causes
of this price decline were complex, the dwindling silver supply was probably the
critical variable. By 1684, this crisis was drawing to an end. The Manchus had

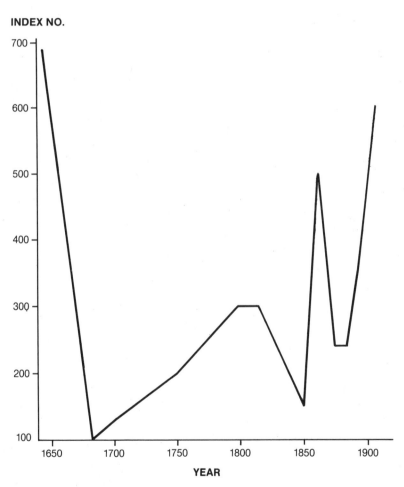

INDEX NO.

YEAR

FIGURE 6.6. The Index Number of Prices in the Qing Period (1682 = 100)
Source: Yeh-chien Wang, ''The Secular Trend of Prices during the Ch'ing Period, 1644–1911,''
Xianggang Zhongwen Daxue Zhongguo Wenhua Yanjiusuo Xuebao (The Journal of the Institute of
Chinese Studies of the Chinese University of Hong Kong), 5, no. 2 (December 1972): 362. Reprinted
by permission.

consolidated their conquest of the empire, and they therefore reopened the coastal ports. Domestically at peace and its foreign trade resumed, China entered a remarkable era of economic prosperity and political stability that lasted until almost the end of the eighteenth century.

With the reopening of foreign trade in 1684, and for nearly a century and a half thereafter, the flow of silver into China, which had been largely stanched for half a century, resumed. During this phase of trade with the West, the Europeans' taste for silks, porcelains, and nankeens remained largely unslaked, but now a new item of Chinese produce entered the trade. This was tea. In 1664, a total of 2 pounds, 2 ounces of the leaf had been imported into England. During the next century, tea became the British national drink, and by the early nineteenth century, the British were consuming some 30 million pounds of Chinese tea each year. So important did the drink become to the culture and economy of Britain that Parliament actually required that a year's supply be kept always in reserve. Tariffs on tea, moreover, produced fully one-tenth of the British government's annual revenue—a circumstance directly related to the Boston Tea Party and the American Revolution.

Because China was the world's only producer of tea during these years and because the Chinese were uninterested in British manufactures, England built up a huge trade imbalance as a result of its China trade. Its chief export product in the eighteenth century—woolen fabrics—found little market in China, where "in cold weather a rich Chinese put on silks and furs, a poor Chinese added padding to his cottons."[27] Indeed, so desperate were the British to sell something, anything, to the Chinese in order to balance the trade that they dumped woolens on the China market, for twenty years at a time taking losses on the sales. The most lucrative British import to China—raw cotton—came not from the home islands, but from India. But China was itself a major cotton producer, and it usually bought the Indian fiber in quantity only when domestic supplies were low. To acquaint the Chinese with English goods and to improve the conditions of trade, London in 1793 sent the Macartney mission to Peking. All that Lord Macartney received for his trouble, however, was Emperor Qianlong's classic reply: "Strange and costly objects do not interest me. As your Ambassador can see for himself we possess all things. I set no value on strange objects and ingenious, and have no use for your country's manufactures."[28]

To obtain their precious tea, therefore, the British paid out large amounts of silver (Table 6.1). Such large remittances of silver to China were particularly painful because Britain did not possess ready sources of silver, as had the Spanish and the Japanese, and mercantilist economic theories then in vogue deplored the nation's loss of bullion. No solution to the problem appeared, however, until the Chinese—with the purposeful enticement of the British—developed an appetite for opium.

Used in China medicinally since the Tang Dynasty, opium was first smoked for pleasure there in the seventeenth century. Quickly recognizing the drug's deleterious effects, the emperor in 1729 banned both its cultivation and its importation. Thereafter and until 1860, opium could be brought into China only by smuggling. At the time of the initial prohibition, some 200 chests (each weighing about

Table 6.1. The Flow of Silver Between
Britain and China (in kilograms)*

Periods	Amounts of Silver (outflows from China indicated by minus signs)
1681–1690	7,100
1691–1700	5,200
1701–1710	28,800
1711–1720	236,400
1721–1730	85,700
1731–1740	94,700
1741–1750	24,000
1751–1760	15,500
1761–1770	127,800
1771–1780	283,300
1781–1790	615,400
1791–1800	193,200
1801–1810	998,500
1811–1820	372,000
1821–1830	−85,500
1831–1840	−371,600

Sources: Hsin-pao Chang, *Commissioner Lin and the Opium War* (Cambridge, Mass.: Harvard University Press, 1964), p. 41. Reprinted by permission.
*Taels converted to kilograms based on 1 kilogram = 26.7 taels.

140 pounds) were imported annually, but that figure increased to about 4,500 chests in 1800, to 19,000 chests in the 1820s, and to 40,000 chests on the eve of the Opium War.

The growth of the opium trade completely altered China's international balance of payments. Since the beginning of the European trade in the early sixteenth century, the flow of silver had favored China. But some 300 years later, the tide began to turn. Data on the flow of silver during these years are still woefully unreliable, but several sources suggest that the year 1826 was the turning point, when China became a net exporter of silver. Soon the precious metal flowed from the country in torrents. By one estimate—the numbers may not be precisely accurate, but they suggest the general trend—China's net import of silver from 1801 to 1826 totaled 1.9 million kilograms, but from 1827 to 1849, the net outflow was 3.3 million kilograms.

This drain of silver contributed to a severe economic crisis, worse even than the depression in the first four decades of the Qing Dynasty. The stimulating effects of the silver inflow during the eighteenth century were now reversed and were followed by a period of business recession and economic distress. Prices plummeted, falling some 50 percent between 1815 and 1850 (Figure 6.6). During those thirty-five years, the real burden of the land tax approximately doubled, because peasants (whose incomes were derived largely in copper cash) had to pay the land tax in scarce silver. Thus whereas in 1800, they had to pay about 1,000 cash to meet a tax obligation of 1 tael of silver, by 1850, they had to pay slightly over 2,000 cash.

The loss of silver to the foreigners may, in fact, have been only one of several causes of the economic crisis and the depreciation of copper cash. Throughout the early nineteenth century, for instance, both government mints and forgers had been debasing the cash by reducing the amount of copper in and the weight of their coins. Widespread hoarding of the more valuable silver also exacerbated the shortage of silver. But because Chinese in the 1830s were unfamiliar with—or perhaps chose to ignore—Gresham's Law ("Bad money drives out good"), they angrily blamed the crisis entirely on the foreigners and the opium trade. Although in this they were only partly right, it is patent that the drain of silver resulting from the opium trade seriously damaged the Chinese economy, contributed to the outbreak in 1839 of China's first war with the European powers, and was one cause of the devastating Taiping Rebellion (1851–64).

The State and Commerce: The Brokerage System

Like the Confucian ideology, the Qing government's policies toward merchants and commerce were profoundly ambivalent. They were marked, for example, by three seemingly irreconcilable characteristics:

> 1. *Supportive.* The late imperial government viewed trade both as essential to the public well-being and as a source of revenue. It was concerned, therefore, to ensure the free flow of goods, to create an environment conducive to trading activity, and to guarantee that prices were fair and stable. To do this, it endeavored, for example, to enforce equitable prices, maintain proper business practices, and ensure that each major business enterprise was financially sound.
>
> 2. *Extractive and Repressive.* The wealth of merchants was to officials like catnip to a cat. Mercantile success was an open invitation to governmental intervention, and every sizable, profit-making enterprise became a target of governmental control, taxation, or squeeze—and sometimes of all three. According to the historian Etienne Balazs, "Officials [used] every means of keeping the merchant class down. . . . If [an enterprise] had reached a stage where it could no longer be suppressed, the state laid hands on it, took it under control, and appropriated the resultant profits." [29]
>
> 3. *Indifferent and Neglectful.* The government was not interested in maintaining the infrastructure of trade. The dynasties neglected, as discussed earlier, to enforce a uniform system of weights and measures, to develop a national system of banking, or even to maintain adequate roads and bridges. They also failed to institute a system of commercial and corporate law that would have provided protection of property rights and guaranteed the faithful performance of contracts.

What was the reason for these contradictions in government policy? The answer, I believe, is that they resulted during late imperial times from a distinctive approach to the tasks of local administration. This approach might be called "the brokerage concept of administration." [30]

A broker is an intermediary between two or more parties to a transaction whose function is to facilitate the transaction by helping negotiate a price agreeable to the parties and to guarantee that the terms of the government are faithfully carried out. For these services, the broker customarily receives a commission or some other form of remuneration. During the late imperial period, the government's use of ''brokers''—intermediaries or agents—typified the state's relationship with not just the commercial sector, but also other large segments of society.

The functioning of the brokerage concept was exemplified in the nation's domestic trade by the *yahang,* or wholesale brokers. These brokers had come into existence sometime before the Tang Dynasty, when the volume of interregional trade was still small and itinerant merchants thus had no need to establish permanent stores or facilities in the various market towns. These ''guest merchants'' were usually unfamiliar with the local dialects, customs, and trading conditions, but the brokers, being natives of the region, were able to help them purchase local products, find customers for the goods they sold, and hire boats, animals, or porters to transport their wares.

The merchants, being outsiders, were often totally dependent on the brokers, who could easily take advantage of their ignorance of local conditions. To protect the traders from these voracious brokers, the Song government instituted a system of licensed brokers, selected for their wealth and honesty, who alone would be permitted to serve as agents in wholesale transactions involving major agricultural and handicraft commodities, such as rice, tea, wine, textiles, and cattle. The Ming and Qing dynasties inherited this system, which greatly proliferated with increased commercialization.

The licensed brokers had manifold responsibilities, which included facilitating the trade of the merchants, protecting the consuming public, and serving the government. They thus provided transportation, warehouse, and lodging facilities to their client merchants; mediated between buyers and sellers; provided accurate weights and measures; and ascertained that the terms of the transactions were faithfully carried out by both sellers and buyers. They also safeguarded against collusion between buyers and sellers, thus protecting consumers from artificially inflated prices. And as agents of the government, brokers were also responsible for policing the conduct of their clients and for keeping records of all transactions, including (1) the names, native places, and routes traversed by the merchants, and (2) the prices and amounts of goods exchanged. In addition, the brokers often collected, on behalf of the government, taxes on goods passing through their agencies. At the same time, most of the brokers were wealthy merchants who traded on their own account.

Scholars who stress the extractive and repressive aspects of the government's policies argue that the state's primary, if not only, interest in commerce was as a source of revenue. In the case of the wholesale-brokerage system, however, it is significant that throughout most of the Ming and Qing periods, the central government purposely denied itself a large potential revenue from the sale of brokers' licenses. Brokers were, it is true, required to purchase licenses and periodically thereafter pay a fee to renew them. But the charge for licenses, initially at least, was not extortionate: the average fee paid by 179,000 brokerage firms throughout the empire in 1733, for example, was merely 1.07 taels. The dynasties' primary interest in the brokers, therefore, was less to raise money than to regulate the commercial sector.

From the mid-nineteenth century onward, however, the government increasingly looked on the brokers as revenue producers. Since the burgeoning of commercial activity after the sixteenth century, there had been far more aspirants to the lucrative role of broker than the official quotas allowed, and local officials had frequently sold licenses "illegally," beyond the fixed quotas, in order to raise money for local-government treasuries or for personal profit. During the Taiping Rebellion, the provincial governments became desperate for money and saw the sale of additional brokers' licenses as a rich source of revenue. The provincial governments therefore raised the quotas for the number of legal brokers and increased the number of commodities that were subject to official brokerage. Herbal medicines, for example, had long been traded without government intervention, but Hupei Province in 1856 brought it under the government-licensed brokerage system.

Not until after the Boxer Uprising, however, did revenue raising become the dominant function of the wholesale-brokerage system. As a result of the extravagant claims of the Boxer indemnity and of the heavy expenses of its new programs of political, military, and educational modernization, the Qing government was experiencing a severe fiscal crisis. One of the many ways that the government now raised revenues was by sharply increasing the rates of the taxes collected for it by the brokers. The change in official policy toward commerce generally, as well as toward the wholesale-brokerage system, is suggested by the fact that the government in 1908 derived approximately 65 percent of its revenue from commercial taxes, whereas in 1753, only about 26 percent had come from the commercial sector. The land tax, which made up the remaining share of the tax revenue, had actually doubled between 1753 and 1908, but the taxes on the commercial sector had concurrently increased almost tenfold.

By the 1930s, the wholesale-brokerage system had degenerated into nothing more than a system of tax farming, in which brokerage licenses were auctioned off to the highest bidders. The brokers then pocketed whatever money they collected over and above the commissions and taxes that the government authorized them to charge on a broad range of wholesale transactions.

Salt merchants and the *hong* merchants in the foreign trade at Canton were other examples of the brokerage concept of administration. In these trades during much of the Qing Dynasty, the government recognized a limited number of wealthy merchant middlemen—approximately thirteen *hong* merchants at Canton and, in the salt monopoly, about thirty "factory merchants" on the production side and another thirty "head merchants" on the distribution side. These merchant middlemen, like the licensed brokers in the domestic wholesale trade, were responsible for facilitating the flow of goods from seller to buyer, maintaining standards of quality, providing uniform weights and measures, policing merchant conduct, and often collecting taxes on behalf of the state. In performing these quasi-official functions, the *hong* and salt merchants often became fabulously wealthy. The Wu family of *hong* merchants, for example, had by the 1830s amassed a fortune of Mex$26 million, which was probably the largest personal fortune in the world at the time. And the salt merchants at Yangchow became famous for patronizing scholarship and the arts, for constructing gardens of breathtaking beauty, and for frittering away fortunes in luxurious and ostentatious living. At the same time, however, the salt and *hong* merchants were the targets of sometimes crushing official exactions and bureaucratic peculation.

The brokerage concept of administration was not limited to the commercial sector. In government at the local level, the broad gap between the bureaucracy at the *xian* level and the commoners in the villages and towns was bridged by the "gentry" and other local elites, who constituted a level of "subbureaucratic" or "informal" administration. These elites were not actually licensed by the government, of course, but the government expected them, and sometimes appointed them, to mediate between it and local society, often consulting with them in *ya-men* offices on questions of local administration. In their role as community leaders, they constructed and maintained various forms of public works, such as bridges, waterways, schools, and irrigation projects; promoted and managed welfare and relief activities, such as charity granaries and cemeteries, orphanages, and widows' homes; and established and supported schools and other educational organizations.

Like the brokers in the commercial sector, the local elites were generally well remunerated for their brokerage services. Sometimes, they were paid wages or fees for managing granaries, directing the construction of irrigation projects, and the like; other times, they received income from special surcharges that the government tacked onto the basic land tax in order to pay for those projects. About 17 percent of all gentry income in the late nineteenth century came from these brokerage services.

Chinese governments of the late imperial period employed the brokerage concept of administration as an alternative to the concept of direct bureaucratic controls, which had been the prevailing mode of local administration until about the tenth century. During the early Tang Dynasty, for example, the imperial bureaucracy had attempted to administer the agricultural sector quite minutely through the *Juntian,* or equal-field, system, which predicated that lands would be distributed according to family size and would periodically be subject to reallocation. In the commercial sector, the government strictly regulated all trade in the nation's major markets, where officials were directly responsible for controlling prices, preventing unscrupulous business practices, ensuring the quality of the currency, and maintaining uniform weights and measures. Officials were also responsible for developing and maintaining roads and waterways.

With the commercial revolution of the late Tang and the Song dynasties, and the increase of population during the same period, the tasks of administration exceeded the imperial government's administrative capabilities. As Ye Shi (d. 1223) in the late Song Dynasty remarked, the government was no longer able effectively to control the merchants because of the rapid growth of commercial activity. More recently, a historian also observed that "oppressive and restrictive policies towards commerce which had been traditional since Han times were by the tenth century either dead or dying. *A totally new orientation for state economic policies was the inevitable result.*"[31]

This new orientation, whereby the government relaxed its bureaucratic grip in the economic field, was evident in other areas of administration as well. Indeed, the concept of limited government and the corollary idea that local elites should provide leadership at the local level were given ideological sanction by Song Neo-Confucianism. Zhu Xi and his philosophical descendants seem to have believed that direct governmental rule, through laws and regulations, was less efficacious as a way of creating a well-ordered society than was the exemplary moral conduct of society's leaders.

At least partly as a consequence of this ideological concept of limited government, the realms of Chinese life that were not directly subject to bureaucratic intervention gradually broadened over the course of the next several centuries. There was "a long-term secular trend beginning in the T'ang whereby the degree of official involvement in local affairs—not only in marketing and commerce but also in social regulation (e.g., dispute resolution) and administration itself—steadily declined, a retrenchment forced by the growing scale of empire."[32] Still, the empire had to be governed; there was an irreducible minimum of social and economic activity that needed some form of regulation and direction. The government's use of local-elite leadership, what we here call the brokerage system, was the late imperial solution to this administrative problem.

The contradictions in the government's policies in the commercial sector become comprehensible when seen as the result of this mode of administration. There was indeed *neglect* of the infrastructure of commerce because the government had consciously abdicated responsibility for that area of social life. There was indeed *support* for the well-being of both merchants and the common people; official ideology dictated such a paternalistic concern, even though the limited capabilities of dynastic administration prevented that concern from being strongly reflected in actual policy. And there was *extraction and repression*—of the common merchants by the brokers, who undertook their mediating role as self-engrossing entrepreneurs; and of the brokers by the bureaucrats, who viewed these rich but virtually defenseless middlemen as easily exploitable sources of revenue.

All the ambivalences in the government's administration of commerce were likewise evident in the brokerage system of local administration. There, too, the government was neglectful of basic social and economic functions; there, too, it was concerned for the welfare of the toiling peasants; and there, too, it often tolerated the cruel exploitation of those peasants. These features of imperial rule in local administration are so familiar that we seldom feel perplexed by the evident contradictions. Those contradictions were inherent to the brokerage system of administration and thus were of a piece with the ambivalences of government policy in the commercial sector.

Selected Readings

(See also the works cited in the notes)

Atwell, William S. "Notes on Silver, Foreign Trade, and the Late Ming Economy." *Ch'ing-shih Wen-t'i* 3, no. 8 (December 1977): 1–33.

Hao, Yen-p'ing. *The Commercial Revolution in Nineteenth-Century China: The Rise of Sino-Western Mercantile Capitalism*. Berkeley: University of California Press, 1986.

Iwao, Seiichi. "Japanese Foreign Trade in the 16th and 17th Centuries." *Acta Asiatica* 30 (1976): 1–18.

King, Frank H. H. *Money and Monetary Policy in China, 1845–1895*. Cambridge, Mass.: Harvard University Press, 1965.

McElderry, Andrea. *Shanghai Old-Style Banks (Ch'ien-chuang), 1800–1935*. Ann Arbor: University of Michigan, Center for Chinese Studies, 1976.

Mann, Susan. "Finance in Ningpo: The 'Ch'ien-chuang,' 1750–1880." In *Economic Organization in Chinese Society*, ed. W. E. Willmott, pp. 47–77. Stanford, Calif.: Stanford University Press, 1972.

Metzger, Thomas A. "The State and Commerce in Imperial China." *Asian and African Studies* 6 (1970): 23–46.

Morse, Hosea Ballou. *The Trade and Administration of the Chinese Empire*. London: Longmans, Green, 1908.

Rowe, William T. *Hankow: Commerce and Society in a Chinese City, 1796–1889*. Stanford, Calif.: Stanford University Press, 1984.

Schran, Peter. "A Reassessment of Inland Communications in Late Ch'ing China." *Ch'ing-shih Wen-t'i* 3, no. 10 (December 1978): 28–48.

Transport in Transition: The Evolution of Traditional Shipping in China, trans. Andrew Watson. Ann Arbor: University of Michigan, Center for Chinese Studies, 1972.

Wang, Yeh-chien. "Evolution of the Chinese Monetary System, 1644–1855." *Conference on Modern Chinese Economic History*, pp. 469–96. Taipei: Academia Sinica, Institute of Economics, 1977.

———. "The Secular Trend of Prices during the Ch'ing Period (1644–1911)." *Xianggang Zhongwen Daxue Zhongguo Wenhua Yenjiusuo Xuebao* (Journal of the Institute of Chinese Studies of the Chinese University of Hong Kong) 5, no. 2 (December 1972): 347–68.

7

Manufacturing in the Late Imperial Period: A Failed Industrial Revolution?

Mao Tse-tung in 1939 wrote: ''As China's feudal society developed its commodity economy and so carried within itself the embryo of capitalism, China would of herself have developed slowly into a capitalist society even if there had been no influence of foreign imperialism.''[1] Guided by this pronunciamento, historians in China have attempted to find evidence to corroborate the chairman's historical insight; and since the 1950s, they have published numerous works purporting to show that ''sprouts of capitalism'' had indeed emerged during the late Ming and early Qing dynasties. With hundreds of quotations drawn from poems, literary essays, and the dynastic histories, they attempt to prove the existence of factory manufacturing, a free market in labor, the commercialization of agriculture, and the growth of urban centers of trade and manufacturing.

In the end, of course, these ''sprouts'' never matured into modern industrial capitalism. The first setback, the Communist historians assert, occurred in the mid-seventeenth century when the rebel Li Zicheng led an antifeudal coalition of discontented peasants and workers against the Ming Dynasty. If this rebellion had been successful, it would have created a political regime serving the interests of the emergent bourgeoisie, much as appeared in France following the Revolution of 1789. At the last moment, however, the feudal forces (represented by Wu Sangui and his cohorts), desperate to preserve their economic and political interests, allied with the barbarian Manchus to obliterate the progressive forces under Li Zicheng. The result was the retardation of the growth of capitalist sprouts for over a half century.

But the forces of history could not be permanently repressed, these historians contend, and in the early Qing, the process of capitalistic production again picked up momentum, reaching even higher levels of industrialization than during the late Ming. This time, the Taiping rebels of the mid-nineteenth century represented the progressive force that nearly overturned the oppressive feudal system. But then

136

foreign imperialism joined with the feudalistic Qing forces, and once again, the full flowering of modern capitalism was impeded.

Western historians have been critical of the Communist historians' search for capitalistic sprouts. They regard the effort as being ideologically motivated, attempting to force Chinese realities into conformity with the Marxist model, which was formed on the basis of a nineteenth-century interpretation of the European historical experience.They also believed that the Communist historians' evidence only weakly supports the contention that China from the sixteenth through the eighteenth century was embarking on the road to industrialization. "Most of the 132 references to workshops that have been culled from eighteenth- and early nineteenth-century literary sources," remarks a leading economic historian, "are brief and imprecise and at best refer to enterprises that were very small and served a limited local market." Moreover, "the internal organization of these enterprises so far as we can tell showed no significant departures from the manufactories of the T'ang and Sung periods; the technology of the workshops was entirely traditional." [2]

Although most Western historians tend to dismiss the Communists' research on capitalistic sprouts as mere political polemic—and it must be admitted that the claim that the rebel Li Zicheng represented a progressive bourgeois force does strain credulity—the sixteenth to eighteenth centuries (except from about 1630 to 1683) were a time of tremendous economic vitality and social change. Whether the developments during these centuries did in fact augur the emergence of capitalism, precisely as known in the West, may be debated. Still, the developments in China during those centuries were remarkably similar to those in England during the century and a half before the 1760s and the onset of the Industrial Revolution. Is it possible that China was also making a breakthrough to industrialization?

The "Sprouts" of Industrialism

In seeking an answer to this question, it is essential that we not misconstrue the manner in which modern industrialization developed in the West. Economic change and industrial development during the seventeenth and early eighteenth centuries in England was extremely slow and uncertain. During this period, when sprouts of capitalism" were indisputably appearing in England, manufacturing output rarely grew as a result of using new technologies, but rather as a result of maximizing the potential of medieval techniques. The textile industry, for example, which became the leading edge of the Industrial Revolution, remained basically a cottage industry into the late eighteenth century. The Lombe silk factory, it is true, was established at Derby in 1724; it employed over 300 women and children and used water-powered machinery. Yet after only a decade in operation, the factory folded. Subsequently, a few large clothiers near Leeds operated "factories" with as many as twenty looms. But they were atypical; even as late as the early nineteenth century, the mill at New Lanark—which employed 2,000 workers—was a rarity. Indeed, on the eve of the Industrial Revolution, textile production was still scattered and rural. "Nor, outside the ribbon industry, did progress as yet owe much to mechanization."[3] John Kay had invented a flying shuttle in 1730, and Lewis Paul, a spinning machine—inventions that doubled the output of weavers and spinners. Yet neither of these inventions was put to practical use for several generations. Indeed, the advances leading to the Industrial Revolution were only occasionally attributable to discoveries—such as mechanical spinning or coke smelting—which required long periods of gestation to have an aggregate effect on the system as a whole. Rather,

> even the marked industrial expansion of the 1750s was achieved largely within the confines of the traditional economic organization: essentially, by multiplying the number of existing units of production and applying doses of fresh labour, and by borrowing processes (like dyeing) that were not in themselves new but added substantially to the profitability of the textile industries.[4]

New techniques of organization (such as the greater division of labor and the increased integration of production and marketing through the putting-out system) and incremental changes in technology were, of course, being applied during the century or so preceding England's Industrial Revolution. But these were mere sprouts hidden amid the still heavy foliage of the old society, and if England had not moved on to the Industrial Revolution would hardly have been regarded as more noteworthy by historians than have been the sprouts in China's past. England's industrial sprouts were, moreover, extremely frail. Economic crises in the 1620s and 1690s, and the long slowdown from the 1720s to the 1740s, revealed that the further development of mechanized factory production and the expansion of commodity markets were not inevitable. "Always the forces of mobility and growth were balanced against the forces of inertia, the forces of enterprise against those of custom. This was still so in 1763."[5] In England, of course, the forces of growth won out. In China during the sixteenth through eighteenth centuries, much the same contest of forces was taking place. But there, the forces of inertia ultimately prevailed.

The burgeoning of the Chinese economy beginning in the sixteenth century came in the wake of some three centuries of widespread economic stagnation. The devastation that resulted from the Mongol invasion in the thirteenth century; the deadly assault of the plague in the mid-fourteenth century (perhaps the same Black Death that ravaged Europe after 1347); the worldwide cooling trend associated with the Spörer minimum from about 1450 to 1540, which reduced farm productivity almost as much as the Maunder minimum did in the 1630s and 1640s; and, finally, the isolationist policy adopted during the early years of the Ming, which strangled an active overseas trade—these four factors probably combined to send the economy into a spiraling decline after the centuries of prosperity during the Song Dynasty (960–1279). Symptomatic of this economic depression was the sharp decline of population, from about 110 million in 1200 to possibly only 65 to 80 million at the beginning of the Ming.

Why the economy in much of the empire revived in the sixteenth century can only be surmised. The return of warmer weather following the Spörer minimum was presumably one factor. Also, Ming policies at this time were notably conducive to economic growth: laws and regulations were favorable to merchants; taxes were light; the system of hereditary occupations for certain artisans, salt producers, and soldiers ceased to exist in all but name; and the government increasingly patronized private manufacturers, rather than relying on corvée labor, to produce such goods as porcelain for the imperial court. The large infusion of silver into the Chinese economy from Japan and Spanish America, discussed in Chapter 6, was probably another critical stimulant to China's economic vitality after the mid-sixteenth century.

Whatever the causes of the economic effervescence, cities grew, agriculture became commercialized, and various areas specialized in manufactures that were purveyed throughout the nation. This spurt of prosperity and economic development, which lasted for almost 200 years, ceased from 1630 to 1683, the years of dynastic transition.[6] But then, until about the 1770s, the economy again leaped ahead, this time to even new heights. All these trends were especially evident in three zones within the eastern crescent: Kiangnan (the area in the lower Yangtze delta, encompassing portions of the provinces of Kiangsu, Anhwei, and Chekiang), the coastal areas of Fukien and Kwangtung, and along the Grand Canal extending to Peking.

One of the first signs of economic change was the increased monetization of the economy. The growing use of money was evident in the government's decision to commute the existing taxes, which were paid in labor services, to payment in silver. This policy began gradually in the early fifteenth century and was extended and made more uniform as money became more abundant during the sixteenth century, when it was known as the Single-Whip Tax Reform. The reform served in turn, as a stimulus to further monetization, because the government had to pay silver to the people who provided it with goods and services, such as construction workers, police and military forces, and postal attendants. The reform also forced the people, as never before, to produce goods for the market because they had to acquire silver to pay their taxes—a situation described by a couplet written in the late Ming period:

> Yesterday a tax was imposed forcefully;
> Today a multitude is selling yarn on the street.[7]

As no other single measure, the Single-Whip Tax Reform sounded the death knell to whatever remnants of a "natural," or barter, economy remained in late imperial China.

The rapid population growth that began in the early Ming period may also have nudged the economy into a new path of development. Much of the natural population growth during this time was in the southern half of the eastern crescent, where the demographic pressures caused farms to become smaller and rents and taxes to rise. To maintain a livelihood, peasants took up sideline occupations, which, like the Single-Whip Tax Reform, contributed to the growing tendency to produce for the market.

Accompanying the population increase and the gradual breakdown of the manorial system was the growth of the cities. Peasants who were not tied to the land—

and in the sixteenth century, they constituted the large majority of the peasantry—were free to leave the villages. Landlords, as we have seen, also moved in significant numbers to the cities during the sixteenth century—a trend described as the "urbanization of the landlord class."[8] Thus established urban centers such as Soochow, Hangchow, Nanking, and Canton expanded and became more prosperous. A late Ming gazetteer remarked, for instance, that Hangchow early in the century had been sparsely populated, but by mid-century had become crowded. Soochow by the late sixteenth century had become one of the largest cities in the empire, its shops spilling out for 20 *li* (nearly 7 miles) beyond the city walls. And the capital, Peking, which grew from about 600,000 in 1450 to about 1 million in 1825, was for about three centuries the largest or second largest municipality in the world—possibly exceeded only during the period of interdynastic upheaval in the seventeenth century by Constantinople, and in the eighteenth century by Edo (Tokyo).

More striking still was the growth of rural towns into urban centers of commerce and handicrafts. Shengze, in the center of the silk-producing region along Lake Tai, for example, grew from a village with 50 to 60 households to a city with 50,000 residents in the late Ming; by the mid-eighteenth century, it had grown "a hundred-fold." Songjiang, virtually depopulated in the 1550s because of pirate raids, became a major center of the cotton-textile industry within just two to three decades. And Wuhu, upstream from Nanking on the Yangtze, grew into a crowded center of trade in textiles and paper. The examples could be multiplied many times.

Although the expansion of cities was partly attributable to the general population growth of the period, the principal stimulus to urban growth came from the increasing commercialization. Progressively during the late Ming, local self-sufficiency was breaking down, and various regions began to specialize in the production of higher value crops or commodities for both local and distant markets. About 90 percent of China's sugar in the sixteenth century, for instance, was produced in the provinces of Kwangtung and Fukien; much of the cultivable land in northern Chekiang was turned over to mulberry bushes for silkworm cultivation. Cotton was the big cash crop in large parts of Shantung, Honan, and Hopei; in the lower Yangtze region, Songjiang and Soochow prefectures were especially famous as centers of cotton production.

Those who specialized in cash crops, in turn, purchased food, tools, and clothing on the market for their own use. Fully 70 percent of the consumption goods in six prefectures in Shantung, for instance, came from the Kiangnan area. A huge trade in rice also developed to supply food to areas specializing in commercial crops. Each year, Kwangtung sent thousands of shiploads of rice to Quanzhou in Fukien, which in the sixteenth century had become a sugar-producing center. A late Ming gazetteer tells of the dependence of Jiading (near Shanghai) on outside sources of supply:

> Our county does not produce rice, but relies for its food upon other areas. When the summer wheat is reaching ripeness and the autumn crops are already rising, the boats of the merchants that come loaded with rice form an unbroken line.

. . . If by any chance there were to be an outbreak of hostilities . . . such that the city gates did not open for ten days, and the hungry people raised their voices in clamor, how could there fail to be riot and disorder.[9]

Given impetus by this growing commercialization, the periodic-marketing system expanded. In Zhangzhou prefecture (Fukien), which served as a major entrepôt in the overseas trade, for instance, the number of periodic markets increased from eleven in 1491 to sixty-five in 1628, a rise of nearly 500 percent—a rate far exceeding the growth of population during the same period. An expansion of the marketing system was also evident in Shantung along the Grand Canal, where in Donge *Xian,* the periodic markets increased from ten in 1550, to seventeen in 1600, to twenty-seven in 1700. Not all areas of the country were affected equally by the increasing commercialization, however, and the proliferation of periodic markets was, therefore, not uniform. Sections of the country in the remote interior were probably less affected by the growing commercialization and specialized production for the market. Even in Shanghai *Xian*—although located near the coast—the periodic-marketing system developed most rapidly only in the nineteenth century, a result of Shanghai's development as a treaty port following the Opium War (Figure 6.3).

An integral part of this process of commercialization was the growth of the manufacturing sector. Silk fabrics, for example, were among China's oldest and most important manufactures, and in earlier times, as during the Song Dynasty, sericulture had been practiced virtually everywhere in the empire. During the latter decades of the sixteenth century, however, as the industry became specialized and professionalized, it became concentrated in Kiangnan, especially near Lake Tai.

The size of production units in the Kiangnan silk industry ranged from individual households to sizable factories. Much of the preliminary work—such as feeding the silkworms and reeling the silk from the cocoons—was usually done separately by peasant families. Weaving, particularly of the finer quality fabrics, was a more complex operation and was often done in workshops that contained twenty to forty looms. The scale of operations of these shops was therefore at least comparable with that of Britain's textile factories on the eve of the Industrial Revolution. The largest weaving facilities were imperial silk works, three of which produced the bulk of the fine silks for the government. One of them, the silk work at Soochow, housed 173 looms and employed more than 500 workers during the late Ming; by the early Qing (1685), it had expanded to 800 looms and 2,330 workers. The extent of the silk industry is suggested by the 30,000 satin looms, not to mention looms used for silk fabrics of lesser quality, in Nanking during the eighteenth century. Indeed, the silk-weaving industry then was larger than it was at the end of the nineteenth century.

Other sectors of the manufacturing economy likewise displayed an impressive dynamism and scale of operations. The kilns at Jingdezhen (in Kiangsi), for instance, produced some of the finest porcelains in the world; translucent whites and blues that caught the fancy of royalty from Peking to London and whose beauty still stuns the art world. So vast were the porcelain works at Jingdezhen that at night, the 500-odd furnaces appeared to be "a great city all on fire, or a vast furnace with a great many vent-holes."[10] Ironworks were also found on a large scale. In the late eighteenth century, the smelters in the northwest (along the border of Hupei, Shensi, and Szechwan border) were described as being

> seventeen or eighteen feet in height. . . . More than ten artisans are hired to serve each furnace. The largest numbers of men are needed for transporting timber and building the (charcoal) kilns in the Black Hills, and for opening up seams and extracting ore from the Red Hills. The distances which the ore and charcoal have to be taken vary, but over a hundred men are required for each furnace. Thus six or seven furnaces will give employment to not less than a thousand men. Once the iron has been cast into slabs it is sometimes manufactured locally into pots and farm tools. A thousand and several hundreds of men are also required for this work and for the transport (of the goods). Thus the larger ironworks in Szechwan and the other provinces regularly have two thousand to three thousand persons, and the smaller ones with but three or four furnaces well over a thousand.[11]

Our source does not reveal the output of these numerous furnaces, but another smelter in the eighteenth century, employing 1,000 workers (including the miners, charcoal burners, and other supporting laborers), reportedly turned out 2.5 tons of pig iron a day. This compared favorably with an English ironworks in the seventeenth century, which produced 2 to 3 tons a day.

The largest manufacturing sector in late traditional China was cotton textiles. This sector continued, as in preindustrial England, to be predominantly a domestic occupation, revealing both the potential for and the obstacles to industrialization.

Chinese had known of cotton since about 200 B.C., but during the early centuries, they generally clothed themselves in linens woven from the long-fibred ramie and hemp plants—although silk was by no means uncommon, except among the very poor. By the late thirteenth century, improved varieties of cotton plants had evolved, and new techniques of ginning, carding, and spinning the short cotton fibers had been introduced. Because an acre planted to cotton produces about ten times as much fiber as does an acre of hemp, and because of the superior characteristics of cotton cloth, cotton by the late Ming Dynasty had become China's principal source of clothing.

Most cotton fabrics, especially of the plain and rough variety, were produced in family households, usually by peasant women, children, and the aged, for whom the work was subsidiary to their main task of farming. Whenever possible—and to an extent not at all evident in preindustrial Europe—they performed all stages of the work, from growing and carding the raw cotton through spinning and weaving the cloth, to tailoring it into clothes for the family's own use. Integration of the entire process within a household was possible because the equipment required little capital investment, the work was sufficiently simple that even girls of nine or ten years of age and old women with bound feet could perform it, and the work did not require continual attention (as did silk weaving), so that it could be accomplished in the family's spare time. Equipment for spinning, for example, was often crude in the extreme, bearing only a vague resemblance to the carefully crafted spinning wheels with which museum-going Americans are familiar. The

FIGURE 7.1. A Two-Spindle Spinning Wheel, Late-Nineteenth Century. Photo courtesy
The Peabody Museum, Salem, Mass.

simplest device for spinning consisted of merely a spindle suspended from the
ceiling; the spinner set in it motion with a hand and then twisted the cotton roving
into yarn. Somewhat more common was a foot-treadle spinning wheel, crudely
made of sticks and twine. More sophisticated spinning wheels with three, four, or
even five spindles did exist—and they produced yarn several times faster than did
anything used by English spinners before Richard Arkwright patented his water
frame in 1769—although they required an expertise that most people who produced for only a family's own use did not possess. Looms were rather more
complex and expensive pieces of equipment. Yet according to a famous seventeenth-century work describing the technology of that era, even looms could be
found "in every tenth household." [12]

Although many families continued to produce cotton fabrics for their own use
well into the twentieth century, a significant part of the industry became specialized and commercialized much earlier. In north China, for instance, conditions
were well suited for cultivating raw cotton, but were too cool and dry to be ideal
for spinning and weaving. By contrast, the lower Yangtze region enjoyed favorable conditions for processing the cotton, but not for growing it in quantities
sufficient to meet the needs of the spinners and weavers. A division of labor
between the two regions therefore evolved. A further division of labor appeared

FIGURE 7.2. Cotton Weaving, Shanghai, 1898. Photo courtesy The Peabody Museum, Salem, Mass.

between spinners and weavers, because many families could not afford looms and thus specialized in spinning. As an eighteenth-century book observed, "There are those [near Shanghai] who sell only yarn. If they work night and day and produce about one *chin* [*jin,* or "catty"] of yarn, they are able to support themselves. Good spinners normally use three- or four-spindle (wheels). They at least use two-spindle (wheels)."[13] Specialization in spinning connotes, of course, specialization in weaving, and in the late seventeenth century, there were some 200,000 weavers just in the Shanghai area.

These professional weavers, often working in urban family workshops, produced fabrics far more elegant than the coarse, plain cloth woven by peasants for their own use. There were, for example, the intricate patterns of the "eye-brow knit" and "flying flower" cloths, which were produced for the luxury trade. The famous "three-shuttle cloth" of Songjiang was made of particularly fine yarn and woven with numerous small vents, so cool and comfortable that it won the ultimate accolade: Ming emperors chose it for their underwear! Chinese cotton fabrics were far superior to those manufactured in England at this time, which is why Britain imported substantial quantities of nankeen—the cloth woven near Nanking—until as late as the 1830s.

Despite the large amount of cotton textiles being produced for the market, the work of spinning and weaving was nowhere concentrated in factories. Some of the finest cotton fabrics may have been produced in urban weaving shops that housed twenty or more looms (as in the silk industry), but cotton spinning and weaving remained preponderantly a household industry. Not until the 1880s, indeed, is there any evidence of factory weaving.

Only in the finishing operations—dyeing and calendering—were the work units relatively large because the economies of scale in dyeing were substantial. Indeed, so great were the savings that resulted from bulk processing that most dyers specialized in just one color. As a consequence, just as during the early stages of cotton-textile manufacturing in England, dyeing was usually done in urban factories rather than in rural households. Calendering—the process of pressing the cloth with a heavy stone to give it a smooth and lustrous finish—could have been performed in households. Because large lots of cloth had already been collected for dyeing, however, it would have been impractical to distribute the cloth to individual households for this one operation prior to marketing it. During the 1730s in Soochow, calendering "factories" averaged about 32 workers each; altogether, there were some 20,000 dyers and calenderers in the city.[14]

What particularly characterized the production of the finer weaves of cotton cloth in late imperial China—and distinguished it from that in England during the seventeenth and early eighteenth centuries—was the fragmentation of the entire process, the several segments being loosely linked by a highly efficient marketing mechanism. Typically, farmers sold their raw cotton to merchants or brokers, who delivered and sold it to household handicraft spinners. The spinners sold their completed yarn to another set of merchants, who sold it to individual weavers. Local merchant-brokers then bought the woven cloth, which they, in turn, delivered to the dyeing and calendering shops or sold to wholesale merchants, who marketed the cloth throughout the empire.[15]

Merchants, that is, were the captains of the industry; the producers themselves were usually financially straitened peasants straining to earn just a few additional copper cash. Even locally based merchant-brokers might have an annual turnover of 10,000 taels or more; large wholesalers, with branches in numerous market towns and cities, operated on a proportionately larger scale. In Shanghai during the seventeenth century, for instance, "wealthy [wholesale cloth] merchants came . . . with a capital of many tens of thousands of taels of silver. The richest may have had several hundreds of thousands and the poorest perhaps ten thousand. For this reason, [local] brokerage houses treat them like kings and marquises and compete . . . for their favor."[16]

For all their wealth, the merchants rarely involved themselves directly in the production process. They did not, as in Europe before the Industrial Revolution, rely on the putting-out system, whereby merchants delivered cotton to the spinners and yarn to the weavers (sometimes providing them with spinning wheels and looms) and paid the workers wages for their efforts. Although there exists literary evidence that the putting-out system was not unknown in late imperial China, that system clearly did not predominate. Instead, spinners and weavers supplied their own equipment, purchased the cotton or yarn, and sold the yarn or cloth to local brokers. As a late Ming gazetteer recorded:

> The poor people take what they have spun or woven, namely thread or cotton cloth, and go to the market early in the morning. They exchange it there for raw cotton (or yarn) with which they return to spin or weave as before. On the morrow they again take it to be exchanged.[17]

They were not, therefore, waged employees.

The Chinese reliance on a market-oriented structure of production, rather than on a putting-out system, is significant because, as most economic historians would argue, true industrial capitalism could not develop so long as merchants remained uninvolved in the production process. Without such involvement, there was no stimulus to change; merchants could satisfy increased market demand not by improving the technology or by enlarging the units of production, but merely by purchasing more of the commodity from a larger number of individual producers.

Why did Chinese brokers and wholesale merchants not become involved in the process of production? Why did they, since they were sensitive to the economies of scale in the finishing operations such as dyeing, not organize the rest of the industry into factory units? The answer is that *the market mechanism worked so well* that there was no incentive for the major entrepreneurs to change the system. Indeed, it would have been financially foolish for them to organize production in factories because spinning and weaving in the domestic system were merely subsidiary occupations for farm families. Spinners and weavers thus were willing to work for less than subsistence wages, knowing that any income they earned, however small, was a net benefit to their households—a clear instance of the peasants' self-exploitation. Merchants saw no advantage in altering this system by establishing factories and investing in more productive technologies, because there always was an ample reserve of handicraft workers anxious and willing to spin and weave. Furthermore, if they did establish factories, they would have to pay full-time factory workers something close to a subsistence wage and would have to put capital into buildings and equipment. Under the system of household production, the merchants could avoid those large and risky investments. The system of household production could also respond more flexibly than could factory production to the ups and downs of the market: when necessary to cut back on production, hundreds of thousands of handicraft workers could put aside their simple machines, without any waste of the entrepreneurs' plant investment; when the market revived, the workers could again be quickly recruited. Factory spinning and weaving did not become feasible, therefore, until the introduction of power-driven spindles and looms in the late nineteenth century changed these economic calculations.

The cotton industry reveals both the strength and the weakness of manufacturing in late imperial China. Among its strengths were a high level of commercialization, knowledgeable merchants who "administered" the system with large amounts of capital at their disposal, considerable division of labor that improved labor efficiency, and a high order of technical proficiency. Considering the technology being used, China's cotton industry was highly sophisticated. A critical weakness of the industry, however, was the relative absence of mechanization, for an industrial revolution cannot occur unless machinery is employed to increase labor productivity. Significantly, this weakness probably resulted from a rational economic decision rather than from an inability to devise more advanced technologies, because the basic elements of the appropriate technology were available if needed. In the early Ming, for example, water-driven machines were used for husking rice, pounding incense, and propelling hammers used in paper manufacture. Also in the early Ming, Chinese were using a machine for spinning hemp; it had 32 spindles and was powered by water, animal, or man. It could spin about 130 pounds of thread in 24 hours and was recognized to be "several times cheaper than the women workers it replaces."[18] True, this spinning machine was for hemp, and therefore the technical problems were rather different from those for the short-fibred cotton. Yet this should not have posed an insuperable problem for a people such as the Chinese, with their rich history of technological creativity. Moreover, because—as Carlo M. Cipolla, a leading economic historian, asserts—"an Industrial Revolution is above all a socio-cultural fact,"[19] it is doubtful that the absence of new, more productive machines was the critical factor obstructing China's path to industrialization.

The Late Ming Sociocultural Milieu

Because of the preeminent importance of social and cultural factors in determining whether a nation successfully industrializes, it is striking that traditional social values were being transformed during the late Ming. This was a time of widespread prosperity. The upper classes were given to extreme extravagence and conspicuous consumption. Even among the lower classes, there was an unaccustomed leisure—although extremes of poverty and misery could, to be sure, still be easily found. The late sixteenth and early seventeenth centuries, in particular, were marked by a "romantic, emotional, and sensual mood."[20] It was also a time of rapid social mobility. Education and literacy were spreading; wealthy merchants or their sons were gaining official status; and long-established gentry families—often impoverished by the luxury-loving ways that had become the hallmark of the age—were turning to careers in commerce. As a noted scholar and literary figure living in the Kiangnan region remarked in the latter half of the sixteenth century, "Status distinctions among scholars, peasants, and merchants have become blurred."[21]

As distinctions among the classes diminished, there developed a social pluralism, revealed in the new respect and social standing that was accorded merchants and artisans. Even in the early sixteenth century, Liu Daxia, a prominent official, had taught his children that engaging in trade or agriculture was the most honorable of occupations—and other scholars often quoted him. Later in the century, a minister of the Board of Rites—ordinarily a bastion of conservatism—suggested that government officials be chosen not just from those successful in the civil-service examinations, but also from the ranks of talented peasants, merchants, butchers, physicians, and even fortunetellers. The proposal was never adopted, but that he could even propose the idea indicates how radically social values were changing. At this time, in fact, skilled artisans—those who crafted fine porcelains, bronze ware, lacquer ware, fans, and the like—were so respected that they socialized with scholars virtually as equals, and their artistic works were valued as highly as such literary productions as paintings and calligraphy.

Appearing at the same time as these social and economic changes in the late Ming Dynasty was a new school of Confucianism, sometimes pejoratively called "wild Chan" or "crazy Zen" (kuangchan). In a manner somewhat reminiscent of the dissenting Protestant sects during the European Industrial Revolution—although there were, to be sure, substantial differences as well—wild Chan provided at least partial ideological justification for the increased social egalitarianism and pursuit of profit that characterized the era.

Wild Chan, more properly known as the Taizhou School, formed as an outgrowth of the philosophy of the great Ming Dynasty Confucian philosopher Wang Yangming (1472–1529). Wang, strongly influenced by Chan (or Zen) Buddhism, had rejected the pedantic and highly elitist interpretation of Confucianism—lixue, or the School of Principle—that during the Ming served as the official orthodoxy. His was the School of the Mind (xinxue), which among other things stressed that all people are possessed of perfect virtue and that, to attain Confucian sagehood, they need only to awaken to the fact of their inherent sagehood. This teaching was popularized in the phrase "The streets are full of sages!"

Wang Yangming had failed to explore all the social implications of his philosophy, and it was left to a group of his followers, who established the Taizhou School, to bring those ideas down to the commoners and to develop a mass movement. A principal founder of the Taizhou School, Wang Gen, was a poorly educated commoner who had prospered as a salt merchant. Wang Gen, emphasizing Wang Yangming's conviction that ordinary people are already possessed of perfect virtue, taught that one need only to act naturally to attain sagehood. Do not suppress desires, he said, but act freely on those desires. Then one is truly a sage. This was a joyful philosophy, an affirmation of life and of humanity, without Confucianism's customary moral strictures.

Wang Gen was a genuine eccentric, dressing, for instance, in the attire supposedly worn by Yao, the legendary sage-emperor, and moving about in a cart such as Confucius was thought to have ridden. Whatever the reasons for his unconventional behavior, he was an enormously successful "evangelist," spreading his ideas among the common people and creating a mood of religious revivalism that, said Huang Zongxi, "spread like the wind over all the land." [22] Backed by an extensive organization, Wang Gen's disciples presented lectures and conducted group discussions, followed by group singing. It was a powerful movement in which peasants and merchants, stonecutters and potters, scholars and officials—persons of all and diverse backgrounds and occupations—participated.

The Taizhou School's naturalism and egalitarianism represented a challenge to the orthodox Confucian Establishment, yet it at least arguably remained within the bounds of Confucianism because it retained the traditional Confucian stress on social betterment by means of individual moral improvement (although that improvement was conceived of in a nontraditional way). Emerging from the Taizhou School and the teachings of Wang Yangming, however, was a group of radicals who, although regarding themselves as Confucians, took Wang Gen's stress on the natural goodness of humankind to the logical extreme, totally rejecting Confucian concerns about morality and emphasizing that people should follow their instincts and desires regardless of where they might lead. One of these radicals, Yen Qun, for example, mirroring the more liberal attitudes of the time, reportedly believed not only that "man's appetite for wealth and sex all sprang from his true nature"—which was not a new idea in Confucianism—but also that, being natural, those appetites ought to be given free rein.[23] This *was* a departure from Confucian orthodoxy.

The best known of these radicals was Li Zhi, whose moral iconoclasm applauded selfishness and the desire for profit; he argued that these motivations were no less natural than the traditionally accepted Confucian ethic of sincerity and filial piety. He also advocated such ideas—still extremely radical at the time—as that women were as intelligent as men and that marriage ought to be by free choice. Nor were these ideas merely the musings of an unconventional philosopher, for his books were tremendously popular, widely circulated, and reportedly read even by village women, for female literacy was now increasing. Such popular success in an age before the advent of modern communications is difficult to understand. A contemporary of Li Zhi, however, when asked to explain Li's large following, explained:

> Who does not want to be a sage *[sheng]* or be called virtuous *[xian]*, but it was always so inconvenient to become one. Now [according to Li Zhi] nothing seems to obstruct the path to enlightenment—not even wine, women, wealth, and lack of self-control. This is quite a bargain, and who does not like a bargain?[24]

Wild Chan reveals how the crust of custom was breaking up during this period of economic prosperity in the late Ming. Rejecting the leadership and the values of the Confucian scholar-official establishment, it provided a rationale for the flux and intermingling of social classes and for the values that many in society then placed on naturalism and materialism. Perhaps the Communist historian Hou Wailu exaggerated in asserting that Li Zhi represented a "rising bourgeois capitalist spirit."[25] Nonetheless, it was certainly not a coincidence that prominent figures in this development of Confucianism, such as Wang Gen and Li Zhi, were natives of China's most economically advanced areas, the lower Yangtze region and the port cities of Fukien. Several of them, too, were sons of merchant families.

The Obstacles to Industrialization

Significant changes, then, were coursing through China's society and economy during the sixteenth to eighteenth centuries in ways not fundamentally dissimilar to those during the seventeenth and early eighteenth centuries in England. Indeed, in some ways—such as the size of factory operations, output of the most efficient cotton-spinning machines, and perhaps even the amount of capital held by merchants (and therefore potentially available for industrial investment)—it would seem that China may have been a step ahead of Britain on the path to industrialization. In the end, of course, the momentum was lost. Why?

Putting the question this way implies that in the normal course of events, China should on its own momentum have moved from this period of commercial prosperity and manufacturing vitality to a modern industrial revolution. Such an implication, of course, is unwarranted. In both ancient Rome and Renaissance Florence, for instance, a factory form of organization had been established within a setting of considerable mercantile activity and social affluence, yet these societies had failed to take the next step of devising and employing new technologies that would have significantly increased per capita productivity. During the early seventeenth century, Holland was the focus of tremendous commercial exuberance and scientific creativity. After about 1660, however, for reasons still being debated, the forces that in historical retrospect seem to have been pushing the small nation toward an industrial revolution vanished, and the country lapsed into depression and conservatism. That China in the sixteenth through eighteenth centuries did not evolve farther on the way to an industrial revolution was by no means, therefore, a historical anomaly. "Perhaps," one historian has observed, "the absence of fundamental change calls for no special explanation and only the European miracle [the Industrial Revolution] does."[26]

Still, curious minds will naturally ask why China, with such a strong start, did not develop new industrial technologies. Perhaps, therefore, it is incumbent to offer an explanation. I am daunted from any attempt to do so, however, because some of the best historical minds in the West have attempted to explain why Britain launched the Industrial Revolution; yet after 100 years of research and dispute, there is still no consensus even regarding when the event occurred, not to mention its causes. To explain why an industrial revolution did *not* occur is obviously even more difficult. We can, however, at least speculate about some of the factors that may have obstructed China's advance to modern industrialization.

It is important to remember that the obstacles to industrialization were not primarily technological. Because the spinning jenny and the water frame had been invented virtually contemporaneously with the first clear manifestations of the Industrial Revolution in Britain, historians long assumed that technological innovation was the primary precondition of industrialization. In recent decades, however, historians have realized that in many underdeveloped nations of the world, the industrialization process makes little progress even when modern technology is readily available. Thus it is evident that a people must *want* to use new technologies, must sense advantages in changing their long-established ways, before their society can be industrialized.

In China, the urge to change was small—a characteristic that contrasts starkly with what David S. Landes regards as one of Europe's most distinguishing characteristics: "the high value placed on the rational manipulation of the environment."[27] That is, the Europeans were possessed of a powerful, irrepressible urge to dominate the natural world, to make nature subject to human control. The Chinese, by contrast, tended to view the universe as an organism, in which all elements existed in harmony. Humans were part of this organism; an element integral to nature, not transcending it.[28]

These contrasting Chinese and Western attitudes toward nature are clearly revealed in their respective art forms. Western artists, for example, often choose as their subject a still-life: a bowl of fruit, cut flowers, or a pheasant, recently shot and hanging head-downward, its feet strung to a nail on the wall—a record of the hunter's triumph in the hunt. In Chinese art, those same subjects would be shown alive in their natural habitat: the fruit fresh on the tree or the pheasant feeding amid clumps of grasses. The beauty in which Chinese artists delighted was no more than, but also nothing less than, nature pristine. Or consider Chinese land-scape paintings, which depict water, trees, and massive mountains. In these we see the grandeur of nature—and there, on an outcropping of mountain or in a boat carried along on the stream, is inevitably the figure of a person or two, looking out at and dwarfed by the wondrous landscape. Thus Chinese celebrated the unity of man and nature. To rein in the forces of nature, to dominate and turn the vast organism of the universe to human will, was distinctly less important than estab-lishing a harmony of oneself and society with the way—or *dao*—of the universe.

This is not to assert that the Chinese were incapable of large and extensive modifications of their natural environment. The Great Wall and the Grand Canal amply bespeak that fact. And the Chinese did not live in grass huts on the moun-tain sides; they built houses and cities, and they diked their unruly rivers and created vast irrigation networks. Yet there was something distinctly different in the way that Chinese and Europeans conceived of their place in the universe. Herbert Spencer perhaps put his finger on the nub of the problem when he spoke of the Faustian spirit of Western civilization. Spencer saw this spirit as imbuing the West with a restless drive, energy, and assertiveness, an imperative to struggle and progressively attain mastery over nature and man. The Chinese, by contrast, being imbued with the concept of the individual's unity with the universal scheme of things, had a sense of the limitations of human endeavor. One could, of course, strive—for wealth, for knowledge and moral improvement, for position. But the Chinese were also keenly aware that to attain contentment, they must sometimes be resigned to their subordinate role in the larger order of things. Thus not all change was progress; big was not always better.

To economists of the numbers-crunching school, such metaphysical rumina-tions may seem irrelevant to an explanation of China's failure to industrialize. Yet a nation's economy is rooted deeply in its culture. These contrasting attitudes regarding the role of humans in nature may, therefore, go far toward explaining why technological innovations in China were used and absorbed without radically altering the traditional system, whereas those same innovations, when transmitted to Europe, revolutionized Western civilizations. According to Francis Bacon:

> It is well to observe the force and virtue and consequences of discoveries. These are to be seen nowhere more conspicuously than in those three which were un-known to the ancients, and of which the origin, though recent, is obscure and inglorious; namely, printing, gunpowder, and the magnet. *For these three have changed the whole face and state of things throughout the world,* the first in literature, the second in warfare, the third in navigation; whence have followed innumerable changes; insomuch that no empire, no sect, no star, seems to have exerted greater power and influence in human affairs than these three mechanical discoveries.[29]

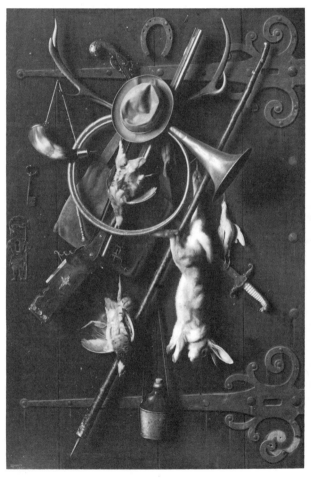

FIGURE 7.3. Typical Chinese Landscape Painting, (A) depicts humankind as small and insignificant amid the awesome grandeur of nature. It is inconceivable that a traditional Chinese artist would have painted anything like William H. Harnett's "After the Hunt" (1884), which celebrated man's domination of nature (B). Wu Li's "Myriad Valleys and the Flavor of Pines" is reproduced with the permission of the Cleveland Museum of Art. Harnett's "After the Hunt" is reproduced with the permission of the M. H. deYoung Memorial Museum, Golden Gate Park, San Francisco.

152

Printing, gunpowder, and the magnet—together with many other major innovations, such as iron and steel technology, an efficient harness for horses, the
sternpost rudder, segmental-arch bridges, and the conversion of rotary to rectilin-
ear motion—were invented in China. The Chinese sometimes put these inventions
to practical use. Gunpowder, for instance, was used by the Song Dynasty in about
1120 against the Jin invaders and a century later against the Mongols. Yet the
Chinese took this awful invention in stride, and their political system remained in
the eighteenth century much as it had been before 1120. In Europe, by contrast,
gunpowder and the gun appeared about 1280; soon, the explosions of guns and
cannons were destroying castle walls, and the entire structure of feudal society
was thereupon transformed. The Chinese were capable of extraordinary technological creativity, yet they placed a higher value on stability and harmony than on
change and domination. Perhaps this is why the "sprouts" of industrialism in the
sixteenth to eighteenth centuries did not grow to full flower.

A second factor working against industrialization in China may have been the
social structure and social values. Of central importance was the status and prestige of the scholar-official class. No other career or profession—not medicine or
law or business or the priesthood—offered comparable rewards. To attain literati
status by successfully participating in the civil-service examinations, therefore,
and thereby to gain a government post was the ultimate career goal of every able
and ambitious young man. Nor was this an utterly unrealistic goal, because participation in the examinations was open to all males, save for a small number of
"mean people"—beggars, sons of prostitutes, slaves, police, coroners, boat-people,
and the like. The instances of young men who graduated from plowing in the
fields to administering the empire, although rare, were sufficiently numerous to
give credence to the myth.

The enormous prestige attached to scholar-official status had profound implications for China's potential to industrialize. First, as soon as a merchant or manufacturer became reasonably well-off, he attempted to attain literati status for himself or his sons, either by procuring the necessary education or by purchasing an
academic degree or bureaucratic post. As revealed in a study of Zhangzhou prefecture, which profited immensely from foreign trade in the sixteenth century,
"there was a direct translation of wealth acquired from expanded commerce into
academic success. One of the first uses to which profits were put was the hiring
of tutors and the acquisition of the expensive education needed to win a *jinshi*
degree." [30]

Second, because of the prestige of literati status, even those who failed to
qualify in the examinations usually attempted, if they could afford it, to emulate
the life style of the scholar-officials. Successful businessmen tended to divert much
of their wealth to purchasing land, buying libraries, and patronizing scholarship
rather than reinvesting in their commercial or manufacturing undertakings.

Finally, the high social value attached to literati status channeled the intellectual interests of China's educated elite away from technical and scientific concerns
and into a narrowly literary scholasticism. From the Song Dynasty to 1905, when
the examination system was finally abolished, literature and the Confucian classics
occupied the interests of China's most educated men, and those who engaged in

manual labor were, at least in the eyes of the elites, objects of derision. Symbolizing these values were the scholar's enfolding gown and long fingernails, which provided concrete evidence that he never undertook any form of physical work. Thus the values of society, resulting from and buttressed by the social structure, diverted the money, time, and interests of China's educated classes from all endeavors that might have fostered economic and technological change.

The contrast with Britain in the seventeenth century is striking. Although British society was, like China's, "open" in the sense that status was not primarily determined by birth—the British peerage was small and of limited influence, rather like members of the imperial families in the Ming and Qing—it differed from China in the relative diversity of its socially respected occupations. Not only landowning and government service brought prestige, but also careers in the church, the armed forces, the law, the theater, and, yes, business. An important reason for this social pluralism may have been the general practice of primogeniture, which dictated that all but the eldest male in each family, even in the "best" families, were compelled to seek vocations and fortunes on their own. Of course, extremely wealthy and influential fathers could usually provide substantially for two or three younger sons, but "the fourth and fifth sons, of gentry and even noble families, would have to be apprenticed to trade—not the trade of the shop, to be sure, but the international commerce that was at once the pride of the English economy and the seed-bed of new houses."[31] The participation of aristocrats in commerce, even if occurring only occasionally, had symbolic value, placing on trade and manufacturing a stamp of legitimacy and respectability.

Among the lesser gentry and middle classes, the same kind of social pluralism made it possible for children with some education to take apprenticeships in the crafts. Not only was participation in manual labor acceptable, therefore, but people of all social classes evinced strong curiosity in and aptitude for things mechanical. Even Samuel Johnson, the eminent humanist and literary scholar, tinkered throughout his lifetime in chemistry and was never loath to be found sooted and rumpled from his experiments. Men in seventeenth- and eighteenth-century England, it has been suggested, "had become mechanics."[32] The contrast with China could hardly be starker.

It is necessary to take issue with the interpretation that Confucianism lay at the root of China's inability to industrialize and modernize. Confucianism, it is claimed, is a doctrine that is opposed to progress—one that envisions the perfect society as having existed in the past—and that, in its stress on a hierarchically ordered society, on virtually unquestioning respect for elders, and on humanistic (as opposed to scientific and technical) learning, served to bolster the existing social order and constituted authority. Thus as Mary C. Wright wrote in her classic study of a failed reform movement in the nineteenth century, "the requirements of modernization ran counter to the requirements of Confucian stability."[33]

While there is undoubtedly some truth in this argument, it is misleading because the parameters of Confucianism were actually exceedingly elastic. Over the years, the character and interpretations of Confucianism shifted dramatically, from a Mencius to a Dong Zhongshu and from a Zhu Xi to a Wang Yangming. Just how far the doctrines of Confucianism could be stretched was revealed in the

Ming Dynasty by the Taizhou School and, in the late nineteenth century, by Kang Youwei.

Moreover, some Westerners, impressed by Japan's recent economic successes, have portrayed Confucianism as a powerful "development ideology." An economist for the Bank of America, for example, citing the Confucian emphasis on industriousness, frugality, and social discipline, asserted that "the Confucian ethic gives these governments [of East Asia] an enormous advantage."[34] The futurist Herman Kahn likewise contended that Confucianism was "in many ways superior to the [Protestant ethic] in the West in the pursuit of industrialization, affluence, and modernization" because it emphasized harmonious human relations and deemphasized selfish, individual interests.[35] These may be rather crude formulations, but they do indicate some of the reasons for thinking that Confucianism may not have been wholly antagonistic to modern change.

A third factor obstructing China's breakthrough into an era of industrialization may have been the insecurity of private wealth and entrepreneurial investments from government exactions. In Chinese political theory, the emperor's power was unlimited; he was the Son of Heaven, the mediator between Heaven and man. In practice, his power was always subject to various political restraints, but the boundaries between state and society and between public and private were poorly defined, offering but slight legal protection to private property. The result was that the security of property—which was, it appears, "an indispensable condition of productive investment and the accumulation of wealth"[36]—was extremely weak.

Among the most successful of China's private entrepreneurs were the *hong* merchants in Canton, who enjoyed monopoly rights in trading with the foreigners. Some of them became enormously rich, while others were frequently ruined as a result of government exactions. In 1720, they formed a guild, the so-called *co-hong*, in an effort to form a united front against both the pressures of foreign traders and the extortionate demands of their own government. Nevertheless, they were frequently required to make "contributions" and "gifts" to government representatives, as they did in 1834:[37]

Tribute to the emperor	55,000 taels
Repairs along the Yellow River	30,000
Expenses of an agent at Peking	21,600
Birthday presents to the emperor	130,000
Birthday presents to the *hoppo*	20,000
Presents to the *hoppo*'s mother or wife	20,000
Annual presents to various officials	40,000
Compulsory purchases of native ginseng	140,000
	456,000 taels

Even more than the *hong* merchants, salt merchants had to pay profusely for the privilege of engaging in trade, contributing over 36 million taels between 1738 and 1804. Government officials, it has been observed, "did not offer protection or assistance to trade. Instead, they drained it with ruinous rapacity."[38] The law provided no effective safeguards from such exactions.

In the West, official exactions on private wealth had, at least by late medieval times, tended to be regularized in the form of specific and anticipatable taxes. The result, paradoxically, probably increased total governmental revenue. Because of this measure of predictability in the relationship between government and commerce, private entrepreneurs felt that capital investments were safe so that they need not conceal their wealth or dissipate it in frivolous show and consumption.

A fourth factor, offering perhaps the most compelling explanation of China's inhibited industrialization, was the relative stability of market demand, which would have provided only minimal stimulus to increase productivity. Entrepreneurs do not automatically adopt new technologies. For them, changes in the methods of production involve risks and dislocations. New buildings and machinery require the expenditures of capital; old equipment must be discarded; laborers must be retrained. Very powerful inducements are needed, therefore, to persuade them to adopt radical technological changes. An entrepreneur might be induced, however, to seek more capital-intensive methods of production if, for example, the labor costs of the old system become exorbitant or if the market demand increases so sharply that old methods of production fall far short of meeting that demand.

Market demand in eighteenth-century England had been particularly conducive to the adoption of new industrial technologies. Not only was the population of the kingdom growing, but also, and more important, the per capita income of that population was gradually rising—not least because of rising productivity in the agricultural sector. An improving transportation system—canals, highways, and (later) railways—also lowered the manufacturers' costs of obtaining raw materials and facilitated distribution of the finished products to the entire national market. At least as important as the growing domestic market was the development of a huge foreign market in the Americas, Africa, and Asia. Confronted with a sharply rising market demand, Britain's manufacturers were gradually persuaded to make the capital investments needed to acquire the machinery that revolutionized the industrial sector.

In China, by contrast, per capita income by about 1800 was probably stagnating; possibly, it was even falling. And foreign trade, although it still brought in significant amounts of silver until the 1820s, accounted for only a minuscule part of the total market demand. As a consequence, the sale of manufactured commodities in China, albeit large in the aggregate, was at best increasing no faster than the population. The large population, growing but still poor, also ensured that labor costs would continue to be low. There was, therefore, little inducement for manufacturers to seek out and use new technologies to increase their laborers' productivity.

Perhaps no one of these four factors, or even all four of them together, suffice to explain why China failed to progress beyond the economic dynamism it experienced in the sixteenth to eighteenth centuries. Perhaps other factors should be taken into account. How much drag, for instance, was created by the irrational monetary system? By the inefficient and costly transportation system? Did the primitive banking system fail to provide an institutional device that would encourage the levels of capital accumulation needed to advance to industrial takeoff? Much further research is required before these questions can be answered with confidence. Whatever the answers may be, it is historically significant that the economy was considerably more vital and prosperous throughout much of the sixteenth to eighteenth centuries than it was later, in, say, the late nineteenth century.

Selected Readings

(See also the works cited in the notes)

Chao, Kang. *The Development of Cotton Textile Production in China.* Cambridge, Mass.: Harvard University, East Asian Research Center, 1977.

Dietrich, Craig. "Cotton Culture and Manufacture in Early Ch'ing China." In *Economic Organization in Chinese Society,* ed. W. E. Willmott, pp. 109–35. Stanford, Calif.: Stanford University Press, 1972.

Elvin, Mark. *The Pattern of the Chinese Past.* Stanford, Calif.: Stanford University Press, 1973.

Feuerwerker, Albert. "From 'Feudalism' to 'Capitalism' in Recent Historical Writings from Mainland China." *Journal of Asian Studies* 18, no. 1 (November 1958): 107–16.

Ho, Ping-ti. "The Salt Merchants of Yang-chou: A Study of Commercial Capitalism in Eighteenth-Century China." *Harvard Journal of Asiatic Studies* 17, nos. 1 and 2 (June 1952): 130–68.

Hsi, Angela Ning-Jy Sun. "Social and Economic Status of the Merchant Class of the Ming Dynasty, 1368–1644." Ph.D. diss., University of Illinois, 1972.

Huang, Ray. *Taxation and Governmental Finance in Sixteenth-Century Ming China.* London: Cambridge University Press, 1974.

Shih Min-hsiung. *The Silk Industry in Ch'ing China,* trans. E-tu Zen Sun. Ann Arbor: University of Michigan, Center for Chinese Studies, 1976.

Sun, E-tu Zen. "Sericulture and Silk Textile Production in Ch'ing China." In *Economic Organization in Chinese Society,* ed. W. E. Willmott, pp. 79–108. Stanford, Calif.: Stanford University Press, 1972.

Sung Ying-Hsing. *T'ien-kung K'ai-wu: Chinese Technology in the Seventeenth Century,* trans. E-tu Zen Sun and Shiou-chuan Sun. University Park: Pennsylvania State University Press, 1966.

Wiens, Mi Chu. "Cotton Textile Production and Rural Social Transformation in Early Modern China." *Xianggang Zhongwen Daxue Zhongguo Wenhua Yenjiusuo Xuebao* (Journal of the Institute of Chinese Studies of the Chinese University of Hong Kong) 7, no. 2, (December 1974): 515–31.

8

Commerce and Manufacturing Under the Impact of the West

Throughout the late imperial period, the Europeans had been kept on the margins of Chinese economic life. They had plugged their trade into the existing commercial networks of the empire, but imparted little influence on either the ways or the values of Chinese life. After the Opium War, however, fueled by the resources and dynamism of the Industrial Revolution and incited by Chinese political and military weakness, the West began pushing China's commercial and manufacturing sectors onto a new evolutionary track. The Chinese, initially at least, resisted the changes being thrust on them, and the nation became an object of international derision because of its backwardness and weakness.

Why China responded so slowly to the economic challenges and opportunities of the nineteenth and early twentieth centuries has been a continuing source of puzzlement and debate. Some historians believe that exploitation and oppression by the imperialist powers inhibited Chinese efforts to develop a modern economy; others hold that the obstacles to economic modernization lay within China itself, in the very culture of the nation and the people. This question is obviously related to the problem of why China did not move into a stage of industrial growth in the sixteenth to eighteenth centuries. But the difficulties that China encountered during the early modern period in borrowing the technologies developed in the West, and in adapting to an expanding commercial world, were special unto themselves.

Foreign Trade

The British had initially ventured to China to *purchase* Chinese products—silk, tea, porcelains, and nankeens. By the nineteenth century, however, the prodigious and unprecedented productive powers of its factories had shifted Britain's ambitions to *selling* to the Chinese. Sir Henry Pottinger, British plenipotentiary in

China, expressed the mercantile optimism of the British when he announced the signing of the Treaty of Nanking in 1842. The treaty, he boasted, opened to the world a trade so vast "that all the mills in Lancashire could not make stocking stuff sufficient for one of its provinces."[1] For a brief time following the opening of the five treaty ports in 1843, it appeared that Sir Henry's optimism was well founded, for the stoppage of the trade during the fighting in the Opium War had created a backlog of demand. After peace returned, therefore, British cotton and woolen fabrics sold out quickly and at good prices. But in 1845, China's purchases fell to two-thirds of those of the preceding year. Throughout the remainder of the 1840s, the trade depression continued. Even by 1850, British exports to China had barely regained the 1843 level, and in 1854, they were again declining. As was to happen repeatedly during the next century and more, the foreigners' dreams of immense sales to China's vast population—the so-called Myth of the China Market—proved to be illusory.

Looking back now, British hopes for the China trade after the Opium War appear incredibly naïve. A leading Sheffield cutlery firm, for example, ignoring the fact that chopsticks are perfectly suited to eating Chinese cuisine, dispatched a large shipment of table knives and forks to China. A piano manufacturer sent a "tremendous consignment of pianofortes," based on the conviction that at least 1 million of the 300 to 400 million Chinese would want to play the musical instrument that had so many devotees in the living rooms of Europe.[2] With respect to the cultural differences between England and China, British merchants retained a monumental indifference or ignorance. And when the Chinese did not purchase their goods in the quantities expected, the merchants faulted not themselves and their economic calculations, but the Chinese and the political obstructionism of the Chinese officials. The problem, they were convinced, was that the post–Opium War treaties had not truly opened the China market, that foreign trade was still confined to the fringes of China, and that it was confronted by a restrictive system of monopoly brokers. They therefore demanded that more treaty ports be opened, especially in north China, and that they be granted the right to travel and conduct business freely in the interior of the country. By 1850, the British prime minister, Lord Palmerston, had likewise become convinced that Chinese political obstructionism was the true reason that the fruits of victory in the Opium War had been so meager. Force was the manifest solution:

> I clearly see that the Time is fast coming [wrote Palmerston] when we shall be obliged to strike another Blow in China, and that blow must be the occupation of a Position on the Yangtse Kiang [River] to cut off communication by the Great Canal. But it would not be advisable to give the Chinese any intimation that such would be our measure. They should be left to reflect upon it when and after it was done. These half civilized Governments, such as those of China Portugal Spanish America require a Dressing every eight or Ten years to keep them in order. Their Minds are too shallow to receive an Impression that will last longer than some such Period, and warning is of little use. They care little for words and they must not only see the Stick but actually feel it on their Shoulders before they yield to that only argument which to them brings conviction, the *argumentum Baculinum* ["persuasion by the stick"].[3]

Table 8.1. Imports of China (in percent)

Year	Total Value (customs taels)	Opium	Cotton Goods	Cotton Yarn	Cotton Raw	Cereals, Wheat Flour	Sugar	Tobacco
1868	63,282	33.1	29.0	2.5	—	0.8	0.8	—
1880	79,293	39.3	24.9	4.6	—	0.1	0.4	—
1890	127,093	19.5	20.2	15.3	—	9.6	0.9	—
1900	211,070	14.8	21.5	14.3	—	7.0	3.0	0.5
1905	447,101	7.7	25.6	15.0	—	2.9	5.1	1.4
1913	570,163	7.4	19.3	12.7	—	5.2	6.4	2.9
1913	570,163	—	19.3	12.7	0.5	—	6.4	2.9
1920	762,250	—	21.8	10.6	2.4	1.1	5.2	4.7
1928	1,195,969	—	14.2	1.6	5.7	8.3	8.3	5.1
1931	1,433,489	—	7.6	0.3	12.6	12.6	6.0	4.4
1938	604,329	—	1.5	0.2	3.8	4.6	2.2	1.8

The result of such cultural arrogance and economic obtuseness was the Second Opium War (1856–1860; sometimes called the Arrow War), which resulted in a second series of treaties. These agreements provided the access that the merchants demanded. Eleven additional treaty ports were to be opened (by 1917, a total of ninety-two ports had been opened to foreign trade),[4] and foreigners gained the privilege of traveling freely in the interior of the country.

The trade, however, developed with frustrating slowness. By 1913, the value of China's total foreign trade had risen almost eight times above the 1868 level, but most of that increase had come only during and after the 1890s. And even in 1913 the exports and imports combined still amounted to only U.S.$1.61 per capita, which figure placed China at the very bottom of a list of eighty-three countries worldwide.

Among the items *imported* by China, only one foreign product found a sure market in China before 1890. That was opium. Ironically, the post-Opium War treaties of 1842 to 1844 had avoided even mentioning the drug, and thus it had continued to be traded as contraband until 1860, when sales were nearly double those on the eve of the Opium War. The treaties of 1860 finally legalized the trade in opium, which continued for the next thirty years to be the foreigners' most valuable import to China. By 1890, however, domestic cultivation of the poppy cut into foreign sales of the drug. After 1908, the British government—its moral scruples finally affecting its policy (besides, the trade was not as profitable as it had been)—imposed progressively tighter limits on sales of opium to China and halted them altogether in 1917. By 1890 opium's place at the top of the list of China's imports was taken by cotton goods and cotton yarn—long the second most important foreign imports to China—partly because opium imports had fallen slightly and partly because sales of cotton cloth increased (Table 8.1).

After World War I, China's import picture changed dramatically. Before 1900, cotton products and opium had together accounted for between 50 and 70 percent of all Chinese imports. But after the war, opium was no longer imported, and the

Table 8.1 *(Continued)*

Paper	Coal	Kerosene	Liquid Fuel	Transportation Materials	Chemicals, Dyes, & Pigments	Iron, Steel, & Other Metals	Machinery	All Others
—	2.1	—	—	—	—	4.8	—	26.9
—	1.2	—	—	—	—	5.5	—	24.0
—	1.6	3.2	—	—	—	5.7	0.3	23.7
—	3.1	6.6	—	—	—	4.7	0.7	23.8
—	1.6	4.5	—	1.8	—	10.4	1.2	22.8
—	1.7	4.5	—	0.8	—	5.3	1.4	32.4
1.3	—	4.5	—	0.8	5.6	5.3	1.4	34.2
1.9	—	7.1	0.4	2.6	6.4	8.3	3.2	24.3
2.4	—	5.2	1.4	2.3	7.5	5.4	1.8	30.8
3.2	—	4.5	1.8	2.3	8.0	6.2	3.1	27.4
4.1	—	4.2	4.1	5.6	10.8	13.2	6.4	37.5

Source: Yu-Kwei Cheng, *Foreign Trade and Industrial Development of China: An Historical and Integrated Analysis Through 1948* (Washington, D.C.: University Press of Washington, D.C., 1956), pp. 19, 32. Reprinted by permission.

importation of cotton goods and yarns declined as domestic manufacturing of those products increased. Indeed, China became a net exporter of yarn by 1928 and of cotton piece goods by 1936. As imports of manufactured cotton products declined, however, those of raw cotton, needed to supply China's growing textile industry, rose from 0.5 percent of total imports in 1913 to a peak of 12.6 percent in 1931. Also reflecting the growing maturity of China's industry was the growth of imports of machinery and industrial raw materials (iron, steel, chemicals, dyes, and the like), which together rose from 12 percent of total imports in 1913 to more than 30 percent in 1936.

The sale of imported goods to China's retail merchandisers was generally dominated by Chinese, not foreign, merchants. After the Chinese interior was opened to foreign travel in 1860, foreign sellers of, for example, cotton yarns and cloth established branch offices in even the smallest treaty ports, where they endeavored to sell their goods directly to Chinese retailers. But Chinese merchants were more familiar with local dealers and conditions, and their distributing and operating costs were lower. As a consequence, the foreign importers soon abandoned their efforts to market cotton goods in the interior and restricted their efforts to making the initial sales at the main ports of entry, such as Shanghai and Hong Kong. As early as the 1890s, many foreign firms had ceased even to import the goods on their own account, acting instead as brokers by taking orders for goods from the Chinese and then receiving commissions on delivery. By 1915, foreign merchants delivered only about 11 percent of all imported goods directly to local Chinese dealers, the remainder being delivered and sold by Chinese wholesalers. "With their knowledge of the Chinese mentality, language, and market conditions," it has been aptly remarked, the Chinese merchants "were able to beat the foreigner at his own game."[5]

Table 8.2.   Exports of China (in percent)

Year	Total Value (custom taels)	Tea	Silk & Silk Goods	Seeds & Oil	Beans	Beans & Bean Cake	Eggs & Egg Products
1868	61,826	53.8	39.7	—	1.0	—	—
1880	77,884	45.9	38.0	0.1	0.2	—	—
1890	87,144	30.6	33.9	0.6	0.4	—	—
1900	158,997	16.0	30.4	2.5	1.9	—	—
1905	227,888	11.2	30.1	3.4	3.0	—	0.9
1913	403,306	8.4	25.3	7.8	5.8	—	1.4
1913	403,306	8.4	25.3	7.8	—	12.0	1.4
1920	541,631	1.6	18.6	9.1	—	13.0	4.0
1928	991,355	3.7	18.4	5.8	—	20.5	4.4
1931	909,476	3.6	13.3	8.4	—	21.4	4.1
1936	452,979	4.3	7.8	18.7	—	1.3	5.9

The import trade, in the final analysis, had a relatively small impact on the average Chinese. Most imported goods never left the treaty ports, being purchased by consumers in those foreign sanctuaries. Except for such commodities as yarn, kerosene, and matches, which patently filled a real need, Chinese consumers in the interior were generally too poor to purchase foreign goods, most of which seemed to be luxuries. "Anyone," Albert Feuerwerker has remarked, "who would claim that the Hunan or Szechwan peasant in the 1930's dressed in Naigaiwata cottons, smoked BAT [British-American Tobacco Company] cigarettes, and used Meiji sugar has a big case to prove."[6]

The export trade, by contrast, had far-reaching consequences on the Chinese people. Critics of imperialism have contended that those consequences were ruinous to the Chinese economy, because Chinese producers concentrated their meager resources on producing for the foreign market and thus became in thrall to foreign markets, whose demand and prices rose and fell with unpredictable and disastrous results. That is, tempted by short-term gains proffered by the international market, Chinese producers first abandoned their traditional self-sufficiency. Then when foreign demand fell, they were ruined. As this indictment implicitly acknowledges, however, producing for the export market could be profitable.

From the 1860s until the eve of World War I, tea and silk were China's chief exports, but the pattern of exports changed significantly. In 1868, tea and silk together constituted 94 percent of the value of all outgoing trade (tea accounting for 53.8 percent; silk, for 39.7 percent). Thereafter, however, China lost its world dominance in these commodities. In the 1880s, teas from India and Ceylon began competing with the Chinese leaf, and by 1910, these countries were selling twice as much on the world market as was China. China's trade in silk, by contrast, remained relatively strong despite growing competition from Japanese suppliers. In 1887, silk, in its raw and its manufactured forms, supplanted tea as China's leading export.

Because Chinese during the decades before World War I had begun producing

Table 8.2 *(Continued)*

Hides, Leather, & Skins	Cotton (mostly raw)	Cotton Yarn & Cotton Goods	Wool	Coal	Ores & Metals	All Others
—	0.9	—	—	—	—	4.6
0.5	0.2	—	0.4	—	—	14.7
1.4	3.4	—	1.6	—	—	28.1
4.3	6.2	—	1.9	—	—	36.8
6.6	5.3	—	3.7	—	—	35.8
6.0	4.1	—	2.4	1.6	—	37.2
6.0	4.0	0.6	—	1.6	3.3	29.6
4.3	1.7	1.4	—	2.3	3.2	40.8
5.4	3.4	3.8	—	2.9	2.1	29.6
4.1	2.9	4.9	—	3.0	1.6	32.7
5.7	4.0	3.0	—	1.6	7.7	40.0

Source: Yu-Kwei Cheng, *Foreign Trade and Industrial Development of China: An Historical and Integrated Analysis Through 1948* (Washington, D.C.: University Press of Washington, D.C., 1956), pp. 19, 34. Reprinted by permission.

other products for the export market, the relative importance of tea and silk in China's export profile had diminished sharply. Tea accounted in 1913 for only 8.4 percent of China's exports, while silk had dropped to 25.3 percent. By 1936, these figures had fallen, respectively, to 4.3 percent and 7.8 percent. Rising in importance on the list of exported items were products from Manchuria, whose soybeans and bean cake had by the mid-1920s become China's most important exports. Manchuria was wrested from Chinese sovereignty in 1931–32, however, and the export of beans and bean cake consequently fell from 21.4 percent of the total in 1931 to only 1.3 percent in 1936. Vegetable oils, leather and hides, and eggs and egg products were other steady exports, revealing the continuing strength of at least some of China's handicraft industries (Table 8.2).

That the livelihood of China's peasants could be profoundly affected, both positively and negatively, by producing for the export market was evidenced by the vicissitudes of the silk industry (Chapter 5). But the fate of the silk producers did not represent that of all Chinese who produced for the export market because China was remarkably successful in the early twentieth century in diversifying its export trade (Table 8.2). Shifts in the international market did not, therefore, have the same pervasive reverberations in China as they did in, say, Brazil or Cuba, where coffee and sugar, respectively, accounted for a large percentage of the exports.

The tribulations of the silk trade, moreover, were only partly attributable to the vagaries of the foreign market. China's competitive position in the world silk market was badly damaged, as we have seen, by the failure of the industry to maintain standards of quality for its products. Similarly, leaf-tea, which had been China's major export item until the end of the nineteenth century, failed to compete with upstart rivals in Japan, Indian, and Ceylon, in large part because of the poor quality of the Chinese product—producers and middlemen alike often adulterating the tea shipments with substandard teas or even with weeds and sand. Other export items, such as vegetable oils, soy beans, and straw braids, also failed to capitalize on their early export potential as a result of adulteration and shoddy workmanship. "As in so many other instances in China," observed the Commissioner of Customs in Hankow in 1923, "a decline in quality upon an increased demand being apparent has already set in, and adulteration [of wood oil] with oils of lesser value, such as sesamum, is already the rule and not the exception."[7] Chinese producers and merchants, it seems, were often afflicted with a bazaar mentality, grasping at short-term profits without regard for long-term development.

On balance, China's producers benefited from the expansion of foreign trade, both import and exports. If the producers had been sufficiently motivated or the government in Peking or Nanking (like that in Tokyo) had been sufficiently strong to maintain quality standards, the benefits would have been even greater.

Banking

Although the primary goal of the foreigners in China had been trade, their activities quickly spilled over into other sectors of the economy. This was largely because the traditional Chinese economy was weak in such services as international banking, insurance, shipping, mining, and manufacturing, all of which were essential to the foreigners' successful conduct of trade.

During late imperial times, China's native banks—the *qianzhuang* and the Shansi remittance banks—effectively met the needs of domestic commerce. The foreign merchants, however, being outsiders, could not easily obtain credit from them. Nor were these native banks equipped to service international financial transactions, such as the exchange of foreign currencies. As early as 1845, therefore, the British-chartered Oriental Banking Corporation established a branch in Hong Kong and three years later in Shanghai. During the next twenty-five years, branches of a dozen other foreign banks, most of which were Anglo-Indian in background, began operations in Hong Kong.

The intricacies of China's domestic trade remained a closed book to the Europeans who ran these new banks, however, and a bank that was created expressly to service the China trade soon overshadowed all competitors. This was the Hong Kong and Shanghai Banking Corporation, chartered in England in 1864. After 1889, banks representing the interests of other foreign nationals quickly followed suit.

The principal function of these banks was financing foreign trade. Foreign traders who were exporting goods from China needed credit to cover the period from the time they purchased goods in China until they received payment for delivery abroad. Importers similarly needed capital to pay for goods until they received payment from Chinese dealers. The largest of the trading firms, such as Jardine, Matheson and Company, were not heavily dependent on such credits, but the bulk of the trade was conducted by a host of lesser merchants who were able to survive only with the loans provided by these foreign banks. The importance of this banking service is suggested by the fact that the thirty-two foreign banks in China and Hong Kong in the early 1930s financed some 90 percent of China's foreign trade.

Foreign banks also served the Chinese. They extended credit to the Chinese government, to private enterprises, and even to *qianzhuang*. Chinese citizens—especially wealthy officials, warlords, and landlords—were major depositors in these foreign banks because they were more concerned about the security of their wealth than about the higher return that they could obtain from the native Chinese banks. The foreign banks also served as depositories for the Chinese government, which customarily repaid its foreign debts, such as loans and indemnities, through these banks. They also issued paper currencies, which circulated widely from the late nineteenth century until the 1930s. Indeed, between 1910 and 1930, these foreign-issued bank notes equaled or exceeded the value of all Chinese-issued bank notes, public and private. The foreign bank notes, solid in value and far more convenient than the silver currency, were highly popular with the Chinese, whether issued in denominations of taels, Hong Kong dollars, Chinese dollars, or foreign currencies. Chinese provincial banks, by contrast, tended to issue un-backed paper money that fluctuated in value and often circulated at a sizable discount.

The first modern-style bank that was owned and operated by Chinese was established in 1897. By the Nanking Decade (1927–1937), Chinese modern banks were outstripping the foreign competition, in large part because of what has been called their "symbiotic relationship" with the Nationalist government.[8] After China regained tariff autonomy and control of its salt revenues in 1929, the Nationalist government opted to use the Chinese-operated, rather than the foreign-operated, banks as its depositories. During the early 1930s, too, the Nationalist government relied heavily on these banks for credit—a circumstance welcomed by the Chinese bankers because the effective yield was often 15 to 20 percent a year. During the Nanking Decade, therefore, the modern Chinese banks initially prospered, multiplying in both number and assets.

This hothouse growth did not produce a robust banking system, however, because the banks' excessive dependence on the government was good for the health of neither the economy generally nor the banks themselves. Because the banks granted a substantial share of their loans to the government (estimates range from 40 to 70 percent of total bank credits), they had relatively few assets left over to lend to the capital-starved private entrepreneurs. In fact, the total of all loans given by the Chinese modern banks to industrial enterprises in the early 1930s amounted to only 4 to 5 percent of their aggregate capitalization. These new-style banks, therefore, made a pitifully small contribution to China's industrial modernization.

The close links with the government, although highly lucrative, also proved to be the banks' undoing. In 1935, in a maneuver designed to halt the government's excessive dependence on private loans, Finance Minister H. H. Kung seized control of the nation's major banks. The result of this so-called Banking Coup of 1935 was that the government gained control of over 70 percent of the nation's banking assets. It also set the stage for the rampant inflation of the 1940s, which proved so disastrous for the Nationalist government, because the government could obtain from the banks new and almost unlimited quantities of paper currency merely by issuing paper securities.

Steamboat Shipping and Railways

Commerce, of course, depends on transportation, and members of the foreign-merchant community were pioneers in promoting modern modes of transportation in China. Shipping in coastal and inland waters is a prerogative usually reserved for a country's own citizens. But China relinquished its monopoly of coastal shipping to the Americans in 1844 in the Treaty of Wangxia, and the other treaty powers gained that privilege through the ratchet-like escalation of the most-favored-nation clause. Subsequently, China also granted the foreign powers the right to trade on inland rivers, beginning in 1858 with a grant to the British to sail on the Yangtze.

Even before the legalization of interport trade by foreigners in the Treaty of Wangxia, however, foreign firms had not hesitated to ship goods in their own vessels from Hong Kong to the newly opened treaty ports. The fast-sailing Western ships easily outdistanced the pirates who then infested those waters, and the newly established foreign insurance companies would not provide coverage on goods sent by native junks. With the legalization of this shipping and then with the arrival of steamboats, foreign tonnage in Chinese waters greatly increased. Initially, this shipping had been undertaken by the trading firms themselves, but in 1862, the American firm of Russell and Company established the first foreign company (Shanghai Steam Navigation Company) that was organized expressly to engage in China's coastal shipping. In 1867 and 1868, two British-owned firms joined the competition. These and later foreign shipping companies were major tools in the opening of China to foreign trade, and the creation of each treaty port was usually followed closely by the opening of regular shipping service between it and Shanghai and Hong Kong. Foreign shippers also ventured into the interior of China, American-built paddle wheelers overcoming the perils of navigating up the Yangtze to Hankow by 1862 and even to Chungking by 1898.

Chinese actually contributed in major ways to the development of steam shipping in China. Although the first steamboat companies to engage in interport hauling were established by the Americans and British, Chinese compradores and merchants were often major stockholders. For example, in the largest of the early firms, the American-operated Shanghai Steam Navigation Company, Chinese probably held the majority of the shares. Most of the cargo carried by these foreign firms, moreover, was owned by Chinese merchants who recognized the advantages of security and speed offered by the foreign ships. As early as 1873, too, the powerful official Li Hongzhang organized the China Merchants' Steam Navigation Company, which soon became a major competitor of the foreign firms. Although this government-dominated company stagnated after 1883, Chinese-owned shipping continued to grow, and by the 1930s was challenging the foreigners' dominance.

Despite this growing competition from a modern technology, native junks persisted with a remarkably tenacity. Indeed, in the 1930s, they still conveyed over 80 percent of the total water freight. Although modern steamers generally dominated the traffic between the treaty ports, the supremacy of the junks outside the treaty-port system remained unchallenged, serving the domestic trade and acting as feeders to the foreign trade in the treaty ports. Because of the increased commercial activity in the twentieth century, moreover, the total number of junks operating in China's waters actually rose, perhaps by more than twofold.

Chinese accepted railroads less readily than steamboats. The first railroad in China was completed in 1876. With the arrogance typical of the foreign-merchant community at the time, the British firm of Jardine, Matheson and Company purchased a 12-mile stretch of land, parcel by parcel, from Shanghai to Woosung and built the railway line—without obtaining official Chinese approval. Local opposition was vehement, but trains began moving on the line in June 1876. Just two months later, the train struck and killed a Chinese. As a result of the furor that ensued, the imperial government bought out the British owners, and in November 1878 tore up the rails and discarded the rolling stock.

Chinese opposition to this railway and to railways generally between the 1860s and the 1880s was based partly on strategic considerations. Most officials in Peking feared that foreign armies could use trains to attack deeply and quickly into the nation's interior, thus undoing all their efforts to build up the nation's coastal defenses. They also feared—with the Taiping and Nien uprisings still etched deeply in their memories—that large numbers of transport workers would be put out of work by competition from the "iron roads," and thus forced into rebellion. Ordinary Chinese, too, were distressed that the railway tracks, the movement of the locomotives, and the stench of their engines would upset the balance of geomantic forces, with catastrophic consequences for both the living and the dead.

Despite such opposition, the pragmatic-minded governor-general of Chihli Province, Li Hongzhang, soon began constructing a railway from the coal mine at Tangshan to the docks near Tientsin. This 7-mile line was completed in 1880, and its manifest utility did much to still the criticisms of the conservatives. China also, of course, felt more comfortable when the railroad was planned and controlled by the Chinese government rather than by the inscrutable barbarians. Yet by the eve of the Sino-Japanese War (1894–95), the Chinese had laid a total of only 195 miles of track, and serious railroad construction did not get under way until after the war. Then in just eight years, 2,513 miles of line were laid, two-thirds of which was constructed by foreigners.

The foreign powers' interest in railroads was only marginally economic. After China's defeat by Japan, they expected the ramshackle empire to collapse, and their scramble for railroad concessions between 1895 and 1903 was motivated largely by the desire to demarcate areas that would fall into their control following the anticipated demise of the empire. This episode, a sordid tale of imperialistic greed that has been told many times in the political and diplomatic histories of the period, had the positive effect of bestirring the Chinese themselves to develop the nation's railways. Popular "national-salvation" movements promoted railroad construction and led to the beginnings of a large number of rail lines, such as those proposed between Canton and Hankow, Hankow and Szechwan, and Soochow and Ningpo. Enthusiasm generally exceeded capability, however, and none of these lines came even close to completion before the dynasty fell in 1912. The imperial government, meanwhile, completed nearly 2,000 miles of track (including lines between Shanghai and Nanking and between Tientsin and Pukow), as compared with just 401 miles of track constructed under popular auspices. By 1911, China had a total of 5,800 miles of railway, 41 percent of which was owned by the foreigners.

During the next twenty-five years, until the beginning of the war with Japan in 1937, nearly 6,800 miles of additional track were constructed, for a total of 12,600 miles. However, almost half of China's total railway mileage lay in Manchuria; just 7,300 miles of railway served China proper. The foreigners' share in the ownership of these lines south of the Great Wall had fallen by 1937 to about 35 percent.

The motives that led to this expansion of the railways were primarily political: the foreign powers used the railroads as a means of staking out territorial claims in China, and later the Nationalist government viewed railroads as an instrument of forging national unity. From the outset, therefore, the economic benefits of the railroads were regarded as of secondary importance.

One economic activity that was revolutionized by the introduction of the railways, however, was coal mining. At least as early as the Tang Dynasty, Chinese had used coal for cooking and in such industries as iron smelting and ceramic- and glassmaking. But the costs of transporting such a heavy, low-value-per-unit commodity as coal by traditional means were nearly prohibitive. Coal, therefore, was traditionally used in places remote from the mines only in the most exiguous amounts.

Following the introduction of railroads, it became economical to ship coal over long distances. Like Li Hongzhang's Tangshan line, several of the railways, especially branch lines, had been designed primarily to move coal from the mines to the industrial centers. The result was to cut the cost of shipping coal to about one-fifth of that in the 1870s. This gave an enormous fillip to the coal industry, output of large mines (there exist no reliable data for small mines) increasing from 1896 to 1936 by a factor of sixty. During the early twentieth century, therefore, it became feasible to use coal extensively in manufacturing and as the principal source of industrial power.

Railroads also contributed to modern industry by serving as the major supply lines for the raw materials used in the production of consumer goods. Approximately 90 percent of the raw materials used by China's consumer-goods industries, which constituted the overwhelmingly largest part of the industrial sector as a whole, were agricultural in origin.[9] And over 60 percent of those raw materials were delivered to the industrial centers by rail. Clearly, the railroads were of signal importance to industrial production.

But the economic benefits of railroads within China proper were largely limited to the modernizing sector. Modern industry and mining in the 1930s still accounted for only 2.95 percent of the net domestic product, however; thus the impact of railroads on the economy as a whole, as transmitted through manufacturing and mining, could not have been large.

Some writers, it is true, have argued that railroads did substantially benefit the agricultural sector, contending that railroads stimulated peasants' involvement in the market economy and consequently led to increases of farm output. The data, however, simply do not bear out these claims. No more than 4 to 7 percent of all marketed agricultural goods, for instance, was transported by rail. And agricultural produce accounted for only 12 to 15 percent of the railways' total tonnage during the 1930s. Some regions that specialized in industrial crops, such as tobacco in parts of Shantung or cotton in parts of Hopei, no doubt benefited considerably from the availability of this relatively cheap, safe, and prompt form of transportation. Judging from the quantities of farm produce transported by rail, however, those regions were not extensive.

Two factors imposed limits on the economic payoff of the railroads. First, the railway system was sparse. A glance at a map reveals that the 7,300 miles of track within China proper in 1937 traversed only a small number of the approximately 1,500 *xian* south of the Great Wall. In fact, railroads in 1937 constituted only about 2.4 percent of all land routes in the country (including Manchuria).[10] Second, most of the railroads constructed south of the Great Wall were redundant of existing trade routes. This was especially true in central and south China, where junks and steamers carried freight on the elaborate network of water routes at prices that were competitive with those of the railroads. Even in north China, much of the rail system was simply superimposed on existing water routes.[11]

Nor did the Chinese economy even benefit from the backward-linkage effects of railway construction, which had been so beneficial to the producer-goods industries in western Europe and the United States. This was because China lacked the iron, steel, and heavy-machine industries that could produce locomotives, rolling stock, tracks, and bridge materials in the quantity and of the quality demanded. Thus only 30 percent of China's expenditures for railway-related industrial goods between 1895 and 1916 was spent in China; the remaining 70 percent was spent on imports from abroad. And of the 1,244 locomotives purchased from 1897 to 1930, only 58 had been manufactured in China; the rest had been made in England, Germany, France, Belgium, and the United States. The result was that foreign industries, not China's, received the strongest boost from Chinese railway construction.

In Manchuria, however, in contrast to the experience south of the Great Wall, railroads did contribute appreciably to economic development. In that vast, underdeveloped, and underpopulated region, railways quickly extended beyond the preexisting transportation networks. There they made possible the exploitation of the forests of the north, the development of the rich coal and iron mines, and the shipment of soybeans and bean products, which by the late 1920s had become China's major export. They also facilitated the large migrations into the region from Hopei and Shantung. After 1931, of course, Manchuria contributed less to the economy of China than to that of Japan.

Table 8.3.   Estimated[a] Number and Capitalization of Foreign-owned
Industries in China in 1894[b]

Type of Firm	Number	Capital (Ch$)
Shipyards: construction and repairs	12	4,943,000
Tea processing	7	4,000,000
Machine silk reeling	7	3,972,222
Processing of exports and imports (other than tea and machine silk)	19	1,493,000
Other light manufacturing	39	3,793,000
Electric power and waterworks	4	1,523,000
TOTAL	88	19,724,222

[a]Table is based on incomplete data.
[b]Includes a small number of firms based in Hong Kong.
Source: Albert Feuerwerker, "Economic Trends in the Late Ch'ing Empire, 1870–1911,"
in *The Cambridge History of China*, vol. 11, ed. John K. Fairbank and Kwang-ching Liu
(Cambridge: Cambridge University Press, 1980), p. 29. Reprinted by permission.

Foreign Manufacturing

Before the signing of the Sino-Japanese Treaty of Shimonoseki in 1895, foreigners
had no legal right to establish manufacturing enterprises on Chinese soil. Nonetheless, foreigners, even before that date, had started various forms of manufacturing in support of their commercial goals. An estimated 103 foreign-owned factories had operated in China before 1895 in defiance of the law.

The first foreign manufacturing firms were ship-repair yards. The number of
foreign ships coming to China increased steadily after the Opium War—by 1865,
some 16,000 entered the treaty ports in any one year—and they were often in
need of repair following long ocean voyages from Europe or America. Initially,
the foreigners relied on Chinese firms for repairs, but they had no confidence in
Chinese workmanship unless supervised by a knowledgeable foreigner. It was one
of these foreign overseers who, sometime between 1845 and 1856, established the
first foreign dockyard in China. Other shipyards were soon established (usually by
the English), although the first large-scale one, Boyd and Company, was not established in Shanghai until 1863. Before 1895, shipbuilding and repair was, in
terms of total capital, the largest foreign-owned industry in China (See Table 8.3).

To facilitate their commercial ventures, foreign merchants also began to process Chinese raw materials for shipment back home. The costs of transporting
goods to Europe and America were high, and the advantages of processing the
Chinese materials in at least a preliminary form prior to export were obvious.
Russian tea merchants, beginning with a plant in Hankow in 1863, were the first
to establish factories for the processing of exports. Merchants from other countries
soon were refining wool, hides, eggs, sugar, tung oil, and vegetable oils in preparation for shipment. Gradually, the foreigners in China also began to manufacture
goods for consumption in China. Some of these commodities were intended pri-

marily for the use of foreigners in the treaty ports: Western drugs (production began in 1853), bread and candies (1855), beer (1864), ice (1880), glass (1882), furniture (1885), and cement (1891). Other foreign factories, taking advantage of China's cheap labor, began to manufacture goods for Chinese consumption in competition with imports from abroad. Matches (production began in 1880), cigarettes (ca. 1902), light bulbs (ca. 1911), metal nails, paper, soap, gramophones, and vacuum bottles were some of the other industries started by foreigners in China.

The largest foreign industry was cotton textiles. Both British and American merchants had planned to establish textile mills in Shanghai and Tientsin in the 1860s, but Chinese opposition forestalled foreign entry into the industry until after the signing of the Treaty of Shimonoseki. By 1913, eight foreign cotton mills (run by British, Japanese, Americans, and Germans) were operating in China, with a total of 345,000 spindles and 2,000 looms. By 1936, those numbers had risen to 2.5 million spindles and 33,000 looms—accounting for only 29 percent of the yarn produced by modern factories in China, but 64 percent of the cotton cloth.

A significant trend in the foreign-owned textile factories during and after World War I was the growing preponderance of the Japanese. By the mid-1930s, the Germans and Americans had long since dropped out of the competition, and British-owned mills ran only 4 percent of the spindles and 7 percent of the looms in China. The Japanese, in contrast, had invested heavily in new equipment so that their mills not only were more efficient, but also dominated the production of high-count yarns—leaving the production of low-count yarns to the relatively antiquated mills owned by Chinese and British.

Foreign industrialists enjoyed significant advantages in China that were denied their Chinese rivals. They were protected in their treaty-port sanctuaries from Chinese governmental interference and squeeze—a factor that, as we will see, was of no small value. They had easier access to the technologies and engineering know-how of the West. And they could obtain loans from foreign banks easily and at relatively low rates of interest, while Chinese industrialists were chronically short of capital. By 1933, therefore, foreign-owned firms were producing more cotton cloth, cigarettes, coal, and electric power than were Chinese-owned facilities. And they controlled fully 63 percent of all industrial capital in the country (including Manchuria).

Chinese manufacturers, however, enjoyed advantages of their own in competition with the foreigners. They were more knowledgeable about local conditions: they knew consumer needs, were familiar with Chinese marketing practices, and could pursue claims against suppliers and debtors more effectively than could the culture-bound and often treaty-port–bound foreign industrialists. The rising tide of nationalism during the early twentieth century, too, led to the antiforeign boycotts and the movements to "Buy Chinese," which put the foreign manufacturers at an "unfair" disadvantage. Despite a slow and halting start during the latter half of the nineteenth century, and despite the higher capitalization of their foreign rivals, Chinese-owned modern factories by the 1930s were outproducing the foreign-owned factories in China proper, in terms of value-added, by a ratio of almost four to one.

Chinese-Owned Modern Industries

The Initial Stage

The Chinese had been slow to emulate the Westerners' industrial model. Even after the defeat in the Opium War, they remained blissfully convinced of the superiority of Chinese ways and deprecated virtually everything foreign. Thus they hunkered down and hoped that this nasty business with the foreigners would go away. It would not, of course, and in 1860, the Europeans used their modern arms to occupy Peking, burn the Summer Palace, and force the emperor to take refuge in Jehol, in southern Manchuria. Further demonstration of the superiority of the Westerners' military technology was provided during the Taiping Rebellion by the Ever-Victorious Army, led by Frederick Townsend Ward and Charles "Chinese" Gordon, which showed that Chinese troops, when armed with Western guns, were more than a match for domestic rebels.

It was, therefore, the military effects of the West's Industrial Revolution that first caught the attention of the Chinese. Soon a small cadre of high-level officials, led by Zeng Guofan, Zuo Zongtang, and Li Hongzhang, established dockyards and arsenals to construct modern gunboats and to produce Western-style guns and ammunition. The initial attempt to apply Western technology to the manufacture of weapons was undertaken by Zeng Guofan when in 1862, he established the Anqing Arsenal in Anhwei during his efforts to suppress the Taiping rebels. He and Li Hongzhang later launched a more grandiose project when they established the famous Jiangnan Arsenal in Shanghai in 1865. Using imported equipment and materials, this arsenal was soon manufacturing its own tools and machinery, and in 1868 launched its first modern gunboat. Li established a similar arsenal in Nanking in 1866; between 1867 and 1874, it built fifteen ships, the largest of which was 280 feet long. These ventures initially appeared to be a grand success, the *North China Herald* observing even as early as 1866 that Li Hongzhang's arsenals "for extent may vie with those of the most powerful nations of Europe," possessed as they were of "enormous magazines" and "vast numbers" of weapons.[12] But these military factories never fulfilled their early promise. The quality of the guns and ships they produced was disappointing. And the costs of production far exceeded the price of imported weapons and ships, largely because most of the materiel had to be purchased abroad and because the Chinese mandarins and the foreign employees in the factories drew excessively high salaries. Never really able to compete with their European counterparts, these arsenals by the twentieth century had fallen woefully below international standards.

By the 1870s, Li Hongzhang realized that modern guns and ships were merely surface manifestations of the Westerners' strength and that the true source of national power lay in economic wealth. "China's chronic weakness," he declared, "stems from poverty."[13] On this premise, he inaugurated a remarkable series of nonmilitary industrial ventures. Li had been perturbed by the large profits that foreigners were drawing from their growing domination of China's interport shipping. Hopeful of stanching this flow of China's wealth to the foreigners, he established in 1873 China's first steamship company, the China Merchants' Steam Navigation Company.

The formation of this company led logically to other industrial innovations. In 1877, he opened the Kaiping Coal Mines, near Tientsin, which provided fuel and cargo for the China Merchants' ships on the return trip to Shanghai (the ships having brought tribute rice from Shanghai). And in 1878, he constructed the 7-mile railway to transport coal from the mines. Other undertakings begun by Li included a copper mine (1881) and gold mine (1887), as well as several iron and coal mines using Western machinery. In 1879, he established China's first domestically owned telegraph line (British and Danes had connected Shanghai by cable to Hong Kong, Vladivostok, and Japan as early as 1870 to 1871), a cotton-spinning factory in 1882, and a cotton-weaving mill in 1890.

Although Li Hongzhang was far and away the most enterprising supporter of industrial ventures in the 1870s and 1880s, a scattering of other provincial officials also launched a number of nonmilitary industries. Zhang Zhidong, governor-general first in Kwangtung–Kwangsi (1884–89) and then in Hunan–Hupei (1889–1907), established cotton-textile mills, silk factories, tanneries, iron and coal mines, and the Hanyang Ironworks (which later became famous as the Hanyeping Coal and Iron Company). Other provincial authorities in Hupei and even faraway Kweichow also established a number of textile mills, match factories, and ironworks.

The form of organization used by Li Hongzhang in most of his industrial ventures was known as *guandu shangban* ("official-supervision, merchant-management"). This was a hybrid device that merged the brokerage concept of administration (chapter 6) with the Westerners' institution of joint-stock companies. It enabled Li to solve the problem of how to establish these enterprises when the potential investors—China's merchants—lacked the needed initiative and the government lacked the needed capital. He therefore provided the initiative himself, using in large part the merchants' money. Of the modern enterprises established during the late Qing period, only about a dozen were formally regarded as *guandu-shangban* operations. "But the essential ingredients of the kuan-tu shang-pan pattern were to be found in virtually every industrial or commercial undertaking organized by Chinese promoters before the end of the Ch'ing dynasty." [14]

The China Merchants' Steam Navigation Company was a typical *guandu-shangban* enterprise. As the promoter of this undertaking, Li was the ultimate authority over it and protected it from the exactions of corrupt and unfriendly officials. He was also an important shareholder, investing 50,000 taels of his own money, and he lent the company an additional 135,000 taels, at interest, from official funds that he controlled. The day-to-day operations of the firm were directed, however, by a former comprador, who served as general manager. Nominally, the company was owned by the shareholders, most of whom were also compradors, who provided 110,000 taels of the original investment. The economic risks were completely theirs. "Profit and loss," Li remarked, "are entirely the responsibility of the merchants and do not involve the government." [15] But the merchants had little, if any, control over the management of the firm. The concepts of shareholders' meetings and boards of directors were alien to China, and the level of official involvement was high. A final feature of the company, common to all *guandu-shangban* enterprises, was a monopoly franchise to help get the company going—in this case, an assurance that it would transport at least 20 percent of the tribute rice sent by the government each year from central to north China.

Beginning in the mid-1880s, a subtle but significant change occurred in the *guandu-shangban* enterprises, because, although the term *guandu shangban* persisted, actual management of these firms fell into the hand of bureaucrats. The first managers had been merchants with purchased official titles and ranks. They had been merchants first and officials second. The managers who took charge of the *guandu-shangban* enterprises after the mid-1880s, such as Sheng Xuanhuai and Zhang Yenmou, tended to be officials first and merchants second. These official-managers had no entrepreneurial experience, received salaries regardless of the level of company profits, and were habituated to a work style markedly different from that in the business world. *Guandu-shangban* enterprises, as a result, soon acquired the organizational traits typical of government bureaus: inefficiency, incompetence, corruption, and disregard for the interests of the shareholders. For a merchant-shareholder to protest to an official-manager, wrote one investor, was "like striking rocks with eggs. Truly we can do nothing." Merchants consequently lost confidence in the *guandu-shangban* enterprises, which thereafter withered for want of private investments or became an even greater burden on the revenues of provincial governments.[16]

Meeting distrust and enmity from the merchant community, official patrons of new enterprises after the late 1880s sought forms of organization that would be more attractive to potential investors. They conjured up numerous new guises, the most common of which was *guanshang hoban* ("official-merchant joint management"), a term that seemed to promise an equal partnership between the officials and the merchants. The first of these was the Kweichow Mining and Iron Works, organized by the provincial governor in 1886. The governor-general of Hunan–Hupei, Zhang Zhidong, who next to Li Hongzhang was the most prominent industrial promoter in the late Qing period, also employed this cosmetic formulation in his several enterprises. The *guanshang-hoban* ventures proved to be no different from the *guandu-shangban* enterprises, however, because the state and the officials invariably overawed and overshadowed the merchants.

During this formative period of China's modern industry, only a few purely private enterprises were established. In 1883, the comprador Zhu Dachun successfully established a machine factory in Shanghai; later, he also started textile, flour, paper, and rice mills. The most famous success story was that of the Rong family, which, starting with a small flour mill in Wusih in 1901, had built a considerable empire of textile factories and flour mills by the 1930s. Pitifully few such private ventures succeeded, however, and those that did flourish were small in scale. The Rong's first cotton mill, for example, was launched with a capital of only 30,000 taels, as compared with over 350,000 taels raised to start the Huasheng Spinning and Weaving Mill in 1881, which was a *guandu-shangban* enterprise. Private promoters, acting on their own, could rarely attract much capital. The concept of joint-stock companies had still not gained popularity, and the private ventures lacked the prestige needed to overcome the potential investors' suspicion of such a strange idea. Moreover, by contrast with patrons of *guandu-shangban* companies, private firms were unable to ensure protection for their enterprises from official exactions.

Wealthy Chinese were, to be sure, looking for investment opportunities—as evidenced by the fact that fully 40 percent of the capital invested in the so-called foreign-owned firms in China in the late nineteenth century was actually provided by Chinese investors. But Chinese, knowing the officials' penchant for squeeze, feared for the security of their investments if placed in Chinese firms. "The major problem in China's economic development was not the lack of capital, but the lack of trust on the part of the investors toward bureaucrats." [17] Virtually everyone, therefore, merchants and officials alike, recognized that a large-scale industrial undertaking could succeed only if officials were participants in it. But therein lay a dilemma, because official involvement was invariably followed by official control, and official control usually resulted in debilitation of the enterprise.

After 1899, however, Zhang Jian and a few other industrial promoters discovered an alternative to official control. Zhang was that rarest of creatures: a preeminent scholar who scorned an official career to engage in business. In 1894, he had placed first among all *jinshi* graduates in that year's metropolitan examination. This achievement assured him a brilliant and remunerative bureaucratic career. After serving in the Hanlin Academy for less than a year, however, he resigned from government service and became an industrial entrepreneur. His first undertaking was the Dah Sun (Dasheng) Cotton-Spinning Mill, started in 1899 with a capital of one million taels, in his native city of Nantong, near Shanghai. Later, he created a veritable industrial complex in Nantong by adding a flour mill, an oil mill, a shipping line, a distillery, and a silk filature.

The secret of Zhang Jian's success was that because he was primarily a private entrepreneur rather than a bureaucrat, he was committed to efficient, profit-making management; yet because he was also a prestigious scholar, he possessed the status that enabled him to cultivate friendships with powerful officials, such as Governors-General Zhang Zhidong and Liu Kunyi, and to procure large loans and investments from the government without having to surrender control of the enterprises to the bureaucrats. Zhang Jian's successes were outstanding among China's early industrial ventures, but he was also representative of a small number of officials and one-time officials who during the last decade or so of the dynasty placed a higher value on entrepreneurship than on bureaucratic success. (Another prominent example was Zhou Xuexi, who developed and ran a large mining operation and the famous Chee Hsin [Qixin] Cement Company.) Their careers reveal how radically social values were changing during the waning days of the dynasty; yet their experiences also demonstrated that official status and connections were invaluable to the success of a sizable industrial undertaking.

Official involvement in industrial enterprises came under sharp challenge during the "rights-recovery movement" between 1903 and 1911. The Chinese Imperial Railway Administration, headed by Sheng Xuanhuai, had relied heavily on foreign loans to finance railway construction. When a wave of antiforeignism swept the country in the early years of the twentieth century, many Chinese expressed the fear that the government was selling out to foreign interests by granting monopoly rights and economic concessions in return for the railroad loans.

In response to the swelling popular sentiment, the government revoked the concessions that it had granted to the foreigners in return for constructing the Canton–Hankow and Shanghai–Ningpo railways. At the same time, it issued charters to nineteen private Chinese corporations to construct railways untainted by foreign funds. To finance the new "popularly owned" *(minye)* Canton–Hankow line, Cantonese leaders of the rights-recovery movement sold shares at such low prices that virtually any supporter of rights recovery—even laborers and students—could purchase them. One share cost only Ch$5, which could be paid in installments over an eighteen-month period. This plan of mass financing proved to be successful beyond anyone's dreams. With subscriptions pouring in from overseas Chinese as well as from the provinces, the company raised some Ch$40 million (about 30 million taels)—double its initial goal—in just four months. Managers of the Shanghai–Ningpo line imitated this scheme and quickly raised Ch$13 million. (These endeavors contrasted sharply with those of other private industrial firms that attempted to raise capital solely by eliciting large investments from the merchant community. Zhang Jian managed to raise 1 million taels for the Dah Sun Company, for example, but only with great difficulty.)

The successes of the Canton–Hankow and the Shanghai–Ningpo railways in fund raising were not matched, however, by operational achievements. The "popularly owned" corporations, it soon became clear, were no less subject to gross mismanagement than were the state-controlled ventures: the corporations' managers let bids at high prices to engineering firms in which they held an interest; embezzlement was rampant; and construction of bridges and other line work was done shabbily. In 1911, when the Qing government nationalized the nation's railways, only 45 of the projected 650 miles of track on the Canton–Hankow line had been completed. The other "popularly owned" railways had been plagued by even greater difficulties, and their achievements were even less notable. Nonetheless, when the imperial government attempted to reestablish its control over these railways, public resentment was so strong that the resulting political protest contributed significantly to the overthrow of the dynasty.

When the dynasty fell in 1912, China could boast of the beginnings of a modern industrial sector. During the initial gestation period, 1865 to 1895, nineteen government arsenals and shipyards and about seventy-five other manufacturing firms had been established by Chinese in all of China. During the next seventeen years—motivated partly by a nationalistic desire to strengthen the nation, and even more by the prospect of substantial profits—private and semigovernmental entrepreneurs established approximately 500 modern industrial plants.

The Golden Age

The golden age of Chinese industry was between 1914 and 1922. After the outbreak of World War I, European industrialists stopped producing for export and concentrated on meeting their own nations' war needs. Japanese yarn exports to

China also fell by 65 percent between 1914 and 1919. As a consequence, foreign competition with China's factories virtually disappeared. At the same time, European demand for Chinese goods—such as strategic ores (tin, antimony, and tungsten), silk, wool, and egg products—increased sharply. Another factor that favored Chinese industry was the increase in freight charges for ocean shipping, which in 1918 and 1919 were some ten to twenty times higher than they had been before the war. Whatever foreign imports did reach the Chinese market, therefore, were available only at exorbitant and often uncompetitive prices—the high shipping costs having the same effect as a protective tariff. The high cost of shipping also dictated that Chinese exports of raw goods, such as vegetable oils and mining products, be more thoroughly cleaned and refined than before, thus greatly stimulating the processing industries. Many of China's industrialists consequently earned unprecedentedly large profits during the Great War.

Even two to three years after the war, the Western nations, now engaged in postwar reconstruction, continued to be big buyers of China's raw and semimanufactured goods, yet they continued to produce largely for their own use. Another factor that favored Chinese industry was the development in China of an antiforeign economic-boycott movement. The first boycott had been organized in 1905 as a protest against America's exclusionary, anti-Chinese immigration policy, followed in 1908 by an anti-Japanese boycott. These economic boycotts became a common means by which Chinese patriots expressed their anger at the foreign powers. Indeed, during the May Fourth Movement (1919) and the emotionally charged years of the 1920s, the boycott of foreign goods and the corresponding call to "Buy Chinese" became semipermanent features of the economic landscape.

Yet China's industrialists were unable to take full advantage of the hothouse atmosphere during and after the Great War, because they could not expand their plants quickly enough to satisfy the potential market. Textile manufacturers, for example, could not purchase the looms, spindles, motors, and other capital equipment needed to increase output. This was because foreign suppliers had converted to war production, and Chinese machine factories still lacked the expertise needed to produce such sophisticated equipment. Chinese industrialists actually placed large orders for European equipment as early as 1916 and 1917, but the new equipment did not reach Chinese docks until 1921 and 1922. Then, however, the industrial plant grew rapidly. During just those two years, thirty-nine textile mills opened. Indeed, the growth of industry during this golden age is suggested by the increase in total spindles, Chinese- and foreign-owned combined, from 866,000 to 3 million between 1914 and 1922 (a gain of 317 percent), and in the total number of looms from 4,800 to over 19,000 (300 percent). Most of that growth came during the latter years of the period. These rates of increase were then the largest in the world.

During the golden age, the industrial sector began to mature, as evidenced by two significant departures from previous practice. First, imports of consumer goods, especially cotton goods, declined, while imports of producer goods sharply increased (accounting in 1920 for 29 percent of all imports). Although the composition of imports and exports suggests that the Chinese economy was still "undeveloped," it was clearly being restructured, indicating a shift to the stage of early industrial growth. Second, industrial development was promoted largely by private entrepreneurs, who had served neither as government officials nor as compradors with foreign firms. It appears, therefore, that the impotence of government during the early Republican period—the warlord period—had the wholesome effect of lessening bureaucratic intervention in the economy.[18]

An industrial crisis beginning in late 1922 marked the end of the golden age. The causes of the crisis were complex: a severe shortage of domestic raw cotton as a result of a poor harvest in 1921 to 1922; the high price of raw cotton on the world market; the fall in the world price of silver, which devalued China's currency; and no doubt, the return of foreign competition as European and American factories completed their reconversion to peacetime production and reentered the international markets. The crisis was short-lived, however, a bumper cotton harvest in the fall of 1925 bringing cotton prices down, and another antiforeign boycott increasing the domestic demand for Chinese goods. Thereafter, China's industry resumed its growth, albeit at a lower rate than during the golden age[19]

The Nanking Decade

A new phase of governmental involvement in the industrial sector began after the establishment of Nationalist rule in 1927. The government of Chiang Kai-shek, in accordance with the writings of Sun Yat-sen, was ideologically committed to economic modernization. And industry in China proper did continue to develop impressively from 1931 to 1936, growing at an annual rate of 6.7 percent. This increase has been attributed to such "growth-inducing measures" of the Nationalist government as attaining tariff autonomy, abolishing the *likin* transit tax, and reforming the currency.[20]

These measures did little, however, to promote industrial growth. The likin, for example, was generally replaced by such euphemistic substitutes as a "special consumption tax." Frequently, too, Nationalist policies obstructed industrial development. The government throughout the 1930s was primarily concerned with the military tasks confronting it. As a result, it invested few resources and little effort in programs of economic development and borrowed heavily to finance its various military undertakings. With the government absorbing more than 40 percent of the nation's bank loans during the 1930s, industrial loans could be obtained only at a premium, often at interest rates of 18 to 20 percent a year. These were rates that "most Chinese industries were unable to pay; as a result, industrial activity was turned into speculative ventures."[21]

Moreover, because Nationalist control of the rural areas was weak, the central government in 1928 surrendered the revenues from the land tax to the provincial governments, despite the fact that the agricultural sector produced most of the national product. Commerce and industry were more easily taxed, and the Nanking government derived its tax revenue almost entirely from three indirect taxes: the customs tariff, the salt tax, and the so-called Consolidated Taxes—excise taxes levied at the place of origin on such commodities as tobacco, flour, cotton yarn, matches, cement, and liquor. Because the government was hard-pressed for revenue, the burden of taxes was sometimes ruinous for the industrialists. During the first three years of Nationalist rule, for instance, two-thirds of Shanghai's 182 Chinese-owned cigarette manufacturers went out of business because, according to the owners, of excessive taxes. As one cigarette manufacturer complained in 1930, "Taxation is more than five times what it used to be. . . . We have been unable to increase our prices because, every time we increase them, the Government, who has promised to do everything to encourage Chinese trade, has hampered us by imposing heavier taxation."[22] By 1937, even Nanyang Brothers, the largest Chinese-owned cigarette firm, succumbed. Staggering from a 38.7 percent tax on its gross income, the owners surrendered control of the company to Chiang Kai-shek's brother-in-law, T. V. Soong.

Foreign-owned companies, because of their political clout, often avoided these crushing taxes. In 1935, the combined cost of taxes and interest on a bale of yarn for a Chinese-owned mill was Ch\$15, whereas the cost for a Japanese-owned mill was only Ch\$2.70.

For all these reasons, it is doubtful that the industrial expansion during the 1930s, was attributable in substantial degree to the Nationalist government's "growth-inducing measures." Indeed, because industrial production grew at a generally constant rate from 1912 to 1937, except during the especially prosperous years of 1914 to 1922, one suspects that economic modernization—electrification, factory production, railroads, foreign trade—had acquired such a momentum that the modern sector was growing almost irrespective of political regimes or policies.

A possible exception to this negative assessment of the Nationalists' policies toward the industrial sector was the Three-Year Plan of Industrial Development, begun in 1936, under the direction of the National Resources Commission. This commission was a secret agency under Chiang Kai-shek's National Military Council, and the purpose of the Three-Year Plan was to create an industrial base in the interior that would enable the country to wage a major war against Japan without dependence on foreign supplies. The plan envisioned the creation of ten major industrial and mining works, ranging from coal, iron, copper, lead, and zinc mines, to a coal liquification plant, chemical and electrical works, a steel mill, and a machinery factory. By contrast with China's existing industrial plant in the large coastal and riverine cities, these projects would constitute an "internal economic center" in Hupei, Hunan, and Kiangsi provinces, where, it was hoped, they would lie outside the reach of Japanese aggression. Germany played a key role in the plan. From the plan's inception, German experts served as advisers to the National Resources Commission, and German industrial firms were to supply all the equipment for the ten projects, including machinery for entire mines and factories. China would pay Germany for these goods through a barter arrangement, sending metal ores, especially tungsten, which German industry needed to produce high-quality steel.

The National Resources Commission's preliminary work of contracting for materials and training personnel had proceeded quickly and with no evidence of corruption, and thus the auguries for the Three-Year Plan were favorable. But assessment of the new industrial strategy is difficult because war broke out after the first year, and the Japanese soon overran most of the area where the mines and plants were to be located.

If the war aborted the Nationalists' Three-Year Plan, however, it may also have saved China's private factories from being taken over by the state. For in the 1930s, Chiang Kai-shek's economic planners were deeply impressed by the seeming advantages of a "planned economy," as was then being implemented in the Western dictatorships. They aspired, therefore, to bring all industry under governmental control. "Had things gone according to plan," recalled an official of the National Resources Commission, "all industry would have been managed by the state *[guoying]*." [23]

The Wartime and Postwar Industries

How China's industries would have fared if the war with Japan had not erupted can only be speculated. In the event, both private and government-sponsored industries in Nationalist China suffered severe setbacks during the war years, 1937 to 1945. The Japanese invaders quickly occupied the major cities in east China, where the bulk of China's modern industry was located, and the government retreated to the mountainous interior in the west. This area—comprising all or parts of Szechwan, Yunnan, Kweichow, Kiangsi, Hunan, Shensi, and Kansu—was almost untouched by modern life. When the war began, the whole region, with some three-fourths of the nation's territory, could claim only about 6 percent of the nation's factories. Anticipating a long war of attrition, the Nationalist authorities removed arsenals, airplane-assembly plants, steel mills, and other war-related industries to the interior. Transportation was difficult and perilous—hundreds of trackers, for instance, were often needed to pull a heavily loaded boat through the swirling waters in the Yangtze Gorges—yet equipment from 639 factories was relocated in west China. Some 42,000 skilled laborers joined this mass industrial migration. During the initial years of the war, moreover, industry boomed in Nationalist China, numerous factories were established, and industrial production nearly quadrupled between 1938 and 1943.

Still, the industrial base in west China had been small, and total industrial output in unoccupied China never exceeded 12 percent of the pre-1937 levels. Beginning in 1943, moreover, crisis struck. The Japanese blockade and bombing, inflation, deteriorating machinery, and impoverishment of the people all took a toll. As a consequence, 56 percent of the factories closed between 1942 and 1944. When the war ended in August 1945, industry in Nationalist China was verging on total collapse.

But industry in Nationalist-controlled China represented only a part, and much the smaller part, of China's total industrial base during the war years. Large areas were occupied by the Japanese; Manchuria, for example, which had fallen to the Japanese in 1931, is larger than Germany and France combined. Although this region since 1932 had ostensibly been governed by the independent state of Manchukuo, the Japanese army dominated industrial policy. The Japanese goal was to

Table 8.4.   Indices of Industrial Production
in Occupied China

Year	Shanghai	North China
1936	100.0	*
1937	85.5	*
1938	74.9	*
1939	138.6	100.0
1940	154.8	121.0
1941	137.8	138.0
1942	—	148.0

*Data not available.
Source: Yu-Kwei Cheng, *Foreign Trade and Industrial Development of China: An Historical and Integrated Analysis Through 1948* (Washington, D.C.: University Press of Washington, D.C., 1956), p. 116. Reprinted by permission.

establish a planned economy, with an industry that would support its military pretensions throughout Asia. Thus in contrast to most colonies, which served as suppliers of raw materials to and markets for the finished goods from the mother country, Manchuria developed into a base for heavy industry. The railway and highway mileage were quickly doubled, and the Japanese conquerors invested heavily in the mining of iron and coal, the generation of electricity, and the production of iron, steel, machinery, and chemicals. Progress was rather slow before 1936, when a Soviet-style five-year plan was instituted; thereafter, development of Manchuria's industrial plant advanced at a furious pace. The annual growth of these basic industries was about 14 percent, which resulted in a total increase of five and a half times between 1931 and 1945—a growth rate unequaled anywhere except in the Soviet Union during the 1930s and in the United States between the depths of the Depression in 1932 and the development of a full war economy in 1943. By 1944 to 1945, therefore, Manchuria was producing eight and a half times as much pig iron as China proper had produced in any peak year, two and a half times as much electrical power, and eight and a half times as much cement.

In China proper, the Japanese also occupied large parts of north and east China after the war began in July 1937. There, much of the industry was destroyed or damaged in the early phase of the war. In Shanghai, fighting devastated 52 percent of the industrial plant, and in the Nanking and Wusih areas of the lower Yangtze Valley, destruction rates ran to between 64 and 80 percent. The Japanese nonetheless worked quickly to restore industrial production, for they viewed this part of China as a vast supply area of raw materials and semifinished products that would feed the advanced industries of the Japanese home islands. As early as 1939, therefore, industrial output was pushed to unprecedented heights (Table 8.4).

As in the Nationalist-held area, industry in Japanese-occupied China suffered severely from the fortunes of war. Especially after 1943, when the Allies assumed the offensive against Japan, industrial production fell precipitously. As United

Table 8.5.   Summary of Damage to Basic
Manchurian Industry

Industry	Percentage Reduction in Productive Capacity
Electric power	71
Iron and steel	51–100
Metal working	80
Non-ferrous mining (coal excepted)	75
Liquid fuels and lubricants	65
Cement	50
Chemicals	50
Textiles	75
Paper and pulp	30
Radio, telegraph, telephones	20–100

Source: Francis C. Jones, Manchuria Since 1931 (London: Royal Institute of International Affairs, 1949), p. 229. Reprinted by permission.

States submarines decimated Japan's merchant fleet, supplies of industrial materials became critically short and the shipment of finished goods even along coastal routes was hampered. As in the Nationalist areas, too, the rising spiral of inflation discouraged industrial investments. When the war ended, industrial output was a mere 25 percent of the prewar levels.

In Manchuria, which had become the major industrial center in East Asia outside Japan itself, the greatest war losses were incurred after V-J Day. The Soviets, having occupied the area late in the war, declared in December 1945 that all Japanese industrial enterprises were "war booty" of the Soviet Union. During the following months, they stripped Manchuria's factories of all the newest equipment, including power generators, motors, and other heavy machinery. Much of what was left behind had been wantonly damaged by the Russians' removal crews. Local Chinese also vandalized the factories, often stealing machinery and even wood for fuel. When the Chinese reoccupied Manchuria in 1946, they found substantial quantities of antiquated machinery still there, but the productive capacity of Manchuria's industry had been seriously crippled (Table 8.5).

A major development during the Nationalist period, which had a crucial impact on the political as well as the economic situation at the time, was the increasing involvement of the government in industry. Critics of the government referred to this policy as "bureaucratic capitalism," a pejorative term connoting that Nationalist officials were enriching themselves by improperly using their offices and influence to engage in industrial and commercial enterprises and to drive private entrepreneurs out of business.

The rise in government ownership of industrial enterprises since the mid-1930s had indeed been remarkable. In late 1936, after nearly a decade of Nationalist rule, government factories still accounted for only about 10 percent of the investment in Chinese-owned industry. By 1944, that figure had risen to 50 percent, and by 1946 had reportedly increased to 70 to 80 percent. During the war with

Japan, the Nationalist government attempted to create an industrial base in west China, emphasizing particularly those industries that contributed to the war effort. Government predominance in this effort was inevitable, because few private entrepreneurs were capable of relocating entire factories to the remote interior or of building large new ones there. As a result, government-controlled industries in the Nationalist area in 1944 produced 78 percent of the iron and steel, 51 percent of the motors, 47 percent of the yarn and cloth, and 100 percent of the petroleum.

After the war, the Nationalist government returned to the areas that had been occupied by the Japanese. There, various governmental agencies took charge of more than 2,000 industrial units that had been operated by the Japanese or their Chinese collaborators, and the question then confronting the government was how to dispose of this considerable industrial plant. Because Japanese investments had greatly added to the value of the factories, the government felt that it ought not return those properties to their original owners without some form of payment from the owners. Popular sentiment also ran high that factories owned and operated by "collaborators"—those who had remained in business under the Japanese—should be confiscated.

The government thus found itself in a dilemma. Official ideology prescribed that the government own and operate only heavy and basic industries, while light and consumer-oriented industries should be privately owned. But an equitable formula for the disposition of the light industries that it had taken over proved to be difficult. Moreover, fewer and fewer investors were willing—especially as the postwar inflation worsened—to put their wealth into industrial properties because manufacturing had become far less profitable than hoarding and speculating in commodities. Critics of the government charged that the officials were purposely delaying the sale of light industries to private entrepreneurs and were enriching themselves through the operation of the factories. Whether or not there was any basis for this accusation, the government had become a major participant in the industrial sector by 1947. It or its subsidiary companies produced 90 percent of the iron and steel and 83 percent of the electric power, and it operated 38 percent of the nation's spindles and 60 percent of the looms. In terms of total production, the share of government-owned industries had increased from 15.6 percent in 1945, to 27.1 percent in 1946, to 42.4 percent in 1947.

This quantum leap in the Nationalist government's industrial involvement became a burning political issue during the postwar years. Mao Tse-tung in 1947 declared that bureaucratic capitalism, together with feudalism and imperialism, was a major target of the Communist revolution. It was also widely believed that the "Four Great Families"—Chiang Kai-shek, T. V. Soong, H. H. Kung, and Chen Li-fu—were acquiring enormous fortunes from bureaucratic capitalism. Soong, for example, was variously rumored to hold over US$47 million just in the United States and to own the controlling interest in General Motors—or was it Dupont? It was also alleged in 1947 that Soong, together with his two sisters, Mme. Chiang Kai-shek and Mme. H. H. Kung, held bank deposits in the United States worth US$800 million.

Such assertions contributed to the popular image of the Nationalists as being hopelessly corrupt. Probably, however, the allegations were grossly exaggerated.

When T. V. Soong left China before the Communist takeover, for example, his total wealth was valued at "less than US$1 million"—not an unreasonable fortune for a man who for most of his career had served as China's preeminent banker—although many thought that figure to be ludicrously low.[24]

A more substantial charge is that the state-run enterprises both during and after World War II operated to the disadvantage of private industry. To support the civil war against the Communists and to obviate the inflationary printing of money, the government ran most of its enterprises undisguisedly to raise state revenues. This put the government in direct and unfair competition with private enterprise, often leading to the bankruptcy of the private firms. State enterprises could, for instance, obtain loans from the government-controlled banks at interest rates of 3 percent a month, whereas private firms had to pay in excess of 15 percent a month. Scarce raw materials were also channeled to the state enterprises; the government's textile mills, for instance, received 80 percent of all imported cotton at a time when the supply of domestic cotton was disrupted by fighting in the civil war. Private firms also suffered as a result of the shortage and high price of fuel and power, whereas state enterprises were assured of steady and cheap supplies from other government monopolies, such as the Fuel Adjustment Corporation.

The Nationalist government's involvement in the industrial sector after 1936 was manifestly a return to the traditions of the *guandu shangban* enterprises in the late Qing period; it also foreshadowed the Communists' nationalization of industrial enterprises in the 1950s. Whenever a Chinese government became strong, it seems, it would attempt to control industrial production. The sources of this tendency presumably lie deeply in China's political culture—perhaps in the general disesteem that officials held for merchants, the Confucian distaste for competition and disharmony, or the tradition that the government must dominate all activities that potentially challenged the preponderance of the state over society. Whatever the reasons, private industry during the past century flourished best when governmental intervention was least.

The Industrial Legacy

During the Nanking Decade, approximately seventy years after Zeng Guofan and Li Hongzhang had established the Kiangnan Arsenal, China had still not reached the point of "industrial takeoff," the stage that is marked by a radical break with the traditional economy and by abrupt structural changes in society. Indeed, the modern industrial sector remained marginal to the Chinese economy as a whole and to Chinese life in general. Handicrafts still outproduced modern factories (in terms of value-added) by more than three times. The entire modern sector—manufacturing, mining, transport, and utilities—in 1933 produced only 7 percent of the gross domestic product. That is, 93 percent of the domestic product was still produced by traditional means. Industrial enterprises by the 1930s, moreover, were concentrated in and around the major treaty ports. Fully a half of the 2,435 factories employing power-driven machinery were located in Shanghai, and approximately 82 percent of the looms and spindles of the cotton-textile industry were in just three locations: Kiangsu Province (including Shanghai) and the environs of Tientsin and Hankow.

This record of industrial growth pales by comparison with that of Japan during the same period and has been the source of much frustration and bitterness to many nationalistic Chinese. There were, however, positive aspects to the record. With the value of industrial output increasing at an annual average rate of 9.4 percent between 1912 and 1936 (including Manchuria), the magnifying powers of compound interest had become wondrously clear by the end of that twenty-four year period. Not only had a foundation of plant and machinery been created that had not existed in 1912, but a substantial corps of experienced managers and disciplined, trained workers now existed.

The significance of this became evident during the 1950s when China impressed the world with its large and rapid industrial expansion. Most observers at the time inferred that this growth was attributable to the large investments in fixed capital that the government had put into the industrial sector during the First Five-Year Plan, 1952–57. In fact, the bulk of those investments had been used for new construction, and most of the new plant did not become operational until after 1957. The large increase in industrial output during that period was largely achieved, therefore, by fully utilizing the capacities of the existing factories—those that had been constructed before 1949. An estimated two-thirds of the increased industrial production came from those pre-1949 plants and only one-third from new industrial facilities.

Several segments of the industrial sector in the pre-Communist period had been especially successful. The most dynamic and fastest growing was the chemical industry, which had been launched after a sharp-eyed Chinese entrepreneur saw that foreigners were making substantial profits in China by importing various acids, ammonium sulfate, soda, and monosodium glutamate. By 1936, Chinese production exceeded the imports of all chemicals except caustic soda.

Machine manufacturing was another area of success. Most of these firms had originated as ship- or machine-repair shops, but the skills required to repair such equipment were readily transferable to original manufacturing. By the 1930s, these firms had expanded and matured, so that they were displacing a large variety of imported goods. There were, for instance, ninety-nine manufacturers of spindles, looms, bowing machines, and other machinery for the textile industry. Chinese industrialists also achieved substantial import substitution of matches, cigarettes, flour, soap, glass, and the like. China's leading cement manufacturer, the Chee Hsin company, is another notable instance of industrial success during the Republican period.

Most Chinese industrial firms, however, limped and struggled merely to survive. Debt burdens were heavy; productivity was low; production costs were high; and the quality of the final product was often inferior. Bankruptcies and foreign takeovers were common. A difficulty afflicting virtually all industrial firms was the limited market demand. The poverty of Chinese society generally, and the continued strength and popularity of handicrafts, meant that the demand for consumer goods was insufficiently strong to encourage dynamic industrial expansion. The small size of the consumer-goods industry meant, in turn, that the demand for producer goods remained exiguous.

The difficulties of Chinese industry were often the consequence, however, of the industrialists' own poor management and incompetent financial planning. For instance, industrialists commonly established their enterprises on too large a scale and with too little capital for the size of their operations. Typical of this tendency was the company that, with only 1.5 million taels in assets, planned to construct a cotton mill that would cost over 2.3 million taels. From the very beginning, therefore, firms were often underfinanced and deeply in debt. Companies also inveterately guaranteed an annual payment of dividends to shareholders, usually at a rate of 8 to 10 percent. This practice of guaranteed dividends was used to attract investors, of course, but the necessity of paying dividends even in years when the company was losing money compounded the firms' financial difficulties.

The pitfalls of undercapitalization and guaranteed dividends should have been painfully evident to every industrialist. Examples of failed factories lay everywhere, and journals at the time frequently pointed out the greater success of Japanese firms, which were financially more prudent. But many, perhaps most, Chinese industrialists and investors were essentially speculators, possessed of a get-rich-quick mentality that damaged long-term development. Injurious though this was to the viability of the country's industries, that mentality was probably a rational response to the instability of political conditions, the insecurity of long-term investments, and the relative shortage of investment capital.

Another difficulty assailing Chinese-owned industry was its tendency toward technological obsolescence. When establishing factories, Chinese industrialists generally imported equipment that was similar to that then in use in European or American plants—although sometimes, to cut costs, they bought second-hand machinery. Having made that initial investment, the industrialists only occasionally purchased new equipment, with the result that their plants, measured by world standards, were soon antiquated. By the 1940s, many of the cotton mills' spindles and looms and the cement industry's kilns were thirty and even forty years old. Being technologically backward, the Chinese factories, as compared with the foreign firms operating in China, were usually less efficient, were more labor-intensive (and hence had higher labor costs), and often turned out goods of inferior quality.

The pervasive tendency for Chinese-owned plants to become obsolete was largely attributable to the fact that most Chinese industrialists operated on the razor edge of solvency. Often operating with inadequate capital, guaranteeing excessively high returns to stockholders, and saddled with heavy debt burdens, the industrialists simply lacked the financial reserves needed to retool. In the West, most industrial firms anticipated the need to update their equipment by setting aside depreciation allowances. The vast majority of Chinese firms had no such funds, or if they did have depreciation allowances, maintained them at ridiculously low levels. Lacking such funds and operating at a low profit margin, Chinese factories fell farther and farther behind their foreign counterparts.

The Impact of Imperialism

Even though some scholars emphasize the positive aspects of the industrial legacy, most observers of China, both in China and abroad, have been convinced that the efforts to create a modern economic sector since the mid-nineteenth century failed. This negative assessment has resulted, first, from the belief that if only China had industrialized more rapidly, it might more successfully have resisted imperialist aggression. And it has resulted, second, from the realization that China's economic modernization was pathetically slow in comparison with that of its neighbor, Japan.

Who or what was responsible for China's so-called tardy modernization? For most patriotic Chinese, the answer has been "Imperialist Oppression!" Their reasoning runs something as follows. As a result of the unequal treaties concluded after the Opium War, China could charge no more than a 5 percent *ad valorum* tariff on foreign imports; it therefore lost the capacity to protect its infant industries from unfair competition with Western manufacturers. After 1895, too, foreigners obtained the right to operate factories in the treaty ports. As a consequence, they had the advantage of using cheap Chinese labor at the same time that they enjoyed ready access to cheap investment capital and to the advanced technologies of the home countries. The imperialists also drained off China's wealth by repatriating the huge profits that they made in China and by exacting large indemnities from the Chinese government after each military victory. By destroying the native handicraft industries, imperialism impoverished the people, thus weakening their purchasing power and inducing political instability. And, finally, by linking China's economy to the world market, Chinese producers were imperiled by the shifts of prices and whims of demand on the world market.

Such an answer was emotionally satisfying to a proud people who were suffering the indignities of foreign poaching on China's sovereign rights. The invidiousness of the opium trade and gunboat diplomacy, of extraterritoriality and the indemnities, of the foreign businessmen's arrogant racism and the missionaries' narrow-mindedness were evident to all Chinese who looked beyond the boundaries of their own villages. The story of the sign in a Shanghai park that read "No Dogs or Chinese Allowed" may have been aprocryphal, but patriotic Chinese believed it because it accorded with their expectations of the foreigners' behavior in and toward China. Most Chinese—including Sun Yat-sen, Chiang Kai-shek, and Mao Tse-tung—have been convinced that a very large share, probably most, of their country's political, social, and economic tribulations since the early nineteenth century were attributable to imperialist oppression.

Economic historians in the West, however, particularly during the past two decades, have become progressively uncomfortable with the contention that imperialism was the principal cause of China's "tardy" modernization. Chinese-owned industry, for instance, grew at about the same rate as did the foreign-owned enterprises in China, and the rates of profit of both foreign and native industrialists in China were almost the same. Foreign manufacturing and investments were concentrated inordinately in the treaty ports and Manchuria, and thus

China's domestic economy remained largely insulated from the Western impact. The huge size of China, combined with the continuing strength of the traditional system of manufacturing and marketing, kept most foreign economic influences at a full arm's length. We are reminded, too, that for all the talk of the imperialists' "unfair advantages," the Chinese enjoyed their own "unfair advantages" over the foreigner, such as greater familiarity with the needs and desires of Chinese consumers and superior knowledge about Chinese marketing and other business practices. And the rising tide of nationalism during the early twentieth century led to the antiforeign boycotts and the movements to "Buy Chinese," which put the foreigners at a disadvantage.

Much of the foreign economic impact is also viewed as having been beneficial. It provided the initial impetus without which China surely would have moved even more slowly along the road to economic modernization. Thereafter, it facilitated the transfer of modern technologies to China. Foreign firms and factories served as "schools" where Chinese acquired management and manufacturing skills appropriate to the new technologies and to international intercourse; they also provided models of orderly, efficient industrial operations. Foreign trade is also depicted as having improved the standard of living of many Chinese by creating commercial opportunities for farmers and handicraft producers. Even those few foreign imports that did succeed in securing a foothold in the Chinese market, such as soap, matches, and kerosene (for lighting), may have improved the general quality of Chinese life; they also inspired Chinese entrepreneurs to start producing domestic versions of those goods.[25]

The debate over the economic effects of imperialism is far from ended. Books and articles, taking one side or the other in the controversy, are still being published, and it would be impossible to resolve this extraordinarily complex question here. What has emerged clearly from the debate thus far, however, is that the effects of economic imperialism were neither uniformly destructive of nor wholly beneficial to China's economic modernization. One might conclude, therefore, at least tentatively, that imperialism was at most marginally responsible for China's "tardy" modernization. The deeper causes lay elsewhere.

What the critics of economic imperialism seem to forget is that economic modernization is not a commodity, but a process. It is like a fragile flower not easily transplanted from one environment to another. This was revealed in the experience of Continental Europe, which, after Britain launched the Industrial Revolution, required several generations to acquire the technologies of modern industry and even longer to attain levels of industrial performance comparable with those of Britain. This tardy response occurred despite the facts that the Continental nations' level of scientific practice and elite education was often at least the equal of Britain's, that their average per capita income and availability of capital were far higher than in China in the nineteenth century, and that they had largely completed the tasks of consolidating political authority and had instituted bureaucratic administrations operating in accordance with established law. Certainly, one would expect these European states, which shared with Britain a basically similar culture and closely related languages, to have absorbed modern industrial practice almost automatically. In fact, even the fastest, France and Germany, required almost a hundred years to accomplish their own industiral revolutions.

On the Continent, economic modernization was retarded by conditions strikingly similar to those in China. The greater size of the Continent, compared with England, together with inadequate roads and waterways, resulted in high shipping costs and fragmented markets. And although average per capita income was fairly high, that wealth was distributed unequally—the elite enjoying considerable prosperity, while the great majority lived close to the subsistence level. There was, therefore, little market for the standardized, mass-produced commodities of modern factories, as opposed to the elegant, specialized, and expensive items that small-scale artisans could turn out. Social structures and values on the Continent likewise worked against the modernization of manufacturing. The aristocracy disdained commercial involvement, while upwardly mobile commoners generally favored the professions or bureaucratic office over business or manufacturing. Wealthy aristocrats put their money into land, and even successful merchants sought to improve their social status by diverting profits from their enterprises to land, governmental position, or aristocratic rank. The Continental people's "worship of thrift," emphasis on family considerations in commercial enterprises, and dislike of competition also worked against the adoption of the British model. Finally, government efforts to promote modern factories were rarely successful because "state assistance was more often than not an encouragement to laxity and a cover for incompetence." [26]

Each of these factors, which worked against the Continent's absorption of the lessons of Britain's Industrial Revolution—large land size, poor transportation, a subsistence-level population, denigration of commerce, and so on—existed also in China. But in spades! When viewed in the light of the experience of the nations in Europe, therefore, China's record of industrial modernization from the 1880s to 1949 was not so dismal as is usually suggested.

Still, the fact remains that China's industrial progress lagged far behind that of Japan during and after the Meiji Restoration, from 1868 onward. Why? The answer is partly to be found in the fact that Japan, for more than a century before the arrival of the Western powers in the mid-nineteenth century, had been undergoing profound social and economic changes that were already propelling the economy toward commercial modernization and rising levels of productivity. When Western industrial technology became available after Commodore Matthew C. Perry "opened" Japan in 1853, it was adopted with astonishing alacrity and encountered relatively little opposition.

Japanese economic modernization was, of course, like that in China, a complex phenomenon. A full explanation would also have to take into account such factors as the political pluralism resulting from Japan's feudal background, which permitted regional experimentation and development and which may be contrasted with the centralized, bureaucratic regime in China that tended to smother industrial and regional initiative. And Japan's ruling elite were samurai, members of a military class, who were far more sensitive to the disparities of power between their country and the West than were the scholar-officials who governed China. There was also Japan's relatively small size and ease of transport by sea. And there was its long tradition of cultural appropriation, which enabled it to borrow from the West without bruising national sensibilities (as it did in China). And, finally, Japanese modernization in the Meiji period was favored by a stable government—in contradistinction to the political disintegration in China—that fostered the development of a modern economic infrastructure, including a nationwide road system, ample industrial energy, a commercial legal code, banking facilities, and popular education.

Japan's rapid economic modernization and attainment of major-power status in less than a half century was an extraordinary achievement. China's course of so-called tardy modernization more closely fits what one should expect when a modern technology is introduced to a largely traditional society.

Selected Readings

(See also the works cited in the notes)

Bergère, Marie-Claire. "The Chinese Bourgeoisie, 1911–37." In *Cambridge History of China*, vol. 12, ed. John K. Fairbank, pp. 721–825. Cambridge: Cambridge University Press, 1983.

Chang, Kia-ngau. *China's Struggle for Railroad Development*. New York: Day, 1943.

Chao, Kang. *The Development of Cotton Textile Production in China*. Cambridge, Mass.: Harvard University, East Asian Research Center, 1977.

Cheng, Yu-Kwei. *Foreign Trade and Industrial Development of China: An Historial and Integrated Analysis Through 1948*. Washington, D.C.: University Press of Washington, D.C., 1956.

Feuerwerker, Albert. *China's Early Industrialization: Sheng Hsuan-huai (1844–1916) and Mandarin Enterprise*. Cambridge, Mass.: Harvard University Press, 1958.

———. "Economic Trends in the Late Ch'ing Empire, 1870–1911." In *Cambridge History of China*, vol. 11, ed. John K. Fairbank and Kwang-ching Liu, pp. 1–69. Cambridge: Cambridge University Press, 1980

———. "Economic Trends, 1912–49." In *Cambridge History of China*, vol. 12, ed. John K. Fairbank, pp. 28–127. Cambridge: Cambridge University Press, 1983.

———. "Industrial Enterprise in Twentieth-Century China: the Chee Hsin Cement Co." In *Approaches to Modern Chinese History*, ed. Albert Feuerwerker et al., pp. 304–41. Berkeley: University of California Press, 1967.

Hao, Yen-p'ing. *The Commercial Revolution in Nineteenth-Century China: The Rise of Sino-Western Mercantile Capitalism*. Berkeley: University of California Press, 1986.

Hou, Chi-ming. *Foreign Investment and Economic Development in China, 1840–1937*. Cambridge, Mass.: Harvard University Press, 1965.

Jones, Francis C. *Manchuria Since 1931*. London: Royal Institute of International Affairs, 1949.

Kuo, Ting-yee, and Kwang-Ching Liu. "Self-Strengthening: The Pursuit of Western Technology." In *Cambridge History of China*, vol. 10, ed. John K. Fairbank, pp. 491–542. Cambridge: Cambridge University Press, 1978.

Li, Lillian M. *China's Silk Trade: Traditional Industry in the Modern World, 1842–1937*. Cambridge, Mass.: Harvard University, Council on East Asian Studies, 1981.

Liang, Ernest P. *China: Railways and Agricultural Development, 1875–1935*. Chicago: University of Chicago, Department of Geography, 1982.

Liu, Kwang-Ching. *Anglo-American Steamship Rivalry in China, 1862–1874*. Cambridge, Mass.: Harvard University Press, 1962.

Murphey, Rhoads. *The Outsiders: The Western Experience in India and China*. Ann Arbor: University of Michigan Press, 1977.

Schran, Peter. "Traditional Transportation and Railroad Development in China Since Late Ch'ing Times." Paper presented at the International Conference on Spatial and Temporal Trends and Cycles in Chinese Economic History, 980–1980, Bellagio, Italy, n.d.

Tamagna, Frank M. *Banking and Finance in China*. New York: Institute of Pacific Relations, 1942.

Wright, Tim. *Coal Mining in China's Economy and Society, 1895–1937*. Cambridge: Cambridge University Press, 1984.

9

New Social Classes in the Early Modern Period

The economic changes experienced by China during the early modern period went hand in hand with far-reaching changes in society. In late imperial times, the nation's social hierarchy had been dominated by just one class—the scholar-officials. But during the early modern period, society became more diversified. By the 1920s and 1930s, and to some degree earlier, successful merchants, military officers, and men of the professional classes enjoyed a prestige that was no less, and in some cases greater, than that of scholars and governmental bureaucrats. A new class of commoners, the urban proletariat, also came into existence with the development of modern industry in the cities. This diversification of society, along with the accompanying transformation of social values, was even more revolutionary in its effect than were the often violent, more dramatic, political upheavals of the time.

Social Elites in Late Imperial Times

The social and political leadership of late imperial China consisted of three distinct strata: the upper gentry, the lower gentry, and the nontitled local elites. Of these, the best known are the first two, the gentry *(shenshi),* also translated as "scholar-officials."

The upper gentry—the most prestigious of the three by far—were those who held bureaucratic office in the government or *were qualified* to hold such office. Before the mid-nineteenth century, most upper gentry acquired that status by earning the *juren* and *jinshi* titles—academic degrees awarded on passing (in the case of the *juren*) one of the provincial examinations or (in the case of the *jinshi*) a provincial examination and then the metropolitan (or national) examination in Peking. Other members of the upper gentry either had succeeded in the military examinations or had purchased their academic titles or bureaucratic ranks, although they did not enjoy the same prestige as those who had passed the civil-service examinations.

The lower gentry, holding the academic title *shengyuan,* were also scholars, but they were not officials. They had passed the preliminary, or first-level, civil-service examinations. This qualified them, however, to be officially recognized as only students and thus recipients of a governmental stipend, but it did not qualify them for bureaucratic office. Their status, while above that of commoners with the same socioeconomic background, was substantially below that of the upper gentry. But they did enjoy some of the same legal privileges as the upper gentry, such as permission to wear distinctive robes and caps, exemption from certain forms of punishment if convicted of a crime, and avoidance of the labor-service tax.

Social historians have long regarded the upper and lower gentry as the only leadership group in late imperial society that merited serious study. During the past fifteen years or so, however, a new generation of historians has focused its research on levels of society below the national and provincial levels, and it is becoming increasingly evident that leadership roles were not restricted to the scholar-official class. During the nineteenth century, the scholars and officials numbered fewer than 1.5 million—or less than 1 member of the gentry for every 300 commoners. Many of them, moreover, resided in the larger towns and cities, and thus there simply were not enough of them to fill all the leadership positions in the empire. Especially as one moved down the administrative ladder, to the lesser towns and villages, and particularly in the poorer and more remote regions of the country, the gentry population became progressively sparse. In such places, even the *shengyuan,* or members of the lower gentry, were seldom seen. At the lower reaches of society, therefore, leadership roles were frequently taken up by non-gentry—men who enjoyed local prominence and authority as a result of their wealth, age, wisdom, or some other attributes of status and leadership.

In Anhwei Province, for example, several lineages dominated affairs in Tongcheng *Xian* uninterruptedly for several hundred years, even though these lineages frequently failed to produce, in every generation, successful candidates in the civil-service examinations. The persisting source of these families' power and prestige was not academic degrees, but wealth derived largely from landholding. "Academic degrees and office were [not, therefore,] the sole precondition of wealth; rather, they were the occasional results of it." [1]

Wealth, therefore, was an important factor in the formation of the late imperial elite. Yet every ambitious youth, whether wealthy or poor, dreamed of passing the civil-service examinations, which since the Song Dynasty had served as the main gateway to official position. In power, prestige, and legal privilege, therefore, the officials and degree holders, were the *crème de la crème* of Chinese society.

The New Elites

The growth of the commercial sector beginning in the 1500s had markedly increased the size and wealth of the merchant classes. And, after 1644, the Manchus constituted a new leadership stratum in the political hierarchy of the empire. For the most part, however, the structure of China's social elite did not change radically from the Song Dynasty until the mid-nineteenth century, when during the suppression of the Taiping Rebellion (1851–64), the old social structure began to crack. And by the second and third decades of the twentieth century, the top layers of the old society had been displaced by new social classes that reflected the growing complexity of a fast-changing economy and of a political system exposed to the pressures of revolution.

Initially, the changes resulted largely from internally generated forces. During the great mid-nineteenth-century uprisings, the Manchu government was financially hard-pressed. Seeking to increase its revenues, it began to sell academic degrees and official posts. Whereas no more than 30 percent of government posts had been filled through purchase before 1850, at least half of the officials in the postrebellion period had risen through purchase, the so-called irregular route. During the same period, the total number of those who obtained academic degrees through purchase also increased by over 50 percent. The result was a major change in the nature of the top stratum of the social structure. Money, rather than academic achievement, was becoming the principal determinant of gentry status.

The long-term significance of this growing importance of wealth in Chinese society, if China had remained in relative isolation from the West, can only be speculated. Perhaps the entire value system would gradually have been transformed, leading to a greater appreciation of commercial and industrial entrepreneurship. We will never know, of course, because shortly thereafter, the Western presence and Western ideas in China imparted their own impetus to social change.

The New Merchant Class

Merchants were the chief beneficiaries of the Qing government's policy of selling academic degrees and official posts; it became common for wealthy businessmen to purchase titles. They did this for the prestige, of course, but gentry status, even when purchased, also made them eligible to enjoy lower tax rates, the privilege of meeting with government bureaucrats on virtually an equal footing, and exemption from many forms of criminal punishment. So attractive was this prospect that in Hankow during the latter half of the nineteenth century, for example, one-half or even more of the major wholesale merchants and large brokers held purchased titles.

At the same time, there was a movement in the opposite direction, regular gentry increasingly engaged in business. Particularly after the 1870s, as commerce and industry in the treaty ports expanded under the influence of the West, scholars and officials began to invest less in land and more in the new entrepreneurial undertakings that were growing up in the treaty ports. Investments in farmland were neither so profitable nor so secure as they had been, whereas Western-stimulated enterprises in the cities promised large returns on investments. Many literati, moreover, were becoming disillusioned with the scholarly life. After many years of preparing for the civil-service examinations, they discovered that their talents were not in great demand and that the majority of the government jobs were going to people who were relatively uneducated but who had the wealth to purchase title or rank.

During the last two decades of the nineteenth century, therefore, the gentry came to view mercantile activity with a less jaundiced eye. In some gentry circles, too, investments in Western-style ventures even acquired a special respectability because they contributed to the goals of national strength and prosperity. Although the compradors were, as noted in Chapter 8, the largest investors in China's modern enterprises, by the turn of the century most gentry residing in the urban centers were engaged in some form of entrepreneurial activity. Emblematic of the changed attitude of the gentry toward commerce is the fact that of twenty-six Western-style textile mills established between 1890 and 1910, twenty had been backed primarily by men who were active or retired officials or were members of the scholar class.

Despite the considerable intermingling of and crossing over between the gentry and the merchant classes in the late nineteenth century, many of the traditional biases against commercial activity persisted. Until almost the end of the nineteenth century, therefore, China remained a gentry-dominated society, and merchants— for all their wealth and influence—were still not fully accepted, socially or politically, unless they purchased ranks and titles so that they could garb themselves in the clothes and aura of scholar-officials.

Particularly between 1890 and 1920, however, the composition of the nation's social and political leadership shifted decisively from the gentry to the new elite classes being spawned by the accelerating process of economic and political change. In the 1890s, the gentry's monopoly of leadership at the upper levels of society began to weaken, but the critical turning point was in 1905, when the Qing government finally abolished the civil-service examinations. Thereafter, the ranks of the old scholar-officials were no longer replenished, and those who had become members of the gentry class before 1905 gradually aged, lost vigor, and died. This was, however, a gradual process. Even in 1909 and 1911, for example, when the Qing government convoked representative assemblies at the provincial and national levels, almost 90 percent of the delegates were members of the gentry class. But the passing years took a toll, and by about 1920, the old gentry constituted only a small minority in such political bodies. In Chekiang, for instance, the number of upper gentry in the provincial assembly fell from 46 percent just prior to the Revolution of 1911 to 6 percent in 1918 to 1921.

At the same time, the merchants, who were long accustomed to subordinating themselves to gentry leadership, gradually moved into positions of social and political leadership and gained confidence with added experience. The entrepreneurial classes were, of course, a heterogeneous group that continued to be highly diverse in economic values and political outlook. Petty tradesmen, for instance, were frequently conservative in outlook, while their more successful and cosmopolitian brethren were acquiring the attitudes of a modern bourgeoisie, favoring economic rationality, free enterprise, and an ideology of economic growth. (Perhaps, when speaking of the merchant classes, one should distinguish between the "upper" and the "lower" bourgeoisie, much as one does in discussing the upper and the lower gentry.) And even among the relatively modern bourgeoisie, there was significant diversity of opinion—especially in the emotionally charged atmosphere of the May Fourth Movement (1919), when more and more of them felt the pull of nationalism and were becoming involved in the political struggles of the time.

Merchants first appeared prominently on the national political scene in 1905 when they led an anti-American boycott to protest the United States ban on the immigration of Chinese laborers. During the following years, they participated in the agitation against the Manchu autocracy, adding their voice to the call for constitutional government and giving financial aid to both the reform and the revolutionary parties. Despite some claims that the Revolution of 1911 was a "bourgeois" revolution, however, the merchants' economic base in 1911 was still too weak, and their political and psychological subordination to the gentry still too strong, for them to have assumed an independent and leading role in national politics.

The rising status of merchants in the early twentieth century was most evident in their role as civic leaders. This was not a wholly new experience for them. Through their guild organizations, they had long participated in various philanthropic undertakings, and during the turmoil of the Taiping Uprising had in some cities taken over such administrative tasks as collecting taxes and directing the police and militia. Increasingly during the twentieth century, merchants assumed a leading role in the governance of the cities. In 1905, for example, when the Shanghai City council was established—this was the first modern, Western-style municipal administration in China—fully twenty of the thirty-eight representatives came from merchant backgrounds.

The merchants usually exerted their growing powers through the chambers of commerce. In 1902, hoping to promote trade and industry as a means of strengthening the nation, the Qing government officially approved the creation of merchant-run chambers of commerce. By 1908, the chambers had been established in 31 major cities and 135 other urban centers, and by 1912, 1,200 chambers of commerce had been organized. The chambers also assumed political and administrative functions in their cities, becoming "the key organization in the urban life of Republican China, central to the running of many cities." [2] They were prime movers, for example, in urban modernization, promoting such public projects as lighting, waterworks, schools, sewage systems, and harbor improvements. They also supported various social-welfare projects and maintained militia for local defense.

The chambers of commerce reached the peak of their influence and prestige during the early and mid-1920s—also, significantly, the high point of the warlord era. The formal administrative powers of government were much diminished, and the merchants—by this time having gained considerable self-confidence—moved at least partly to fill the political void. They assumed leadership in local representative organizations and even, on occasion, as in Shaoxing (in Chekiang Province) in 1922, assumed the duties of the *xian* assembly. Taking a cue from the students in the May Fourth Movement, the increasingly nationalistic merchants were becoming conscious of themselves "as a major, perhaps the major, force around which a new China could be built." [3] They therefore assumed the leadership of the anti-imperialist boycott movement, which remained a potent force from 1919 to 1926.

Following the revolutionary victory of Chiang Kai-shek and the Kuomintang in 1927 to 1928, the political pretensions of the merchants were shattered. The new regime, rather like the Qing Dynasty during the first decade of the twentieth century, was a modernizing bureaucracy; it desired commercial and industrial development of the nation, but it could not tolerate an autonomous merchant class. The turn of events after 1927 seems to bear out the view that Chinese officials felt a permanent hostility toward the bourgeoisie, which could flourish only when central state power was weak.

On the eve of the 1927 revolution, however, the bourgeoisie had welcomed Nationalist rule. Confronted during the preceding years with the depredations of the warlords, the increasing militancy of the labor unions, and the specter of Communist revolution, they willingly accepted, and even helped pay for, the establishment of a political regime that promised to restore political and economic stability. By 1930, however, the new Nationalist government had reorganized the chambers of commerce, arrested or removed most of the former leaders, and effectively broken the power of the once-powerful merchant organizations. The government even wrested control of the antiforeign boycotts from merchant hands. And by using the pretense of enforcing the boycotts to imprison and fine the merchants, the government turned the boycotts into "an instrument of intimidation and terror, another means of subduing the bourgeoisie to the power of the state."[4]

The significance of the new merchant class was not limited, however, to their economic and political roles, for its members were also leaders in China's modern social transformation. Many of the merchants were cosmopolitan and progressive: the most successful of them were usually well educated, and many of them had studied or résided abroad. More than most Chinese, they welcomed innovations from abroad and had a relatively realistic understanding of China's place among the nations of the world. They tended instinctively to be liberals, supportive of government by law, of representative political institutions, and of the preservation of local liberties. They were proponents of industrial growth and economic rationality. In their life style, too, they were among the most Westernized: they often lived in foreign-style homes, dressed in Western-style suits, listened and danced to Western music, drank coffee, and smoked cigars. Many were Christians.

During the early twentieth century, therefore, the new merchant class gradually replaced the gentry as the leading social class, particularly in the cities. Its social status, if not its political power, continued in the 1930s and 1940s to be higher than it had been in, say, the 1870s and 1880s. The merchants' progress and Westernization had, however, been earned at a price. For by the 1930s, the bourgeoisie was profoundly isolated from the peasants and the villages, where beat the true pulse of Chinese life. In this, as in other social characteristics, the new merchant class was remarkably similar to the new intellectual class.

The New Intellectual Class

The new intellectual class, as it had developed by the 1920s and 1930s, was a far more diverse group than its predecessor, the gentry; it was imbued with no common ideology or political outlook, and its social roots were in the cities and in the wealthier strata of society. The new intellectuals were trained specialists—engineers, lawyers, doctors, journalists, and so on—who worked and lived in the cities. Most of them, as a consequence, had lost touch with village life and the common people. Like the gentry, they often aspired to government office, but gone was the traditional commitment to public service.

During the latter half of the nineteenth century, China's educational system began to accommodate the needs created by China's interaction with the West. In 1862, the government established the Interpreters' College, the Tongwenguan, in Peking to teach European languages; soon, engineering, science, mathematics, and international law were added to the curriculum. Similar schools were founded in Shanghai and Canton in 1863 and 1864, and in 1866 the Foochow Arsenal opened a school with instruction in navigation and engineering as well as in English and French. Beginning in 1872, 120 boys, aged 10 to 16, were sent to Connecticut, where they studied in American schools and lived in American homes. Five years later, the Foochow Arsenal sent 30 youths to France and England to learn ship construction and naval strategy.

These various educational efforts during the late nineteenth century were ancillary, however, to the traditional system, which produced candidates for the civil-service examinations; and their products were mostly marginal men in a society that was still predominantly traditional. Perhaps they spoke a foreign language or understood the dynamics of a steam engine, but they gained little or no respect for those achievements. As even Feng Guifen, a prominent reformer, wrote, "Those who study with foreigners are called interpreters; they are all frivolous townspeople . . . their nature is rough, their knowledge slight, and their motives base."[5] Not until after the abolition of the examination system—a measure that proclaimed the disavowal of traditional learning and of the social system built on it—can one truly speak of the emergence of a new intellectual class.

Until 1895, most Chinese literati and members of the upper classes were content with society as they knew it and thus sensed no need to change the traditional educational system. But the military defeat by the Japanese in that year, followed closely by the surge of imperialism that climaxed in the humiliating events of the Boxer episode in 1900, convinced all but the most ignorant or reactionary that China needed new knowledge and new skills if it was to survive as a nation. The result was a pell-mell rush, often poorly planned and badly implemented, to create a new generation of leaders who would understand science, mathematics, and the ways of the West.

The first concerted attempt to revamp the entire educational system—introducing Western subjects into the curriculum and creating a national network of schools, starting with the elementary grades at the *xian* level and culminating in the Imperial University in Peking—was made during the Hundred Days Reform Movement in 1898. That attempt to remake overnight the nation's political and educational system quickly ended, of course, with the emperor a prisoner and the reformers either dead or in flight. The Imperial University survived the Empress Dowager's coup d'état and subsequently became Peking University, the gem of higher learning under the Republic; most of the other reforms, however, were aborted.

The true beginnings of a new educational system, and hence of a new intellectual class, thus began only after the Boxer Uprising, when even the Empress

Dowager became convinced that the Qing Dynasty could survive only if the traditional system were girded up with Western ideas and institutions. In 1901, pulling pages out of the 1898 reformers' playbook—without, of course, giving credit to the emperor or the other now-discredited reformers—she called for the creation of a national system of schools that would teach Western subjects as well as the Confucian classics. She urged that youth be sent abroad to acquire Western learning. And the venerable civil-service examinations were henceforth to be altered by abolishing the "Eight-Legged" form of answers (a highly formalized and stilted form of essay writing) and by adding questions about Western government and science.

Revolutionary though these reforms of 1901 were in theory, actual changes in the educational structure came slowly. There was little money to implement the reforms; teachers who were qualified to give instruction in the new Westernized curriculum were scarce; much time was needed to prepare new textbooks; and schoolhouses were usually obtained by expropriating temples and converting them to the use of the new education.[6] Even by 1909, therefore, a national system of education had not really been brought into existence. Many officials interpreted the imperial policy to mean that there need be only one elementary school in each *xian* (whose average population was about 300,000). And even where the form of schools had been modernized, the content of the education was often dismayingly like that in the past.

Because the new schools were few in number and were not distributed uniformly across the nation, and because many families remained suspicious of the new education (some hoping that the old Confucian emphasis would be restored, and many thinking that Western learning was too fancy and impractical), the old-style private school *(sishu)* continued in existence with astonishing pertinacity. Even until about 1920, the majority of students still studied in these traditional schools, which were "little affected by government decrees or the theories of the educationalists."[7]

The Qing educational reforms, however slow and limited, nonetheless had far-reaching social consequences. As a result of changes in the system of civil-service examinations, culminating in their abolition in 1905, the youth in the nation's better schools ceased to immerse themselves in the study of Confucianism, thus never acquiring the ideological orientation of that profoundly moralistic philosophy. Instead, they devoted themselves to branches of learning that were, in comparison with Confucianism, relatively devoid of moral content. The results of this change should, no doubt, be measured cautiously; ethical change in a modernizing society is inevitable and is attributable to many factors. Still, many Chinese have felt that the jettisoning of Confucianism in the early twentieth century and the failure to replace it with any comparable form of moral training created an ethical vacuum. China's intellectuals, it is claimed, became amoral, devoid of social responsibility, and concerned with only personal advantage.

While it would perhaps be a mistake to overemphasize the amorality of China's educated elite, it does appear that Chinese, during the second, third, and fourth decades of the twentieth century, were no longer part of a moral community, as had existed in earlier times; they were no longer participants in a common culture, sharing values and outlooks. Now there was a sense of cultural confusion, an uncertainty about the conduct and the attitudes that would earn the approbation or censure of their fellow Chinese. The result was that the educated elite in the twentieth century were guided, more often than in late imperial times, by considerations of self-interest and self-enrichment. The ethic of public service and noblesse oblige, which was at least an ideal of the Confucian-educated elite, was sorely attenuated. The official corruption and self-aggrandizement that so marred the rule of the Nationalists in the 1930s and 1940s was doubtless attributable, at least partly, to that attenuation.

Another social consequence of the Qing educational reforms was that the educated elite progressively came from urban and wealthy backgrounds, and became ever more isolated from the rural and impoverished elements of society. Under the old system, education was relatively inexpensive. The *sishu,* the old-style private schools, were generally found in the villages, so that students could live at home; and the price of a set of the Confucian classics and of brush, ink, and paper was within the financial reach of many young peasant boys, especially because relatives, lineages, and villages often assisted bright but needy youth. Limitation of time, rather than of money, was usually the primary obstacle preventing a youth from obtaining an education, because the poor often needed their sons to help in the fields.

Under the new educational system, money became the primary factor determining whether a boy received the kind of education that led to social eminence. Because government policy favored higher education, it provided minimal resources to establish elementary and secondary schools. There were, as a result, few new schools at the village level; the best of those that did exist were located in the cities. This naturally favored the urban youth. Rural youth could attend the new schools only if their families were wealthy, able to afford the expense of boarding at the urban schools, where the cost of living was invariably far higher than in the villages.

Tuition and other costs of the new schooling, moreover, were far more expansive than those of the old private schools. No longer could a student get by with just the basic Confucian canon; the new schools required graduated series of textbooks, reference works, libraries, and laboratory equipment. The new primary education, as a consequence, cost about twice that of the old form of education, and secondary schools and universities cost four to five times as much. Because of the prestige and the high cost of the new education, the wealthy elite stopped providing funds for the village and lineage schools. Thus the poor were losing access to even those schools, and a modern education was becoming a luxury that was available to only the well-to-do.

The most severe social consequences of the new education resulted, however, from the inordinate prestige attached to study abroad. Actually, the first youths to study in Europe and the United States in the 1870s and 1880s came largely from poor families. Those from relatively well-off families, who could afford to study for the civil-service examinations, generally were loath to go abroad and study foreign languages, engineering, and other barbarian subjects. It was, therefore, usually poor boys whom the government or philanthropic Westerners sent to study overseas. After the Qing reforms began in 1901, when the government began concerted efforts to send students to Japan, poor students were not particularly disadvantaged, because government fellowships were readily available. In 1906, for example, when the number of Chinese students in Japan reached a peak of about 15,000, fully 8,000 of them were there under government auspices.

After the dynasty fell in 1912, however, government support for study abroad dwindled quickly. Although the total number of students overseas increased steadily—the number in Europe rose from 565 in 1914 to about 3,180 in 1923; in the United States, the increase during the same period was from 847 to 2,600—the percentage of those studying on fellowships declined. In the United States, for instance, 61 percent of the students received government support in 1905, but that figure fell to 32 percent in 1910, about 19 percent between 1925 and 1935, and down to only 3 percent in 1942. This meant, of course, that most youth who obtained their educations abroad did so with private funds. And because the cost of study abroad, particularly in Europe and the United States, was exceedingly high by Chinese standards, an overwhelming number of these students came from wealthy families. Indeed, the largest single category of students abroad in 1947—over 30 percent—came from merchant backgrounds; 27 percent were sons of professionals (lawyers, journalists, engineers); and 17 percent were sons of government officials. Most of those studying abroad, moreover, came from the most Westernized, urbanized, and prosperous regions of the country. Between 1903 and 1945, for instance, approximately two-thirds of the Chinese students in the United States came from the three provinces (Kiangsu, Chekiang, and Kwangtung) that were close to and centered on either Shanghai or Canton.

Whatever the combination of circumstances that enabled a youth to obtain an education at a foreign university, he would return to China as a member of the upper stratum of the new intellectual class. He was customarily offered high-status positions and good pay, almost without regard for his level of academic achievement and personal merit. By contrast, graduates of China's own universities, and especially of the provincial universities, were consigned to second-class status among the intellectuals. Whereas the foreign-educated youth became university professors or bureau chiefs in the national government, home-bred graduates typically had to settle for teaching positions in middle schools or low-level administrative posts in government. Unemployment among the Chinese-educated was also markedly higher; in 1935, for example, only some 2,000 of 7,000 college graduates found jobs—a particularly explosive situation in any society. The relative prestige accorded those who had been educated abroad is suggested in the salary scale of the Commercial Press in Shanghai, China's most prestigious publishing house (Table 9.1). Although the Commercial Press adopted a more flexible system after 1927, this reveals, in an unscientific but amusing way, the status distinctions within China's new intellectual class.

The favored status of Japanese- and, especially, Western-educated intellectuals had profound social and political consequences during the Republican period. Here was a group that automatically became a leading segment of the national elite. Fully 71 percent of the persons listed in a 1939 *Who's Who*, for instance, had been students at foreign universities. The majority of the high- and middle-level

Table 9.1.   Commercial Press Salary Scale (c. 1912–27)

Education	Monthly Salary (Ch$)	Perquisites
Chinese College (with experience)	80	3′ × 1½′ desk
Japanese College	100–120	3′ × 2′ desk
Japanese Imperial University	150	4′ × 2½′ desk; book shelf; crystal ink stand; and rattan chair
Western College	200	same as the preceding
Harvard, Yale, Oxford, or Cambridge	250	custom-made desk; book shelf; crystal ink stand; and rattan chair

Source: Y. C. Wang, *Chinese Intellectuals and the West, 1872–1949* (Chapel Hill: University of North Carolina Press, 1966), p. 90.

government officials in the Nationalist government after 1927, too, had studied in either Europe or the United States. Yet they were largely ignorant of, and often indifferent to, conditions in the "real China," in the villages and among the peasants. They were for the most part urban and wealthy in background; their studies were oriented to Western rather than to Chinese issues; and, on their return from abroad, they settled in the major cities and rarely ventured into the interior of the country. By comparison with the 41 percent of *jinshi* who had lived in rural China during the latter half of the nineteenth century, for example, not one alumnus of Tsinghua College, after returning from a period of study in the United States, lived in a city smaller than a *xian* capital in 1925.[8] A vast social and intellectual gulf thus separated much of China's social and political leadership from the common people.

The breadth of that gulf varied from individual to individual, of course, as is suggested by a comparison of the social and educational backgrounds of the leadership elites of the Kuomintang and the Chinese Communist parties. Leaders of both parties tended to be young and to be drawn from upper- and middle-class families. Both were also relatively well educated. By contrast with the Russian revolutionaries and the leaders of the Nazi movement in Germany, Chinese revolutionary leaders were typically university graduates and had often studied abroad.

Within these similarities, however, were marked differences. Although both the Communist and the Nationalist leaders tended to come from well-to-do families, the typical Communist leader was the son of a landlord or rich peasant and had been reared in the rural hinterland. The typical Kuomintang leader, by contrast, was the son of a merchant or an urban professional and came from the coastal provinces, such as Kwangtung, Kiangsu, or Chekiang, which had been relatively exposed to Western influences. Furthermore, of the leaders who had studied abroad, those in the Kuomintang had usually studied in the United States or Japan—which tended to make them relatively conservative—while the Communists had typically attended universities in either the Soviet Union or France.

While the factors affecting the fates of these two political parties were far more complex than simply social and geographical backgrounds of their leaders, these differences do suggest that the economic and educational changes in the early modern period did significantly influence China's social structure and leadership.

The New Military Class

Most studies of traditional Chinese society suggest that the soldier was a despised figure who barely clung to the lowest rungs of the social ladder. In the traditional Confucian listing of the social classes—scholar, farmer, artisan, and merchant— the soldier did not even warrant mention. One of the most popular proverbs, too, declared, "Good iron is not used to make nails, and good men are not used to make soldiers."

Yet just as the status of the merchant in traditional times was ambivalent, so was that of the soldier. Most founders of the dynasties had won the empire as leaders of armies, and many of the most revered and popular figures in Chinese history—such as Cao Cao, Guan Yu (later canonized as Guan Di), and Yue Fei— had been generals and military strategists. Works of literature featuring the military and heroic tradition, ranging from the great novels of the Ming Dynasty *(Water Margin* and *Romance of the Three Kingdoms)* to the common tales of knights-errant *(wuxia xiaoshuo),* had been enormously popular for many centuries. In the theater, too, actors who depicted military characters were perennial favorites with both audiences and performers.

In real life, among those living at the lowest economic levels of society, the life of the sword also held a powerful attraction. Life on the farms was grueling and boring, and for many men of ambition, the army often beckoned with the promise of a better and more adventurous life. Thus like the relationship of *yin* to *yang,* the military was a constant complement to the civilian side of Chinese society. In the official ideology and in the more orthodox of popular perceptions, however, it was always less esteemed than were the more peaceable professions.

The first intimation of change in the valuation of the military came during the Taiping Rebellion. In opposition to that great popular uprising, the regular armies of the Qing Dynasty were largely ineffectual, and various officials and gentry, concerned about the security of their homes and native regions, formed and served as the commanders of anti-Taiping militia. Many of these commanders—not only the creators of the armies, such as Zeng Guofan and Li Hongzhang, but also their subordinate officers, such as Cen Yuying, Zhang Shusheng, and Liu Bingzhang— gained national reputations for their military exploits. That these scholars and officials, who indisputably possessed literary talents, would serve as military commanders removed much of the stigma from those holding officers' commissions in the military. Yet most of them left the army and petitioned for posts in the governmental administration after quelling the rebellion, which demonstrates that even in the late nineteenth century, scholar-officials still enjoyed markedly higher status than did members of the military elite.

After about 1895, however, and especially during the last decade of Qing rule, the prestige of the military rose sharply. The concerns of many Chinese had changed.

No longer could they be complacent about the Confucian-dominated agrarianism of old; following the disastrous and humiliating defeats in the Sino-Japanese War (1894–95) and the Boxer Uprising (1900), they feared for the very existence of China. They had become, in other words, nationalistic, and military defense of the nation was central to that sentiment. A new esteem was inevitably felt for those whose job it was to defend the nation.

The type of men who became military officers also changed. To replace the now-discredited and corrupt traditional armies, the imperial government in 1895 approved the formation of Western-style armies—the Newly Created Army of Yuan Shikai, in north China, and the Self-Strengthening Army of Zhang Zhidong, in central China. Subsequently, following the Boxer fiasco, the central government ordered the creation of the "New Army," to be Western-trained and Western-equipped and, ultimately, to consist of thirty-six divisions. The quality of the officers in these new forces was far higher than in the old imperial armies. No longer were officers' commissions given to men who could demonstrate physical strength by lifting a heavy stone and whose intellectual capacity required no more than memorizing about 100 characters in the *Sunzi,* a traditional text of warfare and strategy. By contrast, the educational level of officers in the new armies was high; even many of the common soldiers were able to read and write. By 1906, 36 provincial military academies with over 6,000 cadets were in existence; by 1911, there were nearly 70 military academies. Besides military subjects, these academies gave instruction in science, foreign languages, and even cultural subjects.

As a result of the higher educational level of the officers in China's modernized armies, and because the army symbolized the nation's resistance to imperialism, the social status of military officers improved. Now it became common for sons of gentry families to opt for the army as their first career choice, and even scholars who had won the *shengyuan* and *juren* degrees before 1905 (such as Feng Guozhang, a future president of the Republic, and Cai E, a famous revolutionary leader) turned their backs on the civilian world in favor of careers in the army. Because the army was a leader in the adoption of Western technology, military officers also basked in the admiration that society had begun to feel for things modern and Western.

During the Revolution of 1911, political power fell into the hands of these military officers. Most of the modern army units, especially in the south, had been permeated with anti-Manchu sentiment, and they therefore quickly sided with the revolutionary movement. Amid the political upheaval of the time, they were manifestly the best organized and most powerful forces in the provinces. They were thus in a favorable position to seize control when the dynasty's administration collapsed at the local level. Civilian elites, for the most part, supported this seizure of power because they recognized that the army commanders, most of whom were from gentry and landlord families, would tolerate no radical, popular uprisings against the existing social and economic order. Soon after the outbreak of the revolution, therefore, eleven of the fourteen provinces that declared their independence of Manchu rule were governed by military officers.

Yuan Shikai restored a semblance of civilian authority after he became president of the newborn Republic. During 1913 and 1914, in an effort to lessen provincial autonomy and strengthen the powers of the central government, he stripped the military commanders of their civilian responsibilities and posted civilian governors to direct the provincial administrations. Yuan never succeeded, however, in reducing the power of the military to its pre-1911 level. And by early 1916, during Yuan's ill-fated monarchical movement, the generals reasserted their control over the provinces. The era of warlordism, a dozen years (1916–28) during which regional militarists controlled and fought over the political and fiscal fruits of the nation, had begun.

Militarism, sadly, begat further militarism. During the warlord era, no political party could reasonably hope to attain to national power without a military arm. Thus when the Nationalist revolution nominally unified the nation after 1927, it was Chiang Kai-shek, a military man by training and instincts, who headed the new government. Under his leadership, the Nationalist movement was transformed into a military-authoritarian regime in which the civilian branches, the party and the government, languished and the army served as the regime's principal base of support. Military tasks—suppression of Communist revolutionaries and regional militarists and resistance to Japanese aggression—received top priority. The locus of power within the regime, consequently, resided in such offices as the Military Affairs Commission.

Military officers acquired a prominence during those years that was unparalleled among any of the other major nations in the world. "Among the stable cabinets in the West," it has been observed, "the role of army officers in Germany [was] far greater than in Britain, France, or the United States, although even in Germany they were only about one-third as frequent as in either party [the Nationalists and the Communists] in China." The result was that "in China, revolutionary chaos gave the specialist on violence (i.e., the military careerist) a larger role than anywhere else . . . , and the role of the symbol specialists (lawyers, journalists, teachers) was considerably reduced."[9]

This enhanced role of the military in government and society had consequences for all Chinese, in every walk of life. Military leaders, such as Chiang Kai-shek, instinctively sought military solutions to political problems. Economic, social, and political reforms therefore received only slight attention during the years of Nationalist rule. And warfare cost money, which had to be extracted from peasants and merchants, industrialists and bankers. There was also little security for either person or property. Thus the entire society felt and suffered the effects of militarism. Young men who, in more tranquil times, might have turned to jobs in science, education, industry, or some other constructive career, often chose instead to become military officers; in turning to the profession of violence, they "ultimately destroyed the chances for stable evolution [of government and society]."[10]

Despite the deeply pernicious effects of militarism, the social status of military officers reached its apogee during the era of Nationalist rule, although common soldiers continued to be scorned and often feared. Even more than at the beginning of the century, young men from the "best families" were joining the army, and especially during the early years of the struggles with Japan, they were treated as heroes by an increasingly nationalistic public. "Respect and affection were reserved for them. It was quite common for the young ladies of upper class families or of a women's college to go out with young officers of the army, air force, or the navy, for social functions. Many of the new generals married girls of college education."[11] Not all segments of society shared this adulation for military officers; intellectuals, for example, retained much of the traditional disdain for military men, whatever rank they held. The reputation of the Nationalist military class gradually turned sour, too, as gross corruption spread through the army in the last years of the war against Japan and as the army proved to be almost totally ineffectual in the civil war against the Communists. Throughout the 1930s and 1940s, however, the military wielded predominant political power and influence. The power of the military, together with the rise of the new merchant and the new intellectual classes, which were based largely on wealth, revealed how profoundly China's social structure had been transformed during the early modern period.

The Urban Proletariat

The greatest changes in social structure during the early modern period were evident at the top, among the wealthy, the educated, and the governing classes. Most commoners, such as the peasants, continued to live much as they had 100 or 200 years earlier. One new social group, however, did appear among the commoners during the process of modernization—the industrial proletariat.

The industrial laborers—those who worked in shops and factories using power-driven machinery—were actually but a modest step away from the traditional craftsmen of the past. The levels and sophistication of technology in the factories tended to be low, especially in those factories owned by Chinese, and most factory workers still maintained roots and, often, families in their native villages. But they were also incontestably different from their predecessors, the traditional artisans, because their relations with employers were more impersonal, the output demands on them were more severe, and they were concentrated, as never before, in an urban environment. Moreover, because they became the objects of intensive interest from political agitators (particularly the Communists) during the 1920s, they acquired a significance in China's political revolutionary process that was out of proportion to their relatively small numbers.

China's first industrial workers were those employed in the ship-repair yards and other enterprises established by foreigners in Canton and Hong Kong following the Opium War. Later, in the 1860s, Chinese officials like Zeng Guofan and Zuo Zongtang recruited craftsmen from among these skilled Cantonese to train workers in the shipyards and arsenals that they were then establishing in central and north China. By the 1920s, the industrial work force had grown, by very rough estimate, to 1 million and was concentrated mainly in just six areas: Shanghai, Canton–Hong Kong, Wuhan, Tsingtao–Tsinan, Peking–Tientsin, and southern Manchuria.[12]

The living and working conditions of these industrial workers were remarkably similar to those depicted by Charles Dickens in the early phases of the Industrial

Revolution in England. There was the pallid and undernourished woman laboring at the looms, while her infant lay nearby on the factory floor. Boys just ten to twelve years old labored for twelve hours a day around gears that could, should their attention stray, easily crush a hand, or worked near machine belts that could in an instant rip off a limb. And when the workday was done, they returned to their dormitory quarters to a meal of cold rice gruel and a few vegetables, and to sleep on bug-infested pallets that they shared with others who worked the alternate shift. China's artisans and apprentices in the past had also worked long hours in cold, dank shops, but managers in the modern factories were less paternalistic toward the workers, so that the conditions of employment were probably harsher and more unfeeling than they had been in the small handicraft shops.

Most factories in the 1920s, both those owned by Chinese and those owned by foreigners, operated on shifts that were close to twelve hours each. A survey of twenty-three textile mills in Tientsin in 1923 revealed, for instance, that the workday was fifteen hours in one factory and fourteen hours in two others and that the average among all of them was eleven hours and fifty-five minutes. That was typical of conditions everywhere, except that highly skilled craftsmen, such as trained machinists and printers, tended to work fewer hours, often in shifts of only ten or even only nine hours. The overwhelming majority of China's factory workers, however, were unskilled. The technology in most factories was relatively basic, so most workers were required to perform only simple, repetitive operations that, with more advanced technology, would have been performed by machine. This was especially true of China's major industries, such as cotton and silk mills and tobacco and match factories. In these, a disproportionate number—often 60 to 70 percent—of the workers were women and children who, because their incomes were merely supplemental to their families' main incomes, acquiesced in working for the barest minimum wages.

The conditions of factory labor may be inferred from a reform proposal made in Shanghai in 1924 recommending that no children under ten years of age be employed in the factories, that children ten to fourteen years of age work no more than twelve hours a day, and that children be given twenty-four hours of rest a week. This recommendation for reform was, however, never enforced. The malevolent effects of long hours of work were worsened by the lack of safety precautions around the machines, by poor ventilation, and by malnutrition. Statistics tell something of the situation: of 880 workers in a Shanghai cotton mill, 6 percent of the men, 14 percent of the women, and 22 percent of the boys and girls suffered from tuberculosis. Medical care was, of course, virtually nonexistent.

Factories usually employed one of three forms of recruitment to obtain their workers. Probably the majority of the unskilled workers were hired either as apprentices or as contract laborers. These two systems reduced the workers to semi-slavery. Apprenticeship was a traditional system that had originated in the craft-shops, whereby boys customarily contracted to work for three to four years. During this time, they received little or no remuneration other than their food and lodging, but when they graduated, they were usually able to obtain employment as trained journeymen because the guilds strictly regulated their numbers. In the new factories, this system became corrupted. Apprenticeship ceased to be a method of teaching a trade and became simply a means of employing children at minimal cost. And because the "apprentices" were hired without restrictions on their numbers, few of them had any hope of being promoted to journeyman status after completing their apprenticeships.

In the contract-labor system, which apparently came into existence only in 1928, a labor contractor traveled to the villages of the interior in order to seek out potential workers, usually girls aged fourteen to eighteen. He enticed the girls with promises of a good life in the city—plenteous food, the opportunity to learn a skill, and, as one put it, the chance to enjoy the "strange, amusing foreign sights of Shanghai."[13] The contractors' chief enticement, however, was to the girls' parents, paying them a fee—typically Ch$30 or so—in return for which each girl was obligated to work for a specified period of time, usually three years.

The girls thus "sold" into contract labor rarely had a chance to enjoy the "amusing" sights of the city. In Shanghai, the contractor hired out his girls to various factories. The girls, however, continued to be virtually his property. He collected their wages from the factories and kept most for himself; he forced the girls to live in dormitories or accommodations that he provided, usually not even allowing them to stroll freely outside for fear that they would slip their bondage. Because of overcrowding, exhaustion, inadequate food, and beatings, the girls were often injured or became ill. Any time lost from the job because of illness or other causes was then added to the girls' total contract time, so that many of them worked for four or five years merely to fulfill a three-year contract. The girls were also often exploited sexually, the contractor or his henchmen perhaps forcing them to have sex with them, or sometimes sending them out to work as prostitutes rather than in the mills.

Studies of the Chinese industrial proletariat usually emphasize the brutalizing features of the workers' living and working conditions. The conditions of workers employed under the third system of hiring—the free-labor market—were, however, rather more tolerable. The free laborers, of course, worked in the same insalubrious factories as the contract laborers; they, too, were subject to beatings by the bosses; and their wages were also often wretchedly low, although the wages of skilled technicians were higher than the incomes they would have earned back on the farms. But free laborers customarily received wages directly from the employers—rather than receiving them from, and having to share them with, a contractor—and they thus achieved a degree of economic independence. Many women workers, as a consequence, found that working in the factories was preferable to other alternatives confronting them. Many thus refused to marry when and whom their parents wanted, and they tended to marry later in life than did their rural cousins. When a woman worker did marry, she tended to be—as a Chinese sociologist phrased it in 1935—"a new kind of wife," less willing to be subjugated by her husband and mother-in-law, and likely to bear fewer children.[14] Male workers, too, displayed a more individualistic attitude, and the often suffocating hold of the traditional family on them tended to weaken. The most far-reaching social changes among the lower classes of China during the early modern period were, therefore, found among the industrial workers.

Yet the majority of industrial workers remained close to their peasant roots.

Many had left the countryside to escape hunger and hardship on the farm, but they often left both their families and their hearts back in the villages. Young women, after completing the terms of their contracts, frequently returned home to become peasants' wives. Many male workers who were married lived in factory dormitories, but they returned to visit their wives and children in the villages at least once a year, usually at the New Years. Others returned to their homes in the country in the spring and fall to help with the planting and harvesting. The villages were also the workers' best "unemployment insurance" because when out of work or on strike, they could return to live and work with their families.

Industrial workers were not easily organized into trade unions. With their strong rural orientation, they were slow to develop a distinctive class consciousness. Moreover, many of them were women and children who were, in effect, merely transients in the factories, and industry was fragmented into numerous, small enterprises. As a consequence, the workers often had no sense of a shared destiny or common problems, and there was always a large reservoir of unemployed outside the factory gates waiting to replace "troublesome" workers. Despite these obstacles, the Chinese labor movement became, for a few brief years in the 1920s, a potent political force.

One of the first industrial strikes in China occurred in Shanghai in 1868; between 1895 and 1919, 152 more such strikes were recorded. Most were simply spontaneous protests against hunger and poverty, however, because the proletariat during that early period lacked an organization to formulate labor strategies and to represent its interests exclusively. Instead, the worker organizations then in existence, such as the traditional guilds and a newer breed of "industrial-promotion associations," were usually headed by employers and ostensibly represented the interests of employers and employees alike.

The political potential of the industrial workers did not become evident until the May Fourth Movement of 1919, when urban workers joined young intellectuals and the merchants in a great outburst of resentment against the Versailles peace settlement, Japanese imperialism, and the pro-Japanese Peking government. Participating in the nationwide boycott of Japanese goods and going out on strike in a show of support for the students who had been arrested in Peking, the industrial workers revealed for the first time a hitherto unimagined potential for action that transcended narrow craft and economic issues. Still, the organizational and political immaturity of the labor movement was evidenced by the fact that although the workers often felt genuine outrage at the events culminating in the May Fourth Movement, they remained merely followers. The leadership and organizational work in the movement was supplied by members of the intellectual and merchant classes, not from among the workers.

In the wake of the May Fourth Movement, during 1920 and 1921, the first genuine industrial unions were formed, their purpose being to represent purely working-class interests. At about the same time, young, radical intellectuals who represented diverse political ideologies—anarchists, labor syndicalists, and Marxists—began to look to the proletariat as the driving force in the movement of history. These two factors—the growing class consciousness of the workers and the organizational work of outside agitators—combined to transform the industrial workers into a force that significantly influenced political events leading to the Nationalist revolution in 1927.

The new labor movement first manifested itself in a series of strikes during 1922 and 1923, which began with the Hong Kong seamen's strike in early 1922. In that strike, some 30,000 seamen were joined by sympathetic dock workers, coolies, tram workers, electricians, and domestic servants. By March, the total number of strikers reached 120,000, and they virtually halted shipping in the British colony. After almost two months, the strike ended in a substantial victory for the seamen.

This strike imparted a sharp impetus to the labor movement throughout China. In April 1922, the All-China Labor Congress convened in Canton. At the congress, the Chinese Labor Organizations Secretariat (which had been organized by Communists, probably in 1920 or early 1921) was named to coordinate trade-union activities—evidence that the workers were developing an organizational capability with nationwide implications. Also, Sun Yat-sen, then serving in the revolutionary government in Canton, had been deeply and favorably impressed by the political potential of the Hong Kong workers, which encouraged him to form the first united front with the Soviets and the Chinese Communist party. This historic alliance between the Kuomintang and the Communists was formally consecrated at the Kuomintang's first party congress in January 1924.

The first wave of labor agitation came to an abrupt and tragic end on February 7, 1923, when troops under the command of the warlord Wu Peifu in north China massacred thirty-five striking railway workers. One of those murdered was a union secretary, who was beheaded in front of other workers for having refused to give the order to go back to work. Warlord repression of the labor movement continued during 1923, forcing many of the recently formed unions to disband.

After an interlude of nearly two years, the labor movement revived during 1925. The recent economic depression, which had marked the end of the golden age of Chinese industry, had hurt the livelihood of the workers and had bestirred anti-imperialist sentiment among the bourgeoisie. Thus when a series of labor strikes, beginning in January 1925, culminated in May in the murder of a Chinese striker by a Japanese foreman in a Shanghai mill and then in the shooting of thirteen protesting workers and students by policemen led by British officers, the nation erupted into a paroxysm of antiforeign frenzy. This May Thirtieth Movement, as it was soon called, was a repeat, on a grander and broader scale, of the May Fourth Movement, in the sense that students, merchants, and workers joined in a nationwide, patriotic alliance. This time, however, the students and the bourgeoisie played the supporting roles. It was now the workers, who had grown in number since 1919 and who had a stronger sense of class consciousness and more mature political organizations, who constituted the dominant force in and assumed the leadership of the movement.

The May Thirtieth Movement, whose momentum continued through most of 1926, significantly altered the balance of political forces in China. In the electrified atmosphere generated by the movement, worker and peasant organizations sprouted everywhere in south China, enormously facilitating the Kuomintang's consolidation of its revolutionary base in Kwangtung. Membership in the Communist party also multiplied sixfold, to 60,000. These events, in turn, set the stage for the Northern Expedition, which brought the Kuomintang and Chiang Kai-shek to national power.

The force evinced by the labor movement in this chain of events had, however, provoked a powerful reaction. On April 12, 1927, Chiang Kai-shek—with the backing of the Shanghai bourgeoisie, the foreign authorities in the city, and the Mafia-like Green Gang—began a reign of terror against the Communists and their allies among the workers, killing an estimated 5,000 people in 2 days of fighting. Obviously, the labor movement had badly frightened Chiang Kai-shek and his cohorts.

Throughout the remainder of Chiang's rule on the mainland, therefore, the Nationalists worked sedulously to ensure that the urban proletariat could not again coalesce into a revolutionary force that would threaten their leadership or their conception of the proper ordering of society. Industrial unions were disbanded or their leaders were replaced by the appointees of the government. The purpose of these ''yellow unions,'' as their critics called them, was no longer to represent workers' interests, but to control and supervise the workers. ''Cooperation'' between industry and labor now became the operative word. The labor movement ceased to be a significant factor in the politics of Nationalist China.

This did not necessarily mean that the workers were repressed economically. Indeed, during the postwar years 1945 to 1949, when inflation was rising uncontrollably and intellectuals and most salaried classes were being reduced to penury, the Nationalist government gave especially favored treatment to the industrial work force. The real wages of Shanghai's industrial workers in 1946 (according to a government report) were more than three times higher than they had been in 1936, and the average workday during the same period had shrunk from eleven to ten hours. To protect these advances, even in the face of the inflation, industrial wages were pegged to a commodity-price index. Industrialists bitterly complained about this kid-glove treatment of their workers, warning that the high wages jeopardized the very existence of their factories. By 1947 and 1948, however, the economy was disintegrating everywhere, and even the workers' standard of living dropped sharply. Then worker dissatisfaction broke to the surface again. Nonetheless, the government's labor policy over the previous twenty years had fully revealed that the Nationalists greatly feared this new class, which had formed during the course of economic modernization.

The Political Consequences

The emergence of these new social classes had profound effects on the politics and exercise of state power during the early twentieth century. In late imperial times, the political system had been remarkably stable and long-lived, in large part because of the structure of the relationship between state and society. On the one hand, political power above the local level had been concentrated in the imperial bureaucracy, which was elitist, paternalistic, and authoritarian. On the other hand, the broad masses of the commoners were politically powerless above the village and town level. Their normative role was to be subservient, orderly, and taxpaying. They had no input to the policy decisions of the imperial bureaucracy, and a broad social and political gap separated these two spheres—state and society.

Bridging this gap were the gentry, who served as brokers between the state and the commoners. At base, however, the gentry's loyalties lay with the state, for they had been indoctrinated in the official orthodoxy and they owed their status to the government by way of the civil-service examinations. The result was a marvelous political chemistry because—despite changes of dynasty and the normal vicissitudes of a traditional agrarian society—the political system functioned without fundamental change for approximately 1,000 years.

During the early modern period, however, that political system suffered severe shocks and dislocations. The first tremors had been felt during the mid-nineteenth century, when wealth began to displace learning as the route to elite status. The tremors intensified as a result of the impact of foreign influence, which hastened the formation of the new social classes. Within just one generation, between about 1895 and 1920, the old gentry and the imperial bureaucrats lost their former dominance of politics above the local level, and the newly emergent social groups—the merchant, intellectual, and military classes—came to constitute the social and economic elite. But these groups did not identify as closely with the state as had the traditional gentry. They had, in most cases, gained their status and careers independently of the government, and no longer did they spend their youth immersed in the study of an officially sanctioned doctrine that encouraged acquiescence to the state. All the new social classes, moreover, had become infected with the emotion of nationalism, often leaving them frustrated by the nation's weakness in the face of imperialist bullying and angered by the government's impotence and ineffectuality. Progressively during the early twentieth century, therefore, the traditional polity was breaking up, and from its ruins was rising a new constellation of political forces, which were diverse in economic interests and political loyalties and which progressively demanded a role in the political process.

The consequences of this politicization of the new social classes were farreaching. First, some members of those classes joined the government and gained positions of leadership. The effects of these we have already discussed: being drawn almost exclusively from the wealthier strata of society and being urban in orientation, they were poorly informed about and largely indifferent to the conditions of life in the vast rural areas. They were, therefore, less capable than the traditional gentry of mediating between state and society, and the gap dividing the polity yawned even more widely than in late imperial times.

Second, the leaders of government in the early modern period, regardless of their background, were no less elitist and authoritarian—although perhaps less paternalistic—than their predecessors. As a consequence, they were unable or unwilling to institutionalize the participation of the newly politicized social classes in the political process. The Manchu princes who wielded governmental authority in the last years of the dynasty, followed by Yuan Shikai and Chiang Kai-shek, were forced to accept representative assemblies and other accouterments of democratic government. But nothing in their early socialization or political experience had prepared them to accept popular participation in governmental decision making, which, to them, was as unnatural as if a son were to wield authority over his father. The new social classes thus never gained an institutionalized role in the political process, and so they did not strongly identify with the government. Increasingly, therefore, the army became the government's main pillar of support.

A government whose principal source of support is the military is invariably weak. Ultimately it lacks, as political scientists say, legitimacy. Thus the Chinese government's inability to admit the new social classes into the political process was an important cause of the political instability and weakness that beset China during the decades before the Communist revolution in 1949.

The Challenge to Familism

Amid the proliferation of new social classes and the spread of economic modernization during the early modern period, the values of the old society came under attack. A spirit of individualism and a movement for the liberation of women began to challenge the values of the traditional familism.

Among the educated classes, this attack on the old social ideals began in the wake of the military defeats in 1895 and 1900, the disestablishment of Confucianism as the official ideology in 1905, and the overthrow of the Qing Dynasty in 1912. These events, for many politically aware Chinese, shattered their confidence in traditional ways. By the 1910s, intellectuals like Chen Duxiu and Hu Shi, who cringed at the humiliations inflicted by the foreigners, had become convinced that the source of China's shame and impotence lay in the anachronistic ways of the old society. To achieve a national renewal, China had to emulate the ways of the West. Thus was born the New Culture Movement. This movement, which reached its apogee during the years 1915 to 1922, rejected the familistic ideals of respect for the aged regardless of ability, of supremacy of men over women, and of the sacrifices of the individual to the fortunes and good name of the family. The morality of the old society, declared Lu Xun in his powerful short story "Madman's Diary," was cannabalistic, consuming and destroying the lives of all Chinese in the name of Confucian righteousness. Lu Xun saw hope for the future in the nation's youth, who had not yet been tainted by the false morality of the past. And it was to the youth, to the students and young intellectuals in the universities and middle schools, that the call for a new culture most appealed.

The laboring classes were untouched by the New Culture Movement, but in the cities, they, too, began breaking with tradition. Whereas the old patriarchal family had been a product of and helped perpetuate the traditional agrarian economy, the development of industrial manufacturing imposed strains on the old social arrangements and generated many of the attitudes toward generation, gender, and individualism that young members of the elite classes were acquiring.

In the Chinese peasant economy, where technologies changed slowly, the chief qualification for family leadership was experience. Under these conditions, dominance of the family had fallen naturally to the elders. In the early twentieth century, by contrast, especially in the industrial sector, where technologies and ideas flooded in from the West, reliance on the experience and methods of the past could be an obstruction. The premium there was on new ideas, innovativeness, and a willingness to break with the ways of the past. And these were the virtues of the youth. Youth educated in the new schools were also exposed to a whole universe of thinking and learning that had been a closed book to their fathers' generation. The abandonment of traditional ways, in other words, threatened to leave the older generation behind, and in some areas of society, a new "youth culture" was coming into being. There developed an intoxication with things new and exotic, and a corresponding disdain for the old and the commonplace. Whereas pharmacists had once attracted customers with assurances that their medicines had existed in hoary antiquity, now the allure was provided by the words "science" and "foreign." Students were attracted, John Dewey reported, by any and all ideas, "provided only that they were new and involved getting away from old customs and traditions."[15] Youth who had been influenced by such ideas regarded the older generation with a barely concealed contempt, and they thus challenged the fundamental precepts of the old family structure and values.

A spirit of individualism evolved out of this revolt of the youth. Educated youth acquired their new sense of individual worth and independence largely by reading and talking about Western concepts of freedom and self-reliance, which were propagated in the many new publications of the day. This is called "individualism by ideal." The urban laboring class at the same time was developing "individualism by default," which occurred when young men and women left their villages to work in the cities, living away from the daily dominance of their parents, making decisions for themselves, and earning wages of their own. Such youths developed a spirit of independence to a degree that was inconceivable when they worked every day side by side with their fathers in the fields or with their mothers or mothers-in-law in the kitchens. Whereas in traditional society, children had been regarded primarily as a necessary means to attain familistic goals, the new view stressed that they were important in and for themselves, with concerns and rights that transcended those of the family. This rejection of the basic precepts of familism was revolutionary in its implications. No longer must the son sacrifice his desires to the will of the older generation or his personal well-being to the welfare or reputation of the larger family. And the older generation, perceiving these changes, became fearful that their world was becoming unglued: no longer could they expect absolute obedience or could they feel secure in the knowledge that their sons would remain in the household to care for them in their old age.

Under the impact of the new individualism and the revolt of the youth, the status of women began to change. In the society of late imperial times, most men thought that a woman's proper place was in the house or beside the loom. Although some upper-class women received a modest, literary education—a few of them, indeed, even becoming poets, calligraphers, and artists—the conventional wisdom continued to be that "a woman without talents is virtuous." In the mid-nineteenth century, Christian missionaries began to promote girls' education. Their accomplishments, however, were quantitatively small—in 1877, after 33 years, there were still only 524 students in the 38 schools for girls. By the end of the century, however, some male intellectuals with progressive views took up the cause of women's education, largely on the grounds that ignorant women nurtured ignorant sons. Concerned for the fate of their nation, which was being assailed by the imperialists, these progressive thinkers realized that China could become strong and prosperous only if its citizens were enlightened. They therefore advocated that both boys and girls receive modern schooling.

Footbinding, too, came under attack—again largely for the nationalistic and utilitarian reasons that women, crippled through footbinding, produced physically inferior children. Even the Manchu court in 1902 supported the growing anti-footbinding movement by urging the upper classes "to abstain from the evil practice and by this means abolish the custom forever."[16] Especially after the Revolution of 1911, the practice declined. Yet in China today, one can still see elderly women with bound feet, so it is evident that footbinding was still practiced to some extent, especially in remote areas, even during the 1920s.

The major onslaught on the traditional subjugation of women began only after 1915, when leaders of the New Culture Movement made women's emancipation a major goal of their struggle against the old society. Articles on "the women's problem" in all the progressive magazines of the time deplored the suffering caused by arranged marriages, the prejudice against remarriage, and the submission of women to men. The radical cause proclaimed the revolutionary message that women, too, were individuals.

Women of the lower classes usually remained ignorant of the feminist movement among the intellectuals, but in the cities, they began straining at the bonds of their subjugation. Women and young girls working in the new factories, for example, became economic assets to their families. As a result, they began to acquire a voice in family affairs, and their parents were no longer so eager to marry them off at a young age.

But we ought not exaggerate. All these changes—the emphasis on youth, the development of individualism, and the emancipation of women—were evident in only a small percentage of Chinese families. The professional and educated classes, who were most susceptible to the arguments of the New Culture Movement, represented but a tiny segment within society as a whole. And the number of young men and women who left their villages and became industrial workers was small relative to the total population. Moreover, not all the educated youth and urban workers who were exposed to the new social currents actually changed their behavior and attitudes within their homes. Men and women of the professional class in Shanghai and Peking, it is true, had largely abandoned the old form of arranged marriages and sought out their own mates. A survey in the 1930s, for example, found that eight of ten members of the professional class in Peking, and 16 of the 23 in Shanghai, had married in the modern way; but fully 37 of 46 marriages among members of Peking's middle class, and 98 of 124 marriages among Shanghai's industrial workers, had been arranged in the traditional manner. Among the peasants, tradition remained virtually undisturbed. Only 3 villagers of 170 surveyed, for example, had even heard of "modern marriages."

Politics and governmental legislation had only a marginal effect on the position of women and on relations within the family. In 1930, the Nationalist government proclaimed a new civil code, which provided a legal basis for social change. Women were, for instance, granted the legal rights of selecting their own husbands, of owning property, and of inheriting property from their parents. These laws, however, were seldom put into effect.

In the Communist areas, too, legislation and political pronouncements during the 1930s and 1940s signaled what might have been revolutionary social changes. Women were assured of the freedom of marriage and divorce, mobilized into mass organizations, and often given a rudimentary education. But even here, social change encountered resistance, not least because leaders of the Communist party feared that too strong an emphasis on the movement for sexual equality would detract from the struggle for political and economic revolution. Still, just as factory employment in the cities increased the economic value of women, so the Communists' mobilization of women in war production helped at least marginally to improve women's status in the Communist areas.

Selected Readings

(See also the works cited in the notes)

Bastid-Bruguirre, Marianne. "Currents of Social Change." In *Cambridge History of China*, vol. 11, ed. John K. Fairbank and Kwang-ching Liu, pp. 535–602. Cambridge: Cambridge University Press, 1980.

Chan, Wellington K. K. *Merchants, Mandarins, and Modern Enterprise in Late Ch'ing China*. Cambridge, Mass.: Harvard University, East Asian Research Center, 1977.

Chang, Chung-li. *The Chinese Gentry: Studies on Their Role in Nineteenth-Century Chinese Society*. Seattle: University of Washington Press, 1955.

Croll, Elisabeth. *Feminism and Socialism in China*. New York: Schocken Books, 1980.

Hershatter, Gail. "Flying Hammers, Walking Chisels: The Workers of Santiaoshi." *Modern China* 9, no. 4. (October 1984): 387–419.

———. *The Workers of Tianjin, 1900–1949*. Stanford, Calif.: Stanford University Press, 1986.

Ho, Ping-ti. *The Ladder of Success in Imperial China: Aspects of Social Mobility, 1368–1911*. New York: Columbia University Press, 1962.

Honig, Emily. *Sisters and Strangers: Women in the Shanghai Cotton Mills, 1919–1939*. Stanford, Calif.: Stanford University Press, 1986.

Johnson, Kay Ann. *Women, the Family, and Peasant Revolution in China*. Chicago: University of Chicago Press, 1983.

Lang, Olga. *Chinese Family and Society*. New Haven, Conn.: Yale University Press, 1946.

Levy, Marion J., Jr. *The Family Revolution in Modern China*. Cambridge, Mass.: Harvard University Press, 1949.

Rhoads, Edward J. M. "Merchant Associations in Canton, 1895–1911." In *The Chinese City Between Two Worlds*, ed. Mark Elvin and G. William Skinner, pp. 97–117. Stanford, Calif.: Stanford University Press, 1974.

Stacey, Judith. *Patriarchy and Socialist Revolution in China*. Berkeley: University of California Press, 1983.

10

The *Yin* Side of Society: Secret Societies, Bandits, and Feuds

Thus far, this book has dealt largely with the legal and orthodox aspects of Chinese social life—what might be called the *yang* side of society. But there was also a *yin* side—the shadowy world of the illegal and the heterodox.[1] This is a realm not easily entered; little is known about it because it was disreputable. It did not fit the Confucian elite's image of society the way they thought it *ought* to be, and thus they rarely recorded it in their histories. To the common folk suffering from poverty, insecurity, and injustice, however, this was a real and often attractive alternative to the gentry- and official-dominated way of life. For by banding together in secret societies, turning to banditry, or participating in huge, sanguinary feuds, they could often attain the riches, the solace, or the retribution that the *yang* side of society denied them.

Secret Societies

The term "secret society" is a neologism when applied in the Chinese context. Westerners in China during the mid-nineteenth century, observing a form of organization that seemed to resemble European secret societies, such as the Free-masons and the Carbonari, applied the term "secret society" to the Chinese phenomenon. Subsequently, that term, translated as *mimi shehui,* established itself in the Chinese language. Chinese scholars who have studied what the Westerners called secret societies have, however, generally shunned the term. They have preferred instead to retain two traditional terms, *jiaomen* (folk sects) and *huitang* (secret brotherhoods), that distinguish two distinct species of secret societies. Indeed, the distinction between folk sects and secret brotherhoods is fundamental to an understanding of China's so-called secret societies. Significantly, a form of secret society that shared some of the characteristics of both the folk sects and the secret brotherhoods, what might be called "protective societies," evolved during the early modern period.

Folk Sects

In the autumn of 1813, 100,000 followers of the Eight Trigrams Sect rose against the Qing Dynasty, seizing several cities in the north China plain and penetrating even into the imperial Forbidden City in Peking. Within three months, however, government armies quashed the uprising, and some 70,000 rebels died in their vain attempt to establish a new moral and political order.

The revolt of the Eight Trigrams Sect was but one of many anti-Qing rebellions instigated by millenarian folk sects during the late eighteenth and the nineteenth centuries, and the folk sects are best known as a result of these rebellious activities. But the folk sects were, first and foremost, religious organizations that often existed peacefully for generations without engaging in rebellion. The Yellow Heaven Sect, for example, which was founded in the sixteenth century and survived into the 1940s, never rebelled; and the Wang Sect of Stone-Buddha Village revolted only once during its more than 200-year history—and that time only briefly during the declining phase of the Ming Dynasty. The raison d'être of the folk sects, therefore, was religious, not political, although their religious beliefs did sometimes draw them into rebellion.

The religious beliefs of the folk sects, like those of the popular religion, were radically syncretic. During the late imperial period, the sects belonged predominantly to the White Lotus tradition, which had emerged in the twelfth century as an offshoot of Tiantai and Pure Land Buddhism. Gradually these original Buddhist beliefs had merged with the doctrines and rituals of Taoism, the popular religion, and even Manicheanism. And by the sixteenth century, the supreme deity of many of the folk sects was not Buddhist, but a maternal goddess with antecedents in China's earlier religions: the Eternal Mother *(Wusheng laomu)*.

According to White Lotus cosmology, the Eternal Mother was the original progenitor of all humankind. But humans, living on earth, had lost their original perfection and devoted themselves to evil ways. Grieving, the Eternal Mother sought the return of her earthly children to the Original Home in the World of True Emptiness, which was a nirvana, or paradise, where the karmic wheel of life and death ceased to turn and where suffering and uncertainty were replaced by eternal joy, security, and peace.

To restore her children to this paradise, the Eternal Mother sent Buddhas to earth to teach humans the true way of salvation. These Buddhas came to earth, however, only near the end of a *kalpa,* an era some hundreds of thousands of years in duration. Then a holocaust of floods, fires, or winds would destroy everyone who was not a true believer in the Eternal Mother, and the Maitreya Buddha, which was the Buddha of the Future, would become incarnate on earth to lead true believers in the creation of a new moral order.

This doctrine of salvation in the approaching millennium, which most folk sects taught, was the spark that flared into political rebellion. This was because the sects taught that as the end of the current *kalpa* approached, the members must prepare the way for the new order by destroying the existing government.

Yet for long periods, the sects existed peacefully and almost unnoticed in the recesses of local society. Although banned by the government, they were not clandestine organizations except when threatened by government suppression (which is an argument against calling them "secret" societies), and they even constructed temples and hostels for their members. Only a small part of the population ever joined the sects, and probably most Chinese were barely, if at all, cognizant of their existence. But the sects were sufficiently pervasive that, at least in north China, "in most areas one who was so inclined could locate such a group and attempt to join it."[2]

Organization of the sects was diffuse. Although most of them adhered to the same general theology, the links among them were exceedingly tenuous. Each sect usually numbered only a few score members, who practiced their religion in virtual isolation from one another. The master of each sect, moreover, was free to interpret the teachings of the religion as he or she chose—there was no White Lotus hierarchy above the separate sects to pronounce on doctrinal orthodoxy— and some masters taught from scriptures that only they possessed. There was, consequently, considerable doctrinal variety among the sects, and relations among them—insofar as they had any relations at all—were often marked by intense factionalism and competition for members. Such decentralization and rivalry severely weakened the White Lotus movement, and only rarely could several sects cooperate on a sufficient scale and long enough to pose a real threat to the government. At the same time, that very weakness was a source of the sects' durability, because the government was never able to root out more than a few sects at a time, leaving the rest of the sect structure intact.

Leaders of the folk sects were usually from what might be called the lumpen-intellectual class, people who were literate, but who had not gained distinction in their chosen careers. They might be monks, priests, students who had failed the civil-service examinations, or perhaps simply fortunetellers or failed merchants. Most ordinary sect members, by contrast, were probably peasants, although representatives of every occupation and class status, excepting only the highest elites of Qing society, may at one time or another have joined the sects. Thus landlords and even eunuchs in the imperial palace in Peking are known to have joined the sects.

Most, but by no means all, of the ordinary sect members were probably illiterate, and the sects consequently made minimal intellectual demands on them. Converts to the White Lotus sects during the early nineteenth century, for instance, were taught a basic eight-character mantra: "Eternal Progenitor in Our Original Home in the World of True Emptiness." Repetition of this secret incantation, or some variation thereof, was thought to produce for the believer various magical benefits, such as health, wealth, and protection from calamities. The ceremony accompanying recital of the mantra differed among the various sects, and possibly also among believers at various levels of spiritual sophistication. Some, for example, were expected only to repeat the eight characters silently and an unspecified number of times. Others chanted the mantra twenty-seven times each morning while sitting cross-legged, with closed eyes, and bowing eastward to the rising sun; at noon, they chanted the mantra fifty-four times, again while sitting cross-legged and bowing toward the sun; and in the evening, the believers recited the incantation eighty-one times while bowing westward to the setting sun.

Of the various appeals of the sects to potential members, that of mystical healing was undoubtedly the strongest. In a prescientific society such as that of late imperial China, where the causes of sickness were unclear and the remedies of modern medicine were unknown, illness was a source of special terror. Many of the folk-sect masters, however, claimed to be capable of healing or preventing illnesses, and this was a potent recruiting device. Usually they accomplished healing with yogic meditation or bodily massage. Disciples were taught to sit cross-legged, to close their eyes, and then to circulate their vital breath *(qi)* throughout their bodies and especially to the top of the head. At the lower levels of yogic skill, meditation could result in overcoming diseases, obtaining long life, and gaining immunity from natural disasters. Those attaining higher aptitude could hope even for immortality and rebirth in paradise. Sect masters also achieved the circulation of vital breaths by applying pressure on the "caves and roads" of the disciple's body. Such magical massage, it was thought, would cure illnesses and heal injuries.

Boxing and fencing were other skills that sect masters used to attract followers. The exercises associated with these forms of fighting were believed to confer physical health and thus were regarded as beneficial to the spirit. To Westerners accustomed to claims for the physical and psychic benefits of jogging and other forms of athletic exercise, such beliefs do not seem outlandish. Some of the sects' boxing masters also taught, however, that their skills bestowed physical invulnerability. One adept, for example, repeatedly stabbed himself in the upper body, yet he was reportedly unharmed, marked only by white scars where the knife had penetrated.

Having become a member, a sectarian might find other sources of gratification. For many, the simple act of forming ties with other people as a result of being a member of a semiexclusive organization—especially in Chinese society, where social relationships were so important to an individual's sense of identity and purpose—doubtless resulted in a sense of security and contentment. Another potent appeal was that the multilayered organizations within each sect—often ascending through as many as nine levels, depending on the members' spiritual and magical attainments—provided opportunities for rank and recognition that the official- and gentry-dominated society denied them. The sects also held out a special appeal to women, because they (unlike other secret societies) did not discriminate between the sexes. Women frequently attained positions of leadership in the sects, acting as teachers and even sect masters.

This sexual egalitarianism, exceedingly rare elsewhere in Chinese society, may have been a consequence of the fact that the supreme deity of the White Lotus sects—the Eternal Mother—was female. However that may be, the mixing of the sexes in the congregations provided fuel for the government's charges that the sects engaged in sexual orgies as part of their religious exercises. While the popular Taoist sects in an earlier era had indeed engaged in unusual sexual practices—

such as the one known as the "Union of Vital Breaths"—there is no evidence that folk sects within the White Lotus tradition did so. Sexual promiscuity involving sect leaders and their pupils did, it is true, sometimes occur. When Lin Qing, the future leader of the revolt by the Eight Trigrams Sect in 1813, visited the home of a pupil, for instance, he slept with the pupil's wife and daughter-in-law. In a spirit of reciprocity, Lin Qing told his wife and step-daughters to sleep with the pupil during a return visit. Such promiscuity resulted simply from moral laxity, however, rather than from a doctrinal imperative, and not all sect members approved of it.

Significantly, calls for political revolution and economic reform were not part of the sects' basic appeal. During ordinary times—that is, except in the relatively rare periods when they were rebelling against the state—the sects ignored such questions as landlord exploitation and heavy land taxes. They were religious organizations, and they generally paid little heed to the material or political concerns of specific economic classes.

Periodically, however, folk sects did rebel against the government. In 1622, late in the Ming Dynasty, a White Lotus sect proclaimed the approach of the new *kalpa* and rose in revolt. This uprising was suppressed in just three months, and for about 150 years thereafter, the sects seem to have been politically quiescent. Beginning in the reign of Qianlong, however, predictions of the coming of the Maitreya Buddha and of the turning of the *kalpa* became common. There then began a long series of sect uprisings, the first of which, in 1774, was led by one Wang Lun, who proclaimed to members of his sect that he was the Buddha of the Future. Then, leading 1,000 or so believers, he attacked 3 *xian* governments in Shantung and seized control of the city of Linqing on the Grand Canal. Although the dynasty's forces easily crushed the uprising in just three weeks, this proved to be the forerunner of a century and more of sectarian activities against the state. The most severe and famous of these were the White Lotus Rebellion of 1796 to 1804—which devastated much of central and west China and nearly bankrupted the dynasty—and the Boxer Uprising of 1898 to 1900—whose fury shifted from the dynasty to the foreigners and provoked the intervention of the imperialist powers.

It is puzzling that the folk sects should have lived in peace within their society for such an extended period in the seventeenth and eighteenth centuries, only to erupt thereafter in a century and a half of repeated rebellions. Repression by the government, some scholars have argued, started the wave of rebellions. Being thus denied a permanent and secure place for their activities in the present society, the sects sought such a place in the new social and political order promised by the Eternal Mother.[3] But this explanation overlooks the conditions of political decline in the late Qing period. That sect rebellions increased during precisely the same period that other forms of collective violence—banditry, rioting, feuding, and so on—became widespread indicates that ecological disorder, and not just the sects' revived interest in the promise of the millennium, underlay their increased rebelliousness.

Secret Brotherhoods

Secret brotherhoods, like the folk sects, drew their members from lower levels of the social hierarchy and periodically rose in revolt against the government. They differed from the folk sects, however, in both form and function.

The largest and most active of the secret brotherhoods until the latter half of the nineteenth century was the Triad Society, an organization that exemplified the distinctive traits of this type of secret society. The origins of the Triads are indistinct, hidden behind the veil of secrecy that always surrounded the society. It is clear, however, that the Triads were of much later inception that the folk sects. Traditions of the Triads themselves maintain that the society was organized as early as 1674 by a group of militant Buddhist monks belonging to the Shaolin temple in Fukien—famous because of its links with a style of the Chinese martial arts. An official Qing investigation of the society in the 1780s, however, concluded that the society, while indeed founded by a monk in the province of Fukien, had not been organized until 1767.[4] Whatever the time and place of its formation, the Triads' center of power and activity was in Kwangtung and Kwangsi—although its adherents could be found throughout south China.

By contrast with the folk sects, the Triad Society was not essentially a religious organization. It displayed none of the sects' superstitious beliefs in magical chants, meditation, or physical invulnerability to enemy swords and bullets. It did pay respect to various Buddhist, Taoist, and other deities—even including the Eternal Mother of the White Lotus sect. But its chief objects of worship were historical heroes, most notably Guan Di, the defied general of the second century who personified courage and loyalty.

The basic function of the Triads was to provide mutual aid and protection to its members. Most Chinese satisfied their felt need for a social network through their families and clans. For some—artisans, merchants, and scholars, for example, who resided away from home—guilds and provincial associations partly satisfied this need. But for the poor and downtrodden, for those who had been torn loose from their social roots and had little status in society—such as petty tradesmen, *yamen*-runners, displaced peasants, manure collectors, sedan-chair bearers, dock hands, thieves, and smugglers—the secret brotherhoods often performed this social function. For these marginal members of society, and for a few landlords and wealthy persons as well, the secret brotherhoods served as "substitute clans."[5] Indeed, to foster the sense among Triad members that they had a common kinship, the initiation ceremony included the drinking of blood (drawn from the recruits' pricked finger or from a white rooster) and the conferral on the initiate of the surname Hong, which was common to all Triad members.

What is here termed the Triad Society was known variously in Chinese as, among others, the *Hongmen* (Hong League), the *Sandian hui* (Three Dots Society), the *Sanhe hui* (Three Harmonies Society), and the *Tiandi hui* (Heaven and Earth Society). It was a sprawling organization, spreading from Taiwan in the east to Szechwan and Kansu in the west, and even to Chinese communities overseas, including those in Hawaii and California. But its structure and organization were weak: a common ritual, a common antipathy for the political Establishment, and perhaps a vague sense of community were all that held the many branches of the society together. There existed no centralized leadership, and bitter factionalism—erupting sometimes in bloody fights—often divided the lodges of the brotherhood. Only when faced with a common threat, it seems, could the discrete units of the league cooperate long enough to form a sizable armed force. Even then, however, they might quickly disperse on their own initiative. Parochial interests, that is, dominated the motivations of the Triads' members, and they were never able—as were the Taipings—to form a united force large enough to threaten the very existence of the dynasty. Like the folk sects, the Triads owed their longevity to the hydra-headed character of their organization, too illusive for the government to suppress in its entirety.

Despite the Triads' loose organization, a shared sense of fraternity did link members of the different lodges. Should a Triad be traveling outside his home community, for instance, he could seek the help of a local lodge. By means of an intricate and esoteric system of hand or body movements, or perhaps by positioning teacups in certain ways around a teapot, he could identify himself to and make contact with a local "brother." The generosity accorded such a guest by the host lodge was, however, conditioned by the guest's potential to reciprocate. Thus a guest holding high status in the organization or in a position to repay large favors could expect generous treatment. An ordinary member, by contrast, probably could expect no more than a meal or two and a bed for the night.

Within a lodge, however, the organizational ties were tighter and the members' obligations to one another more wide-ranging. Should a Triad member become involved in a dispute with someone outside the brotherhood, for example, he could be assured of the support of his fellow lodge members. If he ran afoul of the law, his "brothers" were required to help him escape; if he needed money, they must grant a loan. Members would also arrange and pay for the funeral of an impoverished brother. (This, to a Westerner, appears a small matter; to a Chinese who feared that he would become a hungry ghost if not accorded a proper burial, this practice was deeply reassuring.) As in lineages, too, Triad leaders arbitrated disputes among members and provided occasions for feasts and other social get-togethers.

Lodges maintained strict discipline over their members. A brother who revealed secrets of the organization, for example, was to "perish beneath 10,000 swords." (In this sense, the secret brotherhoods, in contrast to the folk sects, were truly "secret" societies.) Having sexual relations with the wife of a fellow lodge member was also a crime to be punished in a similarly dire fashion, as were homosexuality and cheating a brother while gambling. Robbery, rape, drunkenness, cursing, and disorderly conduct were other crimes that might be punished by a beating with the light or heavy bamboo pole or by the cutting off of one or both ears.

The morality of the Triads, however, was that of a counterculture: the disciplinary sanctions were designed to protect and maintain the camaraderie and unity of the lodge members, but did not apply to the members' relations with the Confucian Establishment. The Triads were, in fact, deeply involved in all forms of criminal activity. They often operated or controlled the gambling, narcotics, and prostitution activities of an area; they smuggled salt, the legal trade in which was monopolized by the government; and they sold "protection' to stores, travelers, and brothels. The conduct of the Triads, therefore, was similar to that of the heroes in the novel *Water Margin,* whose relations among themselves were marked by trust, cooperation, and good fellowship, but who preyed on the rich and powerful of the outside world. This popular novel about a band of outlaws in the twelfth century, in fact, profoundly influenced the organization, ritual, and self-image of the secret brotherhoods.

During the latter half of the nineteenth century, following the suppression of the Taiping Rebellion (1851–64), the Triads remained active, especially in Kwangtung and Kwangsi. Elsewhere in the country, however, the Society of Elder Brothers *(Gelao hui)* became the most widespread and active of the secret brotherhoods. The organization, function, mythology, and rituals of the Elder Brothers closely resembled those of the Triads, but the Elder Brothers was not, as is sometimes suggested, just a branch or lodge of the Triads.

Evidence regarding the formation of the Elder Brothers is scanty. The society appears to have originated in Szechwan during the early 1850s. Szechwan was then in a chaotic state as masses of impoverished peasants, together with immigrants fleeing the devastation of the Taiping Rebellion, roamed the province. Within this matrix of poverty and instability, remnants of the White Lotus folk sect came in contact with the Triads and another secret brotherhood known as the Guolu. The Society of Elder Brothers seem to have evolved out of the mix of these several organizations, although the precise process is still unclear. In any case, the Elder Brothers shared many of the Triads' organizational features, but worshiped different ancestors.

The Elder Brothers expanded from Szechwan and Kweichow after some of its members were recruited into the Hunanese army commanded by Zeng Guofan. Thereafter, their influence spread, and by the late 1860s and the 1870s, the Society of Elder Brothers was active throughout the Yangtze River valley and beyond. Even as late as the 1940s, during the war against Japan, the Elder Brothers dominated much of local society in Szechwan.

Much more than the folk sects, the secret brotherhoods had a strong, persistent political orientation. The ritual and literature of the Triads and the Elder Brothers were filled with enmity for the reigning dynasty; their dominant slogan was *Fan Qing fu Ming* (Overthrow the Qing, Restore the Ming). That is, they hoped to overthrow the Manchu rulers, who were foreign conquerors, and restore to the throne a prince of the native Ming Dynasty. When this political revolution occurred, they thought, they would receive the benefits of a just and prosperous society.[6]

But the political orientation of the secret brotherhoods is probably exaggerated. During the late nineteenth and early twentieth centuries, when most is known about them, anti-Manchuism did indeed resonate through their ritual and rhetoric, but smuggling, extortion, and control of gambling operations was the focus of their activities. "The essential aim of secret society operations in these lucrative fields was coexistence with orthodox society in order to exploit it, not dedicated conspiracy in order to destroy it."[7] Even so, the persistence of the ideology of

Fan Qing fu Ming was presumably attractive to Chinese commoners, and especially to deracinated members of society, who generally regarded government as
a baneful force, extortionate and hurtful. The secret brotherhoods provided them
with one of the few means available to vent their real, if often only vague, political discontents.

As the power of the reigning dynasty weakened during the nineteenth century,
secret brotherhoods proliferated and their antigovernmental activities became more
frequent. In 1802, 1817, and twice in 1837, for example, the Triads staged armed
insurrections in Kwangtung; other uprisings erupted in Kwangsi, Kiangsi, Hunan,
and Fukien. Thereafter, following the Opium War of 1839 to 1842 and during the
great rebellions of the mid-nineteenth century, the brotherhoods flourished, their
antidynastic activities thriving on the growth of popular discontent and the dynasty's weakness. For about two decades following the Taiping and Nien rebellions,
brotherhood activity subsided. But during the last decade and a half of the Qing
period, the brotherhoods revived, their traditional anti-Manchuism making them
seemingly natural allies of the growing revolutionary movement. There were, indeed, extensive contacts and collaboration between these two antidynastic forces,
but the parochialism and diffuse social composition of the Triads and Elder Brothers limited their contribution to the final overthrow of the dynasty.

This parochialism always limited the political impact of the secret brotherhoods, whose interests seldom, if ever, transcended immediate economic concerns. Their insurrections were usually of only local importance, therefore, and
they never attempted a massive assault on the central government, as did the
Taipings—although they did on occasion join the Taipings. But cooperation between the Taiping God-Worshipers and the Triad Society was short-lived. The
Triads were not deeply dedicated to overthrowing the Qing, as were the Taipings,
and they often engaged in pillage and mistreatment of the common people rather
than in anti-Manchu campaigning. Hong Xiuquan, leader of the Taipings, remarked that the Triads' "real object has now turned very mean and unworthy"[8]—
an assessment that accurately reflected the secret brotherhoods' self-regarding and
often criminal character.

Protective Societies

China's secret societies were organizationally decentralized and doctrinally syncretic. Over the course of their long history, therefore, they easily metamorphosed
as they responded to the changing social and political environment and to local
diversity. Not surprisingly, therefore, in the markedly different political climate
of China after the Revolution of 1911, a new strain of secret-society organization,
which differed sharply from the principal sects and brotherhoods of the earlier
periods, became predominant. This emergent strain might be called "protective
societies." They were led by local elites, were paramilitary in function, and were
conservative in political orientation.

This form of secret society did, it is true, have antecedents in earlier times.
During the 1780s in Taiwan, for instance, a lodge leader of the Triads was a rich
landlord who had found in the Triad organization "a framework for communal

self-defense.''[9] During the 1860s, too, wealthy merchants on occasion used the Society of Elder Brothers to protect their property and holdings. And the Boxers in 1898 to 1900 likewise had a background in communal defense, and scholars are still working to sort out the influence of local militia from that of White Lotus sectarianism in the Boxer Uprising. The characteristics of the protective societies were not wholly new, therefore, but in the aftermath of the Revolution of 1911, the protective societies became for a time the predominant form of secret society in China.

The best-known protective society in the Republican period (1911–49) was the Red Spear Society, so named from the red tassels with which the members decorated their spears. The origins of the first Red Spear units are unclear: one scholar puts their founding back in the Yuan Dynasty; another asserts that they were a "resurrected" form of the Boxers, which had been suppressed in 1900. Whatever the precise antecedents, it is certain that the society had coalesced into a large and complex organization by 1920 or 1921. In 1927, it numbered more than 3 million followers and had become a major political force in the north China plain, especially in the provinces of Honan (home of half the Red Spears), Shantung, Anhwei, Kiangsu, and Shensi.

Impetus for the formation of the Red Spear units, at least in their twentieth-century incarnation, came out of the virtual anarchy into which north China had fallen. By the 1920s, warlordism was at its apogee; the governmental apparatus had deteriorated; and tens of thousands of bandits preyed on the area. Villages formed "self-defense corps" to fend off the various predators, but they were often ineffective against large bandit gangs because the militiamen often lacked fighting spirit and the villagers quickly lost interest in financing the militia after the bandits moved on to other prey. In an effort to create a more effective local defense force, some local leaders hit on the idea of inviting religious masters to oversee the training of their armed units. The result was the Red Spear Society.[10]

Religion, therefore, was what primarily differentiated the Red Spears from the regular village self-defense corps. Like the sects and brotherhoods of the nineteenth century, Red Spears worshiped a variety of dieties, ranging from Guan Di and the bodhisattva Guanyin to Confucius and Laozi (Lao-tzu). The Red Spear religion strongly emphasized the belief in physical invulnerability, its rituals and beliefs directed toward bestowing on its members the powers of resistance to even the most deadly weapons. Each new member was subjected to a period of purification and training that lasted anywhere from three weeks to three months. Besides learning to recite numerous incantations, drinking water that was infused with the ashes of written charms, and participating in ceremonies that required him to kneel for two to three hours at a time, the recruit received military training. During this training, he was beaten sharply on the body, an experience designed to harden his muscles and prepare him for combat. The master would also strike bricks that had been placed on the initiate's head, breaking the bricks. If he felt no pain, he could advance to the next stage of training.

At the more advanced levels, slashes of a sword at the trainee's chest would leave no mark at all, or at worst a white scar. If the initiate successfully completed this training and abided by the rules of the society—such as maintaining secrecy about the group and abstaining from opium smoking and card playing—then the society's deities would possess him and bestow invulnerability on him. Like the Boxers—of which they may have been direct descendants—the Red Spears were often utterly convinced of their supernatural powers. They even publicly demonstrated their ability to withstand bullets. A skeptical Kuomintang official in the late 1920s once watched as a Red Spear master cut at the torsos of his followers with a sword and fired rifles at their bare chests, without wounding them. After the official examined the weapons and found them to be real, he concluded that "I who was once highly suspicious of Red Spear claims to invulnerability, now believe that they undergo a physiological change which renders them resistant to bullets and sword wounds."[11]

Sometimes Red Spears died in such demonstrations. The deaths were explained away, however, by asserting that the deceased had been ritually impure or had lacked true belief.[12] Even after seeing their comrades die in such demonstrations, most Red Spears reportedly remained convinced of their own invulnerability, and this faith enormously increased their morale and daring in battle.

The Red Spears were relatively effective fighting units, also, because they coordinated their operations more successfully than did the customary village self-defense corps, which often refused to fight in defense of a neighboring village. A gathering of several thousand Red Spears from neighboring villages was not unusual, and in at least one instance, Red Spears from several *xian* in Honan combined to form a force of 300,000 men.

Still, the Red Spears were no more able than the sects and brotherhoods of the nineteenth century to overcome the parochialism of the peasants or the political divisiveness of their leaders. Even when the society had assembled in a sizable joint operation, cooperation was usually ephemeral, because units soon began filtering back to their home villages and families. A more serious weakness was the fissiparous tendency of the leaders, who split off from the original body to form their own protective societies. As a consequence, Red Spear–type organizations, calling themselves the Yellow Spears, Heavenly Gates, Small Swords, and a bewildering variety of other names, could be found across north and central China. Thus while the protective societies became a significant factor in the interplay of political forces in the late 1920s, they had little staying power. For a time during the mid-1930s, under Nationalist rule, they largely disappeared from the scene, although they revived amid the chaotic conditions created in rural China after the Japanese invasion in 1937.

Although group defense was the chief motivation leading to the formation of most protective societies, they soon acquired a reputation for being political rebels. This was because in performing their task of local defense against bandits, they also clashed with warlord armies, which were every bit as extortionate as bandit gangs. To finance their ever-growing armies, for example, the warlords levied new and progressively heavier taxes on the villagers. These levies were especially onerous, because the warlords often demanded payment in gold, silver, or other high-value currency—even though the peasants were usually paid for their produce in the virtually worthless paper currencies that warlord regimes issued in great quantities. The rural elites opposed such extortion, of course, and by 1925 in north China, the Red Spears served as their instrument of tax resistance. Their opposition to the unslakable tax appetites of the warlord regimes and, later, of the Nationalist government sometimes erupted into full-scale war. A proclamation that the Red Spears delivered to the citizens of Kaifeng, a major city in northern Honan, during the battle with the warlord army of Wu Peifu in 1926 reveals the motivation of the defense-oriented secret societies:

> Brethren of Kai-feng city. . . . Now that [Wu Peifu] has arrived he proves even more ferocious than his predecessor. Here a surcharge, there a surtax. . . . Sell your grain and pawn your clothing—still you haven't enough to pay his cursed taxes. See how his army is even more vicious than bandits. He watches bandits running rampant everywhere but does nothing to interfere. No longer can we stand for this. . . . Down with Wu Peifu! Everyone, unite with one mind! To action![13]

The height of the Red Spears' military activity came in 1927, when they became "a pivotal element in the balance of power in North China."[14] Then, waging war with the Nationalists as well as with various warlords, they even captured and took over the administration of Kaifeng and of several *xian* capitals.

Despite the Red Spears' prolonged and sanguinary rebellion against taxes, they never, so far as is known, expressed similar opposition to the heavy land rents that weighed on the lowest strata of rural society. This was because the leadership of the Red Spears was generally controlled, directly or indirectly, by local elites. Indeed, membership in Red Spear units was sometimes barred to peasants who did not own land. Although this limitation still allowed the majority of the peasants to participate—because landownership was widespread in the north China plain—it reveals that the social composition of the Red Spears was radically different from that of most earlier Triad Society lodges and White Lotus congregations.

The participation of local elites in secret societies was seemingly a pervasive phenomenon in the twentieth century, and signaled a change in their general character after the Revolution of 1911.[15] In searching for an explanation of this change, it has been speculated that after the participation of secret societies in the revolution, their prestige had risen and hence the elites were more willing to join. Alternatively, it has been suggested that as a result of the collapse of the monarch and of Confucian orthodoxy, the local elites lacked an "institutional or ideological vehicle" toward which they felt loyalty.[16]

Without denying the partial validity of these explanations, it is probable that the changed attitudes of the elites toward membership in secret societies lay within the processes of social change at that time. During the first years of the Republic, local government was breaking down and, as a consequence, the level of violence was rising. Local elites, having lost the power and legitimacy resulting from the backing of the dynastic bureaucracy, sought other means to assure themselves of security of self and property and to provide themselves with an organizational web that would enable them to perpetuate their controls over village political and economic life. Probably only after a process of trial and error did many of them discover the efficacy of the secret-society system of organization, discipline, and communication networks, and of the "muscle" of the societies' criminal elements. It is also probable that as a result of the process of "social erosion," which was effecting a change in the nature of the village elites, the new elites were less scrupulous than the old gentry about their social relationships and the methods they employed.[17]

Whatever the precise explanation, the protective societies, as the organizational vehicle of the local elites, frequently became the dominant political force on the local level, and even the Society of Elder Brothers had by the mid-twentieth century evolved into a form of the protective societies. In the Szechwanese village of Xiemaxiang in 1948, for instance,

> Everybody who is anybody belongs to [the Society of Elder Brothers], and it operates quite openly. The fact that it is outlawed by the Central Government does not seem to bother anyone concerned, or, it might be added, deter anyone from becoming a member if he is invited. . . .
>
> In Xiemaxiang . . . the society does not operate directly in politics. . . . But it does have great political power. Almost all the people of wealth and education in the *xiang* [an administrative district or group of villages] are members. . . . Membership in the Brothers' Society is virtually the *sine qua non,* in fact, for participation in local government. . . . The membership in Xiemaxiang includes some representatives of all economic classes, but it is heavily weighted in favor of upper-class and educated groups.[18]

Despite the participation of the rural elites, the protective societies of the Republican period frequently engaged in criminal activities, as had the secret brotherhoods of the nineteenth century. The Elder Brothers in the 1940s, for instance, was deeply involved in the opium trade in Szechwan. The Green Gang *(Qingbang),* which in the nineteenth century was a society whose members were largely boatmen and transport workers in the lower Yangtze Valley, became during the twentieth century a Mafia-like gang that dominated the opium trade, prostitution, gambling, and other branches of criminal life in Shanghai. The Red Spears, too, often degenerated into bandit gangs, kidnapping and looting when away from their home villages. Thus in the anarchic political conditions of warlord China, as in the North American frontier experience evidenced in the legends of Wyatt Earp and Matt Dillon, there was often a thin and shifting line between the roles of law enforcer and robber, of protector and predator.

Bandits

Banditry, a problem for China's ruling authorities throughout the centuries, became pandemic in the early twentieth century. Twenty percent of the population of Hopei resorted to banditry during the famine-struck year 1928. In both Shantung and Manchuria, 1 million men, and in Szechwan, 1.5 million, were bandits in the early 1930s. These figures, although perhaps not precisely accurate, suggest the magnitude of this social phenomenon.

The nation's elite, being prime targets of the bandits, naturally deplored the pillage, murder, and mayhem wreaked by the brigand gangs. Yet banditry was a venerable tradition, and in some villages, it was a socially sanctioned vocation, often passed on from fathers to sons. In northern Anhwei, elaborately decorated temples were dedicated to Dao Zhi, a legendary bandit chief. And successive generations of readers of the novel *Water Margin,* including Mao Tse-tung, fantasized over the daring exploits of the 108 bandit heroes on Liangshangpo—a tale with even more romantic appeal in China than the stories of Robin Hood and his Merry Men had in the English-speaking world. Whatever moral judgment one might render about the bandits, they were indisputably a perennial force in Chinese society.

Two factors underlay the pervasiveness of banditry. First was the weakness, superficiality, and passivity of governmental administration at the local level. Bandit gangs could operate for long periods without ever coming to the attention of local authorities. When a *xian* magistrate did learn of bandit activities within his area of jurisdiction, he frequently took no action. In the bureaucracy of the Qing Dynasty, popular disorders reflected poorly on an official's administration. Reports of banditry, therefore, could easily result in demerits on the magistrate's periodic service ratings, and thereby mar his chances for promotion within the bureaucracy. If, of course, the bandit activities became so blatant that they could not be ignored, he might attempt to "exterminate" or "pacify" the outlaws. This course was chancy, however, because local police forces were notoriously ineffective—indeed, they were occasionally in league with the bandits. Or the magistrate might request that higher authorities dispatch troops to quell the bandits, but government troops were often so poorly disciplined and rapacious that they might easily create greater mayhem that the bandits. Bandits, therefore, stood a good chance of survival, especially in areas sufficiently remote from administrative centers that local officials were relatively free from the prying eyes of higher level bureaucrats.

The second factor that contributed to the bandit phenomenon was the customary destitution of much of the rural population. Poor peasants and the lumpen proletariat in the villages, hovering on the narrow and ragged edge of subsistence, frequently faced the reality or threat of hunger. Most continued to till their fields, dig in the mines, or shoulder their burdens, stolidly accepting their fate in life. But others—perhaps poor peasants during the slack season in farming, or young, unemployed men with neither land nor career prospects—realizing that they had little to lose but much to gain, chose the "dangerous path" of outlawry.

Most of these were merely "seasonal bandits," turning to brigandage only when opportunity presented itself or when driven by economic necessity. The late summer in the north China plain, for example, when farm work was slow and the fields of 8- to 10-foot sorghum offered splendid cover for ambush and escape, was a typical season of heightened banditry. Another bandit season was in the weeks prior to the lunar New Year, when debts traditionally came due. For the seasonal bandits, loot supplemented, rather than supplanted, their legitimate incomes. The gangs were transitory, therefore, dispersing when farm work beckoned or when the authorities threatened suppression.

Sometimes, however—particularly in years of natural disasters—the gangs of seasonal bandits did not disperse so readily. With little opportunity for legitimate employment, these gangs began raiding full time. These "permanent" or "semi-permanent" gangs of bandits then roamed farther afield, relying on their mobility for safety and often striking at villages that had been spared the crop failures that had impoverished their own home areas. Seldom did they raid their native villages, the bandits being guided by the popular maxim "A rabbit never eats the grass around its own hole." Their own villages were, therefore, a haven from suppression for many of these gangs. There they received the protection and support of their families and frequently of the village population as a whole, because it was not uncommon for them (after gratifying their own needs) to share the loot with relatives and those who gave them aid and protection. The bandits who were feared elsewhere might, therefore, be hailed as heroes at home.

Leaders of permanent bandit gangs were often drawn not from the poor peasantry, but from the lower strata of the elite. They might be the unmarried sons of landlords or rich peasants who had "turned bad" or were simply sowing their wild oats. Many of them were merely frustrated—young and ambitious, but without the educational or family backgrounds necessary for successful careers in the bureaucracy or in business. Bai Lang (White Wolf), probably the most famous of Republican-period bandits, expressed this sense of frustration in explaining why he had chosen his perilous profession: "I wished to be an official, but was not adept at intrigue; I then wished to be an assemblyman, but was not adept at agitation; hence I have taken the dangerous path of rebellion, willingly risking Heaven's righteous anger." [19]

Yet another common source of bandit leaders were men who had been forced to flee their homes, perhaps because of a disastrous lawsuit, because of a troublesome encounter with the government, or because of the enmity of people in positions of power. A police captain became a bandit, for instance, after he had been forced to flee when his superior picked him as a scapegoat for his own crimes. Another bandit had so angered his former boss, the warlord Zhang Zuolin, that he had fled for his life. Yet another had taken refuge in banditry after having killed a bully who had murdered his brother. Banditry, therefore, served as a major avenue of social mobility for lesser members of the elite whose chances for careers elsewhere had been spoiled.

A third level of bandit organization, beyond the simple permanent or semipermanent gangs, was the "complex gang." Complex bandit gangs were usually formed of alliances among several independent gangs and often totaled several hundred or even several thousand members. The more successful of them actually functioned as sizable armies. Both Bai Lang's gang in 1914 and that of the bandit known as Lao Yangren (Old Foreigner) in the early 1920s, for example, may have numbered, at their peaks, several thousand men. These large bandit forces usually acquired a quasi-military structure, consisting of brigades, battalions, and other units, all under the supreme command of a chief. Such an army was weakly held together, however, for each subchief customarily retained autonomous control over his own band of followers. The bandit armies thus had a cellular quality, and long-term cooperation among these gangs was rare.

Permanent bandits often operated out of bases where the arm of the government was especially weak. Mountains, forests, and marshy shores provided natural hideouts; newly colonized areas in Manchuria were also filled with gangs. Regions lying athwart *xian* or provincial borders were traditional bandit haunts because should authorities in one jurisdiction launch a suppression campaign, the bandits could slip across the border into the neighboring jurisdiction. Government officials were notoriously uncooperative with one another. Some areas—such as western and southern Honan, northern Anhwei, the Fukien–Chekiang border, and various regions of Szechwan—thus gained renown as bandit territories. Out of these base areas, the gangs attacked the trade routes or swooped out on the more prosperous villages in the plains. In north China, where there were few isolated lairs, the bandits relied on mobility for security. Mounted on horseback, perhaps taking advantage of the cover provided by the crops of sorghum, the bandits would raid on area and then quickly move on before defense forces could react.

While both seasonal and full-time bandits continued in existence throughout the Republican period, a different kind of bandit proliferated and overshadowed all other forms of banditry during the early years of the Republic. This was the soldier-bandit. Perhaps soldier-banditry had always existed; certainly, it had been in evidence in the nineteenth century during the Taiping and Nien rebellions. During the warlord period of the twentieth century, however, as a result of the bloated armies and widespread warfare, soldier-banditry reached unprecedented levels. Soldiers defeated in battle, demobilized by the political authorities, or without pay and food had little chance of making a legitimate livelihood, for they were mostly landless and unskilled. But they possessed guns and knew how to use them. It was common—indeed, almost taken as a matter of course—for these troops to turn to banditry.

Soldier-bandit gangs differed from the permanent bandit gangs in two ways. First, they tended to be considerably larger, better armed and organized, and therefore better able to inflict extensive destruction. Second, the primary object of their brigandage was frequently less to enrich themselves with loot than to gain reinstatement in the regular army, indicating, perhaps, that their chief motivation was simply to obtain a secure livelihood.

To accomplish this, they had to bring their presence forcefully to the attention of the authorities. This required not stealthy and petty pillage, but devastation on a scale that the authorities could not ignore. Because of their desire for attention, the soldier-bandits, beginning in the 1920s, were particularly keen to kidnap foreigners. The kidnapping of foreigners not only was more profitable than was that of Chinese, but also created international pressures on the authorities to free the captives and resolve the bandit problem—which could be accomplished most efficaciously by enlisting the gang into the regular army. In 1923, for example, the famous Lincheng bandits in Shantung, led by the twenty-four-year-old Sun Mei-yao, derailed a train and kidnapped about twenty foreigners who were among the passengers. The incident became an international cause cèlèbre—especially because one of the captives was a sister-in-law of the Rockefellers—and was resolved only after all the bandits were given posts in the regular army.

There were obvious dangers for the bandits in going over to the government side. Several times, many of them were massacred after surrendering, but enlistment of the bandits into the army occurred with sufficient frequency that gang leaders regularly looked to it as a means of career advancement. A bandit chieftain was confronted by a nice dilemma, however, because the larger his gang, the higher the rank that he could expect to receive after capitulating. An ambitious chieftain, therefore, had to calculate the moment of surrender carefully, because surrendering too late might result in annihilation.

The flip side of soldier-banditry was that soldiers who were already in an army customarily engaged in brigandage. Poorly paid and badly fed, yet armed and blusterous—and, perhaps, having been bandits before joining the army—the soldiers preyed on the civilian population hardly less than did their illegitimate counterparts. Particularly when on a campaign away from their home quarters, the soldiers pillaged, raped, and murdered so extensively that authorities of civilian governments were often loath to allow them into their territories.

For the civilian population, rich and poor alike, there was little to choose between soldiers and bandits; a common saying was "Soldiers and bandits are indistinguishable" *(bing fei bufen)*. Or as a one-time president of the Chinese Republic, Li Yuanhong, observed, "If the policy is disbandment, soldiers turn bandits; if it is recruiting, bandits turn soldiers. Therefore there is no brigand who is not a soldier, and no soldier who is not a brigand."[20] Thus soldier-banditry was a major factor affecting the economic climate and the people's welfare during the early twentieth century.

In 1959, Eric Hobsbawm introduced into the social-science literature the concept of the "social bandit." Social bandits, he wrote, differ from ordinary robbers and gangsters—in the eyes of themselves and of the peasants, but not in the eyes of the law—because they are champions of the poor and oppressed. They rob the rich and kill the evil officials, but their predatory activities appear to the peasants to be motivated by the desire for equality, justice, and freedom. Robin Hood was the preeminent exemplar of a social bandit, although Hobsbawm contended that social bandits could be found universally, in all peasant-based societies.[21]

Students of Chinese banditry, stimulated by Hobsbawm's writings, have looked closely for evidence of social bandits in China. In the twentieth century, however, if they existed at all, they were exceedingly rare. Some Chinese bandit chiefs did indeed rationalize their plunder with claims that they were seeking a more just society. The Lincheng gang, for instance, proclaimed:

> We signal the masses of the green forest [that is, all bandits] to assemble for one end—liquidation of the corrupt elements in our society. The common folk are our concern and communal property our goal. First we must beat to death all greedy officials and evil rich, destroying the root of China's trouble and transforming this into a pure new world.[22]

Bai Lang may for a time also have fit the mold of a social bandit, because his hints of more equitable government and lighter taxes (but not of changes in the system of government or land tenure) won him a large following in Shensi during

1914. One of Bai Lang's subordinates composed the following song about his chief:

> White Wolf, cunning and bold,
> The Will of Heaven will uphold.
> He calls the hungry to his door,
> Friend of the friendless and the poor.
> Two years hence the world shall see
> For rich and poor equality.[23]

But actions of China's bandits seldom, if ever, corresponded to Hobsbawm's idealized image of the social bandits. Of Bai Lang's gang, it was said that "their cruelties are sometimes fiendish, and when they seize a city they behave like insensate demons."[24] And even the Lincheng bandits, whose proclamation hints at social banditry, released their captives and capitulated to the government that they so deplored after they were incorporated as a brigade into the governmental army: they received a ransom of $85,000, and Sun Meiyao was awarded the rank of brigadier general. Some of the bandit *chiefs* may indeed have fit the image of social bandits because they had often been forced into banditry not by cupidity, but as a result of suffering a social or political wrong. Most bandit chieftains and especially the rank and file, however, having been forced into banditry largely by economic want, did not evince the idealism that Hobsbawm attributed to social bandits.

Usually, therefore, banditry wreaked terrible suffering and devastation on the law-abiding population, rich and poor alike. A memoir written by a medical missionary who worked in Fukien during the 1920s and 1930s recounts some of the horrors inflicted on the common people by the bandit gang of one "Precious Cloud." Once, for example, a man brought his two sons to her clinic:

> The two little boys were five and eight years old and came to have their lacerated faces repaired. Each child had several deep gashes up to six inches long; every one was cut right down to the bone. "How did this happen?" I asked, as I sewed up cut after cut.
>
> "We could not pay the bandit tax," the father answered sadly.
>
> When the faces had been treated, I examined the boys and found large areas of old scar tissue from burns. "What does this mean?" I asked the father.
>
> "Last year we could not pay our taxes, so Precious Cloud's men wrapped my two sons in straw and set them on fire." His face was white, drawn, desperate. The five-year-old son had lost his mind.[25]

Precious Cloud's 1,000-man gang had acquired a reputation for massacring, burning, and raping, and whole villages fled on hearing of its approach. That the common people held no love for these bandits was shown when the authorities captured one of Precious Cloud's subchiefs:

> When Increased Privilege was caught, he was sent to Third Town to be punished by the women there. He had been responsible for the seizure of the seventy

women from that town, so the judgment seemed apt. The women decided on death by the shoe awl. They first tied him in a chair. Then the women went into his room in a never-ending procession. Each carried her sharp shoe awl. They pierced him with the awls hour after hour, night and day for three days till he was finally dead.[26]

Such stories, which could be multiplied many times, suggested the baleful effects of banditry, which helped brutalize not just the bandits, but also their victims.

Feuding

Seldom does imperial China evoke comparisons with the state of Tennessee. Yet in one sense they were similar, for just as Tennessee had its Hatfields and Mc-Coys, so Qing Dynasty China had its feuding lineages. Indeed, since at least the eighteenth century, feuding was a common feature of the Chinese social landscape, involving fighting between organized armed bands, kidnappings, assassinations, and the destruction of rivals' villages and ancestral tombs. Feuding was less pervasive than banditry, surely, but was nonetheless an enduring form of collective violence that for over two centuries affected the lives and property of many millions of Chinese.

The root causes of feuds during the two centuries before the establishment of Communist rule were much the same as those of banditry: weak political authority and intense economic pressures. Feuding was, therefore, a nationwide phenomenon, frequently being reported, for example, in Honan, Kiangsu, Anhwei, Shantung, Hunan, Hupei, and Kansu. Yet for reasons that are not wholly clear, feuding was particularly rife in south China, especially in Kwangtung, Fukien, and Taiwan. Contemporaries often attributed the feuding in the south to the bellicose temperament of the people there. A high official in Fukien in 1821, for instance, spoke of the "disturbed and ungovernable state of that province; arising from the cruel, fierce, and quarrelsome dispositions and habits of the people, who form themselves into armed clans; who fight together, and oppose the ordinary police by force."[27]

In all probability, however, the frequency of feuding in Kwangtung and Fukien was more directly attributable to the highly developed system of lineages there. Still, feuds were by no means always fought along lineage lines, but were sometimes fought between branches of common lineages, and between villages, common-surname groups, secret societies, and ethnic groups. In Taiwan, much of the feuding was between Han Chinese who had immigrated from different regions on the mainland. Those from Quanzhou prefecture in Fukien, for instance, feuded with their fellow provincials from Zhangzhou prefecture; and both these groups feuded with Hakka from Kwangtung. Elsewhere, as in Anhwei, Han Chinese feuded with Chinese Moslems. Frequently, too, the scope of vendettas was enlarged when the combatants formed alliances with other village or ethnic groups.

Disputes over scarce economic resources, such as water rights or land boundaries, were the most common causes of feuds. As often happened, a lineage that was farming upstream of another might channel off so much irrigation water that it adversely affected the fields of the lineage downstream. Then a quarrel, a fight, and, ultimately, a feud might ensue. Quarrels over honor, women, defilement of burial mounds, accusations of thievery, and so on could also spark armed feuds. Occasionally, a powerful lineage or group purposely provoked a feud, using the quarrel as a pretext to seize the property or to eliminate the economic competition of the weaker group. "In most cases . . . the exploitation of the weak lineages by the strong [was] the root of the trouble."[28] As in most warfare, the desire for conquest was present in feuding.

Feuds varied greatly in scale. Some lasted for years and involved thousands of combatants. In the two prefectures of Quanzhou and Zhangzhou in Fukien during the late 1830s, for example, not a day passed for three years in which feuding did not result in at least one death, and sometimes the hostilities there involved 100,000 armed men. Some of the most intense feuding in Kwangtung was between native Cantonese (Punti, or *bendi ren*) and later arrivals, the Hakka. The Hakka, like the Cantonese, were Han Chinese, but they adhered to distinguishing cultural traits, such as a distinctive dialect, hair style, and clothing, and the refusal of women to bind their feet. The regional and particularistic prejudices of the Chinese have always been intense—witness, for example, the enmities between native Szechwanese and refugees from the eastern provinces during the war with Japan and, later, those between the local people and the "mainlanders" on Taiwan. Not surprisingly, therefore, the largest vendetta reported during the Qing period was between the Punti and the Hakka, a struggle that lasted for almost 12 years (1856–67), during which some 100,000 people were killed and thousands of villages were destroyed.

Feuding was expensive. Contrary to expectations, they were not usually fought by rabble masses, but were carried on by organized forces that had to be trained, fed, and equipped. Professional mercenaries were sometimes hired. During the eighteenth century, the weapons ranged from farm implements to fowling guns, although iron-tipped lances were seemingly the most common. During the nineteenth century, modern firearms and even cannons were increasingly employed, with the result that expensive fortifications had to be constructed. In addition, government officials frequently had to be bribed not to interfere in the fighting. Feuding groups also usually paid benefits to the families of those who had died fighting for their cause.

Because of the large expenditures required, feuding occurred more often between prosperous groups in urban and suburban areas than in the rural and impoverished backwoods. Lineage or community temples, which often derived substantial revenues from their holdings of vast ancestral or other communal lands, were the most common sources of funding for these feuds. The belligerents sometimes collected "contributions" or "taxes" from their constituents. Economic distress was often the result. In Fukien, poor families occasionally dared to refuse payment of taxes to the government, but they did not dare to refuse the bullies who collected on behalf of their feuding leaders. Even rich families could be reduced to destitution by feuding. As a nineteenth-century writer observed, "Good members of the lineage who have families must suffer the worst. When there is one fight the rich lose their riches; after the second fight the rich become the poor; after the third fight the poor become paupers and they perish.''[29] Indeed, lineage leaders who had started a vendetta frequently lost control of the fighting to rascals and professional fighters, who profited by perpetuating the fighting. Many lineages were reduced to ruin when they were unable to end the feud.

Society in Turmoil

Even in the best of times, local Chinese society was often wracked by violence. In southeast China, for instance, "many localities . . . never experienced the peace and order that historians have postulated for the 'high Qing' period of eighteenth-century China."[30] Yet the incidence of violence intensified and became even more widespread during the late Qing and Republican periods. The increasing levels of social turbulence during the last 100 years or so of the Qing Dynasty is graphically demonstrated by the record of incidents of violence involving five or more people that were reported to the central government between 1796 and 1911 (Table 10.1).

The especially large number of violent incidents recorded for the decades 1846 to 1855 and 1856 to 1865 reflects the chaotic conditions associated with the Taiping, Nien, and Moslem rebellions. Significantly, however, the incidence of violence during the last forty or so years of the dynasty never fell back to the prerebellion levels. There exists no analysis of violence in the twentieth century comparable with this one for the nineteenth century, but it is clear that the disturbances attributable to banditry, secret societies, and feuding in the Republican period were substantially more numerous than in the last decades of the nineteenth century.[31]

Worsening economic distress may appear to be the obvious explanation for this growing violence. Yet profound poverty is more likely to reduce a people to a despairing struggle for survival than to prod them to collective and violent action. "It is only when the [economic] bonds are loosened and when expectations are high for preserving their lives that people can think seriously of the luxury of a rebellion."[32] No doubt, the chronic poverty of Chinese society underlay the incidents of mass violence, but poverty was at most a necessary, not a sufficient, cause of those incidents. Many areas of the empire, for example, were afflicted at various times by disastrous harvests, yet only occasionally did those areas suffer food riots or other popular disturbances. Moreover, as noted in Chapter 5, there is simply no convincing evidence that China was experiencing a general process of immiseration during the early decades of the twentieth century.

The chief reason for the rising levels of mass violence in the early modern period was probably political. China's administrative structure was showing the effects of the dynastic cycle in its declining phase: the bureaucracy had lost its earlier vitality and was becoming increasingly corrupt. At the same time, the imperial armies—the Banner forces and the Army of the Green Standard—had atrophied; they were no longer effective tools for maintaining political control and social order. One result of this military deterioration was that local elites had moved into the void, collecting taxes and forming village-defense forces that were

Table 10.1. Incidents of Mass Action

Forms of Action	1796–1805	1806–1815	1816–1825	1826–1835	1836–1845	1846–1855	1856–1865	1866–1875	1876–1885	1886–1895	1896–1911	Total
Secret and Sectarian Societies	8	37	31	28	24	25	19	29	27	36	29	293
Banditry and Piracy	42	51	46	97	85	266	302	183	204	156	240	1,672
Feuds and Property Destruction	0	5	2	3	6	16	30	3	12	8	21	106
TOTAL	50	93	79	128	115	307	351	215	243	200	290	2,071

Source: C. K. Yang, "Some Preliminary Statistical Patterns of Mass Actions in Nineteenth-Century China," in Conflict and Control in Late Imperial China, ed. Frederic Wakeman, Jr., and Carolyn Grant (Berkeley: University of California Press, 1975), p. 190. Reprinted by permission.

loyal only to their commanders. Yet the interests of these commanders frequently did not coincide with those of the dynasty. This devolution of power into the hands of local elites thus contributed to the process of political breakdown.

Underlying the entire process was the failure of the imperial administration to adjust to the growing burdens of government. The bureaucracy still numbered only some 20,000 civil officials—approximately the same number as had administered the empire in the middle years of the Ming Dynasty, when the population had been roughly one-third of that in the nineteenth century. Nor had the concepts or institutions of government changed to accommodate the demographic, economic, and political changes that had occurred since the Ming. It was as though the United States in the 1980s continued to be ruled by the same institutions and administrative concepts and the same sized bureaucracy that President Thomas Jefferson had employed in the early nineteenth century. As the population grew and spread, as the economy became more diversified and commercialized, as popular dissatisfaction with the worsening bureaucratic corruption increased, and as local elites acquired greater autonomy, the social strains outgrew the dynasty's governing capabilities. The rising crescendo of violence during the nineteenth century, followed by the chaos of warlordism, marked the culminating phase of this process of political collapse.

China's three great revolutions of the twentieth century—the Republican Revolution of 1911, the Nationalist revolution of 1927, and the Communist revolution of 1949—grew out of this context of collective violence. Should the secret societies and bandits, therefore, be viewed as progressive forces that contributed to the revolutionary movement? Were they, as they have been called, "primitive revolutionaries"?[33]

It is true that Sun Yat-sen did on occasion collaborate with secret societies, and Mao Tse-tung in 1927 joined forces on Jinggangshan with two bandit gangs. These alliances were fraught with contradictions and quarrels, however, because the ultimate goals of the traditional rebels and of the modern revolutionaries were different. The secret brotherhoods and bandits were, as we have seen, inveterately parochial in outlook; they were not opposed to the existing political order per se, but only to oppression or injustice within that political order. They sought, essentially, to win a more remunerative and satisfying place in the system, not to overthrow the system.

The revolutionaries, by contrast, endeavored to overthrow it. Their goals were fundamentally incompatible, therefore, with those of the traditional rebels. The revolutionaries represented not a continuation of the violence engendered by the traditional rebels, but a *reaction* against it.

Selected Readings

(See also the works cited in the notes)

Billingsley, Philip R. "Bandits, Bosses, and Bare Sticks: Beneath the Surface of Local Control in Early Republican China." *Modern China* 7, no. 3 (July 1981): 235–88.
Blythe, Wilfred. *The Impact of Chinese Secret Societies in Malaya: A Historical Study.* London: Oxford University Press, 1969.

Cai Shaoqing. "On the Origin of the Gelaohui." *Modern China* 10, no. 4 (October 1984): 481–510.

Chesneaux, Jean, ed. *Popular Movements and Secret Societies in China, 1840–1950.* Stanford, Calif.: Stanford University Press, 1972.

Comber, L. F. *Chinese Secret Societies in Malaya: A Survey of the Triad Society from 1800 to 1900.* Locust Valley, N.Y.: Augustin, 1959.

Harrell, Stevan, and Elizabeth J. Perry. "Syncretic Sects in Chinese Society: An Introduction." *Modern China* 8, no. 3 (July 1982): 283–303.

Lamley, Harry J. "Belligerent Lineages at Feud under the Ch'ing." Paper presented at the conference "Orthodoxy and Heterodoxy in Late Imperial China: Cultural Beliefs and Social Divisions," Montecito, California, August 20–26, 1981.

Liu, Cheng-yun. "Kuo-lu: A Sworn-Brotherhood Organization in Szechwan." *Late Imperial China* 6, no. 1 (June 1985): 56–82.

Naquin, Susan. "Connections Between Rebellions: Sect Family Networks in Qing China." *Modern China* 8, no. 3 (July 1982): 337–60.

———. *Millenarian Rebellion in China: The Eight Trigrams Uprising of 1813.* New Haven, Conn.: Yale University Press, 1976.

———. *Shantung Rebellion: The Wang Lun Uprising of 1774.* New Haven, Conn.: Yale University Press, 1981.

Overmyer, Daniel L. *Folk Buddhist Religion: Dissenting Sects in Late Traditional China.* Cambridge, Mass.: Harvard University Press, 1976.

Perry, Elizabeth J. "Social Banditry Revisited: The Case of Bai Lang, A Chinese Brigand." *Modern China* 9, no. 3 (July 1983): 355–82.

———. "Tax Revolt in Late Qing China: The Small Swords of Shanghai and Liu Depei of Shandong." *Late Imperial China* 6, no. 1 (June 1985): 81–112.

Shek, Richard. "Millenarianism Without Rebellion: The Huangtian Dao in North China." *Modern China* 8, no. 3 (July 1982): 305–36.

———. "Religion and Society in Late Ming: Sectarianism and Popular Thought in Sixteenth and Seventeenth Century China." Ph.D. diss., University of California, Berkeley, 1980.

Tai Hsuan-chih. "Origin of the Heaven and Earth Society," trans. Ronald Suleski. *Modern Asian Studies* 11, no. 3 (July 1977): 405–25.

———. *The Red Spears, 1916–1949,* trans. Ronald Suleski. Ann Arbor: University of Michigan, Center for Chinese Studies, 1985.

Tiedemann, R. G. "The Persistence of Banditry: Incidents in Border Districts of the North China Plain." *Modern China* 8, no. 4 (October 1982): 395–433.

Wong, R. Bin. "Food Riots in the Qing Dynasty." *Journal of Asian Studies* 44, no. 4 (August 1982): 767–88.

Conclusion:
Constancy and Change

Never let it be said again that China in late imperial times was stagnating, the country of "eternal standstill"! True, technology remained essentially unchanged. True, the changes that did occur before the latter half of the nineteenth century were best measured by half-centuries, rather than, as in the early modern period, by decades or even years. Yet China during the 300 or so years prior to the 1860s experienced changes that in many respects transformed the social landscape of the empire and the lives of its people.

The two forces primarily responsible for those changes were population growth and commercialization. We have seen how the increase in numbers of people pressured the Chinese to move into areas of the empire that had hitherto remained relatively wild and untilled. At the same time, the older, more settled areas of the empire filled up. More and more villages dotted the landscape, the population pressing on itself and the land. Never, it seems, did the population reach the stage of Malthusian crisis, at which available resources can no longer sustain the people at even minimal levels. But the increasingly adverse ratio between land and population forced the peasants to work the land ever more intensively, usually to the point of "self-exploitation." Increasingly after about the 1770s, too, the harshness of life contributed to social and political instability, manifested in feuds, fights, banditry, and secret-society uprisings. All of these were, in the lives of the Chinese people, very real changes.

The growth of the market economy likewise produced vast changes. The rural manors of the early Ming Dynasty, often worked by hundreds and even thousands of serfs, disappeared from the countryside, to be replaced by a system of small-peasant freeholders. Both peasants and elite became progressively oriented to the marketplace, and by the eighteenth century, there existed a national market for raw materials and food products produced throughout the empire. Fortunes were made in trade and manufacturing; market towns proliferated; towns grew into cities. And new institutions, such as the native banks, remittance banks, and *huiguan* (native-place associations) came into being to accommodate the growing trade.

Sadly, the emperors of the Qing Dynasty did not, in like manner, accommodate the vast changes in the economy and population by adopting new policies and institutions. They conceived that the role of government should be little more than collecting taxes, maintaining order, and preserving the dynasty in power. They had no sense that government should assume a *positive* role in society to promote economic growth—for the benefit of both themselves and their subjects. This is not to suggest that the emperors or their chief advisers should have introduced central economic planning à la the Soviet Union, or even that the government should have assumed a leading role in the economy. Such concepts of government are products of the twentieth century and would not have been feasible, or even conceivable, in China in the eighteenth or early nineteenth centuries. But if the Qing had maintained, at a minimum, a modest interregional transportation network or had introduced some order to the currency system, the conditions favorable to economic prosperity would have been markedly improved. Even better, it might have adopted a law code to protect private entrepreneurs from official exactions; or it might have created a school system to spread literacy and nurture creative minds. Such measures were not beyond the imagination's reach during those years—in Japan, the Tokugawa rulers adopted comparable policies—yet the dynasty's rulers had no vision except to expand the empire's dignity externally and to maintain the status quo internally. So low were the rulers' expectations regarding the role of government that even in the late nineteenth century, the dynasty's revenues still amounted to only 1 or 2 percent of the gross national product—a ridiculously low figure even at that time. With such extraordinarily low revenues, the dynasty was forced to employ the "brokerage concept of administration" to perform functions that we would regard as the responsibility of the government itself. Such a minimalist form of government was unable to cope with the dynamics of population growth and commercialization that pulsed through the empire in the eighteenth and nineteenth centuries. The result was administrative paralysis and economic deterioration.

The pace of social and economic change accelerated during the early modern period. The stimulus to change, it is important to note, was generated partly by domestic forces. Commercialization, monetization, and urbanization, which became so evident from the sixteenth century onward, were producing fundamental changes in the social structure by the mid-nineteenth century. By then, merchants were rising in power and prestige; money, not Confucian education, was becoming a significant, if not the prime, determinant of status. Yet the major stimuli to social and economic change after the mid-nineteenth century did undoubtedly result from contact with the West.

The changes that occurred during the early modern period were of immense significance, but equally interesting to the historian is what did *not* change. For in the midst of the technological, institutional, and political transformations of the past 100 and more years, the traditional sociocultural traits have held on with a remarkable tenacity. We saw in Chapter 9 that the emergence of a youth culture, the development of individualism, and the emancipation of women in the first decades of the twentieth century posed a challenge to the weighty tradition of familism. But we also saw that the challenge was evident only in the cities, and even there only among a small fraction of the population. Since the 1930s, the challenge to familism has grown, but even today, after another fifty years of political revolution and economic development, the traditional sociocultural traits endure in all areas of Chinese life.

In the villages of the People's Republic, where the vast majority of Chinese still reside, the traits of familism still reign supreme. The eldest male is head of the family and controls the income of all family members. Rarely do young men and women marry without the active involvement of their parents. And the chief goals of marriage, for all persons concerned, are economic production and biological reproduction—rather than love or even companionship. The birth of a son is a matter of rejoicing, for he will serve as his parents' social security in their old age, whereas the birth of a daughter is regarded as a waste, for she will have to be reared only to leave and become part of someone else's family. The old attitudes thus persist in the countryside, even if some of the more brutal aspects of traditional family life appear to have moderated. Even today, however, female infanticide is sometimes reported, and we can hear of a husband who, after his wife presents him with a third daughter but no son, beats her into unconsciousness.

Sociocultural changes in the cities of post-1949 China—just as in the cities of the 1920s—have been more far-reaching than in the rural areas. Both women and youth have improved their places in the social hierarchy, and the patriarchal ideology of the traditional family has weakened. No longer, for instance, does the eldest male in the family ordinarily manage the purse for the entire family. Youth have considerable voice regarding whom they will or will not marry, although because dating is still an unfamiliar form of courting, boy usually meets girl by means of an "introduction" by a friend or relative, who performs something of the function of the traditional matchmaker. And the birth of a daughter to urban parents is not the devastating disappointment it used to be; indeed, some city parents even take comfort in the discovery that daughters are frequently more filial and reliable after they grow up than are sons.

Thus changes in urban families have been profound. Yet even in the cities, vestiges of the old patriarchal traditions remain strong. Wives usually have to work a "second shift" after returning home from their regular jobs because their husbands expect them to bear all responsibility for housekeeping, shopping, cooking, and laundering. And although the law prescribes that women receive equal pay with men for equal work, male factory managers and male village leaders generally believe that women are incapable of the more highly paid "heavy" and "technical" jobs. Women's pay, therefore, in city or country, is usually less than that of men. (Take, for example, the man and two women whose job it was to water some wheat fields near Peking. The women's task was to channel the water onto the crops, which required scurrying back and forth in order to dig and dike; this was "unskilled" labor, for which they received 6.5 workpoints a day. The man was a "skilled" worker whose task was to squat by the water pump and, at a hail from the women, turn the switch on or off. For this, he was paid 10.5 workpoints a day.)[1] China is still a nation of male chauvinists.

Another part of the sociocultural realm that has been largely resistant to change comprises the three major characteristics of social behavior discussed in Chapter 2: the emphasis on hierarchical status, the importance of personal relationships, and sensitivity to matters of "face." In China today, one quickly encounters the continuing importance of the attitudes associated with authority–dependency relationships—government cadres, for instance, expecting and receiving what we regard as extreme deference from common citizens. And the surest way to get things done, to gain entry to a university, and to advance in one's career is to "know somebody" who can pull the necessary strings. Some American political scientists doing research on China have exulted in their discovery that the most important dynamic in Chinese Communist politics is what they call "clientalist ties." This, however, is nothing more than a jargon term for the *guanxi* and *ganqing* of old.

One wishes that more research had been done regarding the persistence of these traditional social-behavioral traits in China. We are somewhat better informed about another area of the sociocultural realm, that of popular religion.

For four decades, the Communist authorities have been actively discouraging the "feudal superstitions" of the popular religion. Most priests, shamans, geomancers, and other religious specialists were forced to abandon their vocations soon after 1949. Private worship of the gods and ancestors was also discouraged, and during the Great Leap Forward in 1958, most of the remaining village temples were either destroyed or converted into offices of the newly established communes. Not until the Cultural Revolution in the 1960s, however, did suppression of the popular religion become draconian. Then, rampaging Red Guards destroyed ancestral tablets and altars and other religious relics, and it became politically dangerous for anyone even to burn incense and spirit-money.

Despite such repression, the popular religion did not die, and today, in the less repressive atmosphere following the Cultural Revolution, it is showing a considerable resurgence. The Qingming Festival, during which people visit and clean the graves of deceased relatives, is still widely observed, and many peasant families, within the privacy of their homes, regularly present sacrifices to their ancestors. Some areas even report the reconstruction of village temples. And the official press continues to wage a strong campaign against magical healing, spirit exorcising, and geomancy—complaining that such beliefs are "rampant."[2]

Even in Taiwan, where the political pressures against the folk religion have been less severe but the forces of economic modernization have been stronger than on the mainland, signs of the enduring belief in a distinctly Chinese spiritual world are everywhere. Newly constructed houses contain ancestral altars; in multistoried apartment complexes, stove gods continue to superintend the families assigned to them; taxicab drivers often carry with them small sachets, containing magical writing or the blood of a *tongji,* to protect them from accidents. In the villages, the fire-walking ritual is still performed, although now sometimes on a field where baseball is usually played. With such juxtapositions of the old folk religion with the modernized society and economy of Taiwan, it seems that "everything has changed, and yet nothing has changed."[3]

Through the storm and stress of political revolution and economic transformation, therefore, a sociocultural substratum of attitudes, values, and social behavior—that ineffable quality of "Chinese-ness"—remains intact. This truth, from my point of view, is in some ways regrettable. For the persistence of the old values works against political liberalization in both the mainland and the Taiwan regimes, against the attainment of sexual equality, and for the perpetuation of the less estimable manifestations of authority–dependency relationships. But the persistence of the old attitudes and values also means that the Chinese continue to be among the most friendly, indifferent, hard-working, indolent, enterprising, conservative, generous, selfish, paradoxical—and therefore fascinating—inhabitants of this earth.

Notes

Preface

1. Evelyn S. Rawski, "Economic and Social Foundations of Late Imperial China," in *Popular Culture in Late Imperial China,* ed. David Johnson et al. (Berkeley: University of California Press, 1985), p. 3.

2. Ramon H. Myers, "Transformation and Continuity in Chinese Economic and Social History," *Journal of Asian Studies* 33, no. 2 (February 1974): 273–75, and "On the Future of Ch'ing Studies," *Ch'ing-shih Wen-t'i* 4, no. 1 (June 1979): 107–9; Frederic Wakeman, Jr., "Introduction: The Evolution of Local Control in Late Imperial China," in *Conflict and Control in Late Imperial China,* ed. Frederic Wakeman, Jr., and Carolyn Grant (Berkeley: University of California Press, 1975), pp. 1–2.

3. Lin Yu-tang, *My Country and My People* (New York: Day, 1936), p. xiii.

Chapter 1

1. Fernand Braudel, *Civilization and Capitalism,* Vol. 1, *The Structures of Everyday Life: The Limits of the Possible* (New York: Harper & Row, 1979), p. 48. See pp. 31–51 for a discussion of world population from the fifteenth through the mid-nineteenth centuries.

2. Geoffrey Parker, *Europe in Crisis, 1598–1648,* p. 22, quoted in William S. Atwell, "Some Observations on the 'Seventeenth-Century Crisis' in China and Japan," *Journal of Asian Studies* 45, no. 2 (February 1986): 225–26.

3. Quoted in Ping-ti Ho, *Studies on the Population of China, 1368–1953* (Cambridge, Mass.: Harvard University Press, 1959), p. 146.

4. Actually, the predecessors of the Han people were a Sinitic people known as the "Hua-hsia." By the third century B.C., the Hua-hsia had intermingled with several non-Sinitic peoples to form the Han.

5. A fascinating and delightful study of the Chinese diet and attitudes toward food over the centuries, which constitutes a veritable social history of China, is K. C. Chang, ed., *Food in Chinese Culture: Anthropological and Historical Perspectives* (New Haven, Conn.: Yale University Press, 1977).

6. Quoted in Johanna Menzel Meskill, *A Chinese Pioneer Family: The Lins of Wu-feng, Taiwan, 1729–1895* (Princeton, N.J.: Princeton University Press, 1979), p. 40. Ellipses in source.

7. Stephen C. Averill, "The Shed People and the Opening of the Yangzi Highlands," *Modern China* 9, no. 1 (January 1983): 85–86.

8. Quoted in Evelyn S. Rawski, "Agricultural Development in the Han River Highlands," *Ch'ing-shih Wen-t'i* 3, no. 4 (December 1975): 68.

9. Meskill, *Chinese Pioneer Family*, p. 50.

Chapter 2

1. Daniel Harrison Kulp, *Country Life in South China: The Sociology of Familism* (New York: Columbia University Teachers College, 1925), pp. 187–88, 105.

2. C. K. Yang, *The Chinese Family in the Communist Revolution* (Cambridge, Mass.: Technology Press, 1959), p. 20.

3. Ibid., p. 9.

4. Gerald F. Winfield wrote: "In most of the modern hospitals of China pregnant mothers give a history of five to twelve, or even fifteen, pregnancies from which they have one or two children still alive, and frequently none at all" (*China: The Land and the People* [New York: William Sloane Associates, 1948], p. 109).

5. Maurice Freedman, "Ritual Aspects of Chinese Kinship and Marriage," in *Family and Kinship in Chinese Society,* ed. Maurice Freedman (Stanford, Calif.: Stanford University Press, 1970), p. 178. Myron L. Cohen saw evidence of solidarity among brothers in fraternal joint families—at least until family partition became imminent (*House United, House Divided: The Chinese Family in Taiwan* [New York: Columbia University Press, 1976], pp. 142–44, 195–96).

6. Some lineage organizations so proliferated that they had branches in several communities, but their unity was often symbolized by an ancestral hall representing all the branches. By convention, such umbrella-type organizations are termed *higher-order lineages. Clans* were superficially similar to lineages, often possessing the same external attributes of corporate property, ancestral halls, and such. Strictly speaking, however, clans differed from lineages because, although the members shared a surname and claimed a common pedigree, they were not demonstrably descended from a common ancestor.

7. Quoted in R. H. van Gulik, *Sexual Life in Ancient China* (Leiden: Brill, 1961), pp. 98–99.

8. Quoted in Margery Wolf, *Women and the Family in Rural Taiwan* (Stanford, Calif.: Stanford University Press, 1972), pp. 70–71.

9. Before the twentieth century, the mean age of marriage for women was about seventeen years; men were approximately two years older when they married.

10. A wedding, for families of every social stratum, was a matter of high finance, costing both the bride's and the groom's families at least a half-year's income, and often much more. The groom's family was expected to pay a substantial bride-price, which became the possession of the bride's natal family. In return, the bride brought to her new home a dowry—typically consisting of clothing, cloth, furniture, and money—which was openly carried to the groom's home so that the entire neighborhood could see the items and appraise their value. These items did not usually become the property of the groom's family, but were retained by the bride and her husband. Other expenditures were for cakes to announce the engagement, large feasts at the time of both the engagement and the

wedding, and gold jewelry for the bride (bought by the groom's parents). Concern for "face" dictated that the expenditures for all these items be substantial.

11. Quoted in Arthur P. Wolf, "Gods, Ghosts, and Ancestors," in *Religion and Ritual in Chinese Society,* ed. Arthur P. Wolf (Stanford, Calif.: Stanford University Press, 1974), p. 148.

12. The concept of the uterine family is presented in Margery Wolf, *Women and the Family in Rural Taiwan* (Stanford: Stanford University Press, 1972), pp. 32–41. The quote is in ibid., p. 33.

13. The concept of the uterine family, for all its theoretical brilliance as an insight into the psychological and social differences between men and women in China, may be more problematic than is suggested here. The extent to which women internalized the values of the male-centered concept of family, for instance, is not known. If they did deeply absorb those values, then the uterine-family concept, however rational that response may seem to us, may have had little claim on the thinking of a Chinese bride. Second, the concept of the uterine family is probably valid primarily for stem and joint families, where mothers-in-law and daughters-in-law reside together. Actually, as we have seen, some two-thirds of Chinese families—most of which were probably poor—were conjugal, composed of only the parents and the unmarried children. In such a family, the husband's commitment to the line of descent was likely to have been relatively weak, and his ties to his wife and their conjugal family were probably relatively strong. The concept of the uterine family may, therefore, apply less to the poor than to those sufficiently well-to-do that they could maintain stem or joint families.

14. The principal source for this discussion is the brilliant book by Arthur P. Wolf and Chieh-shan Huang, *Marriage and Adoption in China, 1845–1945* (Stanford, Calif.: Stanford University Press, 1980).

15. A man was permitted to take a second wife on such rare and special occasions as when the first wife had committed a grave offense against the family by having lost her virginity before marriage or by having severely harmed her in-laws.

16. Margery Wolf, *Women and the Family,* p. 208.

17. Wolf and Huang suggest that widows without a child and without property "usually" remarried (*Marriage and Adoption,* p. 228). Burton Pasternak, however, insists that the crucial factor determining a widow's remarriage was the absence of a male adult in her household to assist with the family labor ("On the Causes and Demographic Consequences of Uxorilocal Marriage in China," in *Family and Population in East Asian History,* ed. Susan B. Hanley and Arthur P. Wolf [Stanford, Calif.: Stanford University Press, 1985], p. 321).

18. Wolf and Huang, *Marriage and Adoption,* pp. 159–60.

19. Margery Wolf, *Women and the Family,* pp. 182–83.

20. See, for example Jonathan D. Spence, *The Death of Woman Wang* (New York: Viking Press, 1978), pp. 104–05, 108–09, 117; William Hinton, *Fanshen: A Documentary of Revolution in a Chinese Village* (New York: Monthly Review Press, 1966), pp. 163, 164, 181, 228, 229.

21. Quoted in Stuart R. Schram, *The Political Thought of Mao Tse-tung* (New York: Praeger, 1983), p. 187. Emphasis added. This quotation was excised from the official, revised version of Mao's report in *Selected Works of Mao Tse-tung,* 1: 45.

22. Quoted in Simon Leys, *Chinese Shadows* (New York: Penguin Books, 1978), p. 181.

23. Wolfram Eberhard, *Moral and Social Values of the Chinese: Collected Essays* (Taipei: Chinese Materials and Research Service Center, 1971), p. 6.

24. Kuo-heng Shih, *China Enters the Machine Age: A Study of Labor In Chinese War Industry* (New York: Greenwood Press, 1968), pp. 118–19.

25. Richard H. Solomon, *Mao's Revolution and the Chinese Political Culture* (Berkeley: University of California Press, 1971), p. 112.

26. Francis L. K. Hsu, *Under the Ancestors' Shadow: Kinship, Personality, and Social Mobility in China* (Stanford, Calif.: Stanford University Press, 1971), p. 265.

27. Francis L. K. Hsu, *Americans and Chinese: Purpose and Fulfillment in Great Civilizations* (Garden City, N.Y.: Natural History Press, 1970), p. 109.

28. During the late imperial period, institutions that cared for orphans, the elderly, the crippled, and the blind were occasionally maintained by monasteries, lineages, and private charities. My impression is that they were few and far between.

29. Lien-sheng Yang, "The Concept of 'Pao' as a Basis for Social Relations in China," in *Chinese Thought and Institutions,* ed. John K. Fairbank (Chicago: University of Chicago Press, 1957), p. 294.

30. The story is related in Hu Hsien-chin, "The Chinese Concept of 'Face,' " in *Personal Character and Cultural Milieu,* ed. Douglas G. Haring (Syracuse, N.Y.: Syracuse University Press, 1956), p. 460.

31. Lawrence Stone, *The Family, Sex and Marriage in England, 1500–1800* (New York: Harper & Row, 1977), p. 190.

32. Ibid., p. 103. Ellipses in source.

33. Ibid., p. 112.

34. Ibid., p. 162.

Chapter 3

1. Hu Shih, *The Chinese Renaissance, The Haskell Lectures, 1933* (Chicago: University of Chicago Press, 1934), p. 80.

2. C. K. Yang, *Religion in Chinese Society: A Study of Contemporary Social Functions of Religion and Some of Their Historical Factors* (Berkeley: University of California Press, 1961), p. 17.

3. Despite its institutional weaknesses, Buddhism by no means disappeared from China. For example, it enjoyed a considerable revival among the laity during the late Ming period—a movement that shared, incidentally, many of the populist characteristics of the Taizhou school of Confucianism discussed in Chapter 7 (see, for example, Chün-fang Yü, *The Renewal of Buddhism in China: Chu-hung and the Late Ming Synthesis* [New York: Columbia University Press, 1981]).

4. R. F. Johnston, *Lion and Dragon in Northern China* (New York: Dutton, 1910), pp. 359–60.

5. Yang, *Religion in Chinese Society,* p. 53.

6. Like other aspects of the popular religion, the relationship between the ancestors and the living was complex. Maurice Freedman stressed that the ancestors were typically benevolent (*The Study of Chinese Society* [London: Athlone Press, 1966], pp. 301–12). Emily M. Ahern, however, found that the ancestors were often punitive and malevolent: "The people of Ch'inan feel the ancestors to be unreasonable to the point of capriciousness" (*The Cult of the Dead in a Chinese Village* [Stanford, Calif.: Stanford University Press, 1973], p. 200).

7. Arthur P. Wolf, "Gods, Ghosts, and Ancestors," in *Religion and Ritual in Chinese Society,* ed. Arthur P. Wolf (Stanford, Calif.: Stanford University Press, 1974), p. 147.

8. Michael Saso, "Orthodoxy and Heterodoxy in Taoist Ritual," in *Religion and Ritual in Chinese Society,* ed. Arthur P. Wolf (Stanford, Calif.: Stanford University Press, 1974), p. 335.

9. Jack M. Potter, "Cantonese Shamanism," in *Religion and Ritual in Chinese Society,* ed. Arthur P. Wolf (Stanford, Calif.: Stanford University Press, 1974), pp. 208–15.

10. Maurice Freedman, *Chinese Lineage and Society: Fukien and Kwangtung* (London: Athlone Press, 1966), p. 126.

11. Quoted in Ahern, *Cult of the Dead,* p. 181.

12. Saso, "Orthodoxy and Heterodoxy," p. 325.

13. Arthur P. Wolf, "Introduction," in *Religion and Ritual in Chinese Society,* ed. Arthur P. Wolf (Stanford, Calif.: Stanford University Press, 1974), p. 17.

14. Yang, *Religion in Chinese Society,* p. 333. Romanization modified.

15. Quoted in ibid., p. 157.

16. Ibid., p. 134.

17. Ibid., p. 134.

17. Ibid., p. 145.

18. Clarence Burton Day, *Chinese Peasant Cults: Being a Study of Chinese Paper Gods,* 2d ed. (Taipei: Chengwen, 1969), p. 191.

19. Ibid., p. 193.

20. Sidney D. Gamble, *Ting Hsien: A North China Rural Community* (Stanford, Calif.: Stanford University Press, 1968), p. 405.

Chapter 4

1. Quoted in Arif Dirlik, "Chinese Historians and the Marxist Concept of Capitalism: A Critical Examination," *Modern China* 8, no. 1 (January 1982): 106.

2. F. H. King, *Farmers of Forty Centuries: or Permanent Agriculture in China, Korea, and Japan* (Madison, Wis.: Mrs. F. H. King, 1911), p. 194.

3. John Lossing Buck, *Land Utilization in China* (Nanking: University of Nanking, 1937), p. 265.

4. A. V. Chayanov, *The Theory of Peasant Society,* ed. Daniel Thorner et al. (Homewood, Ill.: American Economic Association, 1966), pp. 70–89.

5. The following discussion is based largely on the superb dissertation by Chin Shih, "Peasant Economy and Rural Society in the Lake Tai Area, 1368–1840" (Ph.D. diss., University of California, Berkeley, 1981). See also Joseph P. McDermott, "Bondservants in the T'ai-hu Basin During the Late Ming: A Case of Mistaken Identity," *Journal of Asian Studies* 40, no. 4 (August 1981): 675–701.

6. Quoted in Shih, "Peasant Economy," p. 51.

7. This shift is indicated graphically by the fact that from 1449 to 1644, most *juren* in Lake Tai's Tongxiang Xian were from the rural areas—although from 1505 to 1644, the percentages of *juren* from the towns was rising. After 1644, fully 80 percent of the *juren* in the *xian* came from the towns (Ibid., pp. 135–38).

8. Quoted in ibid., pp. 178–79.

9. Ibid., pp. 169–70.

10. James L. Watson has estimated that slavery in the Hong Kong region in 1900 accounted for no more than 2 percent of the population ("Transactions in People: The Chinese Market in Slaves, Servants, and Heirs," in *Asian and African Systems of Slavery,* ed. James L. Watson [Berkeley: University of California Press, 1980], p. 250).

Chapter 5

1. R. H. Tawney, *Land and Labor in China* (Boston: Beacon Press, 1932), p. 77.

2. Fei Hsiao-t'ung. *Peasant Life in China: A Field Study of Country Life in the Yangtze Valley* (New York: Dutton, 1939), pp. 282, 285. Emphasis added.

3. Tawney, *Land and Labor,* p. 103.

4. Albert Feuerwerker, *The Chinese Economy, 1912–1949* (Ann Arbor: University of Michigan, Center for Chinese Studies, 1968), p. 27.

5. Nicholas R. Lardy, "Food Consumption in the People's Republic of China," *The Chinese Agricultural Economy,* ed. Randolph Barker and Padha Sinha (Boulder, Col.: Westview Press, 1982), pp. 147–58; Richard E. Barrett, "Population Process in China since the Nineteenth Century" (unpub. ms., July 1984), chap. 2, p. 16.

6. Dean T. Jamison et al., *China: The Health Sector* (Washington, D.C.: International Bank for Reconstruction and Development, 1984), pp. 12–18.

7. Martin C. Yang, *A Chinese Village: Taitou, Shantung Province* (New York: Columbia University Press, 1965), p. 32.

8. Philip C. C. Huang, *The Peasant Economy and Social Change in North China* (Stanford, Calif.: Stanford University Press, 1985), pp. 108–09. Emphasis added. Huang bases this conclusion on the evidence that the number of land sales in *one village* increased after farmers there began producing cotton for the market and that the bulk of the purchases were by the relatively wealthy farmers. This sample base is too small, and the evidence of increasing tenancy too indirect, to support the larger generalization. A review criticizing Huang's use of data is by Loren Brandt in *Economic Development and Cultural Change,* 35, no. 3 (April 1987): 670–82.

9. Available survey data of landholding patterns, often calculated down to the tenth of a percentage point, have strong verisimilitude. But they can be grossly misleading. First, the data on landholding patterns during the first decade or two after 1900 were usually based on interviews taken many years after the fact, rather than on on-the-spot surveys. As a consequence, all data prior to about 1920 are especially suspect. Second, comparisons of landholding patterns in different years are usually based on surveys that employed different reporting techniques, and the definitional categories were often misleading. The definitions used for "landlord," for example, often varied wildly; and a "part owner" could be a farmer who rented 99 percent, or only 1 percent, of his land. Moreover, even the more scientifically constructed surveys from the 1930s have now come under heavy clouds of suspicion. Some segments of John Lossing Buck's classic study, for instance, are now recognized to be so seriously skewed in sampling techniques (for example, by taking a disproportionate percentage of surveys in localities near major transport lines), and so inconsistent within themselves and in relation to other surveys conducted at about the same time, that many scholars now regard Buck's statistics with deep suspicion; some even eschew their use completely.

10. David Faure, "The Plight of the Farmers: A Study of the Rural Economy of Jiangnan and the Pearl River Delta, 1870–1937," *Modern China* 11, no. 1 (January 1985): 7–8. I have not included here a discussion of the tenants' burden of rents because the available evidence is too indeterminaate to draw clear or definite conclusions. First, the evidence is extremely murky about whether rents were generally rising, remaining constant, or even falling. Second, the actual burden of tenancy depended not only on the nominal rent, but also on such variables as whether or not, and how much of, a deposit *(yazu)* was required; the form in which the rent was paid (sharecropping, fixed rent, and so on); and the harshness or geniality of the relations between tenants and landlords. And third, rising rents did not necessarily connote increased exploitation, for they could be attributable to the greater

value of the land's product. Conversely, if rents were falling, it could be because the land's productivity had declined. Regional variation should also be factored into this extremely complex set of considerations.

11. See Chapter 7, pp. 138–41.

12. Dwight H. Perkins, *Agricultural Development in China, 1368–1968* (Chicago: Aldine, 1969), p. 164.

13. Lillian M. Li, *China's Silk Trade: Traditional Industry in the Modern World, 1842–1937* (Cambridge, Mass.: Harvard University, Council on East Asian Studies, 1981), p. 198.

14. See below, pp. 163–64.

15. Quoted in Jack M. Potter, *Capitalism and the Chinese Peasant: Social and Economic Change in a Hong Kong Village* (Berkeley: University of California Press, 1968), p. 176.

16. Kang Chao, "The Growth of a Modern Cotton Textile Industry and the Competition with Handicrafts," in *China's Modern Economy in Historical Perspective,* ed. Dwight H. Perkins (Stanford, Calif.: Stanford University Press, 1975), p. 175.

17. Quoted in Mark Elvin, "The High-Level Equilibrium Trap: The Causes of the Decline of Invention in the Traditional Chinese Textile Industries," in *Economic Organization in Chinese Society,* ed. W. E. Willmott (Stanford, Calif.: Stanford University Press, 1972), p. 152. On the boom in handicraft weaving, see Kang Chao, "Growth of a Modern Cotton Textile Industry," pp. 175, 183, 194.

18. Hou Chi-ming, *Foreign Investment and Economic Development in China, 1840–1937* (Cambridge, Mass.: Harvard University Press, 1965), p. 169; Ramon H. Myers, "The Agrarian System," in *Cambridge History of China,* vol. 13, ed. John K. Fairbank and Albert Feuerwerker (Cambridge: Cambridge University Press, 1986), p. 264.

19. Hsiao-t'ung Fei, *China's Gentry: Essays in Rural–Urban Relations* (Chicago: University of Chicago Press, 1953), pp. 127–37.

20. Ibid., p. 134.

21. C. K. Yang, *A Chinese Village in Early Communist Transition* (Cambridge, Mass.: Technology Press, 1959), p. 118.

22. Ibid., p. 114.

23. R. Bin Wong also points out, however, that in times of want, the poor in the early-nineteenth century at least *expected* doles of grain from the rich—and that probably their expectations were sometimes realized ("Food Riots in the Qing Dynasty," *Journal of Asian Studies* 44, no. 4 (August 1982): 769, 782.

24. William Hinton, *Fanshen: A Documentary of Revolution in a Chinese Village* (New York: Monthly Review Press, 1966), pp. 51–52.

25. Morton H. Fried, *Fabric of Chinese Society: A Study of the Social Life of a Chinese County Seat* (New York: Praeger, 1953), pp. 108–09.

26. Y. C. Wang, *Chinese Intellectuals and the West, 1872–1949* (Chapel Hill: University of North Carolina Press, 1966), p. xii.

27. Diana Lary, "Violence, Fear, and Insecurity: The Mood of Republican China," *Republican China* 10, no. 2 (April 1985): 57–58. Romanization modified.

28. Another type of tax that increased greatly during the course of the twentieth century was the *yashui,* a commercial tax on sales of domestic animals, meat, tobacco, alcohol, and other products. It was usually collected by tax farmers, and the system was frequently very corrupt. Ultimately, the consumers presumably had to bear the burden of these taxes.

29. John Lossing Buck, *Land Utilization in China* (Nanking: University of Nanking, 1937), pp. 458–60. Emphasis added.

30. There are serious problems with both pieces of evidence. It is possible that the

increased cloth consumption in China resulted not from a rising standard of living, but from other causes. Perhaps, for example, more cloth was sold simply because modern manufacturing techniques had made cloth cheaper and thus more affordable to the masses. Or perhaps increased cloth purchases reflected the fact of increased urban populations, which generally spend more on clothing than do peasants. Buck's survey data must also be used with caution, because the farms that Buck surveyed were much larger than—nearly double—the average size of farms in each area. Buck admitted that "it is probable" that the data were consequently excessively optimistic (Ibid., p. 437).

31. Quoted in Hung-mao Tien, *Government and Politics in Kuomintang China, 1927– 1937*, p. 168.

32. Arthur H. Smith, *Village Life in China: A Study in Sociology* (New York: Revell, 1899), p. 310.

33. Ibid., p. 246.

Chapter 6

1. James Legge, ed. *The Chinese Classics,* Vol. 2, *The Works of Mencius,* 3d ed. (Hong Kong: Hong Kong University Press, 1960), pp. 125–26.

2. Quoted in Mary Clabaugh Wright, *The Last Stand of Chinese Conservatism: The T'ung-Chih Restoration, 1862–1874* (Stanford, Calif.: Stanford University Press, 1957), p. 156.

3. Legge, *Chinese Classics,* p. 199.

4. Arthur H. Smith, *Village Life in China: A Study in Sociology* (New York: Revell, 1899), p. 49.

5. Hosea Ballou Morse, *The International Relations of the Chinese Empire* (London: Longmans, Green, 1910–18), vol. 1, p. 81.

6. Quoted in Shiba Yoshinobu, *Commerce and Society in Sung China* (Ann Arbor: University of Michigan, Center for Chinese Studies, 1970), p. 4.

7. Quoted in Ping-ti Ho, *Studies on the Population of China, 1368–1953* (Cambridge, Mass.: Harvard University Press, 1959), p. 199.

8. Smith, *Village Life In China,* p. 36.

9. Quoted in "Inland Communications in China," *Journal of the North China Branch of the Royal Asiatic Society,* n.s., 28 (1893–94): 148–49.

10. Quoted in Karl A. Wittfogel, *Oriental Despotism: A Comparative Study of Total Power* (New Haven, Conn.: Yale University Press, 1957), p. 38.

11. Quoted in Mark Elvin, *The Pattern of the Chinese Past* (Stanford, Calif.: Stanford University Press, 1973), p. 133.

12. Smith, *Village Life in China,* p. 35.

13. "Inland Communications in China," p. 56.

14. Han-sheng Chuan and Richard A. Kraus, *Mid-Ch'ing Rice Markets and Trade: An Essay in Price History* (Cambridge, Mass.: Harvard University, East Asian Research Center, 1975), p. 71.

15. Ibid.

16. Ibid., pp. ix, 40, 74. Chuan and Kraus's contention that interregional trade in the eighteenth century was more extensive than it was during much of the nineteenth century is borne out by evidence cited in William T. Rowe, *Hankow: Commerce and Society in a Chinese City, 1796–1889* (Stanford, Calif.: Stanford University Press, 1984), pp. 55, 60.

17. Morton H. Fried, *Fabric of Chinese Society: A Study of the Social Life of a Chinese County Seat* (New York: Praeger, 1953), p. 110.

18. Oscar Handlin, *Truth in History* (Cambridge, Mass.: Belknap Press of Harvard University Press, 1979), p. 26.

19. Besides silver coins of Spanish and Mexican origin, those from Hong Kong, Japan, and Saigon circulated in China. Another form of "money" was opium, which acquired considerable use in the late-nineteenth century as a medium of exchange, especially in the wholesale trade.

20. G. William Skinner, "Marketing and Social Structure in Rural China," *Journal of Asian Studies* 24, no. 1 (November 1964): 3–43; 24, no. 2 (February 1965): 195–228; and 24, no. 3 (May 1965): 363–99. This section is based largely on Part 1.

21. Until the publication of Skinner's study of China's periodic markets, the village was generally thought to have been the basic geographical unit of Chinese society. The concept of the standard-marketing community fundamentally altered that perception. Still, it is probable that Skinner overemphasized the cultural importance of the standard-marketing area. Chinese society was obviously complex, and the loyalties and emotions of peasants were drawn in many directions. Some standard-marketing communities were frequently fragmented within by diverse lineage, class, and religious divisions. At the same time, commitments to ethnic, secret-society, and (again) religious groups could cause peasant interests to transcend the outer reaches of the marketing area (see, for instance, Arthur P. Wolf, "Introduction," in *Religion and Ritual in Chinese Society,* ed. Arthur P. Wolf [Stanford, Calif.: Stanford University Press, 1974], pp. 5–6). Thus the concept of periodic-marketing units contains powerful insights into the functioning of China's peasant society, but it would be a mistake to conclude that the standard-marketing area represented the totality of social forces at the local level.

22. The essential description of the macroregional thesis is in G. William Skinner, "Regional Urbanization in Nineteenth-Century China," and "Cities and the Hierarchy of Local Systems," in *The City in Late Imperial China,* ed. G. William Skinner (Stanford, Calif.: Stanford University Press, 1977), pp. 211–36, 281–301. Skinner identified Manchuria as the ninth macroregion, but did not include it in his analysis.

23. Skinner's analysis of China's macroregions has strong persuasive power, but it has been sharply criticized for erroneously distinguishing between core and peripheral areas in some macroregions and for exaggerating the isolation of the macroregions from one another (Barbara N. Sands and Ramon H. Myers, "The Spatial Approach to Chinese History: A Test," *Journal of Asian Studies* 45, no. 4, [August 1986]: 721–43; Randall E. Stross, "A Hard Row to Hoe: The Political Economy of Chinese Agriculture in Western Jiangsu, 1911–1937" [Ph.D. diss., Stanford University, 1982], pp. 6–7; Norton Ginsburg, "The City in Late Imperial China [a review article]," *American Ethnologist* 6, no. 1 [February 1979]: 146–47. Skinner's analysis is defended in Daniel Little, "Theory versus Data in Skinner's Macroregions Argument" (Paper presented to a colloquium at the John K. Fairbank Center for East Asian Studies, Harvard University, Cambridge, Mass., October 24, 1986).

24. William Lytle Schurz, *The Manila Galleon* (New York: Dutton, 1939), p. 32.

25. Quoted in C. R. Boxer, *The Christian Century in Japan, 1549–1650* (Berkeley: University of California Press, 1951), pp. 105–06.

26. Quoted in William S. Atwell, "Notes on Silver, Foreign Trade, and the Late Ming Economy," *Ch'ing-shih Wen-t'i* 3, no. 8 (December 1977): 2.

27. Peter Ward Fay, *The Opium War, 1840–1842* (Chapel Hill: University of North Carolina Press, 1975), p. 54.

28. Quoted in Michael Greenberg, *British Trade and the Opening of China, 1800–42* (Cambridge: Cambridge University Press, 1951), p. 4.

29. Etienne Balazs, *Chinese Civilization and Bureaucracy: Variations on a Theme* (New

York: Columbia University Press, 1964), p. 41. For a fuller description of this aspect of state suppression of commerce, see Chapter 7, p. 155.

30. The analysis here has been much stimulated by the work of Prasenjit Duara on state brokerage in, for the most part, the twentieth century. See *Culture, Power, and the Modernizing State: Rural North China, 1900–1940* (Stanford, Calif.: Stanford University Press, 1988), Chap. 2.

31. Denis Twitchett, "Merchant, Trade and Government in Late T'ang," *Asia Major,* n.s., 14, no. 1 (1968): 95. Emphasis added. An excellent study of the evolution of the Chinese governments' commercial policies after the Song Dynasty—including discussions of the role of brokers—is Susan Mann, *Local Merchants and the Chinese Bureaucracy, 1750–1950* (Stanford, Calif.: Stanford University Press, 1986). I received a copy of Mann's book too late to incorporate many of its valuable insights into the discussion here.

32. G. William Skinner, "Introduction: Urban Development in Imperial China," in *The City in Late Imperial China,* ed. G. William Skinner (Stanford, Calif.: Stanford University Press, 1977), p. 25.

Chapter 7

1. Mao Tse-tung, "The Chinese Revolution and the Chinese Communist Party," in *Selected Works of Mao Tse-tung,* vol. 3, p. 77, quoted in Albert Feuerwerker, "From 'Feudalism' to 'Capitalism' in Recent Historical Writings from Mainland China," *Journal of Asian Studies* 18, no. 1 (November 1958): 107.

2. Albert Feuerwerker, *State and Society in Eighteenth-Century China: The Ch'ing Empire in Its Glory* (Ann Arbor: University of Michigan, Center for Chinese Studies, 1976), p. 84.

3. Charles Henry Wilson, *England's Apprenticeship, 1603–1763* (New York: St. Martin's Press, 1965), p. 297.

4. Ibid., pp. 359–60. On the technological continuity between medieval times and the early Industrial Revolution, see Samuel Lilley, "Technological Progress and the Industrial Revolution, 1700–1914," in *The Fontana Economic History of Europe,* vol. 3 *The Industrial Revolution,* ed. Carlo M. Cipolla (London: Collins [Fontana Books], 1973), pp. 187–92.

5. Wilson, *England's Apprenticeship,* p. 359.

6. The causes of the economic and political difficulties during this period, aside from the Manchu military incursions, are complex. William S. Atwell noted that Japan was also going through a turbulent period, and he suggests that climatic change, perhaps related to the "little ice age" in Europe at this same general time, may have underlain this time of troubles. Geiss argues that the inflation of silver was a source of profound economic problems in the late-Ming. See William S. Atwell, "*Sakoku* and the Fall of the Ming Dynasty: Some Observations on the 'Seventeenth-Century Crisis' in China and Japan," *Journal of Asian Studies,* 45.2 (February 1986): 225–27; and James Geiss, "Peking Under the Ming (1368–1644)" (Ph.D. diss., Princeton University, 1974), pp. 143–75; Mio Kishimoto-Nakayama, "The Kangxi Depression and Early Qing Local Markets," *Modern China,* 10.2 (April 1984): 227–56.

7. Mi Chu Wiens, "Cotton Textile Production and Rural Social Transformation in Early Modern China," *Xianggang Zhongwen Daxue Zhongguo Wenhua Yenjiusuo Xuebao* (Journal of the Institute of Chinese Studies of the Chinese University of Hong Kong), 7.2 (December 1974): 523.

8. Mark Elvin, "Market Towns and Waterways: The County of Shanghai from 1480

to 1910,'' in *The City in Late Imperial China*, ed. G. William Skinner (Stanford: Stanford University Press, 1977), 459, 460.

9. Elvin, ''Market Towns and Waterways,'' pp. 446–47.

10. P. J. B. Du Halde, *A Description of the Chinese Empire and Chinese Tartary*, I: 80–81, cited in Ping-ti Ho, *Studies on the Population of China, 1368–1953* (Cambridge, Mass.: Harvard University Press, 1959), p. 201.

11. Quoted in Mark Elvin, *The Pattern of the Chinese Past* (Stanford, Calif.: Stanford University Press, 1973), pp. 285–86.

12. Sung Ying-Hsing, *T'ien-kung K'ai-wu: Chinese Technology in the Seventeenth Century*, trans. E-tu Zen Sun and Shiou-chuan Sun (University Park: Pennsylvania State University Press, 1966), p. 63.

13. Quoted in Craig Dietrich, ''Cotton Culture and Manufacture in Early Ch'ing China,'' in *Economic Organization in Chinese Society*, ed. W. E. Willmott (Stanford, Calif.: Stanford University Press, 1972), p. 129.

14. A distinctive feature of these ''factories'' was that the workers were not paid wages; rather, they received piece rates from the contractor who owned the ''factory,'' and, in turn, paid the contractor a fee for the use of the equipment and for food and housing.

15. It is unclear who, in this chain of transactions, ginned the raw cotton. Nishijima Sadao concluded that ''a separate and distinct ginning unit must have existed and that the cotton that the old women bought was ginned cotton which was making its second appearance in the market'' (''The Formation of the Early Chinese Cotton Industry,'' in *State and Society in China*, ed. Linda Grove and Christian Daniels [Tokyo: University of Tokyo Press, 1984], p. 56.).

16. Wiens, ''Cotton Textile Production,'' p. 524.

17. Quoted in Mark Elvin, ''The High-Level Equilibrium Trap: The Causes of the Decline of Invention in the Traditional Chinese Textile Industries,'' in *Economic Organization in Chinese Society*, ed. W. E. Willmott (Stanford, Calif.: Stanford University Press, 1972), p. 158. For evidence of the use of the putting-out system, see E-tu Zen Sun, ''Sericulture and Silk Textile Production in Ch'ing China,'' pp. 95–96, and Dietrich, ''Cotton Culture and Manufacture'' pp. 131–32, both in ibid.

18. Elvin, ''High-Level Equilibrium Trap,'' p. 137.

19. Carlo M. Cipolla, ''Introdution,'' in *The Fontana Economic History of Europe*, Vol. 3, *The Industrial Revolution*, ed. Carlo M. Cipolla (London: Collins/Fontana Books, 1973), p. 12.

20. Takehiko Okada, ''Wang Chi and the Rise of Existentialism,'' in *Self and Society in Ming Thought*, ed. Wm. Theodore de Bary (New York: Columbia University Press, 1970), p. 121.

21. Quoted in Ping-ti Ho, *The Ladder of Success in Imperial China: Aspects of Social Mobility, 1368–1911* (New York: Columbia University Press, 1962), p. 73.

22. Quoted in Wm. Theodore de Bary, ''Individualism and Humanitarianism in Late Ming Thought,'' in *Self and Society in Ming Thought*, ed. Wm. Theodore de Bary (New York: Columbia University Press, 1970), p. 174.

23. Ibid., p. 178.

24. Quoted in Nelson I. Wu, ''Tung Ch'i-ch'ang (1555–1636): Apathy in Government and Fervor in Art,'' in *Confucian Personalities*, ed. Arthur F. Wright and Denis Twitchett (Stanford, Calif.: Stanford University Press, 1962), p. 280.

25. Quoted in De Bary, ''Individualism and Humanitarianism,'' p. 206.

26. Ernest Gellner, quoted in E. L. Jones, *The European Miracle: Environments, Economies, and Geopolitics in the History of Europe and Asia* (Cambridge: Cambridge University Press, 1981), p. 225.

27. David S. Landes, *The Unbound Prometheus: Technological Change and Industrial Development in Western Europe from 1750 to the Present* (Cambridge: Cambridge University Press, 1969), p. 21.

28. Why the two cultures differed in their respective approaches to nature can only be speculated. Perhaps Europe, being a relatively small and poor region that was deficient in precious metals and desiring goods that were available only elsewhere (such as spices, silk, cotton, tea, and porcelain), felt a yearning and dissatisfaction that produced the urge to expand, dominate, and explore. China, on the contrary, being a large continental-size land mass, had since time immemorial been adequately endowed with all the material commodities required for a civilized, reasonably comfortable existence. Sir Robert Hart, writing in the nineteenth century, expressed the Chinese condition well: "Chinese have the best food in the world, rice; the best drink, tea; and the best clothing, cotton, silk, fur. Possessing these staples and their innumerable native adjuncts, they do not need to buy a penny's worth elsewhere."

Another source of differentiation between China and Europe may have been the contrasting forms of writing. The Chinese possessed a pictographic script that contributed to the cultural and political unity of the Chinese people, whereas the alphabetic writing of the Europeans actually promoted the linguistic, and hence cultural and political, fragmentation of the people. These divisions, in turn, produced tensions, rivalries, and warfare among the European peoples that may have engendered the craving to transcend, rather than merely accommodate to, the material environment.

In short, the Europeans' success since the sixteenth century in overcoming the material deprivation and cultural handicaps of their region is probably evidence of the *virtue of adversity*—a concept propounded by the great British historian Arnold J. Toynbee. China, being relatively well endowed and lacking the stimuli of great adversities, became self-satisfied and complacent (Arnold J. Toynbee, *A Study of History*, abridgement of volumes 1–6 by D. C. Somervell [New York: Oxford University Press, 1947], pp. 80–87).

29. Quoted in Joseph Needham, "Science and China's Influence on the World," in *The Legacy of China*, ed. Raymond Dawson (Oxford: Clarendon Press, 1964), p. 242. Emphasis added.

30. Evelyn Sakakida Rawski, *Agricultural Change and the Peasant Economy of South China* (Cambridge, Mass.: Harvard University Press, 1972), p. 90. Romanization modified.

31. Landes, *Unbound Prometheus*, pp. 67–68.

32. Cipolla, "Introduction," p. 10.

33. Mary Clabaugh Wright, *The Last Stand of Chinese Conservatism: The T'ung-chih Restoration, 1862–1874* (Stanford, Calif.: Stanford University Press, 1957), p. 9.

34. Steve Lohr, "Four 'New Japans' Mounting Industrial Challenge," *New York Times,* August 24, 1982, p. D-5.

35. Herman Kahn, *World Economic Development: 1979 and Beyond* (Boulder, Colo.: Westview Press, 1979), p. 121. See also Thomas A. Metzger's contention that a "transformative orientation" in Confucianism imparted an impetus to modernizing change during the past century. *Escape from Predicament: Neo-Confucianism and China's Evolving Political Culture* [New York: Columbia University Press, 1977], especially pp. 191–235).

36. Landes, *Unbound Prometheus*, p. 16.

37. Hsin-pao Chang, *Commissioner Lin and the Opium War* (Cambridge, Mass.: Harvard University Press, 1964), p. 14.

38. Ibid.

Chapter 8

1. Quoted in Nathan A. Pelcovits, *Old China Hands and the Foreign Office* (New York: King's Crown Press, 1948), p. 16.

2. G. C. Allen and Audrey G. Donnithorne, *Western Enterprise in Far Eastern Economic Development: China and Japan* (London: George Allen and Unwin, 1954), pp. 17–18.

3. Quoted in John King Fairbank, *Trade and Diplomacy on the China Coast: The Opening of the Treaty Ports, 1842–1854* (Cambridge, Mass.: Harvard University Press, 1953), p. 380.

4. Albert Feuerwerker, "The Foreign Presence in China," in *Cambridge History of China* (Cambridge: Cambridge University Press, 1983), vol. 12, ed. John K. Fairbank, p. 129.

5. Robert F. Dernberger, "The Role of the Foreigner in China's Economic Development," in *China's Modern Economy in Historical Perspective,* ed. Dwight H. Perkins (Stanford, Calif.: Stanford University Press, 1975), p. 31.

6. Albert Feuerwerker, "Handicraft and Manufactured Cotton Textiles in China, 1871–1910," *Journal of Economic History* 30, no. 2 (June 1970): 377.

7. Quoted in Allen and Donnithorne, *Western Enterprise in Far Eastern Economic Development,* pp. 74–75.

8. Wang Yejian, *Zhongguo Jindai Huobi yu Yinhang de Yenjin, 1644–1937* (The development of money and banking in China, 1644–1937) (Taipei: Academia Sinica, Institute of Economics, 1981), pp. 79–90.

9. In 1933, consumer-goods industries contributed 76 percent of the value added by factories.

10. If China had possessed an efficient system of roads and highways to provide feeder lines to the railway terminals, the railroads would have had a larger impact on the rural economy, despite their limited spatial coverage. Such a system of feeder lines did not exist, of course, and the use of pack animals, carts, and human backs did not provide a serviceable alternative.

11. For instance, the Lunghai line ran roughly parallel to the Huai–Ying river route, and the Tientsin–Pukow line followed the Grand Canal. In fact, in the 1930s, the only major railroads in north China that were not serving areas beyond the Great Wall and that clearly were not redundant of existing water routes were the Chengchow–Hankow, the Tsingtao–Tsinan, and the Taiyuan–Chengting lines.

12. Quoted in Mary Clabaugh Wright, *The Last Stand of Chinese Conservatism: The T'ung-chih Restoration, 1862–1974* (Stanford, Calif.: Stanford University Press, 1957), p. 212.

13. Quoted in Immanuel C. Y. Hsu, *The Rise of Modern China,* 3d ed. (New York: Oxford University Press, 1983), p. 284.

14. Albert Feuerwerker, *China's Early Industrialization: Sheng Hsuan-huai (1844–1916) and Mandarin Enterprise* (Cambridge, Mass.: Harvard University Press, 1958), pp. 9–10.

15. Quoted in Kwang-Ching Liu, "British-Chinese Steamship Rivalry in China, 1873–85," in *The Economic Development of China and Japan: Studies in Economic History and Political Economy,* ed. C. D. Cowan (New York: Praeger, 1964), p. 53.

16. Wellington K. K. Chan, *Merchants, Mandarins, and Modern Enterprise in Late Ch'ing China* (Cambridge, Mass.: Harvard University, East Asian Research Center, 1977), pp. 77–78, 81.

17. Yen-p'ing Hao, *The Commercial Revolution in Nineteenth-Century China: The Rise*

of Sino-Western Mercantile Capitalism (Berkeley: University of California Press, 1986), p. 258.

18. This is not to assert that warlordism was, on balance, economically beneficial. In Chapter 5, we discussed the negative effects of political instability and economic insecurity that were engendered by the warlord situation.

19. John K. Chang, *Industrial Development in Pre-Communist China: A Quantitative Analysis* (Chicago: Aldine, 1969), pp. 70–74.

20. John Chang, "Industrial Development of China, 1912–1949," *Journal of Economic History* 27, no. 1 (March 1967): 80–81.

21. Frank M. Tamagna, *Banking and Finance in China* (New York: Institute of Pacific Relations, 1942), p. 212.

22. Quoted in Sherman Cochran, *Big Business in China: Sino-Foreign Rivalry in the Cigarette Industry, 1890–1930* (Cambridge, Mass.: Harvard University Press, 1980), p. 189.

23. Quoted in William C. Kirby, "Kuomintang China's 'Great Leap Outward': The 1936 Three-Year Plan for Industrial Development," in *Essays in the History of the Chinese Republic* (Urbana: University of Illinois, Center for Asian Studies, 1983), p. 58. I have altered Kirby's translation of *guoying* from "state-owned" to "managed by the state."

24. Interview with William S. Youngman, Cambridge, Mass., May 24, 1987. Mr. Youngman, who had been Soong's lawyer since the 1940s and was executor of his estate, adds that Soong's net worth when he died in 1971 was about US$12 million.

25. A good place to start examining the question of the effects of imperialism in China is "Imperialism: Reality or Myth?" Paul A. Cohen, *Discovering History in China: American Historical Writing on the Recent Past* (New York: Columbia University Press, 1984), pp. 97–147.

26. David S. Landes, *The Unbound Prometheus: Technological Change and Industrial Development in Western Europe from 1750 to the Present* (Cambridge: Cambridge University Press, 1969), p. 136.

Chapter 9

1. Hilary J. Beattie, *Land and Lineage in China: A Study of T'ung-ch'eng County, Anhwei, in the Ming and Ch'ing Dynasties* (Cambridge: Cambridge University Press, 1979), p. 131.

2. Shirley S. Garrett, "The Chambers of Commerce and the YMCA," in *The Chinese City Between Two Worlds,* ed. Mark Elvin and G. William Skinner (Stanford, Calif.: Stanford University Press, 1974), p. 217.

3. Joseph Fewsmith, *Party, State, and Local Elites in Republican China: Merchant Organizations and Politics in Shanghai, 1890–1930* (Honolulu: University of Hawaii Press, 1985), p. 64.

4. Marie-Claire Bergère, "The Chinese Bourgeoisie, 1911–37," in *Cambridge History of China,* vol. 12, ed. John K. Fairbank (Cambridge: Cambridge University Press, 1983), p. 813.

5. Quoted in Sally Borthwick, *Education and Social Change in China: The Beginnings of the Modern Era* (Stanford, Calif.: Hoover Institution Press, 1983), pp. 39–40.

6. See Chapter 3, pp. 59–60.

7. Borthwick, *Education and Social Change,* p. 80.

8. Tsinghua College had been established in 1911 for students who were preparing to study in the United States.

9. Robert C. North, with the collaboration of Ithiel de Sola Pool, *Kuomintang and Chinese Communist Elites* (Stanford, Calif.: Stanford University Press, 1952), p. 55.

10. Ibid.

11. Martin M. C. Yang, *Chinese Social Structure: A Historical Study* (Taipei: National Book Company, 1969), p. 267.

12. Estimates of the size of the industrial work force vary wildly, particularly because those making the estimates maintained no consistent definition of an industrial worker. The estimate in the text follows Nym Wales, *The Chinese Labor Movement* (New York: Day, 1945), pp. 9–10, 152–55. Albert Feuerwerker cites the figure of 1 million for 1933. ("Economic Trends, 1912–49," in *Cambridge History of China*, vol. 12. [Cambridge: Cambridge University Press, 1983], p. 61). But Jean Chesneaux estimates 1.5 million in 1919 (*Chinese Labor Movement, 1919–1927* [Stanford, Calif.: Stanford University Press, 1968], p. 43); while Lynda Norene Shaffer concludes that "4 million workers is a better estimate than that offered by Chesneaux" ("The Chinese Working Class: Comments on Two Articles," *Modern China* 9, no. 4 [October 1984]: 461).

13. Quoted in Emily Honig, "The Contract Labor System and Women Workers: Pre-Liberation Cotton Mills of Shanghai," *Modern China* 9, no. 4 (October 1984): 426.

14. Quoted in Chesneaux, *Chinese Labor Movement*, p. 111.

15. Quoted in Tse-tsung Chow, *The May Fourth Movement: Intellectual Revolution in Modern China* (Cambridge, Mass.: Harvard University Press, 1960), p. 183.

16. Elisabeth Croll, *Feminism and Socialism in China* (New York: Schocken Books, 1980), p. 49.

Chapter 10

1. *Yin* and *yang*, in ancient Chinese thought, were opposite but complementary forces whose dynamic interrelationship informed all things in the universe, uniting each into an integral whole. *Yin* was the negative principle—female, water, moon; while *yang* was the positive principle—male, earth, sun. The idea sounds simplistic, but it is philosophically and psychologically profound. The turn of the seasons, from winter to summer, is an expression of the *yin–yang* principle at work.

2. Daniel L. Overmyer, "Alternatives: Popular Religious Sects in Chinese Society," *Modern China* 7, no. 2 (April 1981): 185.

3. For elaborations of this interpretation, see Susan Naquin, *Shantung Rebellion: The Wang Lun Uprising of 1774* (New Haven, Conn.: Yale University Press, 1981), pp. 53–56, 163–64; Overmyer, "Alternatives," pp. 162–63.

4. A 1925 study saw predecessors of the Triads in earlier Chinese history and asserted that "there is little doubt that what took place towards the end of the 17th Century [that is, the formation of the Triads] should be regarded as a re-organisation rather than as the creation of an entirely new Body" (John S. M. Ward and W. G. Stirling, *The Hung Society: Or the Society of Heaven and Earth* [London: Baskerville Press, 1925], vol. 1, p. 2).

5. Fei-ling Davis, *Primitive Revolutionaries of China: A Study of Secret Societies in the Late Nineteenth Century* (Honolulu: University of Hawaii Press, 1971), p. 73.

6. Jerome Ch'en states that the Elder Brothers were not so virulently opposed to Manchu rule as were the Triads ("Rebels Between Rebellions: Secret Societies in the Novel, *P'eng Kung An,*" *Journal of Asian Studies* 29, no. 4 (August 1970): 814–16).

7. Susan Mann Jones and Philip A. Kuhn, "Dynastic Decline and the Roots of Rebellion," in *Cambridge History of China*, vol. 10, ed. John K. Fairbank (Cambridge: Cambridge University Press, 1978), p. 134.

8. Quoted in Jen Yu-wen, *The Taiping Revolutionary Movement* (New Haven, Conn.: Yale University Press, 1973), p. 69.

9. Johanna Menzel Meskill, *A Chinese Pioneer Family: The Lins of Wu-feng, Taiwan, 1729–1895* (Princeton, N.J.: Princeton University Press, 1979), p. 64.

10. An excellent review of the historiography of the Red Spear Society is Elizabeth J. Perry, "The Red Spears Reconsidered: An Introduction," in Tai Hsuan-chih, *The Red Spears, 1916–1949* (Ann Arbor: University of Michigan, Center for Chinese Studies, 1985), pp. vii–xxi.

11. Quoted in Elizabeth J. Perry, *Rebels and Revolutionaries in North China, 1845– 1945* (Stanford, Calif.: Stanford University Press, 1980), p. 191.

12. An important cause of ritual impurity was sexual intercourse. Because of this invidious effect of contact with females, women were allowed only a very subordinate role in the Boxer and Red Spear organizations.

13. Quoted in Perry, *Rebels and Revolutionaries,* pp. 165–66. Romanization modified.

14. Ibid., p. 174.

15. As noted earlier, some local elites had been members of the secret brotherhoods in earlier times.

16. Ch'en Yung-fa, "The Wartime Bandits and Their Local Rivals: Bandits and Secret Societies," in *Select Papers from the Center for Far Eastern Studies* (Chicago: University of Chicago Press, 1978–79), vol. 3, p. 15; Perry, *Rebels and Revolutionaries,* pp. 200– 01.

17. Parallels exist between China's new local elites in the twentieth century and the Sicilian Mafiosi. Anton Blok has suggested that the Mafiosi were political middlemen in a society where the local elites were "poised between incongruent political cultures." The Mafiosi were able to "exploit the gaps in communication between the peasant village and the larger society rather than closing or destroying them: they thrive upon these interstices and prevent others from making their own connections" (*The Mafia of a Sicilian Village, 1860–1960: A Study of Violent Peasant Entrepreneurs* [New York: Harper & Row, 1974], p. 8).

18. A. Doak Barnett, *China on the Eve of Communist Takeover* (New York: Praeger, 1963), pp. 127–28. Romanization modified.

19. Quoted in Philip R. Billingsley, "Banditry in China, 1911 to 1928, with Particular Reference to Henan Province" (Ph.D. diss., University of Leeds, 1974), p. 133.

20. Quoted in ibid., p. 161. On soldier-banditry, see also Diana Lary, *Warlord Soldiers: Chinese Common Soldiers, 1911–1937* (Cambridge: Cambridge University Press, 1985), pp. 59–70.

21. E. J. Hobsbawm, *Primitive Rebels: Studies in Archaic Forms of Social Movement in the 19th and 20th Centuries* (New York: Praeger, 1959), pp. 13–25.

22. Quoted in Perry, *Rebels and Revolutionaries,* pp. 73–74. Billingsley identifies the source of this quote as the Lincheng gang ("Banditry in China," p. 209).

23. Quoted in Billingsley, "Banditry in China," p. 209.

24. *Times* (London), March 7, 1914, quoted in ibid., p. 368.

25. Ruth V. Hemenway, *A Memoir of Revolutionary China, 1924–1941,* ed. Fred W. Drake (Amherst: University of Massachusetts Press, 1977), p. 108.

26. Ibid., p. 134.

27. Quoted in Maurice Freedman, *Lineage Organization in Southeastern China* (London: Athlone Press, 1966), pp. 106–07.

28. Ibid., p. 108.

29. Quoted in ibid.

30. Harry J. Lamley, "*Hsieh-tou:* The Pathology of Violence in Southeastern China," *Ch'ing-shih Wen-t'i* 3, no. 7 (November 1977): 34. Romanization modified.

31. The figures cited in Table 10.1 for the decade before the Revolution of 1911 are probably too low. See Marianne Bastid-Bruguière, "Currents of Social Change," in *Cambridge History of China,* vol. 11, ed. John K. Fairbank and Kwang-Ching Liu (Cambridge: Cambridge University Press, 1980), p. 594.

32. Carl Leiden and Karl M. Schmitt, *The Politics of Violence: Revolution in the Modern World* (Englewood Cliffs, N.J.: Prentice-Hall, 1968), p. 43.

33. Davis, *Primitive Revolutionaries,* pp. 5, 174–77.

Conclusion

1. Margery Wolf, *Revolution Postponed: Women in Contemporary China* (Stanford, Calif.: Stanford University Press, 1985), pp. 83–84.

2. Ann S. Anagnost, "Politics and Magic in Contemporary China," *Modern China* 13, no. 1 (January 1987): 43–44; Elizabeth J. Perry, "Rural Collective Violence: The Fruits of Recent Reforms," in *The Political Economy of Reform in Post-Mao China,* ed. Elizabeth J. Perry and Christine Wong (Cambridge, Mass.: Harvard University, Council on East Asian Studies, 1985), pp. 180–85.

3. Arthur P. Wolf, "Gods, Ghosts, and Ancestors," in *Religion and Ritual in Chinese Society,* ed. Arthur P. Wolf (Stanford, Calif.: Stanford University Press, 1974), p. 133.

Index

Agriculture, 62–78
  commercialization of: pre-19th century, 73, 84, 139–41; 19th and 20th centuries, 84–86, 95–96. *See also* Commerce, increase of
  crops, 63, 82, 84, 140; early-ripening, 7; increasing yields, 6; from New World, 5, 7, 8
  fertilizing, 7, 68–70
  irrigation and water control, 6, 63, 92
  landholding: absentee landlordism, 73, 80–81, 83; difficulty of calculating, 252 *n;* manors and bondservants, 71–74; size of farms, 17, 66–68, 81; small freeholders, 71–72, 74;
  multiple cropping, 70
  tenancy, 75–78, 83, 91; permanent tenure, 77–78; rents, 75–78, 83, 252 *n*
Ancestral worship, 19–20, 45–47, 48, 59, 250. *See also* Popular religion

Bacon, Francis, 151
Bai Lang, 231, 233–34
Ban Gu, 101
Ban Zhao, 19
Bandits, 90, 92–93, 97, 229–35; "social bandits," 233–34
Banks: Chinese modern, 165–66, 178, 184; foreign, 164–65; native *(qianzhuang),* 112–13, 114, 165; Shansi remittance, 114, 164
Boycotts, antiforeign, 177, 196, 209
Braudel, Fernand, 5, 6
Brokerage system: and commerce, 130–33, 134,

146; as concept of government, 130, 133–34
Buck, John Lossing, 70, 95; data questioned, 252 *n*

Chambers of commerce, 196–97
Chen Duxiu, 213
Chen Lifu, 183
Chiang Kai-shek, 183, 187, 205; quoted, 97
Chinese:
  attitudes toward nature, 150–53
  personality traits and social behavior, 13–14, 34–39, 199–200; "face," 37–38, 244; importance of personal relationships *(guanxi),* 36–37, 244; increased individualism, 208, 213–14, 243; status-oriented, 34–36, 244
Cipolla, Carlo M., 147
Clans, contrasted with lineages, 248 *n*
Climate, effects of, 5–6, 96–97, 138–39, 256 *n*
Commerce, 13. *See also* Brokerage system; Macroregions; Merchants; Periodic-marketing system; Weights and measures
  foreign trade: pre-19th century, 123–29; 19th and 20th centuries, 85–86, 156, 158–64, 176–78, 188
  increase of, 241; pre-19th century, 102, 106–7, 133–34; 19th and 20th centuries, 102–3. *See also* Agriculture, commercialization of
Concubines, 31–32; sons of, 17

265